Property and Prices shows arbitrage and speculation in the stockmarket to be a capitalist economy's most fundamental mechanism of price determination and resource allocation.

Once a stockmarket is incorporated into general-equilibrium theory, the classical analysis of value (à la Ricardo, Marx, and Sraffa) and the neoclassical theory of price (descending from Walras, Hicks, and Arrow–Debreu) can be seen to possess the same mathematical structure. The modern theory of arbitrage pricing in financial markets thus is capable of bringing together the two great rival schools of economic thought.

Property and prices

Property and prices

Toward a unified theory of value

André Burgstaller

CAMBRIDGE
UNIVERSITY PRESS

Published by the Press Syndicate of the University of Cambridge
The Pitt Building, Trumpington Street, Cambridge CB2 1RP
40 West 20th Street, New York, NY 10011-4211, USA
10 Stamford Road, Oakleigh, Melbourne 3166, Australia

First published 1994

Printed in Great Britain at the University Press, Cambridge

A catalogue record for this book is available from the British Library

Library of Congress cataloguing in publication data

Burgstaller, André Charles
Property and prices: toward a unified theory of value / André Burgstaller.
p. cm.
Includes bibliographical references.
ISBN 0 521 41903 4 (hc)
1. Value. 2. Prices. 3. Property. 4. Equilibrium (Economics)
5. Stock-exchange. 6. Arbitrage. I. Title.
HB201.B863 1994
333.33'2–dc20 93-11075 CIP

ISBN 0 521 419034 hardback

SE

Contents

II Primary resources

SUPPLEMENTS

Figures

Acknowledgments

I owe a special debt to my colleague Duncan Foley, with whom I have discussed the matters addressed in this book over many years. His comments on successive versions of the manuscript have been invaluable. My gratitude to Cem Karayalcin is great as well: From student he has become trusted interlocutor, who repeatedly helped me to see more clearly. Ron Findlay's aliveness to the theoretical tensions that pervade our discipline has been a constant source of stimulation, starting in my student days and continuing into the present.

I have also benefited from communication with O. Blanchard, J. Broome, W. Darity, L. Mainwaring, P. Samuelson, and I. Steedman.

Introduction

In what follows, I propose an approach to the theory of value that unifies the classical (Ricardo–Marx–von Neumann–Sraffa) and the neoclassical (Walras–Hicks–Arrow–Debreu) perspectives. My thesis is that classical and neoclassical value theory both operate through arbitrage and speculation in the financial markets. Key among these markets is the bourse or stockmarket. The latter is governed by the requirement that the owners of the economy's real resources be at all times satisfied with the composition of their portfolios of ownership claims. They must be so, for titles to ownership – equities for short – are alienable by definition of private property.[1] It follows that rates of return expected on equity must be uniform at all times – a requirement embodied in the so-called arbitrage, or stock-equilibrium, equation.

Forward-looking asset arbitrage is a capitalist economy's most fundamental mechanism of decentralized valuation – a mechanism theoretically more primitive than the classical principle of the uniform long-run rate of profit, or the neoclassical principle of utility maximization and flow-market clearing. The foundational status of asset arbitrage is due to the weak axiomatic base on which it rests. For the only behavioral postulate it appeals to is nonsatiation, in the following sense: Whatever goal one may attribute to an economic agent – be it a maximal Marx–von Neumann rate of capitalist accumulation or maximum Walras–Fisher utility from household consumption – it must be true that he will never spurn an opportunity to get something in furtherance of that goal, if it is offered to him at no cost.

Asset-arbitrage arguments are thus the most basic theoretical propositions in economics. That they *are* theoretical (and not merely axiomatic)

[1] As I will show, the prohibition of the self-enslavement of labor can be financially circumvented and does not alter the logic of my argument.

follows from the fact that they produce, independently from optimization and flow-equilibrium arguments, falsifiable causal predictions.[2]

I

The concept of freely alienable private property, though traceable to the Roman *dominium*, is essentially modern. Medieval theology, especially its Franciscan strand, took the resources of the earth to be the property of God and merely under the stewardship of humans. Rights over resources were rights of usufruct, not rights of ownership. When writers such as Duns Scotus or William of Occam talk about a man's "property," what they have in mind is his entitlement to use, for consumption or for consumption-oriented exchange, the revenue flow from the stock of resources under his trusteeship. In feudal practice, too, laws of subinfeudation, primogeniture, and entailment severely restricted the alienation of resource stocks – in particular, of land and serfs, which represented the bulk of wealth. Consequently, medieval markets were almost entirely contract (flow), not equity (stock) markets. This is not contradicted by the fact that the fifteenth and sixteenth centuries saw the emergence of a European capital or loanable-funds market. The latter was based on large resource holders' desire to borrow – and the Augsburg and Genoese merchant and banking houses' willingness to lend – against the discounted value of future rent and tax incomes. However, what neither borrowers nor lenders could do was to quickly and easily ("speculatively") change the composition of their current stock of wealth. That is, though late medieval and Renaissance Europe may be said to have possessed a capital market, it lacked well-developed markets in ownership claims – stockmarkets.

The early 1600s saw the establishment, by merchant and trading company interests, of the Amsterdam stock exchange. Subsequent decades witnessed the rapid disintegration of the remnants of the feudal order and the first outlines of the modern capitalist system. One of its enduring characteristics – visible early on already and frequently remarked upon by seventeenth- and eighteenth-century observers – was the contrast between two types of wealth owners: Proprietors whose fortune was concentrated in

[2] See chapter 1. Understanding of arbitrage arguments has been hampered by the dominance of the Jevonian concept of goods arbitrage: The idea that (physically, temporally, and locationally) *identical goods* must have a single market price. This is trivial compared to the much more demanding requirement that *heterogeneous ownership claims* possess a structure of competitive prices such that expected equity yields are instantaneously uniform. From the perspective of optimal resource allocation, the price structure in question is dual to the primal requirement that – irrespective of its boundary conditions (in other words, whatever its history and its goal) – an economy must approach its objective along a path which is dynamically efficient [Dorfman, Samuelson, and Solow (1958)].

a single productive asset (or a single group of functionally related real assets), and owners of yield-maximizing portfolios of instantly tradable financial claims. The contrast was that between the landlord or the capitalist-entrepreneur, on the one hand, and the capitalist-financier (or rentier, banker, projector, stock jobber), on the other. The former were owners of "fonds fixes" or "sunk" capital, the latter of "fonds mobiliers" or "floating" capital – a terminology no commentator, be it Quesnay, Marx, or Marshall, could do without.

Despite its increasing real-world prominence over the centuries, floating or financial capital never gained analytical status within the hard core of economic theory. In particular, unlike real capital, it failed to be integrated into the theory of value and distribution. Instead, it was banished to the looser, more applied or policy-oriented branches of the discipline, such as balance-of-payments theory or the theory of finance. This was true at the time of the classics and continues – despite important integrative developments in recent finance theory – largely to be true today.

Consider, for example, the case of Ricardo. In his corn model, two resource stocks exist at any given moment: A periodically reconstituted wage fund and land. Each provides a stream of services that commands a stream of rental payments in the form of, respectively, a gross capital rental (the fixed subsistence wage plus a variable profit markup) and a land rental. In the two-good version of the model, Ricardo shows how competition entails both a determinate land rental and an intersectorally uniform profit rate on corn stocks. The latter, of course, represents the principle of the uniform rate of profit – the guiding idea in classical and Marxian thinking on capitalist competition.

A fundamental question about resource pricing Ricardo, however, fails to ask. Reflecting the lingering feudal notion of his time that landed property is somehow distinct from other forms of wealth and quasi-inalienable, Ricardo nowhere asks: What are the consequences for the dynamics of a capitalist economy of the equalization of profit rates, not merely across sectoral productive activities, *but across all forms of holding wealth*? That is, what happens if, over and above rental markets for corn and land, a stockmarket allowing the instantaneous and quasi-costless exchange of equity claims to wage funds and land is allowed to emerge?[3]

It is perhaps less Ricardo's failure to pose that question which surprises – only in Marx's time would the division of society's owners into capitalists and landlords seem *passé* – but the failure of modern general-equilibrium theorists to do so. In their models, equity markets are either absent (Heckscher–Ohlin–Samuelson) or rendered invisible (Arrow–Debreu), the

[3] Burgstaller (1989) discusses the consequences of an equity market in the Ricardo–Pasinetti (1960) model.

problem of value being visualized in terms of the flow pricing of inputs and outputs exclusively. The fact that wealth holders must at each instant be satisfied with the stock composition of their instantly tradable portfolios of ownership claims is, wrongly, thought to be of no consequence for the determination of relative prices.

The neglect of financial markets in modern price theory may in part be traced to the decision of its early neoclassical proponents to approach the problem of value by examining single-period pure exchange. Instead of to a focus on the yield-arbitrage equation and the *willingness to hold* storable ownership titles, this led to an emphasis on zero-excess-flow-demand equations and the *willingness to trade* nonstorable consumption goods. Despite his use, early in the *Elements of Pure Economics*, of the stockmarket as an exemplar for the idea of a perfectly competitive market, Walras (1874, 1954) introduces a yield-arbitrage equation only in Part V of his treatise, under the heading of saving and capital formation. There, his interpretation of it is uncharacteristically muddled, suffering from the author's attempt to conflate the stockmarket with the loanable-funds market. That, in turn, seems motivated by a desire to preserve the flow-equilibrium perspective carried over from the pure-exchange and the exchange-and-production models. Had the author approached the problem of pure exchange instead with a finance-theoretic perspective, the question – What are the conditions under which agents are willing to hold their portfolio of equity claims to current and future endowments? – would have imposed itself and received attention at least equal to, What are the terms at which agents willingly trade their current endowments?[4]

As it was, this would remain a road not taken – not taken, at least, in the theory of value. Instead, the concept of portfolio or stock equilibrium gained entry into the discipline through Keynesian macroeconomics. It did so via Keynes's (1936) successful defense of liquidity-preference theory against the Walras–Marshall–Fisher–Robertson flow view of interest-rate determination in the loanable-funds market.[5] Needless to say, the influence of the portfolio-equilibrium concept in macroeconomics has been decisive, even among theorists (such as Friedman or Patinkin) otherwise critical of Keynes. It has led to a progressive diminution in the role attributed to flow-equilibrium considerations in the determination of money prices and interest rates, a tendency intensified in the seventies under the influence of the rational-expectations approach [Arrow (1978)].

The process is well illustrated by postwar developments in the theory of flexible exchange rates. The forties and fifties were dominated by the Bickerdike(1920)–Robinson(1947)–Lerner(1944) elasticities approach,

[4] I discuss Walras's capital theory in supplement D.
[5] See Townshend (1936), Chick (1987).

according to which exchange rates move so as to clear a Walrasian flow market for exports and imports. The fifties saw the Keynesian insight [Alexander (1952)] that any current-account imbalance must reflect a discrepancy between national income and domestic absorption, thus cannot possibly be cured by an exchange-rate adjustment that leaves unchanged that discrepancy. This was followed, in the early sixties, by the overturning of the idea that the magnitude of equilibrium flows of "short-term capital" or "hot money" – the contemporary analogue to eighteenth-century "fonds mobiliers" and nineteenth-century "floating capital" – is a function of the size of international interest-rate differentials. As the Mundell (1963)–Fleming (1962) model showed so arrestingly, international yield arbitrage made such interest-rate differentials an economic impossibility, unless accounted for by transactions costs, risk premia, or expected capital gains. It followed that instantaneous international reserve positions (under fixed exchange rates) and momentary equilibrium exchange rates (under floating rates) were pure stock-equilibrium phenomena. The portfolio approach to flexible exchange rates was to be completed by the incorporation of rational expectations [Dornbusch (1976), Kouri (1976)] and remains today's dominant theory. In it, the exchange rate is viewed as driven by forward-looking asset markets and the instantaneous stock-equilibrium requirement that (appropriately defined) expected yields on alternative forms of internationally tradable wealth be instantaneously uniform. The flow (current-account) equilibrium determinants and variables central to early exchange-rate theory – import demand elasticities, the terms of trade, purchasing power parity – have been relegated to the role of long-run factors that, at given interest rates and expectations, are without purchase on the current equilibrium exchange rate.

II

The motion of a material object, being subject to the laws of physics, uses up time and energy. In contrast, a legal title to that object, being quasi-immaterial, may be transferred without appreciable expenditure of energy and quasi-instantaneously. The price of an ownership title, similarly immaterial, is in principle also instantaneously and costlessly variable.

It is with the consequences for the theory of value of such a distinction between immobile material resources and highly mobile ownership claims thereon that the present work is largely concerned. More precisely, I will argue that any economy that (a) possesses a well-defined system of private property and (b) is competitive, must be governed by two fundamental laws of motion. One traces out the trajectory, through time and across space, of stocks of both produced and primary inputs; the other – an arbitrage or portfolio-equilibrium equation – portrays the accompanying dynamics of prices of ownership claims on such resources:

$$\dot{x} = \psi(\pi, x; \alpha) \tag{0.1}$$

$$\dot{\pi} = \phi(\pi, x; \alpha), \tag{0.2}$$

where x is a vector of input allocations by sector, π a vector of prices of ownership claims, and α a vector of shift parameters. The mathematical consequence of the distinction between immobile inputs and highly mobile ownership claims thereon is this: The elements of x are predetermined at a point in time; those in π may jump instantaneously and discontinuously.

The reader will recognize the above as a quasi-Hamiltonian system, well known in capital theory since Samuelson and Solow's (1956) work on optimal heterogeneous-capital growth, the Hahn (1966) stability problem, and the Cass/Shell (1976b) volume.[6] However, the literature utilizing [(0.1), (0.2)] operates at a very high level of generality and abstraction and has, it is fair to say, had little impact on the average economist's price theory. It is my purpose to make the case for [(0.1), (0.2)] as a powerful alternative to the simple static two-by-two general-equilibrium models he is most likely to use. In particular, I will argue that a dynamical system in π and x is capable of unifying the classical and the neoclassical theory of price and, simultaneously, the theory of capital with the theory of finance.

The arbitraging behavior underlying (0.2) is well known in finance and macroeconomics, but infrequently spelled out in the theory of value and capital. At any point in time, the economy's proprietors hold all existing ownership claims in their portfolios. In a riskless world of perfect asset substitutability, they will willingly hold each type of claim – be satisfied with the composition of their portfolios – if and only if expected yields are uniform. For instance, if aggregate wealth $K \equiv p^C X^C + p^S X^S$ is made up of claims to predetermined stocks of corn X^C and steel X^S, instantaneous uniformity of expected yields requires that the arbitrage equation

$$\rho^C \equiv \frac{r^C}{p^C} - \delta^C + (\hat{p}^C)^e = \frac{r^S}{p^S} - \delta^S + (\hat{p}^S)^e \equiv \rho^S \tag{0.2.1}$$

hold at all times, where ρ^i $(i = C, S)$ is the expected rate of return on an equity claim to X^i; p^i the equity price; $r^i - \delta^i p^i$ the net dividend or rental accruing to owners (net of depreciation $\delta^i p^i$, where δ^i is an exponential rate of depreciation of the stock); and $(\hat{p}^i)^e \equiv (\dot{p}^i)^e / p^i$ the expected percent capital gain. Equation (0.2.1) of course follows from the postulate that ownership claims can be instantaneously and costlessly traded in a competitive

[6] See also Magill (1970, 1977), Brock and Malliaris (1989), and my discussion of Hamiltonian dynamics in supplement A.2.

market. That market is the bourse or stockmarket. A necessary and sufficient condition for it to clear at given dividends r^i and expectations $(\dot{p}^i)^e$ is that the equity prices p^i be such that (0.2.1) obtains. The economy is then said to be in stock equilibrium.[7]

The financial system contains two functionally distinct markets, both of which trade in equity: The stockmarket and the capital (loanable-funds) market. As just seen, the role of the former is to guarantee, via arbitrage, point-in-time uniformity of expected yields and, thus, instantaneous *composition* balance in agents' portfolios. The capital market, on the other hand, lets agents achieve their preferred portfolio *level* over time through saving (accumulation of equity of uniform yield) or dissaving. In the model of pure exchange, flow balance in the capital market determines (given goods-market clearing) the equilibrium level of the uniform equity yield – that is, the momentary-equilibrium real rate of interest. In other models, such as that of von Neumann (1946) or Solow (1956), the capital market helps to determine the relative rate of accumulation (0.1) of capital goods.

The reader may wish to recall at this point that my interpretation of equation (0.1) is broad. I will view it not merely as the law of relative accumulation of new capital inputs, but as descriptive of the process of sectoral reallocation of existing – in particular, of all primary – resources. For I will take it as axiomatic that existing resource stocks are immobile as between alternative employments. They may be *movable*, it is true, but only at a cost and over time – that is, subject to an act of saving and a decision to invest. Both the accumulation of new and the intersectoral movement of existing resources are governed, at each instant, by an arbitrage equation such as (0.2.1). Its function is to make it a matter of indifference how investment is allocated within and across these two uses.

I take the momentary location specificity of existing resource stocks – be they labor or physical capital – to be fundamental. It contradicts the widely used assumption of "perfect factor mobility." According to the latter, existing stocks of real resources can be moved instantaneously and costlessly between sectors or – as in the theory of international capital

7 The reason for my anglicized spelling of "stockmarket" (in lieu of the American "stock market") is to help the reader distinguish between my two uses of "stock": As a market label (stockmarket) and as an equilibrium concept (stock equilibrium, as opposed to flow equilibrium). Chapter 1 shows equation (0.2) to be a simple transformation of (0.2.1) that employs the definitions $\pi \equiv p^S/p^C$, $x \equiv X^C/X^S$, the myopic-foresight assumption, and entrepreneurial profit maximization. It will also be seen that [(0.1), (0.2)] is built on the assumption that the intertemporal felicity function used by households is logarithmic. As noted inalienability of labor presents no problem, provided there exists a capital market that allows borrowing against human capital. Finally, should the economy contain outputs that are nonstorable (pure consumption goods or "nonbasics") [(0.1), (0.2)] will be shown to also incorporate instantaneous clearing of the corresponding flow markets, in addition to stock equilibrium for ownership claims.

movements – even between countries. Obviously, this is wholly metaphysical. What can be so moved are equities, not the physical resource stocks themselves. The assumption of perfect factor mobility thus rests on a fundamental category mistake. Alternatively, it amounts to an inadmissible commingling of steady-state analysis (in which many stocks may be taken as variable) with the study of temporary equilibria (in which all stocks are historically predetermined).

That there should be confusion on this point is surprising. For to distinguish commodities by physical characteristics, date, *and* location is what the Arrow–Debreu model[8] has taught us. The suppression of equity markets in the latter perhaps goes some way in explaining the neglect of location specificity by small-dimensional general-equilibrium models.

To the tripartite taxonomy mentioned, Arrow (1952) and Debreu (1959) add a fourth commodity characterization – by state of nature. The problem of state-of-nature uncertainty I shall neglect in this book. The reader may nonetheless find helpful some remarks on the relationship between my perspective and the modern theory of finance – the field which, more than any other in economics, has taken state-of-nature uncertainty seriously.

III

The influence of time on economic behavior has two aspects. The future generally differs from the present nontrivially – either because the economy has not fully adjusted to a given environment, or because that environment is expected to undergo a change in structure. Current economic behavior will then differ from that obtaining in a steady state – even if no uncertainty attaches to future events. This is the *pure role of time*. The fact that the future state of the environment cannot be known with certitude introduces a second and distinct influence of time on economic behavior: *The role of uncertainty*.[9] Uncertainty I will, as indicated, neglect in this book – despite my frequent use of terms (such as "speculation" or "riskless arbitrage") connoting it. I offer two justifications. Together they reveal the nexus between the work at hand and modern finance theory.

First, I agree that Arrow's (1952) essay on risk-bearing in general equilibrium was pathbreaking, for well-known reasons. However, it also has been severely misleading. It has given rise to the impression that "securities" (bonds and equities) function primarily as instruments for the efficient allocation of risk, and that they only emerge in response to the

[8] Arrow and Debreu (1954), Debreu (1959).

[9] See Burmeister (1980). When information across agents is distributed asymmetrically and/or the latter lack perfect contingent foresight, uncertainty will attach not just to future states of the environment, but also to future market outcomes.

absence of markets for contingent commodities (that is, as insurance substitutes). This is a very peculiar interpretation. For clearly the defining function of a security is to serve as a direct (equity) or indirect (debt) title to private property. In a world of complete certainty, it is in that role that securities are accumulated, held, and traded in financial markets. The introduction of risk will add an insurance (portfolio diversification) motive given the presence of risk aversion – but that is secondary.

It is not true that under certainty ownership claims are economically redundant, that is, reducible to the physical resources themselves. For instance, except in special cases a sequence economy with a complete set of spot markets will behave very differently depending on whether or not the capitalized value of its resource stocks can be bought and sold in a stockmarket.[10] Similarly, the Mundell–Fleming model alerts us to the fact that the international mobility of financial claims will have a profound influence on the dynamics of an open economy – whatever we assume about international movements of real capital.

Second, some of the deepest insights gained in the theory of finance in recent years are in fact independent from the presence of uncertainty. One, in particular, seems noteworthy. It is the idea that the problem of value has a recursive logical structure involving three (not two) steps: Asset arbitrage, optimization, and equilibrium.[11] Since Walras it has been understood that optimization at arbitrary nonnegative prices is a logical prerequisite for the determination of equilibrium prices. Now it is increasingly perceived that optimization is impossible unless agents are confronted with prices that, rather than being arbitrary, already possess a lot of structure. Namely, they must be free of unexploited opportunities for asset arbitrage. The importance of arbitrage arguments in recent finance theory is illustrated by the flowering of "derivative-asset" analysis and the latter's widespread acceptance among market participants. (The Black–Scholes (1973) formula is only the best-known example.) In line with the conventional interpretation of arbitrage as a risk-free transaction, pricing derivative assets involves neither risk preferences, probability beliefs, nor risky endowments.

Such "valuation by arbitrage" of derivative securities finance theory distinguishes from "valuation by equilibrium" of the securities underlying the derivatives. In terms of arbitrage equation (0.2.1), valuation by arbitrage seeks to determine the relative price $\pi \equiv p^S/p^C$; valuation by

10 The special cases are systems – such as the pure-exchange and the Ramsey–Solow economy – with less than two produced capital goods (that is, in which produced capital is either absent or homogeneous); see chapter 2.

11 See, for instance, Duffie (1992) and Huang/Litzenberger (1988). The point was adumbrated by Dorfman, Samuelson, and Solow [(1958), pp.320–1] in their discussion of the conditions necessary for the decentralized achievement of dynamic production efficiency (on the latter, see chapter 2 and supplement A.3).

equilibrium, the corresponding numéraire security prices p^C, p^S. The terminology makes sense insofar as general-equilibrium models in finance are usually of the pure-exchange type.[12] Clearing of the associated Walrasian flow markets then determines the equilibrium p^i as a function of state endowments and of risk preferences (given the absence of unexploited arbitrage opportunities). Risk thus affects the determination of the p^i only, not that of the arbitrage-based relative asset price π.

To summarize: It is increasingly understood in theoretical finance that "no-arbitrage" conditions impart a fundamental structure to the set of all possible equilibrium prices.[13] What is less clearly seen – and what this book will show – is that this insight is completely divorced from the presence of uncertainty.

I close my remarks on some links between the present work and financial economics with the following observation. As noted, recent finance theory has typically restricted itself to an Arrow (1952) contingent-commodity, pure-exchange economy. The logic of that restriction seems unclear, unless it is the wrong-headed insistence on uncertainty as a sine-qua-non for the study of asset-price fundamentals. Why not first examine the asset-price predictions, under certainty, of the full range of intertemporal general-equilibrium models – including those generated by the classical theories of Marx, von Neumann, Leontief, and Sraffa? For instance, the latter's nonsubstitution and nonbasics theorems have fundamental implications for how the interindustry structure of technological innovation affects, and (risk) preferences often fail to affect, the time path of general-equilibrium asset prices. These implications must remain invisible to a student of Walrasian pure exchange.

IV

As mentioned earlier, a principal objective of the study to follow is doctrinal. In a nutshell, I wish to advance the immodest claim that I have found, in system [(0.1), (0.2)], the common theoretical core of classical and Walrasian economics. I will defend that claim by demonstrating that the canonical models of both traditions are special cases of [(0.1), (0.2)].

Three general remarks may serve as a preface to this aspect of my work. First, surely the methodologically most damning criticism of Neo-Ricardian versions of classical theory inspired by Sraffa (1960) is the correct accusation that, being confined to steady states, they are non-causal,

12 See, for instance, Lucas (1978). Brock (1982) is an extension to a production economy.
13 A structure revealed by the martingale property.

therefore incapable of providing what a philosopher or a scientist would call an explanation – a temporal cause-and-effect account anchored in arbitrary initial conditions.[14] This contrasts with Walrasian theory and its emphasis on historically given initial resource endowments and on the sequence of non-steady-state temporary equilibria these and the system's technology, tastes, and expectations give rise to. It suffices to say here that none of the classical models I develop below on the basis of [(0.1), (0.2)] are open to this criticism.

In the second place, important theoretical concerns of Marxian and Neo-Ricardian economics, often unintelligible to Walrasian ears, take on precise analytical meaning within my framework. Two, in particular, shall be emphasized. The *nonsubstitution theorem* asserts that in constant returns to scale, no joint production systems with an unchanging profit rate and not more than one primary input, relative prices are independent of the structure of demand.[15] The *Ricardo–Bortkiewicz–Sraffa theorem* shows that technical changes can be divided into two fundamental kinds: Those affecting the production of basics (which are outputs that enter as inputs directly or indirectly into all other outputs) and those influencing the production of nonbasics. Only the former will have an effect on the economy's rate of profit.[16]

[14] See, for instance, Burmeister (1980) and Dixit (1981) for this criticism. A good illustration of the Neo-Ricardian approach (to the theory of international trade, in the instance) are the papers in Steedman (1979).

[15] What I will call the neoclassical or Samuelson nonsubstitution theorem [see Samuelson (1951, 1959, 1961) and the papers by Arrow, Georgescu-Roegen, and Koopmans in Koopmans (1951); also Mirrlees (1969), Stiglitz (1970), Bliss (1975)] refers to the case of one primary input; the Sraffa nonsubstitution theorem [Sraffa (1960)] to an economy with no primary inputs. The indicated conditions are sufficient for both versions of the theorem. Elementary expositions can be found in Arrow and Starrett (1973), Varian (1984), Ahmad (1991).

[16] Ricardo (1815,1951), von Bortkiewicz (1907), Sraffa (1960); see also Pasinetti (1960). Sraffa's definition of a basic is a produced commodity (an output) that enters directly or indirectly into the production of all commodities; nonbasics are produced commodities other than basics [(1960), §6]. In this book I adopt an alternative definition: Basics are outputs that are storable (they possess a finite rate of depreciation and, thus, can be accumulated as input stocks); nonbasics are outputs that cannot be stored (they are instantaneously perishable – thus, nonaccumulable as input stocks). I offer two reasons for my definition, one of contrast, the other of analogy *vis-à-vis* Sraffa. First, stock prices of basics in my sense and stock prices of primary inputs together exhaust the set of fundamental asset prices π at the center of interest in my book (recall [(0.1), (0.2)]). As will be seen, nonbasics in my sense may contribute to the accumulation of basics (VON NEUMANN III) or to the movement of primary resources (WALRAS III) – thus, be basic in Sraffa's sense – but their price will not figure in the vector π (the value of the services provided by a productive nonbasic output is imputed to the asset value of the basic and primary input stocks that produce it). Second, for the models examined in the present work (excepting the two cases mentioned), Sraffa's definition and mine are exactly coextensive and, thus, may be used interchangeably.

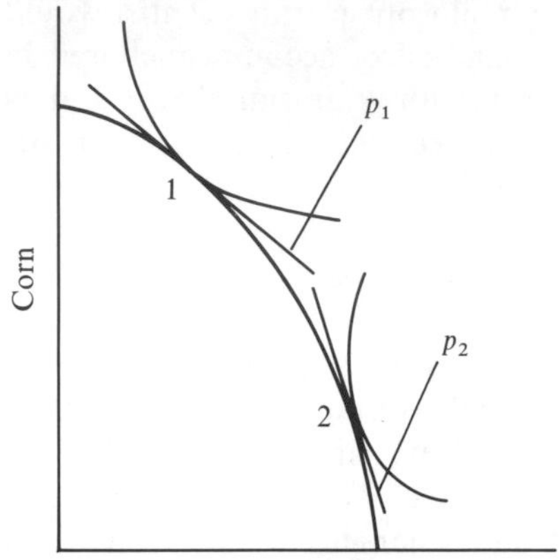

Figure 0.1 Price consequences of a preference shift toward steel (neoclassical case)

In this book I show how these two theorems apply to a non-steady-state environment. Consider, for instance, the canonical question of what the consequences are for the relative price of steel, if – in a two-sector economy with momentarily given and scarce resources – there is a consumption preference shift toward steel away from corn. The standard answer is that depicted in figure 0.1: The price of steel increases. An economically equally justified answer is given in figure 0.2: The price of steel remains unchanged. In the latter case the system responds entirely by means of a progressive shift in capital (thus, output) composition at constant prices along Rybczynski-locus *RR*, a shift triggered by the change in corn and steel inventories that results from the demand disturbance.[17] In the example of figure 0.1, corn and steel are nonstorable outputs produced by two exogenously given primary inputs ("labor" and "land") – the standard neoclassical setup. By contrast, in figure 0.2 storable commodities are produced by commodities under an Uzawa intensity assumption.[18] The two

[17] The change in corn and steel stocks on impact is measured by, respectively, the vertical and the horizontal distance between points 1 and 1′.

[18] Both figures are consistent with intertemporal utility maximization on the part of resource owners. For comparability with figure 0.1, I have assumed in figure 0.2 a (technologically determined) profit rate that happens to coincide with input owners' fixed rate of time preference; this yields a long-run stationary state, rather than the von Neumann steady-growth equilibrium studied in chapter 1. Also, it is for familiarity only that I have drawn the production possibility frontier normally bowed out (implying perfect factor mobility between sectors), rather than rectangular (implying momentary location specificity). For the Rybczynski (1955) locus and the Uzawa (1961/3) intensity assumption, see any text on the two-sector general-equilibrium model [Jones (1965), Johnson (1971), Wan (1971), Takayama (1972)].

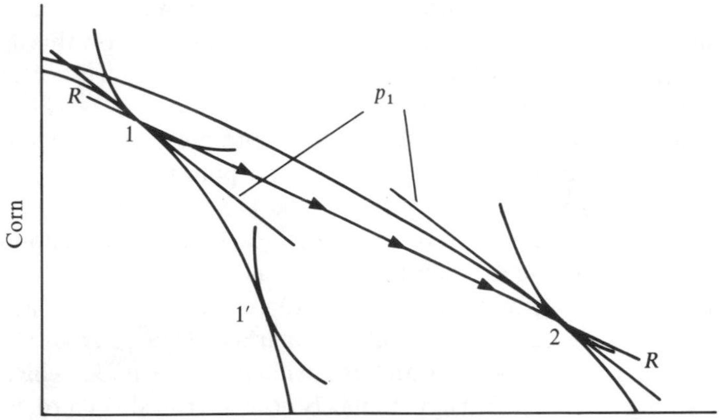

Figure 0.2 Price consequences of a preference shift toward steel (classical case)

answers to the initial question are, from the point of view of economic logic, equally correct – but only the first is part of textbook doctrine. As an antidote, the chapters to follow will repeatedly illustrate the coherence, simplicity, and elegance of dynamic nonsubstitution models. The implied message is, perhaps, less likely to fall on deaf ears now that neoclassical economists have rediscovered Marx–von Neumann models of "expanded reproduction."[19] For endogenous growth is of course inconsistent with ultimate scarcities and, given globally constant returns to scale, cannot help but generate a nonsubstitution theory of long-run prices.

The third and final remark regarding my attempt at doctrinal synthesis concerns the Arrow–Debreu model. It is with the neoclassical "retreat" to the latter that the Cambridge controversies on capital came to an inconclusive halt.[20] In chapter 2 and supplement A.3, I seek to reopen the debate by examining the Arrow–Debreu model from a point of view likely to be understood by economists of classical persuasion. My conclusion will be that, as Hahn (1982a) and others have claimed, the Arrow–Debreu framework is formally consistent with and – not being confined to steady states – more general than the classical models preferred by Cambridge-UK theorists. However, it is also true that it distorts the picture of economic life drawn by these models. It does so by unwarrantedly building up its agent and market categories such that consumer utility maximization and flow-market clearing are highlighted, while the "competition of capitals" (Marx) and the principle of the uniform rate of profit are moved to the shadows.

[19] See Romer (1986), Lucas (1988).
[20] See Harcourt (1972), Stiglitz (1974), Bliss (1975), Hahn (1982a), Ahmad (1991).

The classical visualization of the economic process, though analytically present, remains descriptively implicit. It will be my purpose to show this by translating a simplified version of the Arrow–Debreu model into a classical arbitrage-based von Neumann economy.

Apart from demonstrating how the Arrow–Debreu system lends itself to a classical theory of value, this will help to make three points. First, it yields as a byproduct a long-overdue correction of the Dorfman–Samuelson–Solow (1958) account of decentralized dynamic efficiency. Second, it shows that the Arrow–Debreu model, when interpreted as a sequence economy located in time, possesses an intrinsic dynamic structure driven by arbitrage and forward-looking speculation in the stockmarket. That structure is inconsistent with the extrinsic Walrasian tatonnement process under which the model's stability properties have customarily been discussed.[21] Third, as chapter 1 demonstrates, in a forward-looking, arbitrage-based economy in which all outputs are storable (basics), the problem of the Walrasian auctioneer is solved. It is solved by arbitrageurs who competitively short-sell any equity currently in excess supply. Given simultaneous myopic maximization of profits by entrepreneurs, this is sufficient to instantaneously move all of the economy's prices to their temporary-equilibrium value. Profit maximization by forward-looking speculators then guarantees that these temporary-equilibrium prices are based on correct (saddle-path-consistent) expectations. Speculators thus assure the economy's dynamic convergence to long-run equilibrium, entrepreneurs and arbitrageurs its movement to temporary equilibrium.[22]

My general angle of attack in trying to work toward a meeting of minds between adherents of the Walras–Fisher–Hicks–Arrow–Debreu tradition and the defenders of the Ricardo–Marx–von Neumann–Sraffa legacy can be summarized as follows: I shall (i) argue for [(0.1), (0.2)] as the common theoretical core of both traditions, and (ii) do so by starting from a von Neumann assumption about resource reproducibility. The advantage of the latter as an entry point into the theory of capital was pointed out by Kaldor more than fifty years ago:

> For a proper understanding of the nature of capital and interest one ought to start by analyzing the conditions of equilibrium in a society where *all* goods are capital goods, i.e. where "original" or non-augmentable resources do not exist at all. It is rather unfortunate that, following Böhm-Bawerk and his school, we have been generally accustomed to start with a more complicated set-up, with the picture of Robinson Crusoe engaged in net-making ... Had the analysis started with the "general case" – by imagining a society where *all* resources and the services of all

[21] Arrow and Hurwicz (1958), Arrow, Block, and Hurwicz (1959), Negishi (1962).

[22] Chapter 3 extends this account to an economy containing an instantaneously clearing flow market for nonbasics.

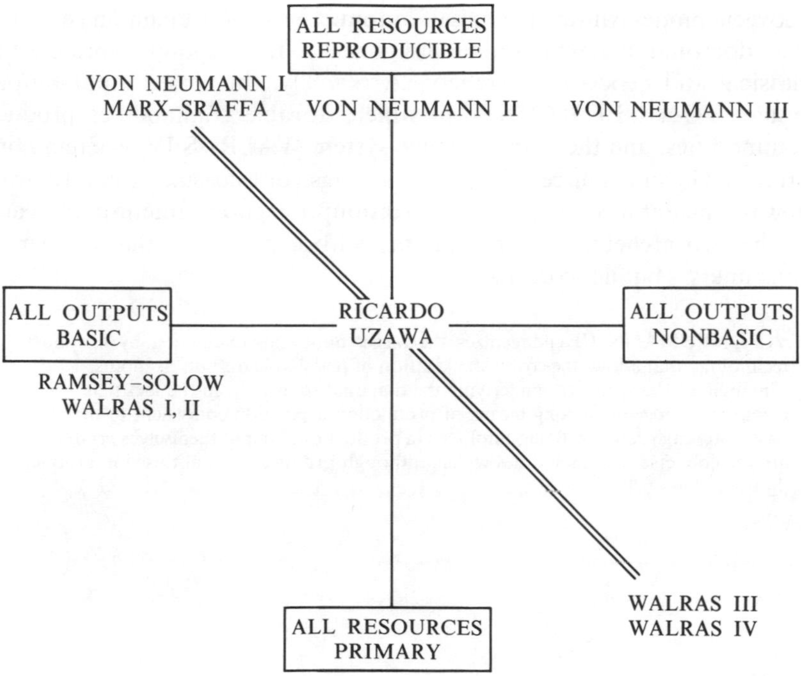

Figure 0.3 Taxonomy of models by input reproducibility and output durability

resources cooperate in producing further resources – a great deal of the controversies concerning the theory of capital might not have arisen. As we shall see, it will be much easier to get back from this world to Böhm-Bawerk's world than to make the journey in the opposite direction.[23]

I will develop a sequence of models, arranged along two axes (see figure 0.3 and the table of contents).[24] One characterizes the system's inputs by reproducibility, the other its outputs by durability. The input axis shows, at one of its poles, primary-input-free variants of the von Neumann–Marx–Sraffa system; at its opposite, Walrasian economies with a multiplicity of primary but no reproducible inputs.[25] The second axis ranks economies according to the durability of their outputs: At one extreme, we find systems in which all goods are storable (or basic in my terminology); at the other, systems producing instantaneously perishable outputs (nonbasics) only; in

[23] Kaldor (1937).

[24] For economy of exposition, I identify models, or groups of models, by the name(s) of the author(s) most closely associated with their spirit or original structure.

[25] Exhaustible resources will not be discussed, though the Hotelling (1931) rule has a Hamiltonian structure identical to [(0.1), (0.2)].

between, models with both types of output.[26] From this taxonomy emerges the "doctrinal diagonal" shown in figure 0.3. Its endpoints represent the classical and neoclassical archetypes: Namely, the closed input–output system VON NEUMANN I, in which storable commodities produce commodities, and the pure-exchange system WALRAS IV, wherein non-produced income sources (Fisherian "springs" or Lucasian "trees") deliver flows of instantaneously perishable consumption goods. Interestingly, each of the two archetypes is an economy with capitalists – that is, owner-consumers – but no workers.[27]

[26] VON NEUMANN III endogenizes the basics-nonbasics distinction by introducing a technology that allows the costly stockization of perishable outputs as inputs.

[27] The logic of the symmetry underlying the diagonal follows from the fact that "[primary] resources ... occupy among means of production a position equivalent to that of 'non-basics' among products. Being employed in production, but not themselves produced, they are the converse of commodities which, although produced, are not used in production" [Sraffa (1960), p.74].

I

Reproducible resources

1

VON NEUMANN I: A basics-only economy

1.1 Introduction

What are the point-in-time and dynamic properties of a decentralized economic universe in which all resources, though momentarily given and scarce, are potentially expandable without limit? This is the question I wish to address in my VON NEUMANN models.

Analytically, the first of these, VON NEUMANN I, is a two-sector, non-steady-state, continuous-time version of the von Neumann (1946) economy.[1] It contains capitalists but no labor – all income is derived from the ownership of nonhuman resources that are capable of aggregate self-replication through a process of automated interindustry production. As a modeling assumption, absence of labor demands no apology: It is an essential ingredient of the Walrasian model of pure exchange, to which VON NEUMANN I will be seen to stand in deep and unexpected symmetry.

Though a complete understanding of that symmetry must await my discussion of WALRAS IV in the final chapter, the reader may wish to keep in mind that this is where I am heading: I shall construct, in this book, a doctrinal circle whose closure will show the Walrasian model of pure exchange to be, like VON NEUMANN I, a two-good, non-stationary-state, intertemporally profit-maximizing economy. Its agents, pure capitalists like their von Neumann counterparts, hold title to nonproduced resource stocks ("fountains") that produce exogenous flows of nonstorable consumption goods ("milk" and "honey"). By contrast, capitalists in VON NEUMANN I hold title to produced input stocks that, via an interindustry network, contribute to the production of storable outputs ("corn" and "steel"). As discussed in the Introduction, I call the former goods non-basics, the latter basics.

[1] Useful introductions to the von Neumann model are Dorfman, Samuelson, and Solow (1958), Vanek (1968), Wan (1971), Brems (1986), Afriat (1987), Ahmad (1991); see also Chakravarty *et al.* (1989).

Apart from developing the basics-only economy VON NEUMANN I and introducing much of the agent and market structure used in the rest of the book, the present chapter offers two results. First, it substantiates the nonsubstitution property discussed in figure 0.2 of the Introduction. It proves the

> *Proposition (dynamic nonsubstitution)*: In VON NEUMANN I, a shift in intra- or intertemporal consumption preferences must leave relative prices unaffected on impact, during the traverse, and across steady states – despite point-in-time scarcity of all resources.

I will contrast this with perturbations that *do* alter relative prices and the rate of profit: Anticipated and unanticipated changes in technology.

Second, for the case of a basics-only system, the chapter solves the problem of the Walrasian auctioneer – the question of who, in a competitive economy with price-taking agents, is left to move market prices to their equilibrium level. The proposed solution may be summarized in two propositions.[2]

> *Proposition (convergence to temporary equilibrium)*: In VON NEUMANN I, the problem of the temporary-equilibrium Walrasian auctioneer is solved. It is so by virtue of profit maximization on the part of entrepreneurs and of stockmarket arbitrageurs. Profit maximization by entrepreneurs anchors output prices in equity prices at all times; profit maximization by arbitrageurs leads the latter to instantaneously short sell – at a price below the current market price – any equity that currently is in stock excess supply. Whatever the state of expectations, this is sufficient to drive stockmarket (thus, output) prices to their temporary-equilibrium value.

> *Proposition (convergence to steady-state equilibrium)*: In VON NEUMANN I, the problem of the intertemporal Walrasian auctioneer is solved. It is so by virtue of profit maximization on the part of well-informed stockmarket speculators. Such profit maximization precludes market bubbles and places the economy on a path of self-fulfilling expectations that is market clearing over an unbounded horizon.

My usual assumption about expectations formation (discussed at length below and in supplement A.2) will be that (i) expectations are formed by speculators and espoused from these by the economy's remaining agents, whose skills lie in areas other than anticipatory ability; and (ii) speculators

[2] Chapter 3 extends the solution to an economy containing a nonbasic.

possess myopic foresight and the capacity to project the latter into the long run (which endows them with "perfect" foresight). Many insights about dynamics do not however depend on the perfect-foresight postulate. At the end of the chapter, I accordingly introduce the static-expectations hypothesis as an alternative to perfect foresight. I will repeatedly make use of this alternative throughout the book.

1.2 The model

Consider an economy in which inputs of corn and steel produce, without a time lag, outputs of corn and steel. Corn and steel are storable and depreciate at a common exponential rate. No labor is used.

The economy's momentary capital or wealth,[3] K, is the value of ownership claims to stocks of corn, X^C, and steel, X^S:

$$K \equiv p^C X^C + p^S X^S, \tag{1.1}$$

where p^i is the stock- or equity-price of capital good $i = C, S$. The economy's numéraire is flow output of corn.

Stocks of steel and corn produce output flows Q^C and Q^S of corn and steel by way of a specific-factors, single-technique Leontief technology of the form

$$Q^C = q^C X^S, \qquad q^C > 0 \tag{1.2}$$

$$Q^S = q^S X^C, \qquad q^S > 0. \tag{1.3}$$

Thus, corn is "steel intensive" and steel is "corn intensive," exhibiting a simple form of the Uzawa (1961/3) factor-intensity assumption.[4]

Four functional categories of atomistic agents exist: Capitalists, arbitrageurs, speculators, and entrepreneurs.[5]

[3] The two terms are used interchangeably throughout, as are capitalist, wealth holder, and owner.

[4] What follows goes through for more complex technologies obeying that assumption in its appropriate form; examples are the standard neoclassical two-sector model with two-factor production functions [Uzawa (1961/3), Jones (1965)], or n-sector extensions thereof [Samuelson (1953), Jones and Scheinkman (1977), Ethier (1984)]. It can be shown that, unlike the latter, VON NEUMANN I does not possess an infinite-horizon path if its technology is anti-Uzawa ($Q^i = q^i X^i, i = C, S$; see my discussion of an anti-Uzawa case in supplement C.2).

[5] Recall the historical distinction, discussed in the Introduction, between the capitalist-financier and the capitalist-entrepreneur. Only capitalist-financiers (called capitalists for short) and pure entrepreneurs appear in my models, reflecting the modern separation of ownership and management. The function proper of capitalists is that of accumulation and consumption; they delegate the management of their portfolios to arbitrageurs and speculators. Though all agents seek maximum profits – and the fact that they do so is, in each case, critical to the behavior of the model – only capitalists have nonzero equilibrium income and, thus, wealth.

Entrepreneurs guarantee that entrepreneurial profits are competitively driven to zero at each instant. This gives

$$p^C = 1 = (1/q^C)r^S \tag{1.4}$$

$$p^S = p = (1/q^S)r^C, \tag{1.5}$$

where p is the flow price of steel and the r^i stand for gross rental rates or dividends of the respective capital goods.[6] The equalities $p^C = 1$, $p^S = p$ preclude pure profits from an excess of stock-demand over flow-supply price,[7] while $1 = (1/q^C)r^S$, $p = (1/q^S)r^C$ rules out pure profits from an excess of flow-supply price over unit flow costs.[8]

I now turn to the economy's bourse or stockmarket. Whereas to the system as a whole the stocks X^C and X^S are rigidly given, to any individual manager of a capitalist portfolio its composition as between ownership claims in X^C and X^S appears as a choice variable subject only to the owner's current wealth constraint.[9] For a portfolio manager to be satisfied with the current composition of his portfolio, each of the equities it contains must carry the same expected yield. Since this is equally true for all portfolio holders, and since portfolio shifts can be executed instantaneously and costlessly, arbitrage equation (0.2.1), or

$$\rho^C \equiv \frac{r^C}{p^C} - \delta + (\hat{p}^C)^e = \frac{r^S}{p^S} - \delta + (\hat{p}^S)^e \equiv \rho^S, \tag{1.6}$$

must be satisfied economy-wide at all points in time. Recall that ρ^i denotes the expected yield (or rate of return) and $(\hat{p}^i)^e \equiv (\dot{p}^i)^e/p^i \equiv (dp^i/dt)^e/p^i$ the expected percent capital gain on an i-type equity ($i = C, S$; e refers to an

[6] Recall from (0.2.1) that net rentals or dividends are given by $r^i - \delta p^i$. Two analytically equivalent ownership assumptions are possible (they are discussed in greater detail in supplement A.3): (i) Capitalists directly own – that is, purchase in the output market and rent out to entrepreneurs in rental markets – physical capital goods; (ii) capitalists own capital goods indirectly via equities issued by entrepreneurs, who use the proceeds to buy physical capital goods and who pay out dividends to equity holders. Thus, r^S equivalently denotes the rental rate on services from steel stocks or the unit dividend paid out to equity holders in the industry (corn) using steel.

[7] $p^C \leq 1$, $p^S \leq p$ would imply the possibility of temporary equilibria with zero gross investment in one or both capital goods; since aggregate gross saving will be strictly positive and expected asset yields equalized at all times (see below), this is ruled out. On the other hand, zero pure profits precludes $p^C > 1$, $p^S > p$. $p^C = 1$, $p^S = p$ follows.

[8] Given my specific-factors technology (which defines a rectangular production possibility frontier), $1 < (1/q^C)r^S$ or $p < (1/q^S)r^C$ – entailing complete specialization in steel or corn, respectively – is ruled out by the finite-price restriction on p and $1/p$. On the other hand, $1 > (1/q^C)r^S$ and $p > (1/q^S)r^C$ is ruled out by the zero-entrepreneurial profit condition. The second equality in (1.4) and (1.5) follows.

[9] Since I assume capitalists to be identical and since I normalize their number to one, the wealth constraint on the representative portfolio is K[(1.1)].

expectation). The exponential rate of depreciation $0 \leqslant \delta < \infty$ is assumed uniform for simplicity.[10]

In a moment, I will interpret (1.6) as the market-clearing condition for the economy's stockmarket. But first observe what (1.6) accomplishes: It guarantees instantaneous uniformity of expected yields across all assets. This uniquely defines the economy's rate of profit $\rho \equiv \rho^C = \rho^S$. It also defines its real rate of interest. For recall that the cost of borrowing – the real rate of interest – is the opportunity cost of acquiring, through asset decumulation, current output in excess of current income. But that opportunity cost precisely is the uniform yield or rate of profit ρ expected from *holding* assets. Rate of profit and rate of interest thus coincide at all times and will be used interchangeably in this book.

Next, rewrite (1.6) as

$$\tilde{\chi}(\pi; p^C, r^C, r^S, \hat{\pi}^e) \equiv \rho^C - \rho^S \equiv \frac{1}{p^C}\left(r^C - \frac{r^S}{\pi}\right) - \hat{\pi}^e = 0, \qquad \pi \equiv p^S/p^C \quad (1.7)$$

where $\tilde{\chi}(\cdot)$ is a yield-differential function. It follows from (1.7) that arbitrage equation (1.6), though it uniquely *defines* the uniform rate of profit ρ, is not by itself capable of *determining* it (that is, of establishing its equilibrium value). What, at given dividends r^i and at given expectations $\hat{\pi}^e$, stockmarket arbitrage *does* determine is the relative equity price π – the number of corn equities one must surrender in the stockmarket in order to acquire one steel equity.[11]

In *some* economies – namely in all those free of nonbasics, such as VON NEUMANN I – the arbitrage equation, however, achieves much more.[12] If combined with entrepreneurial profit maximization, arbitrage is capable of solving for the economy's equilibrium prices p^i and its equilibrium profit rate ρ, given only expectations and parameters. In other words, in economies such as VON NEUMANN I, entrepreneurial profit maximization, as reflected in (1.4), (1.5), and portfolio-yield maximization, as embodied in (1.6), together are necessary and sufficient for full temporary equilibrium.[13]

[10] $(r^i/p^i) - \delta$ is often called the current yield. Unless thus qualified, "yield" always refers to a capital-gain-inclusive magnitude. If the capital gain referred to is expected (as in (1.6)), one is talking about the expected yield; if reference is made to an actual capital gain $\hat{p}^i$, $(r^i/p^i) - \delta + \hat{p}^i$ denotes the actual yield. Under the myopic-foresight postulate, actual and expected magnitudes coincide, in which case I will be talking simply about the rate of return or yield ρ^i on equity *i*.

[11] Note that $\tilde{\chi}_2 = 0$ near a steady state with $\hat{\pi}^e = 0$. (Subscripted numerals throughout refer to partial derivatives, which are always evaluated at a restpoint.)

[12] In what follows recall my claim in the Introduction that arbitrage arguments are theoretical, not merely axiomatic.

[13] Equilibrium at given expectations and parameters (including predetermined variables); see Hicks (1939, 1946), Lindahl (1939).

No goods-market-clearing or other flow-equilibrium condition enters anywhere!

To demonstrate this, I substitute in (1.7) for the dividends or rentals r^i from (1.4), (1.5), obtaining

$$\chi(\pi; \hat{\pi}^e, q^C, q^S) \equiv \pi q^S - (q^C/\pi) - \hat{\pi}^e = 0. \tag{1.7.1}$$

At a given technology q^i and at given expectations $\hat{\pi}^e$, (1.7.1) solves for the unique relative equity price

$$\pi = \pi(\hat{\pi}^e, q^C, q^S) \tag{1.7.2}$$

that makes portfolio holders just willing to hold the claims to the economy's existing corn and steel stocks X^C, X^S and that maximizes entrepreneurial profits – which together are necessary and sufficient for the economy to be in temporary equilibrium. The corresponding temporary-equilibrium rate of profit follows from substitution in (1.5) and (1.6) of $p = \pi(\hat{\pi}^e, q^C, q^S)$ and $p^C = 1$, which gives $\rho = \pi(\hat{\pi}^e, q^C, q^S)q^S - \delta$.

I now delve a little more deeply into the meaning of arbitrage equation (1.6). From an individual portfolio holder's point of view, (1.6) represents an instantaneous portfolio-balance – that is, a zero-excess-stock-demand – condition. Aggregating over all holders, I obtain a corresponding market equilibrium condition. It must refer to a market in which instantaneous portfolio shifts can in fact be executed – the bourse or stockmarket. Thus, (1.6) represents the market-clearing condition for the stockmarket and embodies two well-defined zero-excess-stock-demand correspondences (only one of which is independent), as well as a corresponding equilibrium price that is uniquely defined and stable. This is illustrated in figure 1.1, which shows one of the two equity markets that constitute the stockmarket: The schedule X^S represents the fixed stock supply of steel equity and the schedule $X^{S,d}$ the corresponding downward-sloping stock demand, drawn against the relative price π of steel equity; π^* is the stable stockmarket-clearing equilibrium price.

The agent behavior underlying figure 1.1 is as follows. Capitalists surrender the management of their portfolios to financial specialists, of which there are two types: arbitrageurs and speculators.[14] By assumption, arbitrageurs know and espouse the current myopic expectation $\hat{\pi}^e$ formed

[14] As mentioned earlier, the income of both of these is limited to pure profits, which they seek to maximize and which are zero in the relevant equilibrium (in temporary equilibrium for arbitrageurs and in infinite-horizon equilibrium for speculators). This sidesteps the fundamental issue [Grossman and Stiglitz (1980)] of how financial-market agents can have an incentive to engage in the costly collection of the information necessary to their activities, if they earn zero equilibrium income. The problem is similar to that of accounting for entrepreneurs under zero equilibrium entrepreneurial profits. In both cases the challenge is to model the respective activity as a production process involving the use of (momentarily) scarce resources that command the going equity yield. In the case of entrepreneurship, this leads to models with Penrose investment costs (VON NEUMANN III), Schumpeterian

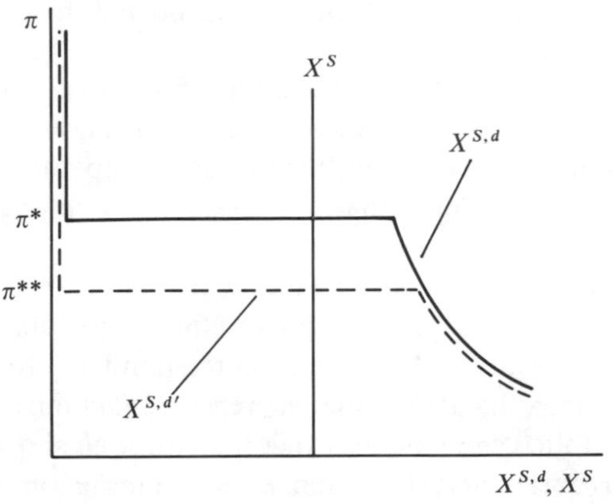

Figure 1.1 The stockmarket

by speculators. They also know current dividends r^i and the sectoral productivities q^i that underlie these by virtue of entrepreneurial profit maximization. From equation (1.7.1), they therefore can infer the price $\pi = \pi(\hat{\pi}^e, q^C, q^S)$ that will currently clear the stockmarket, as well as the corresponding uniform yield ρ.

To arbitrageurs, I thus may assign two functions. First, they seek to instantaneously rid their clients' portfolios of any equity with an expected yield ρ^i less than that available on the best alternative. This behavior guarantees that, whenever $\rho^C > \rho^S$ ($\rho^C < \rho^S$), the stockmarket will show an excess stock supply of steel (corn) equity. Second, whenever such a stock disequilibrium occurs, the representative arbitrageur (i) knows about it, since he is holding some client equity that he is unsuccessfully trying to sell at the prevailing disequilibrium price; (ii) knows the equilibrium price that would clear the market; (iii) knows that (i) and (ii) together offer an incentive to risklessly short sell the equity in excess supply; in consequence, (iv) incipiently short sells that equity in unbounded amounts, thereby driving its price to the equilibrium value.[15] Profit maximization by arbitra-

costs of innovation, or costly intersectoral resource transfers (WALRAS III); in that of arbitrage and speculation, to "noisy" rational expectations models or, equivalently, to perfect-foresight models with an equilibrium gap between the yield expected by the owner and that expected by the manager of a portfolio.

15 In short selling, the arbitrageur borrows the equity in excess supply from present holders of such equity (including from his own clients' portfolios); sells it at a price *set* below (at a yield *set* above) the equity's currently prevailing disequilibrium price (yield), but above the known equilibrium price; and reaps a capital gain, an instant later, by being able to repurchase it – and return it ("with interest") to the original holder – at the new, lower equilibrium price. The key idea is that, unlike consumers and firms in standard Walrasian market disequilibrium, arbitrageurs who hold (instead of short sell) equity in excess supply are *not maximizing profits*.

geurs thus guarantees that the stockmarket price π is moved to its temporary-equilibrium level at each instant.

Since – by virtue of entrepreneurial profit maximization – flow prices are locked into equity prices at all times, this means that the economy's temporary equilibrium is instantaneously established through competition and the search for maximum profit alone – that is, *without recourse to a Walrasian auctioneer*.[16]

The shape of the schedules appearing in figure 1.1 is now easy to grasp, as is the market adjustment that follows parametric shifts in these schedules. Consider the locus marked $X^{S,d}$. It represents a demand correspondence for steel equity that assumes profit maximization by entrepreneurs; maximization of yield on individual portfolio components, other than through short selling, by arbitrageurs; and parametrically given expectations $\hat{\pi}^e$ and technology q^i. Turn now to the excess-yield-differential function $\chi(\cdot)$ in (1.7.1), starting from a zero differential $\chi(\pi;\hat{\pi}^e,q^C,q^S)\equiv\rho^C-\rho^S=0$ and the associated equilibrium price π^*. At any $\pi>\pi^*$, we have $\rho^S<\rho^C$, so that no arbitrageur will want his client portfolio to contain steel equity; therefore, $X^{S,d}=0$. At any $\pi<\pi^*$, one finds $\rho^S>\rho^C$ and arbitrageurs will want to hold the entirety of the steel equity value $K/p^S\equiv X^S+(X^C/\pi)$ of their client portfolios in the form of steel equity; thus, $X^{S,d}\equiv X^S+(X^C/\pi)$ for any $\pi<\pi^*$, varying inversely with π along a rectangular hyperbola with vertical asymptote X^S. At $\pi=\pi^*$, we have $\rho^C=\rho^S$ and arbitrageurs are indifferent about the portfolio composition of their clients' wealth – in particular, they are satisfied to hold the existing stocks of corn and steel equity; thus, $X^{S,d}=X^S$ and $X^{C,d}=X^C$ (from $X^{S,d}+(X^{C,d}/\pi)\equiv K/p^S$).

Stockmarket-clearing short-sales by arbitrageurs may be illustrated as follows. A decline in the percent rate $\hat{\pi}^e$ of steel-equity capital gains expected by speculators, a fall in corn-industry productivity q^C, or a rise in that (q^S) of the steel industry – each of which shifts down the demand curve $X^{S,d}$ to $X^{S,d'}$ – must create, at π^*, an excess stock supply X^S of steel equity. Arbitrageurs will now seek to borrow the latter from current holders (including from their own clients' portfolios), so as to short sell it at a price sufficiently below the current market disequilibrium price to attract a buyer – but not lower than the new equilibrium price π^{**} (which is known by them, given that the parameter shift is public knowledge). Since any short sale realized at a price $\pi^*>\pi>\pi^{**}$ will yield a pure profit $\pi-\pi^{**}>0$, unbounded incipient short selling will instantaneously drive down the price of steel equity from π^* to π^{**}.[17]

I end this already overly long discussion of arbitrage condition (1.6) with

[16] Recall the corresponding proposition in the introduction to this chapter.

[17] Short selling is potentially unbounded, for agents may seek to borrow not just extant steel equity, but steel equity to be created in the future.

a single observation. The reader may have noted that at no point have I found it necessary to set up a problem of utility maximization. In fact – as I formally show in supplement A.2 accompanying the next chapter – the problem of intertemporal utility maximization by decentralized households cannot even be *posed* absent the prior fulfillment of (1.6). Alternatively, (1.6) must be satisfied whatever is being maximized over time.[18] The upshot is that the principle of the uniform expected yield – the instantaneous analogue of the Ricardo–Marx principle of the uniform rate of profit – is *logically prior* to the neoclassical principle of utility maximization.

I now do turn to utility maximization. For it provides *one* important answer to the question of what determines capitalist households' accumulation-and-consumption decision – which in turn determines the quantity dynamics of VON NEUMANN I, as I will show. Recall that I have allowed the capitalist to delegate to other agents many of the functions traditionally attributed to him (in particular, that of entrepreneur and that of portfolio manager). He will, in my scheme, however retain the role of accumulator of capital and householder. In that capacity, I shall have him follow a simple rule. It makes his current consumption spending, E, a fixed proportion, Ω, of his current wealth, K,

$$E=\Omega K, \qquad \Omega>0, \tag{1.8}$$

where E is in turn distributed across consumption of steel, D^S, and consumption of corn, D^C, in the constant proportions γ and $(1-\gamma)$, respectively:

$$D^S=\gamma\Omega K/p,\ D^C=(1-\gamma)\Omega K, \qquad 0\leq\gamma\leq 1. \tag{1.9}$$

Consumption behavior (1.8), (1.9) may be rationalized in two ways: on grounds of strict economic logic, and in terms of more broadly gauged considerations.

Starting with the latter, one may argue that observed consumption behavior is only weakly rational. In particular, it is so when viewed comparatively, namely, against the stringent maximizing logic that, as we have seen, governs the financial-market and entrepreneurial arena. At any given level of wealth beyond that required for subsistence, the behavior of the average consumer is largely myopic and convention ridden – or, in any case, much less impelled toward the relentlessly forward-looking and optimizing stance of the speculator, arbitrageur, and entrepreneur. This would lead one to give (1.8) the following interpretation. First, in his function as householder the representative capitalist acts myopically, that

[18] For instance, in the turnpike literature (1.6) is necessary for maximization, not of intertemporal consumption utility, but of terminal capital stocks [Dorfman, Samuelson, and Solow (1958)].

is, principally in the light of current data (including his current wealth), not on the basis of expectations about the future (the future value of his portfolio). Second, his consumption behavior is strongly influenced by considerations of social class, the prime determinant of which is wealth. This links a household's level of consumption E to its current wealth K via the social norm or convention $\Omega > 0$.[19]

As supplement A.2 demonstrates, consumption rule (1.8), (1.9) also has a standard optimizing explanation. It represents the solution, on the part of the individual wealth holder, of an intertemporal utility maximization problem. The problem is that of maximizing a time-additive logarithmic felicity function of the form $U = U(D^C, D^S) \equiv \ln D(D^C, D^S)$ or

$$U = \ln[(D^S)^\gamma (D^C)^{1-\gamma}] \tag{1.10}$$

over an infinite horizon, where $D(\cdot) \equiv [(D^S)^\gamma (D^C)^{1-\gamma}]$ is a Cobb–Douglas index of quantities consumed. Ω is here interpreted as the fixed rate of time preference used by the representative capitalist in discounting his dynastic household's future felicity.

I am now equipped to discuss capitalist accumulation. Since expected capitalist income is ρK $(= r^C X^C + r^S X^S - \delta K + \dot{\pi}^e X^S)$, desired saving or accumulation must, from (1.8), be $(\rho - \Omega)K$. With stock-equilibrium condition (1.6) assuring that yields are continuously uniform, the representative capitalist will at all times be indifferent about the equity composition of this flow of savings. This means, importantly, that no flow demands for corn and steel equity are defined in the model.[20] Instead, what does determine the equity composition of aggregate savings are the flow supplies $\dot{X}^i$ of the two capital goods, net of replacement δX^i and consumption D^i demands,

$$\dot{X}^i = Q^i - \delta X^i - D^i \equiv Z^i \qquad (i = C, S). \tag{1.11}$$

Note this fundamental point about (1.11): The implied output-market flow-equilibrium conditions $Z^i - \dot{X}^i = 0$ are *identities*.[21] That is, whatever amount of output Q^i is not sold for replacement or consumption purposes will be residually purchased and added to their capital stock by X^i-using firms (or by capitalists renting to these firms).

Each such purchase gives rise to the issuance of a new equity, possessing

[19] A norm that determines the society's thriftiness. The parameter γ in (1.9) may be similarly interpreted as conventional. Steedman (1981) offers an insightful discussion of alternatives to the Fisher–Ramsey view of consumption behavior and the rich doctrinal pedigree of these alternatives [including in Fisher (1907, 1930) himself].

[20] Put differently, the model lacks independent ("Keynesian") investment functions. These emerge only under internal costs of adjustment, as in VON NEUMANN III.

[21] In the sense that flow equilibrium $Z^i = \dot{X}^i$ will obtain for *any* stock equilibrium price $p = \pi(\hat{\pi}^e, q^C, q^S)$.

the same price and expected yield as its seasoned counterparts – that equity must be willingly absorbed into capitalist portfolios. Will aggregate desired saving (net of capital gains) be such that the aggregate value of new equities being issued is so absorbed? That is, will the supply of loanable funds equal the demand for loanable funds? This, of course, is the question about equilibrium in the capital market.

Unlike the stockmarket, the capital market is characterized by a flow-equilibrium condition. It requires $\dot{X}^C + \pi\dot{X}^S = (\rho - \Omega)K - X^S\dot{\pi}$ (where the lefthand side is demand, the righthand side supply of loanable funds), or

$$\dot{K} = (\rho - \Omega)K,\ \dot{K} \equiv \dot{X}^C + \pi\dot{X}^S + X^S\dot{\pi}\ . \tag{1.12}$$

It is easy to show that, since the equation in (1.11) holds identically, so must that in (1.12). This follows from Walras's Law – the requirement that the economy's momentary spending and saving decisions be consistent with its momentary income (output) flows. Walras's Law can be written as the condition that the value of planned flow excess supplies identically equal desired saving net of capital gains:[22]

$$Z^C + pZ^S \equiv (\rho - \Omega)K - X^S\dot{p}^S. \tag{1.13}$$

Since $\dot{X}^i = Z^i$ holds identically, (1.13) implies that (1.12) must hold identically as well. Consequently, given stock equilibrium in the stockmarket, flow equilibrium in the capital market obtains automatically.[23]

Though the economy's three flow markets – for corn, for steel, and for loanable funds – thus play no role in the determination of prices and the profit rate, two of the three provide independent equations that help pin down the system's quantity dynamics. To dynamics I now turn.

From (1.11), $\dot{X}^S$ is given by $\dot{X}^S = Q^S - \delta X^S - D^S$ or by (I use (1.3), (1.5))

$$\begin{aligned} \hat{X}^S &\equiv \dot{X}^S/X^S = x[q^S - \delta x^{-1} - \gamma\Omega(x^{-1} + \pi^{-1})] \equiv \hat{X}^S(\pi, x) \\ x &\equiv X^C/X^S, \end{aligned} \tag{1.14}$$

where x is the economy's capital composition. On the other hand, from (1.12) I have $\dot{X}^C = (\rho - \Omega)K - \pi\dot{X}^S - X^S\dot{\pi}$ or, using (1.1), (1.4)–(1.6), and (1.14),

$$\hat{X}^C = x^{-1}\{[\pi q^S - (\Omega + \delta)](x + \pi) - \pi\hat{X}^S(\pi, x) - \dot{\pi}\}, \tag{1.15}$$

which, like $\hat{X}^S$, would be a function of π and x only, if $\dot{\pi}$ could be shown to be a function of these variables.

22 As a check of consistency, observe that substitution in (1.13) for Z^i, ρK, and ΩK gives $Q^C + pQ^S \equiv r^C X^C + r^S X^S$, the identity between aggregate output and factor income.

23 It follows that, unlike in the pure-exchange economy (WALRAS IV), the capital market cannot solve for the temporary-equilibrium real rate of interest.

I next introduce the myopic-foresight assumption,

$$\dot{\pi}^e = \dot{\pi}. \tag{1.16}$$

According to (1.16), speculators correctly predict the (righthand) derivative of the relative price of steel equity with respect to time. Substitution of (1.16) in (1.7.1) gives the law of motion of the economy's prices $\pi = p^S = p$,[24]

$$\dot{\pi} = \pi(\pi q^S - q^C \pi^{-1}) \equiv \phi(\pi), \qquad \phi' > 0. \tag{1.17}$$

On the other hand, substituting for $\dot{\pi}$ from (1.17) in (1.15), I obtain the sought-after function $\hat{X}^C(\pi, x)$. This, together with (1.14), yields the law of motion of the economy's capital composition,

$$\begin{aligned} \dot{x} \equiv x(\hat{X}^C - \hat{X}^S) = [\pi q^S - (\Omega + \delta) - \hat{X}^S(\pi, x)](x + \pi) - \phi(\pi) \\ \equiv \psi(\pi, x), \qquad \psi_i < 0 \ (i = 1,2). \end{aligned} \tag{1.18}$$

[(1.17), (1.18)] constitutes the economy's myopic-foresight dynamics and represents the VON NEUMANN I version of the quasi-Hamiltonian structure [(0.1), (0.2)]. Since the dynamical system contains one predetermined (x) and one forward-looking (π) state variable,

$$\phi' \psi_2 < 0 \tag{1.19}$$

guarantees a linear approximation of (1.17) and (1.18) near the steady state that exhibits saddle-path stability. In other words, VON NEUMANN I is locally saddle-path stable.[25]

The properties of the economy's steady state, to which I now turn, are easily derived. In long-run equilibrium, π and x must be at rest so that, from (1.17),

$$\bar{\pi} = (q^C/q^S)^{\frac{1}{2}}, \tag{1.20}$$

where a bar indicates a steady-state value. Furthermore, from (1.4)–(1.6) and (1.20),

$$\bar{\rho} = (q^C q^S)^{\frac{1}{2}} - \delta, \tag{1.21}$$

so that the gross profit rate $\bar{\rho} + \delta$ is the geometric mean of sectoral productivities. Accumulation equation (1.12) yields the system's growth rate g along the von Neumann ray,[26]

$$g \equiv \bar{\hat{K}} = \bar{\rho} - \Omega = (q^C q^S)^{\frac{1}{2}} - (\delta + \Omega) \geq 0, \tag{1.22}$$

[24] Unless their sign is self-evident (as in the case of ϕ', for instance), derivatives are presented in explicit form in the chapter appendices.

[25] For a more detailed discussion of stability, see chapter 2 and supplement A.2.

[26] Here, the path of maximal steady growth given consumption program (1.8) (in the original von Neumann (1946) model nonproductive consumption is neglected).

where g is assumed nonnegative for the steady state to be viable. It follows that, at a given technology and rate of depreciation, the higher the rate of capitalist time preference Ω, the lower the system's long-run growth rate g.[27] (1.22) may alternatively be written as the Cambridge equation

$$g = s\bar{\rho}, \qquad s \equiv \frac{\bar{\rho} - \Omega}{\bar{\rho}} > 0, \tag{1.23}$$

where s is the long-run propensity to save out of profits.

I now solve for the steady-state composition of capital, $\bar{x}$. Unlike temporary equilibrium – fully achieved whenever profits are maximized and stocks willingly held at given expectations – steady-state equilibrium in addition calls for flow balance between outputs and consumption-plus-investment demands for these outputs. The reason is simple: Unlike in temporary equilibrium, across steady states flow demands for individual portfolio components are well defined, since each of these components is now required to grow at the rate gX^i. I can thus write *ex-ante* steel flow excess supply as $Z^S - gX^S = [\hat{X}^S(\cdot) - g]X^S$, where gX^S is steady-state flow-investment demand for steel. By Walras's Law, in the steady state it is sufficient to consider one of the two output markets, say that for steel.[28] Setting the function $[\hat{X}^S(\cdot) - g]X^S$ equal to zero for steel-output-market equilibrium and using (1.20)–(1.22), I solve for

$$\bar{x} = \left(\frac{q^C - (1-\gamma)\Omega\bar{\pi}}{q^C - \gamma\Omega\bar{\pi}} \right) \bar{\pi}. \tag{1.24}$$

The following conclusion emerges from (1.20)–(1.22) and (1.24). Across steady states, changes in consumption preferences γ, Ω are without influence on relative prices and the profit rate. This is the Sraffa nonsubstitution theorem.[29] It follows that preference shifts must be accommodated by movements in capital composition $\bar{x}$ and, in the case of Ω, additionally by changes in the growth rate g.

My model's nonsubstitution behavior however also applies to situations *outside* the steady state: Despite the momentary scarcity of all resources, changes in γ and Ω will leave p unaltered on impact and along the traverse to the new steady state. I turn to a discussion of this dynamic nonsubstitution result.[30]

27 Observe that, since steady-state viability hinges on $\Omega \leq \bar{\rho}$, the independence of prices from preference parameters discussed below will not be absolute.

28 Rewrite (1.13) as $(Z^C - gX^C) + p(Z^S - gX^S) \equiv 0$ to see this.

29 See Sraffa (1960), §1–5, and recall my discussion in the Introduction (footnote 15); see also Ahmad (1991), Arrow and Starrett (1973) (the latter notes the qualification mentioned in footnote 27).

30 The VON NEUMANN I example of dynamic nonsubstitution is generic; it extends to more general settings, provided all outputs are basic, all inputs reproducible, and a generalized

It requires a fundamental addition to the set of behavioral assumptions I have made so far. As is typical for saddle-path-stable systems, there exists in VON NEUMANN I a multiplicity of π-values all of which both guarantee temporary equilibrium and validate speculators' myopic expectations on impact of a perturbation and in its immediate aftermath. However, only *one* such π value – that located on the saddle path – will do so over an unbounded horizon. All others must lead, sooner or later, to a stockmarket crisis – a bursting equity price bubble – and correspondingly disappointed myopic expectations. As chapter 2 and supplement A.2 show in detail, it is an assumption about the informational capacity and the profit motivation of stockmarket speculators – additional to the myopic-foresight postulate (1.16) – which assures that the economy is placed on the saddle path on impact and kept there during the subsequent adjustment to the new steady state. According to that assumption, stockmarket speculators possess (i) not only myopic, but infinite-horizon or perfect foresight (that is, the capacity to use their knowledge of the economy's environment and of its dynamic structure [(1.17), (1.18)] so as to calculate the trajectory $\{\pi_t\}_{t=0}^{\infty}$); and (ii) the desire to maximize speculative profits from anticipated bursts in stockmarket bubbles.

Figure 1.2 presents the relevant phase diagram (the system's saddle path coincides with the locus $\dot{\pi}=0$). Consider an unanticipated *ceteris-paribus* shift in capitalists' consumption preferences toward steel ($d\gamma>0$). The steady-state point moves horizontally from A_0 to A_1, illustrating long-run nonsubstitution. Since the speculative behavior just discussed implies that the economy remains pinned down on the saddle path at A_0 on impact and then moves horizontally along that path, price invariance to the demand shift must obtain at each point along the non-steady-state traverse.[31] The economic intuition for this result is straightforward (assume $g=0$ for simplicity): Though steel flow supply (1.3) is completely inelastic on impact of the increase in steel flow demand, that demand increase can be satisfied, and satisfied at an unchanged $p=\pi$, namely out of steel inventories. In fact, it is the ensuing decline in steel stocks and the corresponding rise in corn inventories $[d(1-\gamma)<0]$ that accounts for $\dot{x}>0$ at A_0 and thereafter. By the

form of Uzawa factor intensity obtains. The result may also be viewed from the perspective of macroeconomic theory – namely as a rare instance of a *fix price economy* [Barro and Grossman (1971), Benassy (1975), Drèze (1975), Malinvaud (1977)] in which the fixity of prices in response to relative ($d\gamma>0$) or aggregate ($d\Omega>0$) demand shocks is endogenous to the intertemporal optimization process, rather than exogenously imposed.

[31] As we shall see in WALRAS I, this is not true once a primary input is present (as in the Samuelson nonsubstitution theorem). Nor does it hold under technologies that violate the relevant Uzawa factor-intensity assumption. Finally, it is easy to see that the impact and dynamic-adjustment response to a demand disturbance that has been anticipated is the same. This means that the emergence of expectations of $d\gamma>0$ does not, per se, trigger any adjustment – unlike anticipations of a technology shock, discussed below.

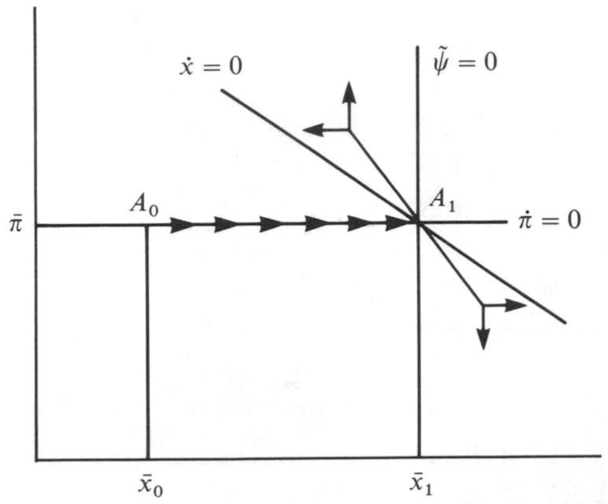

Figure 1.2 Dynamics of VON NEUMANN I; adjustment following an unanticipated preference shift toward steel

time A_1 is reached, the corresponding adjustments $\dot{Q}^C = q^C\dot{X}^S < 0$, $\dot{Q}^S = q^S\dot{X}^C > 0$ – which are Rybczynski (1955) effects – will have pushed flow supplies to a level just sufficient to again allow steady-state flow market clearing, $Q^i = D^i(\gamma^i) + (\delta + g)X^i$. Neither prices, nor the profit or growth rate, need change at any point, all momentary flow "disequilibria" being met by inventory changes. (The argument extends to $g > 0$ in obvious fashion: Instead of to $\dot{X}^S < 0$ and $\dot{X}^C > 0$, $d\gamma > 0$ leads to $0 \gtrless \hat{X}^S < g$ and $\hat{X}^C > g > 0$ on impact.)

Alterations in the rate of time preference also fail to affect π and ρ on impact and thereafter. Apart from capital composition changes, the effect of $d\Omega > 0$ is to instantaneously lower the system's growth rate.

Because they do impinge on long-run relative prices, technology changes differ in their consequences depending on whether or not they are anticipated. Consider the following situation: Faced with a positive productivity shock in the corn industry ($dq^C > 0$), stockmarket speculators correctly anticipate it to last $t_1 - t_0 < \infty$ periods only. The consequent adjustment dynamics are portrayed – for the case $d\bar{x}/dq^C > 0$, and under the informational and behavioral assumptions about speculators introduced earlier – in figure 1.3.[32] Had the rise in the factor productivity of steel been permanent, the economy would have jumped to point a on impact and moved horizontally to A' over time, thus bringing about a lasting fall in the price $1/p$ of corn, as well as a rise in the profit and growth rate. Here, however, the system must ultimately revert to its initial equilibrium A – and

[32] The adjustment path shown is derived algebraically in the chapter appendix.

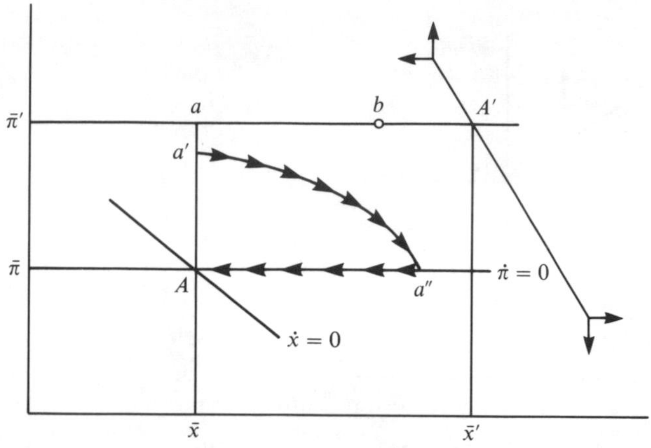

Figure 1.3 Adjustment following a temporary productivity increase in the corn industry

do so, except on impact, without a discrete change in π.[33] On impact (at t_0), the economy jumps to a higher $\pi = p$ (see point a') and experiences a rise in the profit and growth rate. The increase in π will be such as to make dividends $r^C = \pi q^S$ just large enough to render holders of corn equity willing to continue holding it despite the rise in the factor productivity of steel. The fact that the jump in the steel price will be less than that following a permanent shock $dq^C > 0$ reflects speculators' correct expectation of capital losses on steel equity during the period preceding the productivity reversal ($\dot{\pi} < 0$ along path a'–a''). Having thus fully discounted the latter by the time (t_1) it actually arrives, the stockmarket leaves π and ρ unchanged at that moment (see point a''), the drop in the current yield q^C/π on steel being matched by a reduction in expected capital losses.

As shown in supplement A.2 accompanying the next chapter, the perfect-foresight trajectory A–a'–a''–A is intertemporally utility maximizing for capitalists and optimal from a planning point of view. Decentralized optimality will be lost, if I change my expectations assumption to static expectations. My reasons for now doing so are as follows. Some find (1.16) and the associated saddle-path stability hard to swallow as a descriptive postulate.[34] It is, therefore, important to point out that many insights about

[33] Since anticipated discrete changes in future π values offer unexploited opportunities for speculative profits.

[34] For instance, Burmeister (1980); see also the literature on the foundations of rational-expectations theory and the problem of how agents learn. It is well to recall, though, that dropping the perfect-foresight (or rational-expectations) postulate means condoning the not less implausible idea that speculators make systematic mistakes from which they never learn.

economic dynamics developed in this book are independent of the specific expectations hypothesis used. In particular, under static expectations the system's adjustment path following unanticipated perturbations always turns out to be qualitatively the same as that obtaining under perfect foresight. Equally important, the static-expectations story often facilitates an intuitive understanding of the corresponding perfect-foresight dynamics.

Assuming static expectations means that, instead of (1.16), I have[35]

$$\dot{\pi}^{e} \equiv 0, \tag{1.25}$$

so that, from stockmarket equilibrium condition (1.7.1),

$$\pi = (q^{C}/q^{S})^{\frac{1}{2}}, \tag{1.26}$$

whether or not the economy is in steady-state equilibrium [compare (1.20)]. As regards the dynamics of accumulation under static expectations, I continue to assume consumption behavior characterized by (1.8), though now without a basis in intertemporal utility maximization. I also assume that actual consumption always equals planned consumption ΩK, any unexpected capital gains $(\dot{\pi} - \dot{\pi}^{e})X^{S}$ being saved in their entirety,

$$\dot{K} = [\rho K + (\dot{\pi} - \dot{\pi}^{e})X^{S}] - \Omega K, \tag{1.27}$$

where the bracketed term on the righthand side is actual [expected, ρK, plus unexpected, $(\dot{\pi} - \dot{\pi}^{e})X^{S}$] profit income and $\dot{K} \equiv \dot{X}^{C} + \pi \dot{X}^{S} + X^{S}\dot{\pi}$ is actual accumulation of wealth. Under static expectations this yields, instead of (1.12),

$$\dot{K} = (\rho - \Omega)K + X^{S}\dot{\pi} \tag{1.28}$$

as the system's law of accumulation. Given (1.26), the analogue to (1.18) appears as

$$\dot{x} = [\pi q^{S} - (\Omega + \delta) - \hat{X}^{S}(\pi, x)](x + \pi) \equiv \tilde{\psi}(x), \qquad \tilde{\psi}' < 0, \tag{1.29}$$

which guarantees the local dynamic stability of the static-expectations economy. It is easily seen that the dynamics following unanticipated perturbations in γ, Ω, and technology are indistinguishable from those obtaining under perfect foresight [see figure 1.2; $\tilde{\psi} = 0$ stands for $\dot{x} = 0$ from (1.29), while $\dot{\pi} = 0$ now represents the economy's locus of temporary equilibria, as implied by (1.25) and (1.7.1)].[36]

35 The analysis to follow applies, *mutatis mutandis*, to all the models examined in this book and will not be repeated in later chapters.

36 By contrast to the perfect-foresight dynamics discussed earlier, a transitory $dq^{C} > 0$ under static expectations (see figure 1.3; the $\tilde{\psi} = 0$-locus is omitted) moves the economy to point *a* on impact, thus raising π beyond its optimal short-run value. The system then horizontally travels toward A' for $t_1 - t_0$ periods; when $dq^{C} < 0$ at t_1 (say, at point *b*), π drops to its initial value and x asymptotically declines back to $\bar{x}$.

2

Stockmarket arbitrage, intertemporal price coordination, and the Arrow–Debreu model

2.1 Introduction

In what follows I discuss, and place in the literature, a number of theoretical issues raised by the work at hand.[1] Throughout the chapter and its attachments, the basics-only economy VON NEUMANN I will be my reference point. With suitable adjustments for nonbasics and for nonreproducible resources, the same arguments could be developed using any of the other models of the book, since all share the same Hamiltonian structure [(0.1), (0.2)].

Section 2.2 and its associated supplement A.2 cover three main and two subsidiary topics.[2] The main topics are (i) the relative role of consumption optimization and of stockmarket speculation in decentralized price coordination – specifically, their role in solving the Hahn (1966) problem of dynamic instability of the market economy or, technically speaking, their role in assuring the fulfillment of the decentralized system's transversality conditions (TVC's); (ii) a discussion of the sense in which my canonical equations [(0.1), (0.2)] can be said to be (quasi-)Hamiltonian and to embody, together with the associated TVC's, the conditions necessary and sufficient for a market economy to move along a perfect-foresight-competitive-equilibrium (PFCE) path; and (iii) a comparison of these necessary-and-sufficient PFCE conditions with those that characterize the optimal path of a centrally planned economy. The two subsidiary topics (covered only very briefly) are nonlinear dynamics and multiple restpoints; and

[1] The issues receive a formal treatment in the supplements labeled A. The latter are more technical than the rest of the book, are not needed for continuity of argument (given the present chapter) and, therefore, have been placed at the book's end. Their organization parallels that of the first three sections of the present chapter: An introductory note A.1 is followed by two parts that carry the same main titles as sections 2.2 and 2.3 and are referred to as supplements A.2 and A.3.

[2] Only the first of these [(i)] is discussed at some length under 2.2; for the others, the reader must turn to A.2.

attempts in the literature to link Hamiltonian dynamics in physics and economics.

Section 2.3 and supplement A.3 have two goals, one of which is ancillary. Regarding the latter, I wish to critically reexamine the classic Dorfman-Samuelson–Solow (1958) condition for the decentralized achievement of dynamic production efficiency. (I have no quarrel with the authors' analysis of efficiency in the planned economy.) In the supplement I show that the account given – and repeated in the literature[3] – of what firms do and what "pure investors" do in guiding the market economy to dynamic efficiency is flawed. The flaw in question is illuminating, for it suggests what to be alert to in the pursuit of my principle goal – that of unveiling the stockmarket, and the Hamiltonian dynamics its activity generates, in the Arrow–Debreu economy.[4] What Dorfman–Samuelson–Solow and Arrow–Debreu share, is that they subsume part (Dorfman *et al.*) or all (Arrow–Debreu) of the *financial* activity of arbitrageurs and speculators under the mistaken rubric of "profit maximization by firms." Once financial activity and real production have been disentangled, the Arrow–Debreu system is seen to be mathematically isomorphic, in its sequence-economy interpretation, to my Hamiltonian system. To show this rigorously, on the basis of a generic example similar to VON NEUMANN I, is the central purpose of supplement A.3. What the associated section 2.3 of the present chapter does is to indicate why, despite this mathematical isomorphism, I do not consider the Arrow–Debreu model to be a suggestive or useful way of thinking about intertemporal price coordination.

Section 2.4, finally, provides a capsule history, from this book's theoretical perspective, of postwar mainstream thinking on capital theory. It leads up to, but does not in any detail discuss, the Cambridge capital controversies and the subsequent mainstream "retreat" to the Arrow–Debreu model.

2.2 Market, plan, and intertemporal price coordination

It is useful to begin by examining a capitalist household's consumption optimization problem, say in the context of a general constant-relative-risk-aversion (CRRA) utility function.[5] The exercise makes clear that, assuming a household *is* seeking to solve an intertemporal optimization problem, it will be unable to do so unless the interest rate is well defined at each instant – that is, unless the household can expect future rates of return to be uniform across equities at each instant. This presupposes arbitrage

[3] For recent examples, see Burmeister (1980) and Ahmad (1991).

[4] Arrow and Debreu (1954), Debreu (1959), Arrow and Hahn (1971).

[5] See supplement A.2, which shows the latter's special logarithmic form to lead to myopic consumption rule (1.8) used throughout the book.

and stockmarket clearing. The latter, therefore, are *logically prior* to decentralized intertemporal utility maximization. Moreover, it is equally clear that the household views asset prices as parametrically given to it by the stockmarket. Only the shadow price of wealth does it consider as under its control. This, as we will see, contrasts with the view the social planner takes of his shadow prices. Finally, the exercise demonstrates that a household treats maximized utility as if it were one of the components of its portfolio, that is, as subject to the uniform-yield requirement. The problem of intertemporal utility maximization is thereby *subsumed* under the general theory of portfolio arbitrage.

Three general themes may be said to link consumption optimization by households; the market or PFCE solution of VON NEUMANN I and its descriptive Hamiltonian dynamics; and the planning solution of the same model, as obtained from an optimal-control Hamiltonian. The first is that, indeed, both the planning *and* the market version of VON NEUMANN I can be derived from Hamiltonian functions and their associated quasi-canonical equations. In the planning or optimal-control version, the Hamiltonian is given by the maximized sum of discounted utility from consumption plus the utility value of investment; in the decentralized or descriptive version, by the competitively maximized value of national income. In either case, the canonical equations contain perturbation terms not present in Hamilton's formulation of the dual laws.[6] All models in this book – even those that, unlike VON NEUMANN I, contain perishable goods (nonbasics) and corresponding instantaneous flow-market-clearing conditions – are representable as descriptive quasi-Hamiltonian systems that yield the dual dynamic laws [(0.1), (0.2)].[7]

A fundamental attribute of Hamiltonian systems is that, as market systems, they are dynamically highly unstable – namely saddle-path stable. In other words, there exists a multiplicity of equity-price configurations that will clear current markets and validate agents' myopic price expectations regarding the next period – but only *one* such configuration can continue to do so period after period *ad infinitum*. All others will lead, sooner or later, to a stockmarket crisis – a bursting equity-price bubble –

[6] Which accounts for the qualifier "quasi." On the canonical equations of Hamilton, see Lanczos (1970), Goldstein (1950), Magill (1970). I compare optimal control and descriptive Hamiltonians at the end of supplement A.2.

[7] To see this, observe that the zero-excess-flow-demand equations for nonbasics must contain normalized wealth $k(\pi, x)$ and a set of parameters α_1 (intratemporal tastes, the rate of time preference, the technology of nonbasics production) as arguments; the market-clearing prices implied by these equations therefore can be solved for as functions of π, x, α_1, and will enter the nonbasics-sector rentals appearing in the arbitrage equation. This gives [(0.1), (0.2)], with $\alpha \equiv [\alpha_1, \alpha_2]$, where α_2 are parameters other than those in α_1. In other words, one derives the quasi-canonical equations from a *temporary-equilibrium* national-income function.

and correspondingly disappointed expectations. Importantly, this issue of instability only arises in a decentralized economy, and only in one populated by households that take one or more price ratios as given by the stockmarket. It does not arise, first of all, for the social planner in the centralized economy: He freely *sets* all shadow prices so as to maximize the economy's utility integral; this generally requires him to place the system on the convergent saddle path or manifold.

It also fails to arise in two types of decentralized systems, *provided* equity claims to their resource stocks are assumed nontradable in a stockmarket. First, in economies – such as the land/labor Heckscher–Ohlin–Samuelson system and the Walrasian pure-exchange economy – in which all capital goods (or income sources) are nonproduced. Second, in Ricardo–Ramsey–Solow–Uzawa-type economies with a *single* produced and one, or a multiplicity of, nonproduced capital goods. Given absence of a stockmarket, instability will not arise in these two cases, if the economy is populated by myopic or intertemporally consumption-optimizing households. In the latter case,[8] following a perturbation, households reset *both* the shadow price of wealth (λ) *and* the shadow equity price vector of capital goods (π) such that the decentralized economy jumps to its convergent saddle path – that is, fulfills the transversality conditions for λ and π.[9] Since each of the model's forward-looking variables is thus under the control of the optimizing household (which takes as given from markets only non-forward-looking flow prices for input services and nonbasic outputs, plus the interest rate – none of which is dual to a stock variable, that is, subject to a TVC), the economy's convergence along the stable manifold is assured. The key assumption thus is that, despite decentralization, all capital-good price ratios remain non-stockmarket determined, just as in the planned economy.

For *nonproduced* capital goods, such absence of a stockmarket can always be stipulated – sometimes even plausibly so, as in the case of human capital – without imperiling the decentralized system's capacity to replicate the planner's optimal resource allocation. In other words, in the case of an economy containing only nonproduced capital goods, absence of a stock-

[8] Which is the one I wish to focus on, since only it exhibits a potentially unstable Hamiltonian dynamics. For the myopic case, recall my discussion of static expectations in the last chapter.

[9] Two remarks are in order. First, when all capital goods are nonproduced, the saddle path degenerates into a point (the stationary-state point); convergent equity-price dynamics along an unstable trajectory following anticipations of a shock remain, however, well defined (see WALRAS IV). Second, it is insufficiently realized that the standard decentralized Ramsey–Solow model contains *two* household-enforced transversality conditions (not just one, for the shadow price of wealth λ). This follows from the fact that the model needs to invoke the so-called Non-Ponzi-Game (NPG) condition, which can be shown to correspond to a TVC on the shadow price π of human capital.

market creates no "missing-market" problem in the Arrow–Debreu sense – provided the system contains a perfect capital market for borrowing and lending (by means of a Fisherian bond) and markets for the economy's input services and nonbasic outputs. (Since there are no produced capital goods, there are no markets for basic outputs.) In these special circumstances, a stockmarket may thus with justice be said to be redundant: Nothing that can be achieved in the presence of it cannot also be achieved in its absence via intertemporal consumption optimization on the part of decentralized households.[10] In particular, the latters' decisions will replicate the planner's optimal intertemporal resource allocation – which provides one of the two cases in which the so-called "equivalence principle" linking a decentralized economy consisting of households and firms with the planned economy can legitimately be said to hold.

The scene changes dramatically once we introduce *produced* capital goods (that is, basic outputs). More precisely, it does so for all economies containing basics – *except* in the Ricardo–Ramsey–Solow–Uzawa boundary case of a single produced capital good. In the latter, the preceding discussion continues to apply and the equivalence principle receives the second of its two valid instantiations (the first one being the nonbasics-only case just discussed). For, as soon as we have produced capital goods, there must, for each one of them, be an output market in newly produced specimens thereof – output markets that (just like markets for nonbasics or input services) cannot be dispensed with if the decentralized economy is to replicate the planner's allocation. (Their absence, in other words, *would* create a missing-market problem.)[11] Assume, therefore, that the decentralized economy contains *two* produced capital goods and a corresponding *pair* of basic-output markets.[12] It then must also contain a flow relative price of one of these two capital goods in terms of the other – a price I have labelled p in VON NEUMANN I.[13] Two points are noteworthy about p. First, like all other market prices (say, for consumption goods from nonbasic outputs), it is viewed by households as parametrically given to

[10] Observe that I continue to assume absence of uncertainty. Should there be state-of-nature uncertainty, together with differences in state-contingent endowments across agents and/or differences in risk preferences, a stockmarket is needed for full decentralized efficiency, if insurance markets are absent. This is the central insight of Arrow (1952).

[11] More fundamentally, the decentralized economy will not be *viable* in the absence of tradability of basic outputs (recall Sraffa's definition of a basic).

[12] What follows once again confirms that a major fault line in economic theory lies between models that do and those that do not dispense with the assumption of heterogeneous produced capital goods.

[13] In the boundary case of a single produced capital good, no such flow relative price exists – at most flow relative prices of nonbasics in terms of the single basic as numéraire (as, for instance, in the two-sector Uzawa model).

them and outside their influence. Second, household utility maximization is inconsistent with a divergence between the relative flow price p and the relative stock price π (whether shadow or market price π). We now have two choices. We may continue to insist on the assumption that the decentralized economy contains no stockmarket and that π is a forward-looking shadow price set by utility-maximizing households (as in the above account of a system containing only nonproduced capital goods).[14] The implication then is that competitive households also set the *market* price p – which is a contradiction. (By assumption, competitive households take market prices as given.) Alternatively, we may introduce a stockmarket: This turns π into a market price that both households and firms treat as parametrically given to them.[15] The point, of course, is that only the latter assumption involves no contradiction.

The presence of a stockmarket, however, introduces a new and fundamental problem. There now is a forward-looking price or price vector π in the economy whose convergence (TVC) can*not* be assured by appeal to intertemporal consumption optimization on the part of decentralized households. This leads to the second of the three themes of the present section. (The first, to recall, is that the market economy represents a saddle-path-stable quasi-Hamiltonian system.) It is the idea that the market economy contains a group of agents, *stockmarket speculators*, who maximize profits by placing the system on the stable saddle-path – that is, by enforcing transversality (and continuity) of the infinite-horizon relative-equity-price path $\{\pi(t)\}_{t=0}^{\infty}$ of capital goods. Supplement A.2 shows that such convergence and continuity of π implies, and is implied by, maximum speculative profits (which are zero in equilibrium).[16]

The third theme may now be introduced. Recall from VON NEUMANN I that its convergent intertemporal π-path is the combined outcome of *myopic* consumption behavior by households and of *forward-looking* profit maximization by stockmarket speculators. But this means that it is frequently neither sufficient *nor necessary* for dynamic convergence of an economy that households be forward-looking utility maximizers. In other words, for an understanding of infinite-horizon decentralized price

[14] Recall that firms cannot be called upon to set π, given that they maximize profits myopically [Arrow (1964)]. This is a key point in my critique of the Arrow–Debreu model.

[15] Firms now view π as a given (stock-and-flow) demand price into which they lock their flow-supply price p via profit-maximizing variations in output level and/or through entrepreneurial entry into and exit from the industry (recall VON NEUMANN I).

[16] Observe that here I have been focusing on the problem of the convergence of π to its steady-state value; I assume that the problem of π's convergence to its temporary-equilibrium value (at given speculative expectations $\hat{\pi}^e$) has been solved by profit maximization on the part of arbitrageurs as discussed in chapter 1.

coordination, stockmarket speculation is paramount – consumption optimization, by contrast, secondary.[17]

The following considerations on this issue may be useful. Analytically, it is necessary to draw a distinction between the wealth-owning household as an intertemporal optimizer and the wealth-owning household as an intertemporal optimizer *of consumption*. (The distinction is always implied when we talk about the planner: Given initial capital stocks and technology, he espouses whatever maximization goal we proceed to propose to him.) Nothing *fundamental* in our theorizing about the possibilities of coordination inherent in the market mechanism should hinge on the postulate of consumption optimization – which is a naive borrowing from commonsense psychology. For *any* quantity or price decision variable may in principle be turned into an intertemporal maximand, and many decision variables other than consumption have been so turned, especially in a planning context. As an example, the finite-horizon turnpike literature has focused on maximum physical stocks of one or several capital goods or, equivalently, on maximum growth.

On the other hand, households may not be *intertemporal* optimizers at all, be it of consumption or of any other objective. As seen, they may be following a *myopic* consumption rule – for instance, on the basis of status considerations that link a household's current consumption level to its current wealth via a social norm or convention [(1.8)]. Since entrepreneurs (who operate in perfect output and input markets) are behaving myopically as well, this completely removes forward-looking behavior from both firms and households. The saddle-path-stable Hamiltonian structure [(0.1), (0.2)], however, remains (given more than two tradable assets) and with it the question, What forward-looking agent group will competitively stabilize the market economy?

The point, of course, is that convergence – the logical possibility of infinite-horizon decentralized price coordination and (normatively) of an efficient intertemporal allocation of resources – cannot be made to hinge on the very special assumption that households are forward-looking consumption optimizers. To repeat, it cannot be made to so hinge for three reasons: first, intertemporal *consumption* optimization as an objective is one of many conceivable ones; second, *intertemporal* optimization as a behavioral characterization of households is neither very plausible nor enjoys overwhelming empirical support; and third, even if we grant that households optimize consumption intertemporally, the transversality condition assignable to them will involve, as price decision variable, only the shadow price

17 The "equivalence principle" is thus misleading, given that it anchors decentralized convergence in the optimizing behavior of households.

of household wealth – not, of course, the parametrically given asset market prices. These remain unanchored and free to explode, unless stabilized by stockmarket speculation.

2.3 The Arrow–Debreu model: A critique

As mentioned, the supplement that accompanies the present section (A.3) shows the Arrow–Debreu and my Hamiltonian system to be mathematically isomorphic. Nevertheless, as a tool for *causal* theorizing – a tool for dynamics, as opposed to one for existence proofs – the Arrow–Debreu model suffers from distinct disadvantages *vis-à-vis* the Hamiltonian approach. Three of these may be mentioned.

1 The Arrow–Debreu model's time horizon is finite and arbitrary. This leads to a corresponding arbitrariness in its price structure, since the final-period price of commodities needs to be known to determine antecedent prices, but can be so known only by peering into, and valuing, the period subsequent to the economy's ultimate period (which involves a contradiction). This is a well-known difficulty from which models, such as this book's, that possess unbounded horizons and associated transversality conditions are exempt.

There is another reason why the extension to an infinite horizon is critical. Only it reveals the fundamental fact that all but one of the paths that appear market clearing over finite time turn out to be unsustainable over an unbounded horizon. This fact then raises the question of who in the decentralized economy is supposed to place the system on the single convergent path. A Walrasian auctioneer cannot do so.[18]

The second and third drawbacks of the Arrow–Debreu model as a tool for dynamic analysis derive from the interpretation of the model as a futures-market economy (according to which the system possesses a full complement of spot and futures markets, open at the beginning of the first period when contracts for the current and all futures periods are concluded). The criticism here is both one of empirical implausibility – this has led to the Radner–Hahn sequence-economy interpretation, in which some or all futures markets are missing [Radner (1972), Hahn (1970, 1973)] – and of unnecessary sacrifice of analytical structure. It is on the latter I wish to

[18] As is shown by the literature that seeks to extend the Arrow–Debreu model – whether in its futures-market or sequence-economy interpretation – to an infinite horizon. In it, fulfillment of the infinite-horizon transversality condition is invariably *assumed*, rather than derived from the market-clearing process itself. See, for instance, Heller (1975), in which only market disequilibria (and their tatonnement correction by the auctioneer) along the convergent path are considered. See also the symposium on decentralization in infinite-horizon economies in the *Journal of Economic Theory*, No.2, 1988 [Majumdar (1988)].

focus. The essential insight is this:[19] Not all quantity choice variables are the same, and it is analytically wasteful to proceed as if they were. The set of all quantity decision variables naturally divides into two exhaustive and mutually exclusive subsets – a division that facilitates the solution of an economic model by giving it a special structure it would otherwise lack. The division, of course, is that between stock (or state) variables, which are currently predetermined, and flow (or control) variables, which may be currently changed. This distinction the Arrow–Debreu model fails to make, which is the source of its second and third weaknesses: A blurred picture of price formation that mirrors the indistinct picture of quantity choice variables; and the failure to grasp the model's intrinsic price–quantity dynamics. To these defects I now turn.

2 The Arrow–Debreu model is misleading in the picture it draws of the mechanism of decentralized price formation. It is so because it hides from view (though it contains) an essential price-determining equilibrium condition: The arbitrage, or stock equilibrium, condition. Instead of stock and stockmarket equilibrium, the model highlights a system of zero-excess-flow-demand equations as what determines the intertemporal price structure. But in many economies – VON NEUMANN I is an example – flow equilibrium obtains identically for *any* price vector satisfying the arbitrage equation. More generally, both flow- *and* stock-equilibrium conditions must enter into the determination of equilibrium prices.

3 Far from being static, the Arrow–Debreu model contains, but hides, an *intrinsic* causal dynamics that reflects the stock/flow distinction. In particular, all stock choice variables $x(t)$ are predetermined in the aggregate – but must nonetheless be willingly held by decentralized agents in any given period. How is this to be achieved? It is made possible by the fact that neither the prices $\pi(t)$ of equity claims attached to the stocks, nor the latter's increments $\Delta x(t)$ are predetermined. In particular, $\pi(t)$ can jump to make agents just willing to hold $x(t)$, given current and expected future circumstances. $\Delta x(t)$, on the other hand, can be currently set such that $x(t)$ – though unalterable *now* – takes on the desired value *over time*. The result, of course, is Hamiltonian system $\Delta\pi = \phi(\pi, x)$, $\Delta x = \psi(\pi, x)$, possibly augmented by the dynamics of the household shadow price of wealth λ.

Theorists' inability to "see" [(0.1), (0.2)] in the Arrow–Debreu model has had serious consequences. An instance is the long literature on the tatonnement stability of the model.[20] This literature rests on a two-fold

[19] See Dorfman, Samuelson, and Solow (1958), Malinvaud (1972), Dixit (1990).

[20] For example, Arrow and Hurwicz (1958), Arrow, Block, and Hurwicz (1959); see the surveys by Negishi (1962) and Hahn (1982b).

confusion. First, it aims to solve the problem of how, by moving the intertemporal price vector, the Walrasian auctioneer over time brings about "equilibrium." But that problem is badly posed. As shown in VON NEUMANN I, temporary *flow* equilibrium often obtains identically. Temporary *stock* equilibrium, on the other hand, is brought about through profit-maximizing short sales on the part of arbitrageurs – not by a Walrasian auctioneer. Second, the literature imposes an *extrinsic* tatonnement dynamics of the general form

$$\Delta P = \alpha[D(P) - y(P) - \omega], \qquad \alpha > 0, \tag{2.1}$$

on a model that already contains an intrinsic Hamiltonian dynamics $\Delta\pi = \phi(\pi, x)$, $\Delta x = \psi(\pi, x)$ *inconsistent with (2.1)*. (P is the intertemporal Arrow–Debreu price vector; $D(\cdot), y(\cdot)$, and ω denote the demand, supply, and exogenous-endowment vectors, respectively; and α represents a vector of exogenous adjustment speeds.)[21]

2.4 Strands in neoclassical capital theory

Though it is composed of several strands, a clearly defined body of mainstream postwar thought on capital exists.[22] It is with themes raised by that body of thought – not with the Neo-Ricardian [Sraffa (1960)] and Neo-Austrian [Hicks (1973)] heterodoxies – that I have been concerned in this chapter.

What I wish to do in this closing section is to summarize and connect some of these strands in neoclassical postwar capital theory. I do so, of course, in the light of my book's theoretical perspective and without the illusion of offering anything but a highly personal sketch. The strands in question are: 1. The fifties literature on the von Neumann turnpike, the nonsubstitution theorem, and dynamic production efficiency; 2. the sixties literature on consumption efficiency, the Golden Rule, and consumption optimality; and 3. the mainstream "retreat" to the Arrow–Debreu model following the Cambridge capital controversies.

[21] The inconsistency in question is easy to see: Since [(0.1), (0.2)] represents the system's true motions and foresight is perfect, the P-path implied by (2.1) will "soon" be perceived as unsustainable, thus as involving unexploited profit opportunities; the consequent correction in P destroys (2.1). That tatonnement process (2.1) is not derivable from the axioms of optimizing behavior has been noted by a long line of authors, including Arrow (1959), Hahn (1970), Gordon and Hynes (1970), and F.M. Fisher (1983). Moreover, even if one admits (2.1) as a price adjustment mechanism, the latter is known to be dynamically stable only under highly restrictive assumptions regarding income effects (that is, the shape of the market demand curve; see Sonnenschein (1972)). For overall assessments of these and related difficulties, see Hahn (1982b), Ingrao and Israel (1990); for a doctrinal perspective, Currie and Steedman (1990), Weintraub (1991).

[22] See Bliss (1975) and Burmeister (1980).

1 The immediate postwar generation of neoclassical capital theorists was very much alive to the challenge of bringing the classical models of von Neumann (1946) and Leontief (1951) into a unified whole with the Walrasian tradition. The landmark study in these efforts was the book by Dorfman, Samuelson, and Solow (1958) with its discussion of duality theory and dynamic production efficiency under heterogeneous-capital growth. An equally significant contribution was made by the neoclassical literature on the nonsubstitution theorem [see the papers in Koopmans (1951)] and on the turnpike theorem [Dorfman *et al.* (1958), Radner (1961), Morishima (1964), McKenzie (1963, 1982), Furuya and Inada (1962)]. It is in this period also that, following Samuelson's deeply penetrating (1937) discussion of the arbitrage principle, the theory of capital was for the first time clearly perceived to possess a variational, or Hamiltonian, structure [Samuelson and Solow (1956), Samuelson (1960)].[23]

2 However, under the powerful influence of the work of Pontryagin (1962), Hamiltonian analysis in economics increasingly came to be identified with optimal consumption control rather than with the study of dynamic production efficiency and with decentralization in the presence of heterogeneous-capital goods. It did so, despite Hahn's (1966) demonstration that decentralized heterogeneous-capital growth is deeply problematic. The shift in emphasis from the earlier literature was typically rationalized on the grounds that, in a *centralized* economy, consumption optimality – or, more generally, consumption efficiency [Malinvaud (1953, 1961, 1962), Cass (1972a,b)][24] – implied dynamic production efficiency, but not vice versa. The focus on consumption efficiency in turn led to an increasing preference for one-good models, in which the problem of dynamic production efficiency (in the centralized economy) or of Hahn conundra (in its decentralized counterpart) could be ruled out of court.[25] Overall, it is fair to say that the dominant theoretical outlook experienced a dramatic shift away from von Neumann (1946) toward Ramsey (1928) as a source of inspiration.[26] Apparently, among all the reluctant analytical moves the

[23] Apart from Samuelson (1937), early discussions of the arbitrage or present-value principle can be found in Fisher (1907, 1930), Wicksell (1934), Kaldor (1939), and Allais (1943). On the von Neumann economy, see also Kemeny, Morgenstern, and Thompson (1956), Morgenstern and Thompson (1976). Solow (1983) and Hahn (1983) provide useful accounts of developments in neoclassical capital theory during the period under consideration.

[24] See also the literature on the Golden Rule [Phelps (1961, 1965), Koopmans (1965)] and on the possibility of decentralized overaccumulation as implied by Samuelson (1958), Diamond (1965).

[25] Exceptions to this trend are Shell and Stiglitz (1967), Bruno (1969), Magill (1970, 1977), Cass and Shell (1976b), Majumdar, Mitra, and McFadden (1976), and, more recently, Becker (1981), Brock and Malliaris (1989).

[26] The landmark in this development are the papers in Shell (1967).

theorist is continuously forced to make, getting rid of heterogeneous capital must, at this stage, have seemed least objectionable to many workers in the field – less so, in any case, than continuing to operate with the *ad hoc* savings function forced on the heterogeneous-capital literature by the need for tractability [as in Hahn (1966), Shell and Stiglitz (1967), Cass and Shell (1976a)]. One thus ended up with a preferred mainstream approach to the *decentralized* economy, in which the earlier focus on market arbitrage between different varieties of productive capital had vanished from the picture and been replaced by a focus on subjective arbitrage between current and future household consumption. In the light of this drift of mainstream capital theory – away from the concern of the classics with production and the competitive pressure for a uniform rate of profit toward Fisher–Ramsey utility theory and intertemporal consumption smoothing – the emergence of the Cambridge capital controversy is not, perhaps, so surprising.[27]

3 I shall not enter into the details of this controversy here or at any other point in the book.[28] It suffices to state its uncontroversial outcome: Cambridge-UK won the theoretical battle, but lost the war for professional influence. The theoretical battle was won by conclusive demonstration that single-capital-good models capture the range of possible steady-state outcomes of heterogeneous-capital models only imperfectly, and thus should be mistrusted as guides to the theory of capital. The war of influence was lost for at least three reasons. These were (i) Ideological: the philosophical and political threat posed by Marxism – the as yet untamed monster Ricardian economics had sired – was an often disavowed, but in hindsight clearly visible backdrop of the debates.[29] (ii) Analytical: being confined to the straightjacket of steady states, the Cambridge-UK arguments were noncausal; needed instead to really convince neoclassical theorists was a full-fledged dynamic analysis, in which the causal detail of "anomalous" intertemporal interest-rate and price paths could be traced out, starting from historically given initial conditions.[30] (iii) Tactical: when cornered, the Cambridge-US side changed the contest's terrain – from aggregative

[27] On contrasts between the classical and the neoclassical vision of the economic process see Ahmad (1991), Marglin (1984), Broome (1983), Duménil and Lévy (1985), Walsh and Gram (1980), Abraham-Frois and Berrebi (1979); also Dobb (1973), Bharadwaj (1978), Dasgupta (1985). Uniformities across the two traditions are stressed by Morishima (1973, 1977, 1989), von Weizsäcker (1971), Wan (1971), Hollander (1979), Nagatani (1981), Roemer (1982), Hahn (1982a), Afriat (1987); see also the contributions in Chakravarty *et al.* (1989).

[28] For competent and contrasting evaluations, see Harcourt (1972), Bliss (1975), Burmeister (1980), and Ahmad (1991).

[29] See the epilogue of Bliss (1975).

[30] See Burmeister (1980), Dixit (1981), Smith (1984) for this argument.

economies à la Solow (1956) to the Arrow–Debreu (1954) model; since the latter allows for full heterogeneity of commodities, it admits the relevant anomalies in principle, thus is immune to the Cambridge-UK criticisms.[31] Given the model's lack of structure, this move remained however purely formal and defensive, rather than constructive. It disarmed the opponent without showing a way forward in how to improve our thinking about capital.

[31] See, for instance, Stiglitz (1974).

3

Other von Neumann models: Basics and nonbasics

3.1 Introduction

The basics-only framework introduced in chapter 1 was a pure stock-equilibrium model. Even in the short run, consumption preferences – which are expressed through flow demands – could have no influence on price, given that all outputs flowed into inventory stocks.[1] In the present chapter, I drop the basics-only assumption and consider outputs that are instantaneously perishable and, thus, cannot accrue as input stocks.[2] I call them nonbasics and take them to represent consumption services or nonstorable consumption goods.[3] Their import does not derive from any looming significance they possess in real economic life. For, in reality, most consumption goods are held as inventories by both producers and consumers. Rather, it stems from the fact that they – and they alone – can legitimately be theorized as outputs whose point-in-time equilibrium price is determined by a Walrasian cross of (flow) demand and (flow) supply. All other outputs allow carryover of stocks across market periods and, thus, introduce a speculative element of equity holding into the problem of price determination.[4,5]

1 Recall that VON NEUMANN I assumed reproducibility of all inputs and Uzawa factor-intensity, both of which are necessary for price invariance in the short run. (I introduce primary resources into a basics-only economy in chapter 7 and examine the consequences of an anti-Uzawa technology in supplement C.2.)

2 At least not so directly, without a prior process of physical transformation (see VON NEUMANN III).

3 Recall the discussion in the Introduction (footnote 16) of my definition of a nonbasic *vis-à-vis* that of Sraffa (1960).

4 Perishable input (as opposed to consumption) services have a rental that, at given input stocks, is recursively determined from output prices and technology by entrepreneurial profit maximization. At least this is true if we treat input stocks as being on the market at each instant (which is reasonable for the nonhuman stocks considered here, but not necessarily for scarce labor with a labor–leisure choice; see chapter 7).

5 It is useful to think of both input- and output-market exchanges as taking the legal form of *contracts*, whose quantity units are expressed as flows and whose price/quantity terms can be continuously varied in the light of market conditions. For example, when considering

A posthumously published reflection by Hicks (1989) provides a useful doctrinal perspective on the matter:

When in the 1920s at Cambridge a new generation of teachers were set to lecture on Marshall, putting into their own words what he had said, this was one of the things that troubled them. If Marshall's proposition [on equilibrium in the market period] was to be used in the way he had used it, there could be no carryover; so it would be safer to make the article traded perishable – 'fish' not 'corn' ... That is formally correct, but it greatly reduces the scope of the theory ... What was to be done? The right thing, surely, would have been to go on to construct a formal theory of the market for a nonperishable product; that indeed would have turned a corner ... It did not happen, just like that, for two reasons, one general, one more special. I take the special reason first. It was bound to be noticed, as soon as the first step was taken along the road to such a theory, that the market in question would be a speculative market ... Then there was also the more general obstacle. The theory that was needed could not be developed without a considerable change in point of view. The traditional view that market price is, at least in some way, determined by an equation of demand and supply had now to be given up. If demand and supply are interpreted, as had formerly seemed to be sufficient, as flow demands and supplies coming from outsiders, it is no longer true that there is any tendency, over any particular period, for them to be equalized; a difference between them, if it were not too large, could be matched by a change in stocks. It is of course true that if no distinction is made between demand from stockholders and demand from outside the market, demand and supply in that inclusive sense must always be equal. But that equation is vacuous. It cannot be used to determine price, in Walras's or Marshall's manner ... the demand–supply equation can only be used in a recursive manner, to determine a sequence (it is a difference, or differential, equation) ... (pp.10–11)

How does adjustment toward temporary equilibrium take place when, unlike in VON NEUMANN I, a perishable product *is* present? In section 3.2, I offer two processes of quasi-Marshallian adjustment (labeled M1 and M2), neither of which invokes an auctioneer, only competitive profit maximization by atomistic entrepreneurs and arbitrageurs.[6] I summarize M1 and M2 here in a proposition that parallels the earlier convergence proposition for the basics-only economy VON NEUMANN I.

Proposition (convergence to temporary equilibrium): In VON NEUMANN II, the problem of the temporary-equilibrium Wal-

transactions in the newspaper market, think of newspaper subscriptions rather than issue-by-issue purchases at the newsstand. *Equities*, by contrast, are transacted in financial markets, of which, as we have seen, there are two functionally distinct types: the stockmarket (stocks) and the capital market (flows). "Equities" and "contracts" correspond to the fundamental legal distinction between an ownership title (which creates a right *in rem*) and a contract (creating a right *in personam*).

[6] These adjustment processes extend to my other models containing nonbasics, such as RICARDO, UZAWA, and WALRAS III–IV.

rasian auctioneer is solved. It is so by virtue of competitive profit maximization on the part of entrepreneurs and of stockmarket arbitrageurs. The former leads entrepreneurs either (M1) to set the price of the nonbasic so as to clear its market at the momentarily fixed supply and to pay out the entire revenue thus earned as dividends to input owners; or (M2) to set the price of the nonbasic so as to at least (by competition, just) meet the dividend demands of input owners. Profit maximization by arbitrageurs, on the other hand, leads them, under M1, to short-sell any equity currently in stock excess supply at the dividends paid by entrepreneurs and at given capital-gains expectations (thus clearing the stockmarket); under M2, to simultaneously undertake two actions: first, as portfolio managers to demand dividends from entrepreneurs such that, at given capital-gains expectations and at given equity prices, the expected equity yield is uniform (thus, the stockmarket cleared); second, to instantaneously short-sell equity in currently nonreproduced (reproduced) inputs – thereby lowering (raising) the economy's wealth measured in basics-numéraire – whenever there is excess demand (supply) in the market for nonbasics at the price set by entrepreneurs. Whatever the state of speculative expectations, M1 or M2 are sufficient to drive stockmarket and all output-market prices to their temporary-equilibrium value. (The companion proposition concerning convergence to steady-state equilibrium remains unchanged from chapter 1.)

In VON NEUMANN II, a single nonbasic – consumption services (S) – replaces the basic good steel that appears in VON NEUMANN I; the remaining basic – corn (C) – is the economy's sole input. Once installed in a sector, corn is, however, completely immobile. Sectoral resource reallocation can take place only via exponential depreciation and the rechanneling of the economy's flow of current gross investment.[7] Not surprisingly, except across steady states, the nonsubstitution behavior of prices now disappears: Point-in-time supply of the nonbasic being inelastic and nonstorability forcing its market to clear at each instant, demand for it must be price-determining, at least momentarily. A principal purpose of VON NEUMANN II is to discuss the sequence of quasi-Walrasian temporary equilibria that a preference shift across the two goods now gives rise to and to show how this sequence leads the system back onto its von Neumann ray. Another purpose is to provide a first example of the

[7] The implicit assumption is that the costs of reproduction of corn are small relative to the costs of intersectoral movement of existing corn stocks. This is not true for nonreproducible (primary) inputs, whose reproduction costs are infinite and whose yield-maximizing intersectoral movements are the subject of WALRAS III in chapter 8.

> *Ricardo–Bortkiewicz–Sraffa theorem*: Only changes in the technology of producing basics affect the economy's rate of profit; productivity shocks to sectors producing nonbasics do not.[8]

Though seemingly at odds with general-equilibrium thinking, the theorem will be seen to hold up in all the models I examine, and to do so both in and out of the steady state.[9]

The distinction between basics and nonbasics is, thus, fundamental. As indicated, it is so both for our view of how prices adjust to temporary equilibrium and for what influences the rate of profit. To gain a deeper understanding of the distinction, in section 3.3 I endogenize it. That is, VON NEUMANN III introduces a technology which allows the transformation of nonbasics into basics. The technology consists of a storage process which turns – at a nonbasics or "wastage" cost – the economy's two outputs of nonbasics into two input stocks of basics. As will be seen, this has the well-known alternative interpretation of a costly capital-stock-adjustment process [Lucas(1967)], driven by scarce entrepreneurship [Penrose(1959)] and giving rise to a pair of Keynesian flow-investment-demand functions that contain sectoral "Tobin-q's" as arguments [Tobin (1969)].

Two consequences follow. First, *ex-ante* flow-demand functions are now defined for consumption *and* investment. As a result, for each of the two goods independent output-market clearing is required (in addition to stockmarket equilibrium), if the economy's temporary-equilibrium price system is to be closed. (Capital-market balance obtains by Walras's Law.) Of course – and this is the second consequence – such output-market clearing can not be achieved through alterations in a single relative price of nonbasics. Instead it requires changes in the economy's two Tobin-q's – the ratio of stockmarket value to replacement cost of each sector's capital stock.

Unsurprisingly, in VON NEUMANN III a Sraffa-nonsubstitution response to intratemporal preference shifts continues to obtain in the long run (since all inputs are reproducible), but not in the short run (given input immobility and instantaneous flow-market clearing). Also, since nonbasics are virtual basics, perturbations in nonbasics technology *are* transmitted to the economy's rate of profit, in conformity with the Ricardo–Bortkiewicz–Sraffa theorem.

[8] Recall my discussion in the Introduction. Nonbasics were called "luxuries" by Ricardo (1815, 1951) and von Bortkiewicz (1907), meaning consumption goods that do not enter the stock of wage goods – the wage fund – advanced to workers by capitalists (see chapter 4).

[9] The two exceptions VON NEUMANN III and WALRAS III being terminological only.

3.2 VON NEUMANN II: A basics-and-nonbasics economy

Consider an economy whose momentary capital is given by

$$K \equiv p_C X_C^C + p_S X_S^C, \tag{3.1}$$

where X_j^C is industry j's stock of corn capital and where p_j denotes the price of an equity claim on that stock ($j = C, S$).[10] The system's numéraire is, as earlier, flow output of corn. X_C^C and X_S^C help to produce fixed-coefficient output flows of corn, Q^C, and consumption services, Q^S,

$$Q^C = q^C X_C^C, \qquad q^C > 0 \tag{3.2}$$

$$Q^S = q^S X_S^C, \qquad q^S > 0. \tag{3.3}$$

As before, entrepreneurs see to it that pure profits are driven to zero at each instant. The corresponding conditions now appear as [compare (1.4), (1.5)]

$$\max(p_C, p_S) = 1 = (1/q^C) r_C \tag{3.4}$$

$$p = (1/q^S) r_S, \tag{3.5}$$

where p refers to the price of consumption services and the r_j are unit dividends (rental rates) paid by entrepreneurs on equity (corn capital) in sector j. Unlike in VON NEUMANN I, one of the two outputs, consumption services, has no investment uses, whereas the other, corn, has two such uses, only the higher priced of which will be operative at any one time. This leads to the definition of two non-steady-state regimes, termed ALPHA and BETA,

$$\begin{array}{ll} \text{ALPHA:} & 1 = p_S > p_C \\ \text{BETA:} & 1 = p_C > p_S. \end{array} \tag{3.6}$$

In ALPHA, gross investment in the corn industry is zero ($\dot{X}_C^C = -\delta X_C^C < 0$), the entirety of the economy's current investment flowing into the service industry; and vice versa for regime BETA ($\dot{X}_S^C = -\delta X_S^C < 0$). As will be seen, $1 = p_C = p_S$ along the von Neumann ray only, when $\hat{X}_S^C = \hat{X}_C^C = g \geq 0$.

Consider now the bourse. Though the physical capital stocks X_j^C are completely immobile across sectors, claims of ownership to these stocks will be instantaneously and costlessly transferable among the economy's portfolio holders through the stockmarket. As earlier, this enforces instantaneous equality of expected yields among all equity claims [compare (1.6)],

$$\rho_C \equiv \frac{r_C}{p_C} - \delta + \hat{p}_C^e = \frac{r_S}{p_S} - \delta + \hat{p}_S^e \equiv \rho_S, \tag{3.7}$$

[10] Throughout this section, subscripts index sectoral location, superscripts physical type.

where the ρ_j and $\hat{p}_j^e$ refer to expected yields and expected percent capital gains on the two types of equity, and where $\rho \equiv \rho_C = \rho_S$ is the economy's rate of profit. Rewriting (3.7) as an excess-yield-differential function that incorporates entrepreneurial profit maximization, I have

$$\chi(p, p_C, p_S; \hat{\pi}^e, q^C, q^S) \equiv (pq^S/p_S) - (q^C/p_C) - \hat{\pi}^e = 0, \qquad \pi \equiv p_C/p_S \tag{3.8}$$

from (3.4) and (3.5). Note the change in the definition of π from $\pi \equiv p^S/p^C$ in VON NEUMANN I to $\pi \equiv p_C/p_S$ here.[11]

Unlike in VON NEUMANN I, I now need one more equation to close the temporary-equilibrium system. At a point in time, not only must ownership claims be willingly held – that is, stock-equilibrium condition (3.8) obtain – but the flow of instantaneously perishable consumption services supplied must equal the flow of such services demanded. The former equals the fixed amount $Q^S = q^S X_S^C$, while the latter amounts to $D^S = \gamma \Omega K/p$, $0 < \gamma \leq 1$ being the proportion of total consumption spending ΩK that falls on services and $\Omega > 0$ again denoting capitalists' fixed rate of time preference [recall (1.9)].

The corresponding flow-equilibrium condition may be written as $Z^S \equiv Q^S - D^S = Q^S - \gamma \Omega K/p = 0$, or as

$$z^S(p, p_C, p_S; x, \gamma, \Omega, q^S) \equiv q^S - \gamma \Omega (1 + \pi x) p_S/p = 0, \qquad x \equiv X_C^C/X_S^C, \tag{3.9}$$

from (3.1)–(3.3), where $Z^S/X_S^C \equiv z^S(\cdot)$ is a normalized flow-excess-supply function for consumption services and x again denotes the economy's capital composition. The temporary-equilibrium system is now closed: Given expectations $\hat{\pi}^e$; predetermined sectoral capital stocks X_j^C (thus, a predetermined capital composition x); preferences γ, Ω; and technology q^i, equations (3.9), (3.8), and $\max(p_C, p_S) = 1$ in (3.4) are sufficient to solve for the three momentary equilibrium prices p, p_C, p_S (thus, for π and ρ).

By analogy to (1.13), Walras's Law can be written as $Z^C + pZ^S \equiv (\rho - \Omega)K - X_C^C \dot{p}_C - X_S^C \dot{p}_S$ (the value of planned flow excess supplies must identically equal desired saving net of capital gains). Consider, say, ALPHA ($p_S = 1, \dot{X}_C^C = -\delta X_C^C$). Allow the stockmarket to clear and entrepreneurial profits to be maximized at a given p, expectations, and parameters [(3.8)]; then the corn-market flow-equilibrium equation $p_C \dot{X}_C^C + \dot{X}_S^C = Z^C [\equiv Q^C - \delta(p_C X_C^C + X_S^C) - D^C]$ must hold identically. Now

[11] In both cases, the numerator (denominator) refers to the price of the capital good used in the corn-sector (S-sector). Observe that in ALPHA (3.8) appears as $\chi(p, \pi, 1; \hat{\pi}^e, q^C, q^S) = 0$, in BETA as $\chi(p, 1, \pi^{-1}; \hat{\pi}^e, q^C, q^S) = 0$; for given $p, \hat{\pi}^e$, and q^i we may, thus, draw stock demand and supply curves as a function of π analogous to those appearing in figure 1.1.

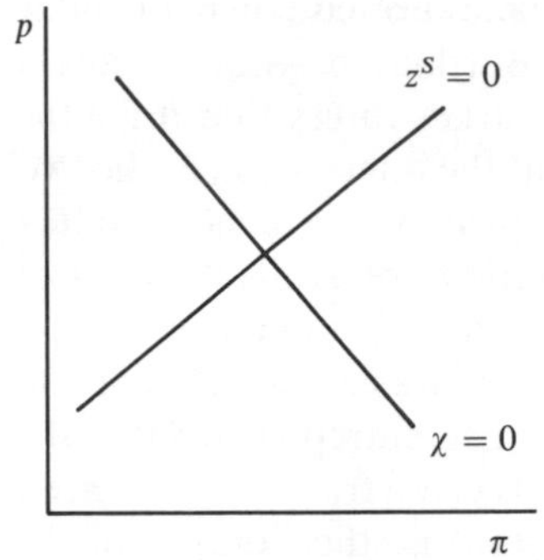

Figure 3.1 Temporary equilibrium in ALPHA

allow the consumption services market to clear [(3.9)]; then $Z^S=0$. Substituting $Z^C = p_C\dot{X}^C_C + \dot{X}^C_S$ and $Z^S=0$ on the lefthand side of Walras's Law, and rearranging, shows that the capital-market flow-equilibrium condition

$$\dot{K} = (\rho - \Omega)K, \qquad \dot{K} \equiv p_C\dot{X}^C_C + p_S\dot{X}^C_S + X^C_C\dot{p}_C + X^C_S\dot{p}_S \tag{3.10}$$

obtains identically at any set of temporary-equilibrium prices satisfying (3.8) and (3.9). In a moment, this identity will help to solve for the economy's relative rate of accumulation, $\dot{x}$.

Figure 3.1 illustrates a temporary equilibrium in regime ALPHA.[12] Loci $\chi(p, \pi; \hat{\pi}^e \ldots) = 0$ and $z^S(p, \pi; x \ldots) = 0$ show combinations of p and π that (at given expectations, capital stocks, and parameters) ensure stock and flow equilibrium, respectively. The $\chi=0$-schedule is downward sloping since a rise in p – by increasing the gross rental $r_S = pq^S$ of service-sector capital, thus the current yield $r_S/p_S - \delta$ on service-sector equity – creates a stock excess supply of corn-sector equity that must drive down its price $p_C = \pi$. On the other hand, the $z^S=0$-curve is positively sloped since a rise in p leads to a decline in demand D^S or $d^S \equiv D^S/X^C_S = \gamma\Omega(1+\pi x)/p$ for services, thus to a positive excess flow supply of them. That excess supply can only be eliminated by a rise in $p_C = \pi$ sufficient to increase wealth by whatever amount necessary to bring demand for services back to its original level.

This explains the slope-configuration of the $\chi=0$- and $z^S=0$-loci.

[12] In regime BETA, the $z^S=0$-locus would be negatively sloped and flatter than the $\chi=0$-schedule; the same comparative-statics results as those discussed below for ALPHA obtain.

However, before performing a comparative-statics exercise on figure 3.1 – in particular, one demonstrating the Ricardo–Bortkiewicz–Sraffa theorem – I need to enquire more deeply about the market forces that drive the system to its temporary-equilibrium position at the intersection of the two loci. (What follows elaborates the convergence proposition in the introduction to this chapter.) Three adjustment scenarios are available, each of which can be shown to be consistent with competitive profit maximization on the part of entrepreneurs and arbitrageurs: Walrasian adjustment and two types of Marshallian adjustment. In the former, entrepreneurs take the price of the nonbasic output and input rentals as given from an auctioneer; they vary their demand for input services – that is, their output of the nonbasic – so as to maximize profits at these given prices.[13] Under Marshallian adjustment, it is the momentary stock of inputs at their disposal and the level of output producible therefrom that entrepreneurs take as given. They then competitively set the price of consumption services so as to maximize profits (which does not involve a contradiction, as I now show).

In the first of the two Marshallian scenarios (M1), they do so by moving p to the S-market-clearing level at the intersection between the vertical supply and the downward-sloping demand curve (see the top diagram in figure 3.2; in the corresponding diagram M1, p is moved on to the $z^S=0$-locus at any given π). Competition between entrepreneurs forces them to pay out the entire revenue pQ^S as gross dividends $r_C X_S^C$ to their firm's shareholders (owners of X_S^C).[14] Given the corresponding net dividend $r_S - p_S\delta = r_S - \delta$, arbitrageurs clear the stockmarket by driving the relative equity price $\pi = p_C$ to a level consistent with a uniform expected yield – that is, on to the $\chi=0$-schedule in diagram M1 of figure 3.2.

In the second Marshallian scenario, M2, the roles of entrepreneurs and arbitrageurs in market clearing are reversed. Output of the nonbasic is again momentarily given and its price is again set by entrepreneurs, but now at a level $p \geq a_{CS} r_S$ at least (by competition, just) equal to that necessitated

[13] Since factors are instantaneously immobile, one output level only is consistent with full employment of the S-sector input, thus, with a positive rental of that input, positive unit costs, and a positive output supply price. Since, given the demand function $D_S = \gamma\Omega K/p$, $\gamma > 0$, a zero nonbasics equilibrium price and output level will never be observed, the set of entrepreneurs' profit-maximizing quantity choices under Walrasian adjustment degenerates into the single point $Q^S = q^S X_S^C > 0$.

[14] The point is that, unlike in the Walrasian account, entrepreneurs will not maximize profits, if they sell at a disequilibrium price – that is, if they sell $q^S \equiv Q^S/X_S^C$ at a supply price below demand price, or if they fail to sell q^S when supply price exceeds demand price. In both cases, they end up making absolute or relative losses (relative, that is, to competing entrepreneurs) and, thus, will be voted out by shareholders. This gives them an incentive to acquire the necessary information on the parameters γ, Ω of the nonbasics demand curve (information here assumed to be free; recall the parallel discussion in chapter 1, footnote 14).

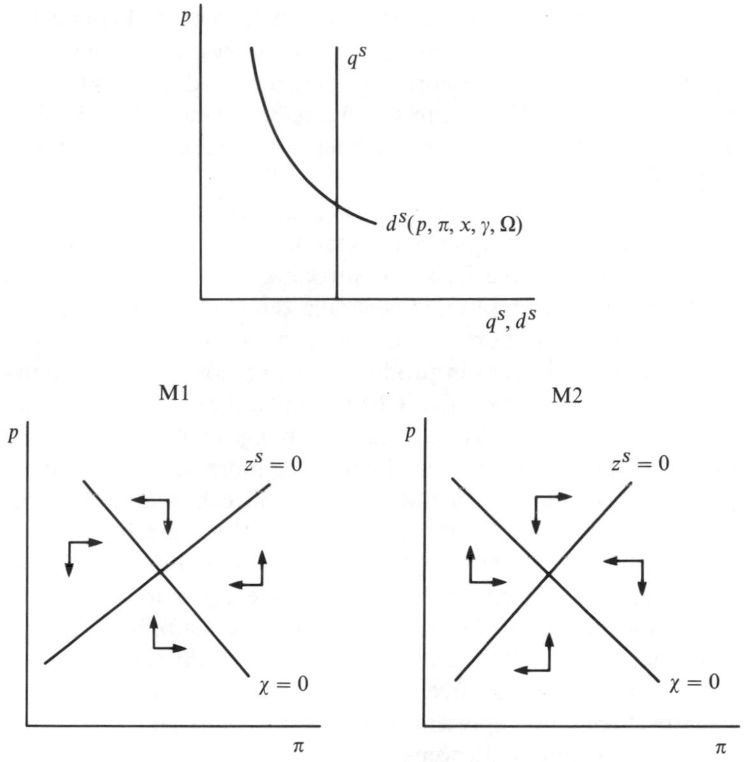

Figure 3.2 Marshallian adjustment toward temporary equilibrium

by the *dividend r_S demanded by shareholders*. r_S, in turn, is determined by portfolio holders' insistence on an equal expected equity yield at the given capital-gains expectations and at a given relative equity price π. Thus, for any given π-value, profit maximization by entrepreneurs and arbitrageurs moves p on to the $\chi = 0$-locus in diagram M2 of figure 3.2. Profit-maximizing short-selling by arbitrageurs now drives π on to the $z^S = 0$-locus – namely to a value resulting in a level of wealth and a corresponding demand for nonbasics $d^S(p, \pi \ldots)$ just sufficient to absorb the given supply q^S at the dividend-determined price p set by entrepreneurs. In particular, when there is an excess demand for (an excess supply of) consumption services – as represented by a point to the right (left) of the $z^S = 0$-locus – arbitrageurs will sell equity in currently nonproduced (produced) inputs $X_C^C(X_S^C)$, thus lowering (raising) the relative equity price $\pi \equiv p_C/p_S = p_C$ of nonproduced inputs and, thereby, the economy's wealth $K = (1 + \pi x)X_S^C$ just sufficiently to move the system on to the $z^S = 0$-schedule.

That the two Marshallian adjustment processes M1, M2 allow the economy to instantaneously converge to the temporary-equilibrium point is supported by the stability of the corresponding pseudo dynamics (see the phase arrows in the M1, M2 diagrams of figure 3.2): Under M1, $\dot{p} \gtreqless 0$ as $z^S \lesseqgtr 0$ and $\dot{\pi} \gtreqless 0$ as $\chi \lesseqgtr 0$, entailing convergence; under M2, $\dot{p} \gtreqless 0$ as $\chi \lesseqgtr 0$ and $\dot{\pi} \gtreqless 0$ as $z^S \gtreqless 0$, also entailing convergence.

Consider now a rise in the productivity q^S of the service sector (at given expectations $\hat{p}_j^e$ and values of other parameters). It illustrates the temporary-equilibrium version of the Ricardo–Bortkiewicz–Sraffa theorem. As against the Walrasian presumption of generalized interdependence, Sraffa (1960) – and before him von Bortkiewicz (1907) and Ricardo (1815, 1951) – has shown that not all changes in production technology have repercussions on the economy's rate of profit ρ: Changes in nonbasics technology do not. Observe from (3.8) and (3.9) that, unlike a change in q^C, $dq^S > 0$ can be accommodated, at given expectations, by nothing more than an instantaneous equiproportionate drop in p on impact. All other variables – in particular π and the profit rate – remain unaltered. (In figure 3.1, the two loci shift down by equal amounts.) $dp/p = -dq^S/q^S < 0$ by itself thus manages to simultaneously eliminate an incipient excess supply of corn-sector equity in the bourse ($\chi > 0$) and an incipient excess supply of services in the output market ($z^S > 0$). The invariance of the profit rate moreover obtains even if expectations are free to vary in accordance with foresight. That is, the impact response represents the system's jump to the new steady state – no traverse dynamics intervene at any point.

This is confirmed by an examination of the model's laws of motion and its steady state. The two temporary-equilibrium conditions may for that purpose usefully be brought together in a reduced form expression. Solving $z^S(p, p_C, p_S; x\ldots) = 0$ for the function $p = p(p_C, p_S; x)$ and substituting the latter into $\chi(p, p_C, p_S; \hat{\pi}^e \ldots) = 0$, I obtain

$$\dot{\pi}^e = \pi\{[p(p_C, p_S; x)q^S/p_S] - (q^C/p_C)\} \equiv \phi(p_C, p_S, x) \tag{3.11}$$

after rearrangement. Under myopic foresight – that is, $\dot{\pi}^e = \dot{\pi}$ – the relative equity price π is an autonomous state variable; (3.11) yields its law of motion, once I specify the prevailing regime and the dynamics of x.[15]

Each of the model's two temporary-equilibrium regimes ALPHA and BETA has associated with it a distinct dynamical system, the two being "spliced" at the von Neumann steady state. Consider, for example, ALPHA ($1 = p_S > p_C = \pi$). Under it, the economy finds itself in a situation in which dividends plus expected capital gains are relatively unfavorable to

[15] Under static expectations, $\dot{\pi}^e \equiv 0 = \phi(p_C, p_S, x)$, which, given specification of the regime, yields $\pi = \pi(x)$. Here, π is endogenous to the temporary equilibrium and, like p, a function of the single autonomous state variable x.

corn-sector capital, which necessitates an equity price p_C below p_S for expected-yield equality across assets. Since the price of new corn output equals 1, neither the purchase of new nor the replacement of worn-out capital – either costs 1 per unit but is worth only $p_C < 1$ – will be profitable in the corn sector. In ALPHA, therefore, the rate of gross investment must be zero in that sector,

$$\dot{X}^C_C = -\delta X^C_C < 0, \qquad \delta \geq 0. \tag{3.12}$$

By contrast, in BETA we have $1 = p_C > p_S = 1/\pi$, so that the economy's gross investment will be flowing in its entirety into the corn industry, forcing the service sector to decumulate its corn stock at the rate[16]

$$\dot{X}^C_S = -\delta X^C_S < 0. \tag{3.13}$$

Of course, neither (3.12) nor (3.13) are consistent with a steady state. A necessary condition for the latter is

$$1 = p_C = p_S, \qquad \pi = 1, \tag{3.14}$$

given that in the steady state growth in capital stocks must be equiproportionate, equalling $g = \hat{\bar{K}} = \hat{\bar{X}}^C_C = \hat{\bar{X}}^C_S = \bar{\rho} - \Omega \geq 0$ from (3.10). The steady-state profit rate and nonbasics price are given by

$$\bar{\rho} = q^C - \delta = pq^S - \delta > 0, \text{ thus } \bar{p} = q^C/q^S, \tag{3.15}$$

from (3.7) and the assumption of long-run viability ($g = q^C - \delta - \Omega \geq 0$). Stockmarket equilibrium thus solves for both the long-period profit rate and the long-run relative price of nonbasics. Flow-equilibrium condition (3.9), on the other hand, yields the steady-state capital composition

$$\bar{x} = (q^C/\gamma\Omega) - 1 > 0. \tag{3.16}$$

Two noteworthy results emerge. First, the model's steady state exhibits Sraffa-nonsubstitution: $\bar{p}$ is unaffected by changes in preferences (γ or Ω), which are accommodated entirely by alterations in the long-run composition of capital. Second, (3.15) provides confirmation, for the long run, of the Ricardo–Bortkiewicz–Sraffa theorem: $dq^S > 0$ has nil effect on $\bar{\rho}$, but lowers $\bar{p}$ proportionately.

I now proceed to analyze the system's perfect-foresight dynamics and examine each of the two non-steady-state regimes in turn. Note that none of the laws of motions to be considered contains q^S as a parameter.

[16] Observe that (3.12) and (3.13) assume that corn consumption is out of current corn output, not out of (the cheaper of the two) corn inventories. Even if we allowed for the latter (as in VON NEUMANN I), short-run nonsubstitution would fail to obtain on account of the nonstorablity of consumption services.

(i) ALPHA

Substituting in (3.10) for ρ from (3.7) and for $\dot{X}^C_C$ from (3.12), I obtain, given (3.6), $-\pi\delta X^C_C + \dot{X}^C_S + X^C_C\dot{\pi} = [(q^C/\pi) - \delta + \hat{\pi}^e - \Omega]K$ or

$$\hat{X}^C_S = [(q^C/\pi) - \Omega](1+\pi x) - \delta + \pi^{-1}\phi^\alpha(\pi, x) \equiv \hat{X}^C_S(\pi, x), \tag{3.17}$$

where, from (3.9), (3.11), I have used

$$\dot{\pi} = \pi[\gamma\Omega(1+\pi x) - (q^C/\pi)] \equiv \phi^\alpha(\pi, x) \equiv \phi(\pi, 1, x), \quad \phi^\alpha_i > 0 \ (i=1,2), \tag{3.18}$$

the law of motion of the relative equity price under ALPHA and myopic foresight. The corresponding relative-stock dynamics are given by

$$\begin{aligned} \dot{x} &\equiv x(\hat{X}^C_C - \hat{X}^C_S) = -x\{[(q^C/\pi) - \Omega](1+\pi x) + [\gamma\Omega(1+\pi x) - (q^C/\pi)]\} \\ &\equiv \psi^\alpha(\pi, x), \quad \psi^\alpha_1 > 0,\ \psi^\alpha_2 < 0. \end{aligned} \tag{3.19}$$

Figure 3.3 shows, under ALPHA, the $\dot{\pi}=0$, $\dot{x}=0$ loci and the associated phase paths defined by (3.18), (3.19). The approach to the von Neumann steady state is through values $x > \bar{x}$ and along an unstable trajectory that reaches $\pi = 1$, $x = \bar{x}$ in finite time.[17]

(ii) BETA

Proceeding as before, I now obtain

$$\hat{X}^C_C = (1/\pi x)[(q^C - \Omega)(1+\pi x) - \delta\pi x + \pi^{-1}\phi^\beta(\pi, x)] \equiv \hat{X}^C_C(\pi, x) \tag{3.20}$$

from (3.10), after substitution for ρ from (3.7) and for $\dot{X}^C_S$ from (3.13). I also have, from (3.9), (3.11),

$$\dot{\pi} = \pi[\gamma\Omega(1+\pi x) - q^C] \equiv \phi^\beta(\pi, x) \equiv \phi(1, \pi^{-1}, x), \quad \phi^\beta_i > 0 \quad (i=1,2), \tag{3.21}$$

the law of motion of the relative equity price in BETA. The dynamics of capital composition now are, from (3.13) and (3.20),

$$\begin{aligned} \dot{x} &= (1/\pi)\{(q^C - \Omega)(1+\pi x) + [\gamma\Omega(1+\pi x) - q^C]\} \equiv \psi^\beta(\pi, x), \\ &\quad \psi^\beta_i > 0 \quad (i=1,2). \end{aligned} \tag{3.22}$$

The loci $\dot{\pi}=0$, $\dot{x}=0$ under BETA are segments of rectangular hyperbolae that intersect the $\pi = 1$-line at the same x-values as do the corresponding loci

[17] The trajectory lies below the stable branch of a notional saddle point at the intersection of the two loci somewhere in BETA. The chapter appendix provides details on the dynamic analysis at hand.

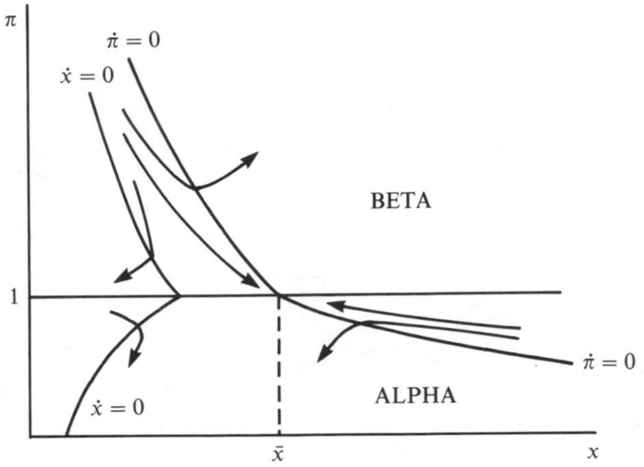

Figure 3.3 Dynamics of VON NEUMANN II

under ALPHA (see figure 3.3). The approach to the von Neumann steady state is now through values $x < \bar{x}$, but again along an unstable trajectory that reaches $\pi = 1$, $x = \bar{x}$ in finite time.[18]

Consider the consequences of an unanticipated permanent shift in consumption preferences away from corn toward consumption services ($d\gamma > 0$; see figure 3.4). Across steady-state growth paths, π remains unaltered at unity and the capital composition shifts away from corn-sector capital ($d\bar{x} < 0$). Since on impact Q^S is fixed, the rise in the flow demand for services leads to a jump in their price p at that moment. The consequent increase in the current gross yield $r_S/p_S = pq^S/p_S$ of service-sector capital lowers the relative attractiveness of corn-sector equity. To preserve expected-yield equality across assets, its price p_C must fall and push the system into regime ALPHA on impact. The bourse, though, correctly foresees the need for a subsequent reversal of this price decline ($\dot{p}_C = \dot{\pi} > 0$ on impact and thereafter) and therefore keeps p_C from falling as much as it otherwise would have to. From what has been said it follows that the momentary profit rate jumps, setting in motion a period of accelerated overall investment $\hat{K} = \rho - \Omega > g$. Point a in figure 3.4 illustrates the economy's position on impact. The steady-state point has shifted from A_0 to A_1 and the system has jumped, at a given capital composition, on to the corresponding convergent perfect-foresight path.

The characteristics of the subsequent adjustment are clear. Since $p_C < 1$,

18 The trajectory lies above the stable branch of a notional saddle point at $\pi = 0, x \to \infty$.

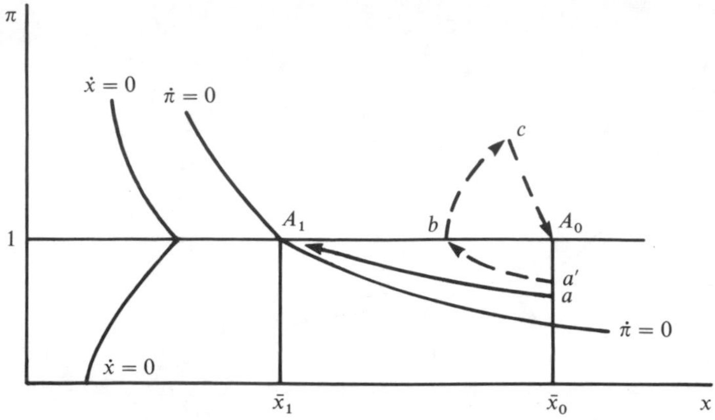

Figure 3.4 Adjustment following a permanent and a transitory preference shift toward consumption services

aggregate gross investment is channeled exclusively into the service industry, making for $\dot{X}^C_C<0$, $\dot{X}^C_S>0$, $\dot{x}<0$ on impact and throughout the traverse to the new steady state. This gives rise to a sequence of Rybczynski effects on output composition that progressively lower Q^C, raise Q^S, and reverse the initial price increase of consumption services. The gain in the value productivity r_S of service-sector capital is, in consequence, also reversed, as is the rise in the economy-wide profit rate, which, in turn, allows the price of corn-sector equity to recuperate. In finite time the system reaches its new steady state at A_1, with $p_C=1$ and the two sectoral capital stocks again growing at the common rate g.[19]

[19] Qualitatively the same adjustment dynamics obtain under static expectations (the $\dot{\pi}=0$-schedules now represent the loci of temporary equilibria in the two regimes, with $\dot{x}<0$ in ALPHA and $\dot{x}>0$ in BETA from (3.19), (3.22)). Dashed path A_0–a'–b–c–A_0 in figure 3.4 shows the consequences, under perfect foresight, of a rise in γ that is purely temporary and confidently expected to last for $t_1-t_0<\infty$ periods only. Its main interest lies in the illustration it provides of an endogenous regime switch from ALPHA to BETA at some well-defined moment t^*, $t_0<t^*<t_1$ (see point b). Adjustment before t^* is similar to that following a permanent $d\gamma>0$. At t^*, the system experiences a complete reversal in the pattern of investment, with the $\dot{X}^C_i$ and $\dot{x}$ all changing sign. This turnabout is forced onto the economy by stockmarket speculators' anticipation of a drop in the equity price of service-sector capital $1/\pi\equiv p_S/p_C$ at the moment (t_1) that sector's temporarily favorable demand conditions vanish. Since such a drop, anticipated with certainty, offers unexploited profit opportunities, it will not be allowed to occur. Therefore, following the rise in $1/\pi$ at t_0 (by less than under a permanent $d\gamma>0$ – see point a'), the economy is launched on a pre-t_1 path along which $1/\pi$ is being continuously depressed – first via $\dot{p}_C>0$, subsequently via $\dot{p}_S<0$. With the

3.3 VON NEUMANN III: Transforming nonbasics into basics

Consider an economy whose momentary wealth is given by

$$K \equiv p^C X^C + p^S X^S, \tag{3.23}$$

where p^i is the price of corn and steel in their form as basics, that is, as input stocks X^i $(i = C, S)$. Such stocks, it will be assumed in a moment, can only be "installed" or "stored" at a cost. (Corn output is, as usual, the economy's numéraire.)

Steel and corn stocks produce output flows Q^C and Q^S of corn and steel which are nonbasic and nonusable as productive inputs (other than into the nonbasics-to-basics transformation process discussed below). Production of nonbasics is by means of a technology identical to that of VON NEUMANN I [recall (1.2), (1.3)],

$$Q^C = a_{SC}^{-1} X^S \tag{3.24}$$

$$Q^S = a_{CS}^{-1} X^C, \tag{3.25}$$

where the $a_{ij} > 0$ are fixed input–output coefficients.

As earlier, entrepreneurs maximize profits. This requires that they increase the capacity X^i of their firm to the point where the marginal entrepreneurial profit of doing so equals the marginal cost they incur. The marginal (or average) entrepreneurial return to capacity expansion is $q^i - 1$, where

$$q^S \equiv p^S/p, \; q^C \equiv p^C \tag{3.26}$$

represents the two-sectors' "Tobin-q" and where p is the output or nonbasics price of steel. Thus, $q^S - 1 \equiv (p^S - p)/p$ is the percent excess of the stock-demand over the flow-supply price of steel, q^S being the ratio of the price at which corn entrepreneurs can float additional equity over what they must pay, in the steel-output market, for the materials necessary to expand capacity. On the other hand, the "effort" cost to them (measured in units of investment resources) of assuming responsibility for accelerating the rate $\dot{X}^i$ of capacity expansion by a small amount depends on the proportional rate $\hat{X}^i$ at which capacity is already expanding; the cost in question is given by (MCE stands for "marginal cost of entrepreneurship")

$$\mathrm{MCE}(\hat{X}^i) \equiv T(\hat{X}^i) + \hat{X}^i T'(\hat{X}^i), \qquad \mathrm{MCE}' > 0 \tag{3.27}$$

reversal thereby fully discounted into the asset price structure by the time t_1 arrives, $1/\pi$ remains unperturbed at that moment (see point c), though stockmarket speculation now correctly changes its forecast to an improvement in service-sector equity prices ($\dot{p}_S^e$ jumps from negative to positive).

and represents the derivative with respect to $\dot{X}^i$ of a sectorally uniform installation-cost function $\dot{X}^i T(\hat{X}^i)$.[20] The idea is that for an i-firm to achieve a rate of growth $\dot{X}^i$ in its capital stock (i-basics), a total amount of $\dot{X}^i + \dot{X}^i T(\cdot)$ units of i-output (i-nonbasics) is required, of which $\dot{X}^i T(\cdot)$ is entrepreneurial compensation; and, furthermore, that the coefficient $T(\hat{X}^i)$ rises as the percent rate $\hat{X}^i$ of investment is increased.

Why is $T' > 0$ rather than zero? As indicated, two explanations are available. One focuses on the basics/nonbasics (storable/perishable) distinction. It views $T(\cdot)$ as embodying a storage technology that is capable of transforming – at a net input or "wastage" cost of $\dot{X}^i T dt$ – an amount $\dot{X}^i(1+T)dt$ of nonbasics into an increment of dX^i units of basics. The other explanation takes the view that the economic system contains an input which, unlike other factors of production, is only required in a dynamic environment of nonstationary output levels: Its function is to facilitate change in the economy's productive arrangements. The input in question is entrepreneurship [Penrose (1959), Uzawa (1969)].[21] Unlike that embodied in my standard zero-pure-profit conditions, the entrepreneurship being considered here is scarce and, thus, able to command a return $\dot{X}^i T(\cdot) > 0$ whenever the economy is undergoing capacity change.[22]

From what has been said regarding (3.26) and (3.27), absence of excess entrepreneurial profits requires

$$q^i - 1 = \mathrm{MCE}(\hat{X}^i), \tag{3.28}$$

which may be solved implicitly for the flow-investment-demand functions[23]

[20] Alternatively interpreted below as a storage-cost function. The specific formulation here adopted is due to Hayashi [(1982); see also Blanchard and Fisher (1989), chapter 2]: $\dot{X}^i T(\dot{X}^i/X^i)$ is linearly homogeneous in $\dot{X}^i$, X^i; it obeys $T(\hat{X}^i) \gtrless 0$ as $\hat{X}^i \gtrless 0$ (so that $\dot{X}^i T(\cdot) \geq 0$, investment and disinvestment being costly both), $T' > 0$, $2T' + \hat{X}^i T'' > 0$.

[21] Schumpeterian entrepreneurship [Schumpeter (1934)] is associated with innovation (roughly, changes in the a_{ij}) rather than with alterations in capacity (changes in the X^i) focused on by the present model.

[22] To simplify the analysis, I do not model, as part of the economy's wealth K, the equity claims that correspond to the entrepreneurial income $\dot{X}^i T$. Along a convergent perfect-foresight path, such entrepreneurial wealth equals $\sum_{C,S} p^{\bar{E}_i}\bar{E}_i$, $p^{\bar{E}_i}\bar{E}_i \equiv \int_0^\infty \dot{X}^i(t) T[\hat{X}^i(t)] \exp[-\int_0^t \rho(\tau) d\tau] dt$, where $\bar{E}_i$ $(i = C, S)$ is a fixed stock of sector-specific entrepreneurship and $p^{\bar{E}_i}$ its (shadow) equity price. This is not innocuous since, unlike in a model with a stationary state – such as WALRAS III, where another problem of costly, entrepreneurially driven change in economic arrangements is analyzed (intersectoral resource movements) – in the model at hand entrepreneurial profits $\dot{X}^i T$ do not go to zero even in the long run (a von Neumann steady state $g = \bar{\hat{X}}^i > 0$). Portfolio and savings decisions on the part of the recipients of $\dot{X}^i T$ are, therefore, also not modeled; instead, it is implicitly assumed that i-type entrepreneurial income is fully spent, at each instant, on consumption of i-type output.

[23] The sign of the derivative $\hat{X}^{i\prime}$ follows from the restrictions on $T(\cdot)$ listed in footnote 20, the equality at equal q^i of rates of investment and their derivatives from the assumed sectoral identity of the T-function.

$$\hat{X}^i = \hat{X}^i(q^i), \qquad \hat{X}^{i\prime} > 0,\ \hat{X}^{C(\cdot)} = \hat{X}^{S(\cdot)} \text{ at } q^C = q^S. \tag{3.29}$$

According to (3.29), a rise in the Tobin-q^i – that is, a rise in the stockmarket's valuation of firms (p^iX^i) relative to their replacement cost (X^C and pX^S) – increases the rate $\hat{X}^i$ of capacity formation by entrepreneurs running these firms.

Total current payout to a firm's stockholders has two components: Cash dividends Π^iX^i and the value of stock dividends $p^i\dot{X}^i$.[24] Unit cash dividends Π^i on equity in corn and steel capital – that is, unit cash dividends paid out by steel and corn firms, respectively – are given by[25]

$$\begin{aligned} &\Pi^C(q^C, q^S, \pi) \equiv pa_{CS}^{-1} - \hat{X}^C(q^C)[1 + \tilde{T}(q^C)] \\ &\qquad \Pi_1^C \gtrless 0, \quad \Pi_2^C < 0, \quad \Pi_3^C > 0 \\ &\Pi^S(q^C, q^S, \pi) \equiv a_{SC}^{-1} - p\hat{X}^S(q^S)[1 + \tilde{T}(q^S)] \\ &\qquad \Pi_1^S < 0, \quad \Pi_2^S \gtrless 0, \quad \Pi_3^S > 0, \end{aligned} \tag{3.30}$$

where $\tilde{T}(q^i) \equiv T[\hat{X}^i(q^i)]$ from (3.29), and where I have used (3.26) and the definition of the relative equity price below to express the nonbasics price p of steel in terms of π and the q^i,

$$\pi \equiv p^S/p^C, \text{ thus } p \equiv \pi q^C/q^S. \tag{3.31}$$

The stockmarket is governed by the condition that arbitrageurs be at all times satisfied with the composition of the portfolios they manage. This requires that the yield ρ^i expected from current cash dividends Π^i, current stock dividends $p^i\hat{X}^i$, and expected capital gains $(\dot{p}^i)^e$ be uniform across the two types of equity,

$$\rho^C \equiv \left[\frac{\Pi^C(\cdot) + p^C\hat{X}^C}{p^C}\right] + (\hat{p}^C)^e = \left[\frac{\Pi^S(\cdot) + p^S\hat{X}^S}{p^S}\right] + (\hat{p}^S)^e \equiv \rho^S, \tag{3.32}$$

which, as usual, may be written in the alternative form of a zero-yield-differential equation $\chi(\cdot) = 0$,

$$\begin{aligned} \chi(q^C, q^S, \pi; \hat{\pi}^e) \equiv{} & (1/q^C)\{\Pi^C(q^C, q^S, \pi) + q^C\hat{X}^C(q^C) \\ & - [\Pi^S(q^C, q^S, \pi) + \pi q^C\hat{X}^S(q^S)]\pi^{-1}\} - \hat{\pi}^e \\ ={} & 0, \quad \chi_1 = -\chi_2 > 0, \quad \chi_3 > 0, \quad \chi_4 < 0. \end{aligned} \tag{3.33}$$

[24] It could alternatively have been assumed that payout consists of cash dividends only. Since accumulation is financed out of retained earnings exclusively (that is, firms do not enter the capital market), this would imply that the *number* of equities outstanding is fixed at all times; accumulation would be entirely reflected in capital gains that persist in the steady state. The present approach has certain expository advantages, but the differences are terminological only.

[25] Thus, cash dividends paid out by (say) steel firms, $\Pi^C X^C = pQ^S - \dot{X}^C - \dot{X}^C T$, equal total revenue pQ^S minus the sum of the output-market cost of investment, $\dot{X}^C$, and normal entrepreneurial compensation, $\dot{X}^C T$. For simplicity, the rate of exponential depreciation is set equal to zero in this chapter.

In the basics-only economy VON NEUMANN I, $\chi(\pi;\hat{\pi}^e\ldots)=0$ solved for π uniquely, thus closing the temporary-equilibrium price system (at given expectations and parameters); in VON NEUMANN II, the presence of one nonbasic required, in addition to $\chi(p,\pi;\hat{\pi}^e\ldots)=0$, a single instantaneous flow-equilibrium equation $z^S(p,\pi;x\ldots)=0$; in VON NEUMANN III, by contrast, *both* of the economy's outputs are nonbasic so that, in addition to stock-equilibrium condition (3.33), I now need *two* of the economy's three flow-equilibrium equations to close the temporary-equilibrium price system.[26] The point is that, unlike in VON NEUMANN I and VON NEUMANN II, each good $i=C,S$ now possesses well-defined *ex-ante* flow-demand functions for consumption *and* investment; only through instantaneous variations in the relevant market price – which is q^i, as we will see – can the sum of i's consumption and investment demand be rendered consistent with the momentarily fixed supply Q^i.

It is convenient to focus on the output-market-equilibrium equations $Z^i\equiv Q^i-\dot{X}^i(1+\tilde{T})-D^i=0$ $(i=C,S)$. Using $z^i\equiv Z^i/X^i$, (3.24), (3.25), (3.29), and my usual consumption-demand assumption $D^S=\gamma\Omega K/p$, $D^C=(1-\gamma)\Omega K$ [(1.9)], this gives

$$\begin{aligned} z^C(q^C,\pi;x,\gamma,\Omega,a_{SC})&\equiv[a_{SC}^{-1}-q^C(1-\gamma)\Omega(\pi+x)]x^{-1}\\ &-\hat{X}^C(q^C)[1+\tilde{T}(q^C)]=0,\quad z_i^C<0(i=1\text{–}3,5,6),\ >0(i=4) \end{aligned}\tag{3.34}$$

$$\begin{aligned} z^S(q^S,\pi;x,\gamma,\Omega,a_{CS})&\equiv a_{CS}^{-1}x-(q^S/\pi)\gamma\Omega(\pi+x)\\ &-\hat{X}^S(q^S)[1+\tilde{T}(q^S)]=0,\quad z_i^S<0(i=1,4\text{–}6),\ >0(i=2,3)\\ x&\equiv X^C/X^S, \end{aligned}\tag{3.35}$$

where x again is the economy's capital composition. The system's temporary equilibrium is now fully determinate: For given expectations $(\hat{\pi}^e)$, capital composition (x), preferences (γ,Ω), and technology (a_{ij},T), equations (3.33)–(3.35) jointly determine the equilibrium values of q^C, q^S, and π. It follows that, given the expectation $(\hat{p}^C)^e$, the uniform temporary-equilibrium yield on equity

$$\begin{aligned} \rho[q^C,q^S,\pi;(\hat{p}^C)^e]=\rho^C&\equiv\frac{\Pi^C(q^C,q^S,\pi)+q^C\hat{X}^C(q^C)}{q^C}+(\hat{p}^C)^e\\ \rho_i>0(i=1,3,4),&\quad\rho_2<0, \end{aligned}\tag{3.36}$$

is (from (3.32)) also determinate and fixes the cost of borrowing nonbasic corn – the corn-numéraire real rate of interest $\rho(\cdot)$. The price of nonbasic steel p, finally, is given by identity (3.31).

Thus, a natural way to think about price determination when outputs are nonbasic, but transformable into basics at a cost, is to view the stockmarket

[26] By Walras's Law [which remains as in (1.13)], only two of the three flow-equilibrium conditions $Z^C(\cdot)=0$, $Z^S(\cdot)=0$, $\dot{K}=(\rho-\Omega)K$ are independent.

as speculatively fixing the relative price π of *existing* stocks of basic corn and steel, whereas output markets determine the own-rates-of-return q^C-1, q^S-1 on *adding* to stocks of corn and steel,

$$q^C = q^C(\pi; x, \gamma, \Omega, a_{SC}), \quad q_i^C < 0(i=1,2,4,5), > 0(i=3) \tag{3.37}$$

$$q^S = q^S(\pi; x, \gamma, \Omega, a_{CS}), \quad q_i^S < 0(i=3\text{–}5), > 0(i=1,2), \tag{3.38}$$

from (3.34), (3.35).

The model's dynamics now follow immediately. Solving (3.33) for $\hat{\pi}^e$, using the myopic-foresight assumption $\hat{\pi}^e = \hat{\pi}$ and (3.37), (3.38), I have

$$\dot{\pi} = (\pi/q^C)\{\Pi^C[q^C(\cdot), q^S(\cdot), \pi] + q^C(\cdot)\hat{X}^C[q^C(\cdot)] - \Pi^S[q^C(\cdot), q^S(\cdot), \pi]\pi^{-1} - q^C(\cdot)\hat{X}^S[q^S(\cdot)]\} \equiv \phi(\pi, x), \quad \phi_1 > 0, \quad \phi_2 < 0. \tag{3.39}$$

The law of motion of capital composition is given by

$$\dot{x} = x\{\hat{X}^C[q^C(\cdot)] - \hat{X}^S[q^S(\cdot)]\} \equiv \psi(\pi, x), \quad \psi_i < 0(i=1,2), \tag{3.40}$$

from (3.29) and, again, (3.37), (3.38).

System [(3.39), (3.40)] – illustrated in figure 3.5 – is locally saddle-path stable,

$$\phi_1\psi_2 - \phi_2\psi_1 < 0. \tag{3.41}$$

Its properties in a steady state,

$$\dot{\pi} = \dot{x} = 0, \qquad \bar{\hat{X}}^C = \bar{\hat{X}}^S \equiv g(\cdot) \geq 0, \tag{3.42}$$

are easily derived. First, (3.42) and output-market equilibrium imply that the Tobin-q^i must be equal and constant. Therefore,

$$\bar{q}^C = \bar{q}^S \equiv \bar{q}, \qquad \bar{p} = \bar{\pi}, \tag{3.43}$$

from (3.31): In a steady state, the relative nonbasics (output) price $\bar{p}$ equals the relative basics (equity) price $\bar{\pi}$.[27] What determines $\bar{\pi}$?

Stock equilibrium (3.33) and the definition of unit cash dividends in (3.30) yield $\bar{\pi} = \bar{\Pi}^S/\bar{\Pi}^C = (a_{CS}/a_{SC})^{\frac{1}{2}}$. The following long-run Sraffa-nonsubstitution result ensues:

$$\bar{p} = \bar{\pi} = (a_{CS}/a_{SC})^{\frac{1}{2}}, \tag{3.44}$$

which is the same as (1.20). That is, the relative output price $\bar{p}$ is determined by relative sectoral productivity alone and independent of consumption preferences.[28]

How then are consumption preference shifts accommodated? To under-

[27] This holds true in VON NEUMANN I *at each instant* – which is what makes it a basics-only economy. [28] Note that the installation technology $T(\cdot)$ does not enter.

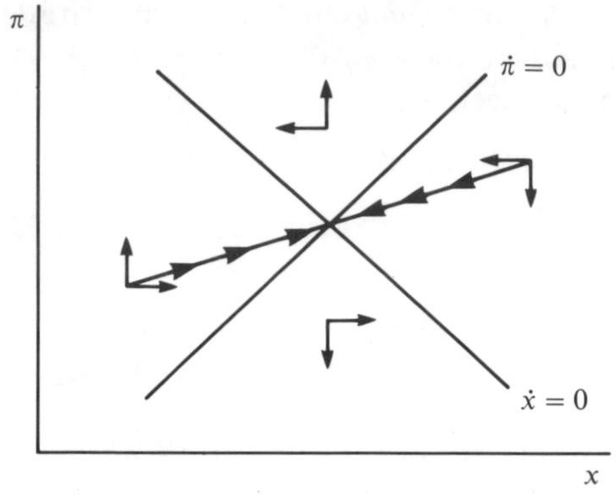

Figure 3.5 Dynamics of VON NEUMANN III

stand this, consider now the model's remaining steady-state variables. Starting with the equity price $\bar{q} = \bar{p}^C$, the rate of interest $\bar{\rho}$, and the long-run rate of growth g, it is easiest to determine them via capital market equilibrium. From the equality between demand $p^C\dot{X}^C + p^S\dot{X}^S$ and supply $(\rho - \Omega)K - X^C\dot{p}^C - X^S\dot{p}^S$ of loanable funds, we have $\hat{K} = \rho - \Omega = (\Pi^C/p^C) + \hat{X}^C + \hat{p}^C - \Omega$ at each instant, thus

$$\frac{\bar{\Pi}^C(\bar{q})}{\bar{q}} = \Omega, \qquad \bar{\Pi}^{C\prime} = \Pi_1^C + \Pi_2^C < 0, \tag{3.45}$$

in a steady-state equilibrium with $\hat{K} = \hat{X}^C$, $\hat{p}^C = 0$. Two things follow from (3.45). First, since $\bar{\Pi}^C/\bar{q} = \bar{\Pi}^S/\bar{\pi}\bar{q}$ from (3.32), in the long run consumption spending $\Omega K \equiv \Omega(\bar{q}X^C + \bar{\pi}\bar{q}X^S)$ just equals dividend income $\bar{\Pi}^C X^C + \bar{\Pi}^S X^S$. Second, (3.45) solves for the long-run Tobin-q, thus for the system's long-run rate of endogenous growth $g = \hat{X}(\bar{q})$ and rate of profit $\bar{\rho} = \Omega + \hat{X}(\bar{q})$, as functions of the rate of time preference:

$$\bar{q} = \bar{q}(\Omega \ldots), \bar{q}' < 0; \; g = g(\Omega \ldots), g' < 0; \; \bar{\rho} = \bar{\rho}(\Omega \ldots), \bar{\rho}' > 0. \tag{3.46}$$

The intratemporal preference parameter γ is still absent as a determinant.[29]

Only one variable remains to accommodate changes in γ: The compo-

[29] Dots in the $\bar{q}(\cdot)$, $g(\cdot)$, $\bar{\rho}(\cdot)$-functions stand for the output and installation technologies a_{ij}, T. As can be seen from $\bar{\Pi}^C = (a_{CS}a_{SC})^{-\frac{1}{2}} - \hat{X}(\bar{q})[1 + \tilde{T}(\bar{q})]$ and (3.45), any productivity advance $da_{ij} < 0$ must raise $\bar{q}$, g, and $\bar{\rho}$. That $\bar{\rho}$ is affected confirms the status of the VON NEUMANN III outputs as basic in the sense of the Ricardo–Bortkiewicz–Sraffa theorem. It is also interesting to note that a high $\bar{\rho}$ (a high real rate of interest) may be associated either with a low $\bar{q}$ (a depressed stockmarket, following a demand shock $d\Omega > 0$) or a high $\bar{q}$ (a booming stockmarket, due to a generalized jump in productivity).

sition x of the economy's physical capital stock. Using one of the two output-market-equilibrium conditions, say (3.34), I obtain[30]

$$\bar{x}(\gamma, \Omega \ldots) = \left(\frac{\gamma \bar{\pi} a_{CS}^{-1} + (1-\gamma)\hat{X}(\bar{q})[1+\tilde{T}(\bar{q})]}{(1-\gamma)\bar{\pi} a_{CS}^{-1} + \gamma \hat{X}(\bar{q})[1+\tilde{T}(\bar{q})]} \right) \bar{\pi} > 0$$
$$\bar{x}_1 > 0, \quad \bar{x}_2 \gtrless 0 \text{ as } \gamma \gtrless \tfrac{1}{2}. \tag{3.47}$$

At given technologies, $\bar{x}$ depends on intra- and intertemporal preferences. In particular, across steady states a permanent shift in preferences γ toward steel moves capital composition toward the input, corn, used intensively in the production of steel: $d\bar{x}/d\gamma > 0$. The consequent Rybczynski expansion in relative steel supply is sufficient to accommodate the change in the pattern of consumption demand at an unchanged consumption price of steel $\bar{p}$.

The result becomes transparent once the system's responses on impact of $d\gamma > 0$ – when all resources are rigidly given – and along the subsequent traverse are clearly understood (see figure 3.6a–c). On impact of the preference shift toward steel, the stockmarket correctly foresees a period of sustained pressure on steel industry capacity (corn stocks) and a period of slack demand for the inputs used intensively in corn (steel stocks). For some time, it reckons, the profitability q^C of additional capacity in the steel industry will be high and the rate of return q^S on investment in the corn industry, low. The stockmarket knows, furthermore, that unless the relative equity price $\pi \equiv p^S/p^C$ falls, the rise in q^C and the drop in q^S will – via increases in current payout $\Pi^C X^C + p^C \dot{X}^C$ on steel industry equity and decreases in current payout $\Pi^S X^S + p^S \dot{X}^S$ on corn industry shares – open up an inadmissible yield differential $\rho^C - \rho^S > 0$. It follows that stockmarket speculators must instantaneously lower p^S relative to p^C on impact, $d\pi < 0$.

Will the observed equilibrium response in the two output markets be consistent with the stockmarket adjustment just outlined? To see this, assume that π has indeed been speculatively lowered on impact and consider the consequent situation, *at given* q^S, in the flow market for steel. Steel consumption demand is higher, both because of the exogenous preference shift toward steel and because the steel-value of wealth, $K/p \equiv q^S(X^C \pi^{-1} + X^S)$, has risen. It follows that there must exist, at the prevailing own-rate-of-return q^S, an excess demand for steel that can only be eliminated by lowering q^S (which brings down investment demand $\hat{X}^S(q^S)$ and the steel-value of wealth, thus consumption demand $\gamma \Omega K/p$ for steel). I conclude that, as postulated in my account of stockmarket clearing, the equilibrium value of q^S will indeed have to fall on impact [see (3.38)]. Similar reasoning and inspection of (3.37) reveals that the drop in the

30 Of the three flow-equilibrium conditions – only two of which are independent, as we recall – I have employed one (capital market equilibrium) to solve for $\bar{q}$ in (3.45); another remains free to solve for $\bar{x}$. In deriving (3.47) from (3.34), I have used (3.30), (3.46)–(3.49).

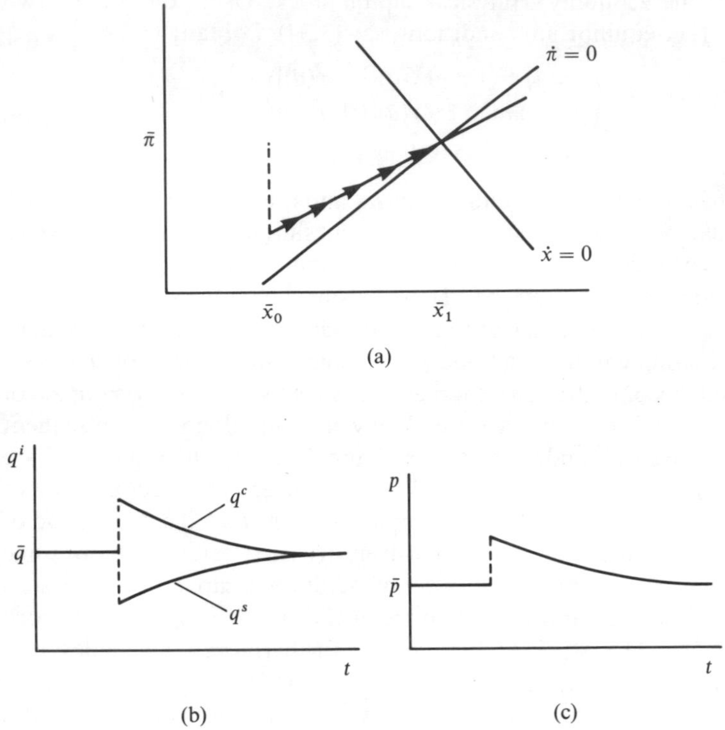

Figure 3.6 Adjustment following a preference shift toward steel

consumption demand for corn must elicit a corn-market clearing jump in corn's own-rate-of-return q^C on impact. This is illustrated in figure 3.6b.

The drop in q^S and the jump in q^C in turn lead to a drop and a jump, respectively, in rates of corn and steel capacity expansion ($d\hat{X}^S < 0$, $d\hat{X}^C > 0$), so that $\dot{x} > 0$ on impact. In other words, the system sets in motion the process of dynamic capital-composition adjustments mentioned earlier. Moreover, as can be seen from figure 3.6a, $\dot{x} > 0$ and $\dot{\pi} > 0$ throughout the subsequent traverse to the von Neumann ray, which allows successive Rybczynski expansions in relative steel supply $Q^S/Q^C = (a_{CS}^{-1}/a_{SC}^{-1})x$ to progressively reverse all impact price changes.[31]

[31] It is only the steady-state response of p that is at odds with the conventional Walrasian result. Despite a seeming ambiguity on impact – in (3.31) π drops, but q^c/q^s rises – the appendix shows $dp/dy > 0$ to always obtain in the short run; see figure 3.6c.

4

MARX–SRAFFA: Labor and the struggle over the surplus

4.1 Introduction

The presence of labor poses no fundamentally new theoretical issues: Like the study of nonhuman assets its analysis is a problem in capital theory.

Two polar assumptions are available. Labor may be viewed as the services of a resource – called human capital – that, like land, is nonproduced and exogenously given. Like the landlord, the nonreproducible worker looks forward to a capitalizable stream of rents from the ownership rights in his human capital. This is the Walrasian conception, discussed in chapters 6–8. Alternatively, labor may be considered a resource endogenously reproducible by the economic system. This is the classical viewpoint, adopted in one form or another by Malthus, Ricardo, Marx, von Neumann, Sraffa, and Lewis. In this chapter, I entertain the latter.[1]

Apart from the reproducibility assumption, two elements distinguish the classical concept of labor. First, workers are not capitalists. That is, without a wage contract, a worker by definition has zero ownership claims, thus no access to extant stocks of goods. Second, production takes time – inputs precede outputs by a nonzero interval. The production period, moreover, is longer than the survival span of an unfed worker. It follows that workers are compelled to borrow the means of survival against the contribution to future output their services make.

This gives rise to the fundamental classical idea of a wage advance by the capitalist: *Wages come out of capital, not out of income*. Put differently, worker subsistence comes out of stocks of goods, not out of flows of output. Of course, ownership titles to these wage-good inventories must compete with other equity in the portfolios of capitalists, thus are subject to the principle of uniform yield.

[1] The central idea of the recent neoclassical theory of endogenous growth [Romer (1986), Lucas (1988), Sala-i-Martin (1990)] – that human capital is a reproducible input which may be accumulated (or allowed to depreciate) like physical capital – is formally indistinguishable from the classical concept of labor. I argue this and related points concerning post-Solovian neoclassical growth theory in supplement B.

It is easiest to model these ideas by assuming a homogenous *wage fund* – inventory stocks of a single type of storable consumption good, say corn. Consumption of workers is thus nondiversified. This gives rise to the subsistence-wage variant of the von Neumann model examined in section 4.2.

I next consider the possibility of allowing for utility-maximizing diversification of worker consumption. A natural way to proceed is as follows. Workers may succeed in introducing a nonsubsistence element into the standard wage contract – a "bonus" paid at the end of the production period out of the emergent output. This leads to a Marx–Sraffa version of the von Neumann model, developed in section 4.3. Here, the social – that is, economically underdetermined – division of the surplus between capitalist profits and worker bonuses occupies center stage.

Apart from demonstrating that my Hamiltonian equations [(0.1), (0.2)] subsume a Marx–Sraffa system, this chapter formally develops two ideas:

> *Proposition (Marx's law of the falling rate of profit)*: At a given technology, at a given subsistence wage, and notwithstanding the absence of steady-state scarcities, such as Ricardian land, increasing mechanization of the capitalist economy must lead to a decline in its rate of profit.
>
> *Proposition (Sraffa's inverse relation between workers' share of the surplus and the rate of profit)*: If the class struggle allows workers to raise their share of the economy's surplus, the rate of profit must fall, both on impact and across steady states.

Throughout this and the next chapter, the presence of a wage fund forces my analysis into discrete time.[2]

4.2 A subsistence-wage economy

Consider a capitalist economy to which labor services are offered – out of a Marxian reserve army or a Lewisian hinterland – infinitely elastically at the corn subsistence wage $\bar{w}$.[3] Capitalist production takes one period in all

[2] By definition, the wage fund represents circulating capital that fully depreciates within the production period. In continuous time, this implies an infinite rate of depreciation ($\delta \to \infty$), which contradicts the mathematical idea of a stock (a stock persists through a nonzero interval of time). By contrast, a circulating-capital stock lasting for one period in discrete time is mathematically well defined ($\delta = 1$).

[3] The underlying idea [Marglin (1984)] is that capitalism never operates without *some* form of hinterland: In its infancy, because the modern sector remains small relative to the traditional economy (Lewis); in its maturity, because the system endogenously recreates a hinterland – through macroeconomic crises, capital exports, or increased immigration – whenever the disappearance of a labor reservoir threatens the stability of the distribution of income between profits and wages.

sectors. The subsistence wage is advanced by capitalists to workers via entrepreneurs at the beginning of the production period, out of a stock of wage goods that will have been fully consumed by the time output emerges at the end of the period. Capitalists ensure the period-by-period reproduction of the economy by reaccumulating a wage fund at the end of each production cycle.

The simplest way to formalize the above is to recast VON NEUMANN I in discrete time and to let the variable X^C stand for the corn wage fund. The definition of capital then remains formally as in (1.1),

$$K \equiv p^C X^C + p^S X^S, \tag{4.1}$$

where X^C and X^S now refer to (equity claims on) the economy's wage fund and steel stock, respectively. The p^i are the associated equity prices. As before, the numéraire is corn output.[4]

The steel industry is "labor intensive" – for simplicity, uses only labor; the corn industry is "highly mechanized" – for simplicity, does not use labor, only steel. Steel-industry entrepreneurs hire workers to the point where the wage fund they have rented from capitalists is fully exhausted,

$$L = X^C/\bar{w}, \tag{4.2}$$

L being aggregate and steel-sector employment ($L_S = L$). A wage fund X^C thus makes possible the production of $Q^S = q^S L$ or

$$Q^S = q^{S*} X^C, \qquad q^{S*} \equiv q^S/\bar{w} > 0 \tag{4.3}$$

[4] The model's timing notation and "beginning-/end-of-period" terminology obey the following. (i) To save on symbols, I generally omit the time index; unless otherwise noted, all variables refer to period t. Thus, $x \equiv x(t)$; $\Delta x \equiv \Delta x(t) \equiv x(t+1) - x(t)$; $\hat{x} \equiv \hat{x}(t) \equiv \Delta x(t)/x(t)$; $t+1$ refers to the end of period t, which is the same as the beginning of period $t+1$. (ii) Inputs are applied at the beginning of period t and current outputs emerge at the end of period t. Workers consume the wage fund at the beginning or during the period, that is, before current output emerges; capitalists consume and save out of current output, that is, at the end of the period (thus, any output saved in the form of stocks carried over into period $t+1$ is unavailable for capitalist consumption until the end of period $t+1$). (iii) Markets are open; current production and capitalist consumption and savings plans are formulated; and all period-t contracts and prices are unalterably fixed *at the beginning* of the period: When current outputs emerge at the end of the period (concurrently with the opening of markets for period $t+1$), period-t contracts and consumption/savings decisions are simply executed; they are not open to revision in the light of period $t+1$ information. Such execution is always possible since, by assumption, no disappointment of (say, output) expectations are ever allowed to occur within the period – all perturbations hit the economy at the beginning of the period when markets are open. (iv) Though intra-period expectations are thus correct by definition, this is not true for inter-period expectations. In particular, beginning-of-t expectations about the beginning-of-$t+1$ price of a claim to a stock carried over into $t+1$ are speculative and require an assumption about expectations formation. (v) From (iii), the zero-entrepreneurial-profit condition, and the definition of the numéraire it follows that $p^C = 1$, thus $\hat{p}^C = 0 = (\hat{p}^C)^e$; that is, the equity-price of corn is, as earlier, locked in by the unitary flow price of corn. (Note that $(\hat{p}^C)^e = 0$ is also implied by the circulating-capital assumption $\delta^C = 1$.)

units of steel. The production function for corn is

$$Q^C = q^C X^S, \quad q^C > 0. \tag{4.4}$$

Clearly, production structure (4.3), (4.4) is identical to that of VON NEUMANN I [(1.2), (1.3); I normalize $\bar{w}$ to unity]: Stocks of corn (steel) produce output flows of steel (corn). The zero-excess-profit conditions are, as in VON NEUMANN I,

$$p^C = 1 = (1/q^C) r^S \tag{4.5}$$

$$p^S = p = (1/q^{S*}) r^C, \tag{4.6}$$

where r^S, r^C are the gross unit-dividends (rental rates) paid by entrepreneurs out of end-of-period corn and steel outputs. The latter have flow prices 1 and p, respectively.

The presence of discrete time slightly complicates the stockmarket arbitrage equation *vis-à-vis* the continuous-time version (1.6) of VON NEUMANN I.[5] This is due to the fact that end-of-period-t outputs of basics and the corresponding income payments accrue as discrete stock increments. The equity claims thereon may be sold at beginning-of-$(t+1)$ stockmarket prices that usually differ from those obtaining upon contract conclusion at the beginning of t. In particular, owners of corn inputs X^C receive a steel rental of $r^C(t)/p(t) = r^C(t)/p^S(t) = q^{S*}$ and a corresponding steel income (steel-stock increment) of $q^{S*} X^C = Q^S$. Upon its receipt at the end of t (the beginning of $t+1$), they may sell it at $p^S(t+1)$ and earn a unit capital gain $[p^S(t+1) - p^S(t)][r^C(t)/p^S(t)] \equiv \hat{p}^S(t) r^C(t)$ (in corn) that is additional to the corn value $r^C(t)$ of the rental received from steel entrepreneurs. Therefore, at the beginning of any period holders of equity in corn expect a one-period yield of $\rho^C \equiv (r^C/p^C) + [(\hat{p}^S)^e r^C/p^C] - \delta^C + (\hat{p}^C)^e$. They will be holding such claims willingly only if [compare (1.6)]

$$\rho^C \equiv [1 + (\hat{p}^S)^e] \frac{r^C}{p^C} - \delta^C + (\hat{p}^C)^e = \frac{r^S}{p^S} - \delta^S + (\hat{p}^S)^e \equiv \rho^S, \quad \delta^C = 1, \quad \delta^S < 1, \tag{4.7}$$

which is the arbitrage equation of a discrete-time analogue of VON NEUMANN I that contains a circulating corn wage fund ($\delta^C = 1$) and fixed steel capital ($\delta^S < 1$). Using (4.5), (4.6), this may as usual be rewritten as

$$\begin{gathered} \chi(\pi; \hat{\pi}^e, q^C, q^{S*}) \equiv \pi q^{S*} - (q^C/\pi) - (1 - \delta^{S*}) - (1 + \pi q^{S*}) \hat{\pi}^e = 0, \\ \pi \equiv p^S/p^C, \end{gathered} \tag{4.8}$$

which solves for the temporary-equilibrium stockmarket price and profit rate

[5] See also supplement A.3, where I show that (4.7) below is necessary for decentralized dynamic efficiency.

$$\pi = \pi(\hat{\pi}^e, q^C, q^{S*}), \qquad \rho = \rho^C[\pi(\cdot), \hat{\pi}^e, q^{S*}] \equiv \rho(\hat{\pi}^e, q^C, q^{S*}), \tag{4.9}$$

whose properties are identical to their VON NEUMANN I counterparts.[6]

As in continuous time, capitalist consumption spending E is proportional to wealth. However, since such spending takes place at the end of the production period, it is proportional to end-of-period wealth,[7]

$$E = \Omega(K + \Delta K) = \frac{\Omega}{1+\Omega}(1+\rho)K, \tag{4.10}$$

where $K + \Delta K$ and $(1+\rho)K$ are end-of-period wealth, net and gross of end-of-period consumption spending E, respectively. Observe that only current (that is, beginning-of-period) prices and the current interest rate enter (4.10), so that the latter is a myopic-consumption function like its continuous-time counterpart (1.8).

Given demand functions $D^S = \gamma E/p$, $D^C = (1-\gamma)E$, the output-market-balance equation for steel appears as $\Delta X^S = Z^S \equiv Q^S - \delta^S X^S - D^S = q^{S*}X^C - \delta^S X^S - [\gamma\Omega/(1+\Omega)](1+\rho)K/p$ [and similarly for corn; as in VON NEUMANN I, $\Delta X^i = Z^i$ will hold as an identity, given (4.8)]. Substituting for K and $\rho = \rho^S$ from (4.1), (4.6), (4.7), I have

$$\begin{aligned}\hat{X}^S &\equiv \frac{\Delta X^S}{X^S} = q^{S*}x - \delta^S - \gamma\frac{\Omega}{1+\Omega}\left[\frac{q^C}{\pi} - \delta^S + \hat{\pi}^e\right](x\pi^{-1}+1) \\ &\equiv \tilde{\hat{X}}^S(\pi, x, \hat{\pi}^e), \quad \tilde{\hat{X}}^S_i > 0 \ (i=1,2), \quad \tilde{\hat{X}}^S_3 < 0, \quad x \equiv X^C/X^S,\end{aligned} \tag{4.11}$$

which is similar to (1.14) except that, through the interest-rate factor $(1+\rho)$, it involves the expectation $\hat{\pi}^e$.

Finally, under (4.10) capital-market equilibrium requires [compare (1.12)],[8]

$$\Delta K = \frac{(\rho - \Omega)K}{1+\Omega}, \qquad \Delta K \equiv \Delta X^C + \pi\Delta X^S + (X^S + \Delta X^S)\Delta\pi, \tag{4.12}$$

and will, given (4.8), also obtain identically.

The model's dynamics are now easily derived. I start by imposing the myopic-foresight assumption $\hat{\pi}^e = \hat{\pi} \equiv \Delta\pi/\pi$ and solve (4.8) for the corresponding steel-equity-price motions,

$$\Delta\pi = \frac{\pi}{1+\pi q^{S*}}[\pi q^{S*} - (q^C/\pi) - (1-\delta^S)] \equiv \phi(\pi), \qquad \phi' > 0. \tag{4.13}$$

[6] Observe that, near a steady state ($\hat{\pi}^e = 0$), changes in the capital-gains coefficient $(1+\pi q^{S*})$ specific to discrete time leaves $\chi(\cdot)$ unaffected.

[7] The chapter appendix shows (4.10) to be the optimal consumption rule of a capitalist household that maximizes an infinite-horizon sum of discounted felicities $(1+\Omega)^{-t}U[D^C(t), D^S(t)]$, where $U(\cdot)$ is a logarithmic function identical to that used to derive (1.8). I have employed the household budget constraint $\Delta K = \rho K - E$ to derive the second from the first equality in (4.10).

Substituting $\phi(\pi)/\pi$ for $\hat{\pi}^e$ in (4.11), I obtain $\tilde{\hat{X}}^S[\pi, x, \phi(\pi)/\pi] \equiv \hat{X}^S(\pi, x)$ which, when combined with the myopic-foresight solution of (4.12) for $\hat{X}^C$, yields the capital-composition motions $\Delta x \equiv x(\hat{X}^C - \hat{X}^S)$,

$$\Delta x = \left\{\frac{[1+\phi(\pi)/\pi]\pi q^{S*} - (1+\Omega)}{1+\Omega} - \hat{X}^S(\pi, x)\right\}(x+\pi) - [1+\hat{X}^S(\pi, x)]\phi(\pi)$$
$$\equiv \psi(\pi, x), \quad \psi_1 \gtrless 0, \quad \psi_2 < 0. \tag{4.14}$$

The linearized version of dynamic system [(4.13), (4.14)] has roots

$$\eta_1 = \phi' + 1 > 1, \quad \eta_2 = \psi_2 + 1 = -(\bar{\rho} + g + \delta^S) < 0, \tag{4.15}$$

so that a condition necessary and sufficient for saddle-path stability – involving damped oscillations, since $\eta_2 < 0$ – is that $\eta_2 > -1$, or

$$\bar{\rho} + g + \delta^S < 1, \tag{4.16}$$

where $\bar{\rho}$ and g are the steady-state rates of profit and growth, and where I have used $\bar{x}$ to calculate η_2. These long-run values are given by

$$\bar{\rho} = \bar{\pi} q^{S*} - 1, \quad g = \frac{\bar{\rho} - \Omega}{1+\Omega}$$
$$\bar{\pi} = \{(1-\delta^S) + [(1-\delta^S)^2 + 4q^{S*}q^C]^{\frac{1}{2}}\}/2q^{S*} \tag{4.17}$$
$$\bar{x}(\gamma) = \frac{(1+\Omega)(g+\delta^S) + \gamma\Omega(1+\bar{\rho})}{q^{S*}[1+(1-\gamma)\Omega]}, \quad \bar{x}' > 0,$$

from, respectively, (4.7), (4.12), (4.8) and $\tilde{\hat{X}}^S(\bar{\pi}, x, \gamma \ldots) = g$ in (4.11). Since $\bar{\rho}$ and g must be nonnegative for a viable steady state, it follows that a necessary condition for saddle-path stability is $\delta^S < 1$.[9] Given such stability, the system's phase diagram is as in figure 4.1 a, b (the saddle path coincides with the horizontal locus $\Delta\pi = 0$).[10]

The discrete-time analogue to the VON NEUMANN I economy thus exhibits the same long-run and dynamic nonsubstitution properties as its continuous-time counterpart in chapter 1. In particular, an intratemporal preference shift $d\gamma > 0$ toward steel is accommodated, at unchanged $p(t) = \bar{p} = \bar{\pi}$, $t \epsilon [0, \infty)$, by a long-run change in capital composition $\bar{x}' d\gamma > 0$

[8] Note that I am not imposing the assumption that $\Delta X^S \Delta\pi$ is second-order small.

[9] Thus, if both corn *and* steel are assumed to be circulating capital ($\delta^i = 1$, $i = C, S$), (4.16) is violated and any multi-period motion will be explosive. However, all adjustments are achievable through single-period PFCE jumps across steady states. Should (4.16) fail to obtain under $\delta^S < 1$, the PFCE dynamics can be shown to be as follows: Subsequent to a disturbance (at $t = 0$) and a period of explosive oscillations it initiates, the economy will specialize in the production of corn for exactly one period (at $t = \tau - 1$); it returns to the steady state immediately thereafter (at $t = \tau < \infty$).

[10] Since the changes in π and x are discrete – and since a continuous-time approximation of the system's dynamics is not available (as it would be, if $0 < \eta_2 < 1$) – figure 4.1a,b cannot be used to trace motions off the saddle path.

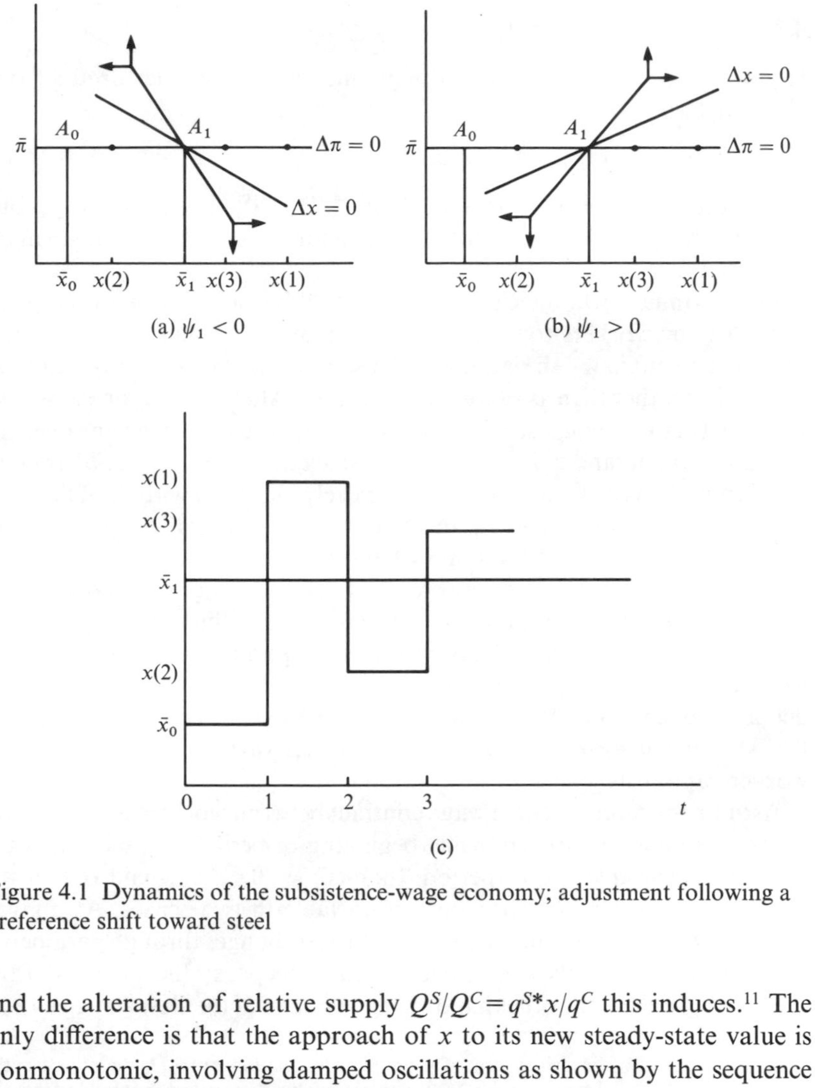

Figure 4.1 Dynamics of the subsistence-wage economy; adjustment following a preference shift toward steel

and the alteration of relative supply $Q^S/Q^C = q^{S*}x/q^C$ this induces.[11] The only difference is that the approach of x to its new steady-state value is nonmonotonic, involving damped oscillations as shown by the sequence $x(0) = \bar{x}_0, x(1), x(2) \ldots \bar{x}_1$ in figure 4.1a–c.[12]

[11] Observe that the motions of π in (4.13) are governed by the unstable root $\eta_1 > 1$ exclusively; given saddle-path stability and an invariant $\bar{\pi}$, π thus cannot change at any point.

[12] This is true as well for a static-expectations version of this model, which is a discrete-time analogue of (1.25)–(1.29) in VON NEUMANN I: Instead of (1.27) one has $\Delta K = [\rho K - (\Delta\pi - \Delta\pi^e)(X^s + \Delta X^s)] - \Omega(K + \Delta K)$ from (4.10) and the definition of capital gains in (4.12). Under static expectations $\Delta\pi^e \equiv 0$, which gives, instead of (1.28), $\Delta K = [(\rho - \Omega)/(1 + \Omega)]K + (X^s + \Delta X^s)\Delta\pi$ and, instead of (1.29), $\Delta x = \{[\pi q^{s*} - (\Omega + 1)][1 + \Omega]^{-1} - \hat{X}^s(\pi, x)\}(x + \pi) \equiv \tilde{\psi}(x)$, $\tilde{\psi}' = -(\pi + x)\hat{X}^S_2 = \psi_2 < 0$, where π is fixed at $\bar{\pi}$ [(4.17)] from

4.3 The social division of the surplus

In the model considered up to this point, the system's net product (the classical surplus),

$$Y \equiv Q^C + pQ^S - (X^C + \delta^S p X^S), \tag{4.18}$$

went entirely to profits, $\rho K \equiv Y + (\Delta p^S)^e[X^S + Q^S]$, since the wage bill, $\bar{w}L = X^C$, simply was an element of the economy's depreciation allowance, $X^C + \delta^S p X^S$.

In this framework, the class struggle could be viewed as an attempt by capitalists or workers to influence the *size* of the surplus by means of a parametric shift in $\bar{w}$ – the latter now interpreted, in the manner of Marx, as a historical rather than as a biological datum.[13] Alternatively, one may take the view that $\bar{w}$, being a secular phenomenon, is largely invariant over the relevant horizon and consider the class struggle to be over the *division* of the surplus. This is the viewpoint most closely identified with Sraffa (1960). The model to follow *combines* the Marxian and the Sraffian perspectives and, in doing so, removes some of their respective weaknesses. These include, for the Marxian perspective, its inability to generate one of the fundamental predictions of Marx – the law of the falling rate of profit; for the Sraffian perspective, the absence of a wage advance, which requires workers to be owners (of stocks of wage goods) in violation of the classical definition of a worker. By contrast, my MARX–SRAFFA model generates the Marxian law and operates with classical workers, not neoclassical worker-capitalists.[14]

Assume the representative wage contract between workers and entrepreneurs contains, apart from a beginning-of-period subsistence-wage advance, a variable end-of-period "bonus" ϵy, $0 \leq \epsilon < 1$, paid out of the current surplus $Y \equiv yL$. The bonus is variable in two senses. At a given momentary value of the per-capita surplus y, it changes through parametric shifts in the distributive coefficient ϵ; such shifts proxy the vagaries of the class struggle.[15] On the other hand, at a given state of the class struggle ϵ, the

$\Delta \pi^e \equiv 0$ in (4.8). The linearized form of the difference equation $\Delta x = \tilde{\psi}(x)$ therefore has the root $\eta = \tilde{\psi}' + 1 = \psi_2 + 1 = -(\bar{\rho} + g + \delta^S) < 0$, which is identical to η_2 in (4.15). It follows that the static-expectations economy is locally stable (exhibiting damped oscillations), whenever its perfect-foresight analogue is saddle-path stable [that is, whenever (4.16) holds].

13 In this sense, $\bar{w}$ expresses society's changing consensus on what constitutes poverty – a consensus upset by advances in the economy's productivity and wealth or by bursts of migration from the world's hinterlands.

14 Below, I follow Sraffa and depict the division of the surplus exclusively in terms of a labor-market outcome. Today it is, of course, also importantly mediated by the electoral cycle between left- and right-leaning governments and the change in the extent of public income redistribution this entails.

15 The determination of ϵ could – but, in this instance, will not – be endogenized game-theoretically, say along the lines of Lancaster (1973).

bonus will change with $y \equiv Y/L$, that is, with the economy's aggregate productivity. Therefore, in the model to follow total worker compensation depends on the subsistence wage $\bar{w}$, the economy's aggregate productivity Y/L, and the state of the class struggle ϵ.

The bonus – labor's "discretionary income" – leads workers to diversify their consumption. Whereas beginning-of-period subsistence continues to fall on corn exclusively, workers now optimally divide their end-of-period consumption ϵy across steel and corn outputs (saving remains zero, by the classical definition of a worker). Assuming that a representative worker's utility function is Cobb–Douglas, this gives

$$D_L^S = \gamma_L \epsilon Y/p, \quad D_L^C = (1-\gamma_L)\epsilon Y, \quad 0 \leq \gamma_L \leq 1, \tag{4.19}$$

as labor's end-of-period consumption demands for steel (D_L^S) and corn (D_L^C), γ_L being the corresponding propensity to consume steel. p again denotes the flow price of steel in terms of flow corn.

Vis-à-vis the wage fund economy previously studied, the preceding yields the following new model. The definitions of capital, employment, and outputs remain as in (4.1)–(4.4). However, whereas the end-of-period cost to the steel entrepreneur of hiring a worker was $r^C X^C/L = r^C \bar{w}$ before, it will now amount to $r^C \bar{w} + \epsilon y$ and be competitively equalized with labor's end-of-perio value product pq^S. The corresponding zero-entrepreneurial-profit conditions appear as [compare (4.5)–(4.6)]

$$p^C = 1 = (1/q^C) r^S \tag{4.20}$$

$$p^S = p = (1/q^{S*})(r^C + \epsilon y/\bar{w}). \tag{4.21}$$

Thus the end-of-period gross rental or dividend r^C a capitalist expects for the wage-fund services of his corn stocks now equals $pq^{S*} - \epsilon y/\bar{w}$ rather than pq^{S*}: A bonus ($\epsilon > 0$) acts like a tax on the value produced by corn capital and, consequently, reduces the dividend r^C entrepreneurs are willing to pay for its services. This in turn will bring down the yield ρ^C of equity in wage funds relative to what it would be had no bonus been paid.

Before developing further the general-equilibrium implications of $\epsilon > 0$, I introduce the per-capita surplus or aggregate-productivity function $y(\pi, x)$,

$$\begin{aligned} y(\pi, x) &\equiv \bar{w}[q^C x^{-1} + q^{S*}\pi - (1 + \delta^S \pi x^{-1})], \quad y_1 > 0, \quad y_2 < 0 \\ \pi &\equiv p^S/p^C, \quad x \equiv X^C/X^S, \end{aligned} \tag{4.22}$$

from (4.18), (4.20), and (4.21). The function $y(\pi, x)$ has two fundamental properties:[16] (i) At a given composition $x \equiv X^C/X^S$ of capital between wage funds X^C and fixed capital X^S, an increase in the price of steel $p = \pi$ must raise the value of net per-capita steel output $p(Q^S - \delta^S X^S)/L =$

[16] In what follows, the reader may find it helpful to draw an analogy to the per-capita income function $y(p, k)$ of the standard neoclassical two-sector model [Uzawa (1961/3)].

$\pi(q^{S*} - \delta^S x^{-1})$ and, thus, aggregate productivity ($y_1 > 0$); (ii) at given prices, a shift $dx > 0$ in the system's capital composition away from fixed toward wage-fund capital will decrease aggregate productivity ($y_2 < 0$). Putting (ii) differently, at given prices and at a given technology the economy's aggregate productivity Y/L depends positively on its *degree of mechanization* $X^S/L \equiv \bar{w}/x$.[17]

As in the subsistence-wage economy $\epsilon = 0$ studied earlier, the model's temporary equilibrium is established exclusively via the bourse. The latter's search for continuous yield uniformity across ownership claims again imposes arbitrage condition (4.7) at each moment. After substituting in the latter for $p^C = 1$ and $p^S = \pi$, this gives

$$\rho^C = (1 + \hat{\pi}^e) r^C - 1 = \frac{r^S}{\pi} - \delta^S + \hat{\pi}^e = \rho^S. \tag{4.23}$$

Though entrepreneurial profit maximization again implies $r^S = q^C$, we now have, instead of $r^C(\pi) = \pi q^{S*}$,

$$\begin{aligned} r^C(\pi; x, \epsilon) = \pi q^{S*} - \epsilon y(\pi, x)/\bar{w}, \quad & r_1^C > 0, \quad r_3^C < 0 \\ & r_2^C = -\epsilon y_2/\bar{w} \geq 0 \text{ as } \epsilon \geq 0, \end{aligned} \tag{4.24}$$

from (4.21), (4.22). That is, the dividend r^C and expected yield ρ^C on wage fund equity depend not just on π ($r_1^C > 0$) and on expectations $\hat{\pi}^e$ as under $\epsilon = 0$, but also on the degree of mechanization $\bar{w}/x$ (capital composition x) and the state of the class struggle ϵ. In particular, a *ceteris-paribus* increase in the system's degree of mechanization $(dx < 0)$[18] – by raising aggregate productivity y, thus the bonus ϵy received by the typical worker – will lower

[17] To be distinguished from its *capital intensity* $k \equiv K/L \equiv \bar{w} + \pi(\bar{w}/x) \equiv \bar{w}(1 + \pi x^{-1})$. The latter is closely related to what Marx calls the "value" composition of capital $\delta^S \tilde{\pi} \tilde{x}^{-1} \equiv \delta^S \tilde{\pi} X^S / \tilde{w} L \equiv C/V$, where C is "constant" and V "variable" capital, $\tilde{w}$ being the "value of labor power" (measured in Marxian labor value, as indicated by a tilde). The "rate of exploitation" is given by $\tilde{Y}/V \equiv \tilde{Y}/\tilde{w}L$, where $\tilde{Y}$ is the Marxian surplus, the entirety of which is assumed to go to capitalists. Note that the rate of exploitation increases whenever labor's productivity $\tilde{Y}/L$ rises at a given value of labor power. Assuming the rise in $\tilde{Y}/L$ is due to an increase in the "technical" composition of capital X^S/L ($-y_2 > 0$ in (4.22)), we get the well-known ambiguity in the behavior of the "value" rate of profit $\tilde{\rho} \equiv \tilde{Y}/(C + V) \equiv (\tilde{Y}/V)/[1 + (C/V)]$ following $d(C/V) > 0$. My model fails to fit this standard Marxian framework in three essential ways. First, I assume that workers receive a fraction $\epsilon > 0$ of the surplus Y (in Marxian terms, total worker compensation exceeds the value of labor power $\tilde{w}$). Second, as shown below, my model predicts that $d\rho/d(X^S/L) < 0$ unambiguously, if $\epsilon > 0$. Third, since my production assumptions imply a widely divergent composition of capital across sectors, prices and values will fail to be proportional. In the absence of an explicit transformation algorithm (which remains to be developed for the model at hand), the translation into Marxian value categories remains unclear. I nonetheless feel entitled to call this chapter's proposition regarding $d\rho/dx^{-1} < 0$ a "Marxian" law of the falling rate of profit.

[18] Since I am keeping $\bar{w}$ fixed throughout, $d(\bar{w}/x) > 0$ implies and is implied by $dx < 0$.

the dividend and yield of wage-fund equity ($-r_2^C<0$). The same will be true if workers succeed, through the class struggle, in shifting the distribution of the surplus in their favor ($r_3^C<0$).

My usual characterization $\chi(\cdot)=0$ of stockmarket equilibrium under entrepreneurial profit maximization therefore appears as

$$\chi(\pi; x, \epsilon, \hat{\pi}^e \ldots) \equiv r^C(\pi; x, \epsilon) - (q^C/\pi) - (1-\delta^S) - [1 + r^C(\cdot)]\hat{\pi}^e = 0, \tag{4.25}$$

which solves for the system's temporary-equilibrium price and uniform profit rate,

$$\begin{aligned} &\pi = \pi(x, \epsilon, \hat{\pi}^e), \quad \pi_1 < 0, \quad \pi_i > 0 \; (i=2,3) \\ &\rho = \rho^S[\pi(\cdot), \hat{\pi}^e] \equiv \rho(x, \epsilon, \hat{\pi}^e), \quad \rho_i > 0 \; (i=1,3), \quad \rho_2 < 0. \end{aligned} \tag{4.26}$$

The signs of the partial derivatives in (4.26) are important and easy to grasp. Consider, first, $\rho_1>0$: Increases in the system's degree of mechanization ($dx<0$), by lowering the rental and rate of return on wage funds, must trigger a rush into steel equity and a jump in its equilibrium price ($-\pi_1>0$) that brings its yield into alignment with ρ^C at an unambiguously reduced-equilibrium profit rate $\rho^C=\rho^S=(q^C/\pi)-\delta^S+\hat{\pi}^e$. In other words, as claimed in one of the two propositions in this chapter's introduction, I have here at hand a version of the Marxian law of the falling rate of profit. Recall that what the law asserts has seemed to most economists[19] a logical impossibility: That the rate of profit ρ will secularly decline under increased mechanization despite absence of ultimate scarcities such as Ricardian land. $\rho_1>0$ in (4.26) (when applied to a path along which x is declining) shows the impossibility to be possible after all. Observe that the law is strictly a consequence of my assumption that, over and above the subsistence wage they receive, workers successfully lay claim to a share of the current surplus[20]: It is $\epsilon>0$ that allows the temporary-equilibrium profit rate to become a function, though the relative asset price π, of x and the degree of mechanization $X^S/L=\bar{w}/x$.

Consider next the temporary-equilibrium effects of fluctuations in the class struggle, the subject of the second proposition: By raising aggregate worker bonuses at the expense of capitalist dividends, a *ceteris-paribus* increase in ϵ lowers the return on wage funds ($r_3^C<0$, $\partial\rho^C/\partial\epsilon<0$). The induced stockmarket-clearing jump in the price of steel ($\pi_2>0$) guarantees a reduction in the uniform yield ($\rho_2<0$). The temporary-equilibrium model therefore exhibits an inverse Sraffian relation between workers' share in the surplus ϵ and the system's profit rate ρ.

19 Samuelson (1957) among them.

20 This runs counter to Marx's typical assumption that the surplus goes to profits exclusively.

I now turn to the dynamics of capitalist accumulation. I maintain my earlier characterization (4.10) of capitalists' consumption decision and use (4.19) to describe nonsubsistence expenditures by workers. This gives $D^S \equiv \{\gamma_L \epsilon Y + \gamma_K[\Omega/(1+\Omega)](1+\rho)K\}/p$ as the aggregate flow consumption demand for steel (where γ_k refers to capitalists' propensity to consume steel). Substituting for D^S in the steel output-market-equilibrium equation $\Delta X^S = Z^S \equiv q^{S*}X^C - \delta^S X^S - D^S$ and using (4.22)–(4.24), I obtain

$$\begin{aligned}\hat{X}^S &= q^{S*}x - \delta^S - \{\gamma_L \epsilon y(\pi, x)\bar{w}x^{-1} + \gamma_K \frac{\Omega}{1+\Omega}\left[\frac{q^C}{\pi} - \delta^S + \hat{\pi}^e\right](x+\pi)\}/\pi \\ &\equiv \tilde{\hat{X}}^S(\pi, x, \hat{\pi}^e), \quad \tilde{\hat{X}}^S_1 > 0; \quad \tilde{\hat{X}}^S_2 \gtrless 0, \quad > 0 \text{ if } \epsilon \text{ small}; \quad \tilde{\hat{X}}^S_3 < 0,\end{aligned} \tag{4.27}$$

so that the rate of steel accumulation behaves as under $\epsilon = 0$ [see (4.11)], provided I choose $\epsilon > 0$ sufficiently small.[21] The capital-market-equilibrium condition remains as in (4.12).

Solving stockmarket-equilibrium condition (4.25) for $\hat{\pi}^e$ and imposing myopic foresight, $\hat{\pi}^e = \Delta\pi/\pi$, one has the law of motion of prices [compare (4.13) and recall r^C_2 in (4.24)]

$$\begin{aligned}\Delta\pi &= \frac{\pi}{1+r^C(\cdot)}[r^C(\pi, x) - (q^C/\pi) - (1-\delta^S)] \equiv \phi(\pi, x) \\ \phi_1 &> 0, \quad \phi_2 = -\epsilon\frac{\pi y_2}{\bar{w}(1+r^C)} \geq 0 \text{ as } \epsilon \geq 0.\end{aligned} \tag{4.28}$$

Equation (4.27) thus again can be reduced to $\hat{X}^S = \tilde{\hat{X}}^S[\pi, x, \phi(\pi, x)/\pi] \equiv \hat{X}^S(\pi, x)$ which, when used in conjunction with (4.12) as earlier, yields the law of mechanization [compare (4.14)]

$$\begin{aligned}\Delta x = &\left\{\frac{[1+\phi(\pi, x)/\pi]r^C(\pi, x) - (1+\Omega)}{1+\Omega} - \hat{X}^S(\pi, x)\right\}(x+\pi) \\ &- [1+\hat{X}^S(\pi, x)]\phi(\pi, x) \\ \equiv &\ \psi(\pi, x), \quad \psi_1 \gtrless 0, \quad \psi_2 < 0 \text{ if } \epsilon \text{ small.}\end{aligned} \tag{4.29}$$

It follows that

$$\phi_1\psi_2 - \phi_2\psi_1 < 0, \tag{4.30}$$

if ϵ – thus ϕ_2 – is sufficiently small. Diagrammatically (see figure 4.2a,b and recall figure 4.1), as ϵ increases from zero to positive, the formerly horizontal $\Delta\pi = 0$ locus takes on a negative slope. (4.30) restricts ϵ to values – always attainable, since I can make ϵ as small as I like – such that the $\Delta\pi = 0$ locus remains less steep than the $\Delta x = 0$ schedule when $\psi_1 < 0$.

[21] See the chapter appendix. ϵ may be set arbitrarily close to zero.

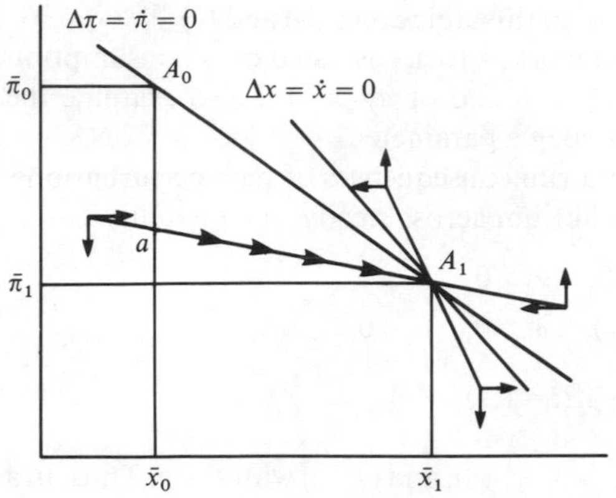

(a) $\psi_1 < 0$

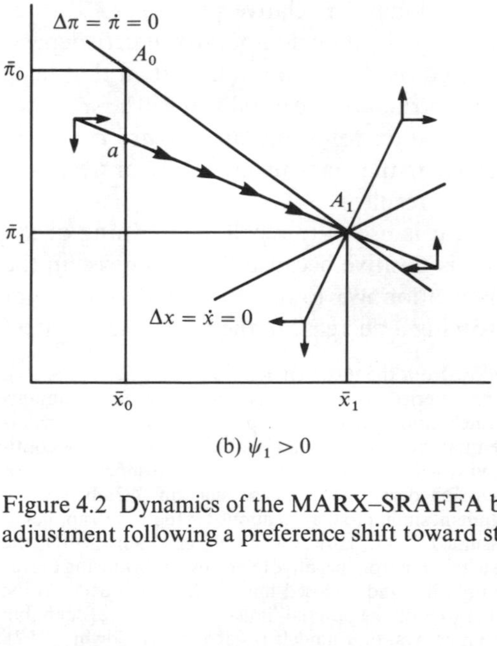

(b) $\psi_1 > 0$

Figure 4.2 Dynamics of the MARX–SRAFFA bonus-wage economy; adjustment following a preference shift toward steel

In what follows, I will assume that (4.30) obtains. This leaves three possible configurations for the system's characteristic roots:

$$\begin{aligned} &\text{(a)}\ \ \eta_1 > 1,\ \eta_2 < -1 \\ &\text{(b)}\ \ \eta_1 > 1,\ -1 < \eta_2 < 0 \\ &\text{(c)}\ \ \eta_1 > 1,\ 0 < \eta_2 < 1. \end{aligned} \tag{4.31}$$

I shall concentrate on the saddle-path-stable cases (b) and (c).[22]

To put MARX–SRAFFA to work, I focus as usual on a consumption preference shift toward steel ($d\gamma_L > 0$ and/or $d\gamma_K > 0$). I also examine the effects of changes in the class-struggle parameter ϵ.

I start by considering the long-run consequences of such perturbations. Stock- and capital-market equilibrium across steady states entail[23]

$$\begin{aligned} \bar{\pi} &= \bar{\pi}(\bar{x}, \epsilon), \quad \bar{\pi}_1 < 0, \quad \bar{\pi}_2 > 0 \\ \bar{\rho} &= \bar{\rho}^S[\bar{\pi}(\cdot)] \equiv \bar{\rho}(\bar{x}, \epsilon), \quad \bar{\rho}_1 > 0, \quad \bar{\rho}_2 < 0 \\ g(\bar{x}, \epsilon) &= \frac{\bar{\rho}(\cdot) - \Omega}{1 + \Omega}, \quad g_i = \bar{\rho}_i \ (i = 1, 2), \end{aligned} \tag{4.32}$$

from, respectively, (4.26) with $x = \bar{x}$, $\hat{\pi}^e = 0$, and (4.12) with $\hat{K} = g$. Thus, in a MARX–SRAFFA world steady-state relative prices and the long-period profit rate depend not just on technology – as in the VON NEUMANN universe – but, in addition, on the composition of capital $\bar{x}$ and on the state of the class struggle ϵ. Moreover, long-run relative prices $\bar{p} = \bar{\pi}$ do not depend on demand preferences. At least, they do not *proximately* depend on γ_i and Ω. They can be influenced by these only to the extent that taste changes call forth alterations in the structure of capital $\bar{x}$. It will be seen that alterations in $\bar{x}$ are such as to require, following an *increase* $d\gamma_i > 0$ in consumption demand for steel, a *fall* in the long-run price $\bar{p} = \bar{\pi}$ of steel – the opposite of the expected Walrasian result.

Before developing this further, it is useful to recall the meaning of the partial derivatives in (4.32). $-\bar{\pi}_1$ is positive because a long-run rise in the degree of the economy's mechanization $\bar{w}/x$ lowers the rental and rate of return on wage funds, thus enforcing a decrease in their steady-state asset

22 The three cases (a)–(c) in (4.31) follow from the fact that $\phi_1\psi_2 - \phi_2\psi_1 \equiv J \equiv (\eta_1 - 1)(\eta_2 - 1)$, where η_1 and η_2 are the system's characteristic roots. Observe that case (c) – it obtains whenever $\phi_1 + \psi_2 + 1 + J \equiv \eta_1\eta_2 > 0$, which unlike under $\epsilon = 0$ is possible – yields nonoscillating saddle-path motions. These are qualitatively indistinguishable from those of a continuous-time approximation $\dot{\pi} = \phi(\pi, x)$, $\dot{x} = \psi(\pi, x)$ to [(4.28), (4.29)]; this justifies the use of such an approximation when discussing discrete-time phase diagrams 4.2a,b (see my labeling of the dynamic loci). An argument similar to that mentioned in footnote 9 applies to unstable case (a). So far I have assumed (4.30). However, if ϵ is raised sufficiently, the Jacobian determinant in (4.30) will switch sign from negative to positive, introducing the (as yet unexplored) possibility of a bifurcation and a closed limit cycle. This opens up the prospect of linking MARX–SRAFFA to both the optimal-limit-cycle literature [Benhabib and Nishimura (1979)] and the dynamic Marxian models inspired by Goodwin (1967). Finally, a static-expectations version of the economy – constructed as in the $\epsilon = 0$-case (recall footnote 12) – will have the single law of motion $\Delta x = \{[r^C(\pi(x), x) - (1 + \Omega)](1 + \Omega)^{-1} - \hat{X}^S[\pi(x), x]\}[x + \pi(x)] \equiv \tilde{\tilde{\psi}}(x)$, $\tilde{\tilde{\psi}}' \gtrless 0$, where $\pi(x)$ is the same as $\pi(x, \epsilon, 0)$ in (4.26). As $\epsilon \to 0$, $\tilde{\tilde{\psi}} \to \tilde{\psi}$ and the discussion in footnote 12 applies. However, a stable monotonic approach ($0 < |\tilde{\tilde{\psi}}'| < 1$, implicitly assumed below) is now possible as well, as is, of course, instability ($|\tilde{\tilde{\psi}}'| > 1$).

23 As in my discussion of the model's temporary equilibrium, technology q^C, q^{S*}, and time preference Ω are suppressed as explicit functional arguments.

price $1/\bar{\pi}$ for yield uniformity. Just as in temporary equilibrium [recall (4.26)], the decline in wage fund profitability *at given* π $(-\partial\bar{\rho}^C/\partial x = -r_2^C < 0)$ must thus push down the equilibrium yield $\bar{\rho}^C = \bar{\rho}^S \equiv (q^C/\bar{\pi}) - \delta^S$. It follows that the economy is experiencing a secular mechanization-induced decline in the uniform rate of return on capital $(-\bar{\rho}_1 < 0)$ – which is the Marxian law of the falling rate of profit. Furthermore, and in line with Marx, the decline in the secular profit rate leads to a long-run slowdown in the economy's rate of endogenous growth $(-g_1 < 0)$.

Exactly the same chain of reasoning as that just applied to the consequences of $d\bar{x} < 0$ can be used to show that, at a given capital composition, worker success in the class struggle $(d\epsilon > 0)$ – by making labor, therefore wage funds, relatively less profitable as an input $(r_3^C < 0)$ – must lower the uniform long-run rate of return on capital $(\bar{\rho}_2 < 0)$. As we shall see presently, this result obtains even once we let capital composition adjust. It follows that the model confirms, for the long run, the Sraffa proposition on the inverse relationship between the rate of profit and the worker share of the surplus.

I now do allow capital composition (the degree of long-run mechanization) to adjust. As in all my models, the determinants of $\bar{x}$ come from the requirement for long-run flow equilibrium in the output markets. I again focus on the market for steel, invoking Walras's Law. From (4.27) (with $\hat{\pi}^e = 0$) and (4.32) I have

$$\bar{z}^S(x, \epsilon, \gamma_L, \gamma_K \ldots) \equiv \tilde{\tilde{X}}^S[\bar{\pi}(\cdot), x; \epsilon, \gamma_L, \gamma_K, \Omega] - g(\cdot) = 0 \qquad (4.33)$$

as the model's long-run flow-equilibrium condition, where $\bar{z}^S(\cdot) \equiv Z^S/X^S$ is normalized steady-state flow excess supply of steel. (4.33) closes the steady-state model since it yields[24]

$$\bar{x} = \bar{x}(\epsilon, \gamma_L, \gamma_K \ldots), \quad \bar{x}_1 \lesseqgtr 0, \quad \bar{x}_i > 0 \ (i = 2,3). \qquad (4.34)$$

Observe that, in complete analogy to VON NEUMANN I, a shift in consumption preferences toward steel must lead to a shift in long-run capital composition toward the input, corn, used intensively in steel production $(\bar{x}_2 > 0, \bar{x}_3 > 0)$. The following results, promised earlier, emerge. Substituting $\bar{x}(\cdot)$ from (4.34) into (4.32), I obtain

$$\bar{\pi} = \bar{\pi}[\bar{x}(\epsilon, \gamma_L, \gamma_K), \epsilon] \equiv \bar{\bar{\pi}}(\epsilon, \gamma_L, \gamma_K), \ \bar{\rho} = \bar{\rho}^S = [q^C/\bar{\bar{\pi}}(\cdot)] - \delta^S \equiv \bar{\bar{\rho}}(\epsilon \ldots)$$
$$\bar{\bar{\pi}}_1 > 0, \quad \bar{\bar{\pi}}_i < 0 \ (i = 2,3), \quad \bar{\bar{\rho}}' < 0. \qquad (4.35)$$

That is, a permanent preference shift toward steel must lead to a long-run *decline* $(\bar{\bar{\pi}}_2 < 0, \bar{\bar{\pi}}_3 < 0)$ in the relative price of steel; and an inverse Sraffian

[24] The signs of the partial derivatives in (4.34) and (4.35) are subject to the condition that ϵ be not too large (see the chapter appendix).

relation $\bar{\bar{\rho}}' < 0$ obtains between the share of the surplus going to workers and the long-run rate of profit earned by capitalists – thus, between ϵ and the secular rate of accumulation $g(\epsilon) \equiv [\bar{\bar{\rho}}(\epsilon) - \Omega]/(1 + \Omega)$.

To further clarify the price consequences of a preference shift and to pull together my short- and long-run analysis, I now turn to a diagrammatic discussion of the system's evolution through time. I rely on the phase space generated by the continuous-time approximation of [(4.28), (4.29)]; see figure 4.2a,b.

Consider the short-run effects of $d\gamma_i > 0$, assuming to begin with that expectations are static (the $\dot{\pi} = 0$-schedule then represents the system's locus of temporary equilibria). On impact, the economy remains at A_0 (the $\dot{\pi} = 0$-locus does not shift): $\pi = p$ is unchanged and the flow disturbance is, at given stock levels, entirely accommodated by alterations in the latters' rate of change – $\hat{X}^S$ falls below and $\hat{X}^C$ rises above g, making for $\dot{x} > 0$. This exactly parallels the short-run adjustment in VON NEUMANN I. Differences only emerge in the post-impact period. With the degree of mechanization now lower (x higher), the system's aggregate productivity y and thus the worker bonus ϵy will be lower as well. This raises the current gross yield $r^C/p^C = pq^{S*} - \epsilon y/\bar{w}$ on wage funds and makes them relatively more attractive as an asset. An incipient stock excess supply of steel equity ensues. The consequent drop in the asset price π of steel lowers its output price p *pari passu*. I conclude that the shift in consumption preferences toward steel has led, a period after its impact, to a stockmarket-induced *decline* in the flow price of steel. With p continuing to fall subsequently, the static-expectations economy travels down the $\dot{\pi} = 0$-locus to reach a new steady state at a permanently lower $\bar{\pi} = \bar{p}$.

What has happened is that the preference shift has acted, on impact, not on the structure of prices, but on the structure of accumulation. In this instance, the shift has been toward steel "luxury" goods, for which steel equipment intensively used in the production of corn wage goods is a close substitute. Consequently, on impact the relative rate of accumulation $\hat{X}^S - \hat{X}^C$ of such equipment falls and (starting from a steady state) turns negative. By the Rybczynski theorem, this must give rise to a contraction in the steel-intensive relative to the labor-intensive sector of the economy. The consequent growth in total employment L relative to net national product Y means that aggregate labor productivity $y \equiv Y/L$ will fall. (Recall $y_2 < 0$ and observe that prices and the factor productivities q^i are unaltered; thus, the change in y is due to the shift in the sectoral composition of output toward labor-intensive products alone.) The decline in aggregate labor productivity in turn entails an economy-wide cut in labor's bonus ϵy – a cost reduction particularly beneficial to the profitability of the labor-intensive sector of the economy. This the stockmarket honors with a revaluation of that sector's equity (claims to corn stocks) relative to equity of the highly mechanized sector (shares in steel stocks; thus, $\pi_1 < 0$). Since flow-supply prices in output markets are rigidly locked into stock-demand prices as determined by the bourse, there results a fall in the output price $p = \pi$ of steel.

The point, of course, is that *what determines the relative price of a good is the profitability of holding it as a stock – not its relative marginal utility to the consumer*. In the case at hand, because corn is used intensively in the production of steel (consumption demand for which has exogenously risen), the profitability of holding corn stocks, thus the equity and output price of corn, must *rise* – despite the fact that consumption preferences have shifted *away* from corn.[25]

[25] If $d\gamma_i > 0$ is unanticipated and permanent, the only difference between a perfect-foresight and the static-expectations story just presented resides in the economy's response on impact: Under foresight, π and p must drop on impact already (to point a in figure 4.2a,b), as opposed to with a one-period delay. The capital loss on steel-equity (which is unexpected) simply reflects the capitalization into asset values of the stockmarket's correct expectation that the price of steel will henceforth be declining: $\dot{\pi} < 0$ at a and along the saddle-path aA_1. The impact response and the saddle-path motions of perfect-foresight system [(4.28), (4.29)] qualitatively coincide with those of its continuous-time approximation, if the stable root η_2 is positive; if that root is negative, the motions will exhibit damped oscillations (recall footnote 22).

II

Primary resources

5

RICARDO: Basics, nonbasics, and land

5.1 Introduction

If, in the subsistence-wage version ($\epsilon = 0$) of MARX–SRAFFA, I let nonreproducible land take the place of reproducible steel as an input and if, as in VON NEUMANN II, I allow steel output to become a nonstorable consumption good, I have at hand the essentials of Ricardo's corn model:[1] Scarce land produces corn and corn produces, via subsistence labor, a nonbasic Ricardian luxury. The great fruitfulness of Ricardo's two-sector framework derives from the fact that it successfully straddles – doctrinally, is the common source of – the von Neumann and Walrasian models. In the most economical way conceivable, it incorporates central elements of both: On the von Neumann side, surplus labor, a linear manufacturing technology, and a uniform profit rate; on the Walrasian side, an exogenous endowment of a nonproduced resource, input substitutability in corn production, and flow-market clearing for the consumption good.[2]

Though the Ricardian story could, in all its essentials, also be told within a VON NEUMANN framework of complete sector specificity of each input, I shall follow Ricardo in the present chapter and broaden my technological assumptions: Circulating corn capital will be used in both sectors and be instantaneously mobile across them. My reasons for proceeding in this way are twofold. First, it shows how the Hamiltonian approach accommodates multiple-input technologies and various degrees of input substitution. Second, the Ricardian model enables me to examine these issues without violating the substance of my axiom of input immobility. This follows from the fact that stocks of wage goods constitute circulating capital, which fully depreciates within a single period of

[1] See his *Essay on Profits* [Ricardo (1815, 1951), vol. IV]; also, Samuelson (1959), Pasinetti (1960).

[2] For completeness and future reference (in RAMSEY–SOLOW), I discuss the one-sector version of Ricardo's corn model in the first of the two supplements accompanying this chapter (C.1).

production. It can be shown that sectorally immobilizing wage-good stocks for that period via a specificity assumption – instead of allowing for instantaneous mobility at the period's beginning – has only trivial effects on the model's behavior. Moreover, whatever one's assumption about the mobility of such stocks, at no point is there ever an incentive for the intersectoral reallocation of *labor*. After all, the two sectors represent capitalist islands of employment surrounded by the huddled masses of subsistence job seekers. In this respect, Ricardian land or neoclassical human capital are clearly different. Their fixed supply means that increased use in one sector requires a costly resource transfer from another sector. Since in this chapter I am as yet unwilling to model the corresponding investment decision, I am precluded from adopting the conventional symmetric Heckscher–Ohlin–Samuelson (HOS) structure, with land used in both sectors.[3]

As regards substitutability of labor for land in the production of corn, I will assume that it is neoclassically smooth in the body of the chapter (section 5.2) and pursue discrete alternatives – including single-technique Leontief and "blueprints" technologies, as well as my usual assumption of complete input specificity by sector – in supplement C.2. I also use that supplement to explore the implications of an anti-Uzawa alternative (land-intensive nonbasics, corn-intensive corn) to my usual intensity assumption.

The key results implied by the technological alternatives mentioned are as follows. The neoclassical model exhibits continuous full employment and nonoscillating saddle-path motions.[4] A central insight afforded by the Leontief technology is that its interaction with forward-looking stockmarket speculation allows the emergence of profit-maximizing unemployment of land. Being necessarily transitory – full employment of the primary input is guaranteed in the stationary state – such unemployment gives rise to a zero rental, *but never to a zero equity price*, of land.[5] As we will see, unemployment is not, however, a necessary feature of adjustment in the Leontief economy: Often the latter can optimally respond by a single-period, full-employment jump across stationary states. As regards multi-

[3] One of the beauties of Ricardo's set-up is that, notwithstanding its asymmetric structure, it does yield the two core theorems of its symmetric HOS progeny, namely Rybczynski's and Stolper–Samuelson's. As is well known, this is not true for what has been labeled the "Ricardo–Viner–Ohlin" or "specific-factors" model [Samuelson (1971), Jones (1971)], which contains two permanently sector-specific types of land.

[4] Recall that the presence of circulating capital imposes a discrete-time, difference-equation treatment. Monotonic motions are also characteristic of the nonsmooth technologies I examine in supplement C.2. Convergence then typically takes place, not along a saddle path as in the neoclassical model, but along an unstable trajectory that entails a switch in regime when, in finite time, the stationary state is attained.

[5] Except under static expectations. The reader may want to bear in mind that in RAMSEY–SOLOW I show neoclassical labor to be isomorphic to Ricardian land.

ple-discrete-technique ("blueprints") technologies, they increase the scope for adjustments that need not involve unemployment (the limiting case being the neoclassical production function). Finally, an anti-Uzawa version of my single-specific-input technology is shown to be nonviable in the long run.

Some other results developed in this chapter are these. First, the Ricardian economy with land obeys, across stationary states, the Samuelson nonsubstitution theorem [Samuelson (1959)] and, at each point in time, the Ricardo–Bortkiewicz–Sraffa theorem. Second, when applied to RICARDO, my usual specific-input technology provides a natural setting for a Marshallian adjustment process toward temporary equilibrium (labeled M2 in chapter 3), in which it is stockmarket arbitrageurs who clear the flow market for nonbasics by varying consumers' portfolio wealth.[6]

The structure of RICARDO is similar to Pasinetti's (1960) classic interpretation of the two-sector Ricardian economy. It differs from the Pasinetti model in two key respects (apart from being cast in discrete time):[7] It incorporates a stockmarket in land, and it is consistent with intertemporal consumption optimization.

5.2 The model

Consider an economy in which, as in MARX–SRAFFA, labor is supplied infinitely elastically at the subsistence wage $\bar{w}$, paid out of a corn wage fund that is advanced at the beginning of the unitary production period. Workers have no stake in the surplus ($\epsilon = 0$). Apart from a momentarily given stock of wage goods X^C, capitalists own the system's invariant stock of capitalistically usable land, $\bar{T}$:

$$K \equiv p^C X^C + p^T \bar{T}, \tag{5.1}$$

where K is capital and the p^i $(i = C, T)$ are prices of ownership claims. The numéraire remains corn output.

To produce the economy's two outputs, consumption services (S) and corn (C), j-sector entrepreneurs hire workers L_j, using wage funds $X_j^C = \bar{w}L_j$ they have rented from capitalists ($j = C, S$). For an aggregate level of employment $L \equiv L_C + L_S \equiv (X_C^C/\bar{w}) + (X_S^C/\bar{w})$, entrepreneurial demand for wage funds is $\bar{w}L$ or

$$X_C^C + X_S^C \equiv T(x_C + x_S) \leq \bar{T}x \equiv X^C,\ x_j \equiv X_j^C/T,\ x \equiv X^C/\bar{T},\ T \leq \bar{T}, \tag{5.2}$$

[6] See supplement C.2. The setting is natural because in this instance the nonbasics market-clearing equation only contains the relative equity price as a price variable, not the price of nonbasics.

[7] Following Pasinetti, much of the literature on the corn model has been mistakenly cast in continuous time *ab initio*. The present chapter and its supplements show the circumstances under which this is not misleading.

where $\sum X_j^C$, T denote current demand for (employment of) and X^C, $\bar{T}$ current supply of wage funds and land.[8] x_j is the normalization of X_j^C in terms of employed land and x the system's capital composition.

Labor is the sole input in the production of consumption services; normalizing $\bar{w}$ at unity, I have $L_S = X_S^C$ and a supply of nonbasics given by

$$Q^S = a_{CS}^{-1} X_S^C \equiv a_{CS}^{-1} x_S T \equiv q^S T, \qquad \bar{w} = 1, \tag{5.3}$$

where a_{CS} denotes the constant amount of corn required to produce, via labor, one unit of consumption services and where q^j refers to output of j per unit of T. My usual assumption in this chapter will be that both labor and land are used in the production of corn,

$$Q^C = Q^C(X_C^C, T) \equiv q^C(x_C)T, \tag{5.4}$$

where $Q(\cdot)$ is a constant-returns-to-scale production function, of which (as mentioned) I shall examine three variants: The standard neoclassical Inada (1963) form

$$\begin{aligned} &q^{C\prime} > 0, \quad q^{C\prime\prime} < 0, \quad q^C(0) = 0, \quad q^C(\infty) \to \infty, \\ &q^{C\prime}(0) \to \infty, \quad q^{C\prime}(\infty) = 0, \end{aligned} \tag{5.4.1}$$

which, when paired with (5.3), guarantees full employment of both inputs ($\sum X_j^C = X^C$, $T = \bar{T}$); the single-technique Leontief form

$$Q^C = \min\,[a_{CC}^{-1} X_C^C, a_{TC}^{-1} T], \tag{5.4.2}$$

which, when joined to (5.3), allows spells of unemployment of land ($\sum X_j^C = X^C$, $T \le \bar{T}$); and the blueprints technology

$$\begin{aligned} &Q^C = \begin{Bmatrix} \min[(a_{CC}^{-1})_1 X_C^C, (a_{TC}^{-1})_1 T] \\ \min[(a_{CC}^{-1})_2 X_C^C, (a_{TC}^{-1})_2 T] \end{Bmatrix}, \\ &(a_{CC}^{-1})_1 > (a_{CC}^{-1})_2, \; (a_{TC}^{-1})_1 < (a_{TC}^{-1})_2, \end{aligned} \tag{5.4.3}$$

which, with (5.3), also will be seen to permit temporary unemployment of land. I will, furthermore, briefly comment on the specific-factors technology (5.3) and

$$Q^C = a_{TC}^{-1} T, \tag{5.4.4}$$

entailing $X_S^C = X^C$, $T = \bar{T}$, as well as on its anti-Uzawa alternative

$$Q^S = a_{TS}^{-1} \bar{T}, \qquad Q^C = a_{CC}^{-1} X^C. \tag{5.4.5}$$

These technological variants are illustrated in figure 5.1 by the production-possibility curves a [(5.4.1)], b [(5.4.2)], c [(5.4.3)], and d [(5.4.4) or (5.4.5)]. I

[8] As always, I assume there to be a one-to-one relation between input stocks and the stream of services they generate.

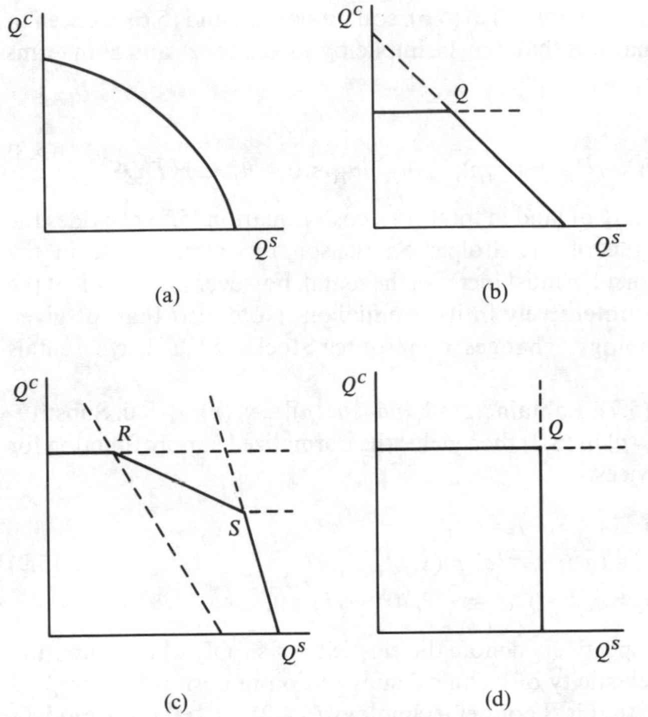

Figure 5.1 Production-possibility curves for RICARDO under alternative technologies

use (5.4.1) in the remainder of this chapter and refer the reader to supplement C.2 for the discussion of (5.4.2)–(5.4.5).

Under [(5.3), (5.4), (5.4.1)] the model's zero-entrepreneurial profit conditions are

$$p = a_{CS} r^C \tag{5.5}$$

$$p^C = 1 = a_{CC}(x_C) r^C + a_{TC}(x_C) r^T, \tag{5.6}$$

where the $a_{iC}(\cdot)$ are the variable input–output coefficients in corn ($a_{TC} \equiv 1/q^C$); the r^i denote end-of-period rentals on wage funds and land; and p and 1 refer to the flow price of consumption services and of corn, respectively.

As is well known, entrepreneurial cost minimization is sufficient to ensure a one-to-one relation between the corn intensity of corn production x_C and corn's relative rental r^C/r^T,

$$x_C = \tilde{x}_C(r^C/r^T), \qquad \tilde{x}'_C < 0. \tag{5.7}$$

Following substitution of (5.7) in (5.6), equations (5.5) and (5.6) are seen to represent two equations that may be implicitly solved for r^C and r^T in terms of p alone,

$$r^C = pa_{CS}^{-1}$$
$$r^T = r^T(p), \quad r^{T\prime} = -(r^T/p)(1-\theta_{TC})/\theta_{TC} < 0, \quad \theta_{TC} \equiv r^T\bar{T}/Q^C, \tag{5.8}$$

where θ_{TC} is the share of land in total corn cost. Equation (5.8) provides the Ricardian analogue of the Stolper–Samuelson theorem: A rise in the relative price of corn $1/p$ must increase the rental, however measured, of the input (land) used intensively in its production. Note also that, at given prices and technology, changes in resource stocks $X^C, \bar{T}$ leave rentals unaltered.[9]

Using (5.8) in (5.7), I obtain $x_C = \tilde{x}_C[pa_{CS}^{-1}/r^T(p)] \equiv x_C(p), x_C' < 0$. Substitution of $x_S = x - x_C(p)$ in (5.3) then yields the normalized supply function for consumption services,

$$Q^S/T = a_{CS}^{-1}[x - x_C(\cdot)] \equiv q^S(p, x)$$
$$q_1^S = (q^S/p)v \equiv (q^S/p)(x_C/\theta_{TC}x_S)\sigma^C \tag{5.9}$$
$$q_2^S = a_{CS}^{-1} > 0, \ \sigma^C \equiv -\hat{x}_C/(\hat{r}^C - \hat{r}^T) > 0,$$

where v and σ^C respectively denote the elasticity of supply of consumption services and the elasticity of technical substitution in corn ($\sigma^C = 0$ implies $x_C = \bar{x}_C = a_{CC}/a_{TC}$, that is, Leontief technology (5.4.2)). $q_2^S > 0$ is the model's Rybczynski effect: At a given p, a shift in capital composition toward corn leads to an expansion of the nonbasics sector.

I now turn to the stockmarket. With ownership titles to wage funds and land costlessly and instantaneously tradable through it,

$$\rho^C \equiv \frac{r^C}{p^C} - 1 = \frac{r^T}{p^T} + (\hat{p}^T)^e \equiv \rho^T \tag{5.10}$$

must hold at all times, where ρ^C is the expected yield ($\equiv$current yield, by $\delta^C = 1$) on equity in the economy's wage fund and ρ^T the expected yield on holdings of imperishable land ($\delta^T = 0$).[10] Substituting in (5.10) from (5.6), (5.8) and rearranging, I obtain

[9] Thus, are reflected exclusively in Rybczynski output-composition changes. This is the difference between Ricardo's corn model and the specific-factors framework mentioned in footnote 3.

[10] Observe that because end-of-period rentals $r^C/p = a_{CS}^{-1}$ received in the form of nonbasics are nonstorable, they do not give rise to an equity increment and a possible capital gain thereon (recall (4.7) and see my critique of the Dorfman–Samuelson–Solow (1958) arbitrage condition in supplement A.3; unlike there, intersectoral input mobility *does* imply rental equality: $r_C^C = r_S^C = r^C$ in (5.5), (5.6)).

$$\chi(p,\pi;\hat{\pi}^e\ldots)\equiv pa_{CS}^{-1}-1-\frac{r^T(p)}{\pi}-\hat{\pi}^e=0, \chi_i>0\ (i=1,2),\ \chi_3<0$$
$$\pi\equiv p^T/p^C=p^T, \tag{5.11}$$

the economy's point-in-time stock-equilibrium condition under zero entrepreneurial profits. According to (5.11), by respectively raising and depressing the current yields r^C-1 and r^T/p^T on wage funds and land, a *ceteris-paribus* increase in the price of consumption services must create an incipient yield differential in favor of wage funds and a corresponding stock excess demand for them ($\chi_1>0$); at given expectations of capital gains on land, this leads to a jump in the relative price $1/\pi$ of claims to corn stocks in terms of titles to land ($-\chi_2<0$). I next consider the model's flow equilibrium condition.

Since consumption services are perishable, their market must clear at each instant. Given optimizing functions $E=[\Omega/(1+\Omega)](1+\rho)K$, $D^S=\gamma E/p$ for end-of-period consumption and nonbasics demand by capitalists [recall (4.10)], this requires $Z^S\equiv Q^S-\gamma[\Omega/(1+\Omega)](1+\rho)K/p=0$ or, when normalized in terms of land ($T=\bar{T}$) and after substitution for $\rho=\rho^C$,

$$z^S(p,\pi;x,\gamma,\Omega)\equiv q^S(p,x)-\gamma[\Omega/(1+\Omega)]a_{CS}^{-1}(x+\pi)=0$$
$$z_i^S>0\ (i=1,3),\ <0\ (i=2,4,5), \tag{5.12}$$

where $z^S(\cdot)$ is normalized flow excess supply of nonbasics, γ capitalists' propensity to consume them, and Ω the rate of capitalist time preference.[11] I can use (5.12) to solve for the temporary-equilibrium price of nonbasics in terms of π, x, and parameters:

$$p=p(\pi;x,\gamma,\Omega),\qquad p_i=-z_{1+i}^S/z_1^S>0\ (i=1,3,4),\ <0\ (i=2). \tag{5.13}$$

An increase in the price of land $\pi=p^T$ raises wealth and consumption of nonbasics, thus pushing up the latter's price ($p_1>0$); so will a shift in intratemporal preferences γ toward nonbasics ($p_3>0$), or a shift in intertemporal preferences Ω toward current consumption ($p_4>0$). On the other hand, a movement in capital composition x away from land toward corn tends, *à la* Rybczynski, to raise output of consumption services by more than it raises demand, thereby depressing their price ($p_2<0$).

Clearly, (5.11) and (5.12) are independent stock- and flow-equilibrium conditions that, together, are sufficient to determine the model's two

[11] Observe that the interest-rate $(1+\rho(p))$ and purchasing-power $(1/p)$ effects of the nonbasics price p on D^S are such as to leave D^S independent of p (since $(1+\rho)/p=a_{CS}^{-1}$, where $\rho=\rho^C$ is the uniform profit rate). Should the price response of supply, q_1^S, vanish as well – as it must, for instance, under (5.4.4) – $z^S(\cdot)$ will be independent of p ($z_1^S=q_1^S=0$) and a function, via wealth, of the single price variable π. Recall footnote 6 and see my discussion in supplement C.2.

temporary-equilibrium variables π and p, given expectations $\hat{\pi}^e$, capital composition x, preferences (γ, Ω), and technology.[12]

I turn to the model's dynamics. By Walras's Law, (5.11) and (5.12) together imply capital-market equilibrium, that is, equality between demand for loanable funds, ΔX^C, and supply of loanable funds, $[(\rho-\Omega)/(1+\Omega)]K-\bar{T}\Delta\pi$; this gives the law of accumulation[13]

$$\Delta K=\frac{(\rho-\Omega)K}{(1+\Omega)}, \qquad \Delta K\equiv\Delta X^C+\bar{T}\Delta\pi. \tag{5.14}$$

The law of motion of the price of land under myopic foresight $\hat{\pi}^e=\hat{\pi}\equiv\Delta\pi/\pi$ is, from (5.8), (5.11), and (5.13),

$$\begin{aligned}\Delta\pi&=\pi\{p(\pi,x)a_{CS}^{-1}-1-r^T[p(\pi,x)]/\pi\}\equiv\phi(\pi,x)\\ \phi_1&=(\phi_2/p_2)p_1+\Omega>0,\ \phi_2=p_2(\pi a_{CS}^{-1}-r^{T'})<0,\end{aligned} \tag{5.15}$$

which, when combined with (5.14), immediately yields the dynamics of the system's capital composition $\hat{x}\equiv\Delta x/x\equiv\hat{X}^C-\hat{T}=\hat{X}^C$,

$$\begin{aligned}\Delta x&=[p(\pi,x)a_{CS}^{-1}-1-\Omega]\left(\frac{x+\pi}{1+\Omega}\right)-\phi(\pi,x)\equiv\psi(\pi,x)\\ \psi_1&=(\psi_2/p_2)p_1-\Omega<0,\psi_2=-\frac{(1-\gamma)\Omega(x_C+\pi)a_{CS}^{-1}}{1+(1-\gamma)\Omega}p_2>0,\end{aligned} \tag{5.16}$$

where the partial derivatives ϕ_i, ψ_i have been evaluated at the Ricardian stationary state $\Delta x=\Delta\pi=0$.

In that state, one finds

$$\bar{\rho}=\bar{p}a_{CS}^{-1}-1=\Omega,\ \text{thus}\ \bar{p}=(1+\Omega)a_{CS} \tag{5.17}$$

$$\bar{\rho}=r^T(\bar{p})/\bar{\pi}=\Omega,\ \text{thus}\ \bar{\pi}=\bar{r}^T/\Omega, \tag{5.18}$$

from (5.16) and (5.10). Consequently, the long-period profit rate $\bar{\rho}$ must equal capitalists' "minimum required rate of return" or rate of time

12 The properties of the temporary equilibrium of RICARDO may be studied with the help of a diagram identical to that used in VON NEUMANN II (recall figure 3.1, keeping in mind the changed definition of x and the corresponding change in the sign of $\partial z^S/\partial x$). It is not difficult to demonstrate that the Ricardo–Bortkiewicz–Sraffa theorem is a feature of RICARDO: From (5.5), (5.6), a doubling of service-sector productivity a_{CS}^{-1} will not require any change in rentals r^i – nor, therefore, in labor allocations x_j – if it is accompanied by an instantaneous halving of the price of consumption services (then $d\tilde{x}_C(r^C/r^T)=0$ in (5.7), thus, $dx_S=d[x-x_C(p,a_{CS})]=-dx_C(p,a_{CS})=-d\tilde{x}_C(\cdot)=0$ in (5.9)); but $\hat{p}=\hat{a}_{CS}<0$ does yield simultaneous flow and stock equilibrium at an unaltered π and profit rate, as inspection of (5.9) [where $\hat{q}^S=-\hat{a}_{CS}$], (5.11) [where $dr^T=0$], and (5.12) shows. Since, as is easily confirmed from the model's dynamic and stationary-state properties, no adjustments beyond those in temporary equilibrium occur, the theorem is verified.

13 Walras's Law implies $(Q^C-X^C-D^C)+p(Q^S-D^S)\equiv[(\rho-\Omega)/(1+\Omega)]K-\bar{T}\Delta\pi$, with $Q^C-X^C-D^C=\Delta X^C$, thus (5.14), holding identically in temporary equilibrium.

preference Ω; the long-run price of consumption services $\bar{p}$ is determined by their long-run unit cost of production $(1+\bar{\rho})a_{CS} \equiv \bar{w}(1+\bar{\rho})a_{LS}$; and the price of land equals the present value $\bar{r}^T/\bar{\rho}$ of stationary-state land rentals. Given (5.17) and (5.18), the long-run version of flow-equilibrium condition (5.12) implicitly solves for the stationary-state wage-fund–to–land ratio,[14]

$$\bar{x} = \bar{x}(\gamma \ldots), \qquad \bar{x}' > 0. \tag{5.19}$$

It comes as no surprise that the long-run Ricardian economy obeys a Samuelson (1951,1959) nonsubstitution theorem (since one nonreproducible input is present, constant returns to scale obtain, and joint production is absent): At the fixed profit rate $\bar{\rho}$, changes in the preference parameter γ leave stationary-state prices $\bar{p}$ unaffected, being reflected instead in capital-composition movements toward the input used intensively in the industry favored by the demand shift.

I now turn to the question of the model's dynamic stability. The simultaneous difference equation system [(5.15), (5.16)] may be linearized and collapsed into the single second-order difference equation

$$\begin{aligned} &x(t+2) + a_1 x(t+1) + a_2 x(t) = c\bar{x} \\ &-a_1 \equiv (\phi_1 + 1) + (\psi_2 + 1) = \eta_1 + \eta_2 > 0 \\ &c \equiv \phi_1\psi_2 - \phi_2\psi_1 = (\eta_1 - 1)(\eta_2 - 1) = (x+\pi)\Omega p_2/p < 0 \\ &a_2 \equiv c - a_1 - 1 = \eta_1\eta_2 = a_{CS}^{-1}[p_1(x_C + \pi) + p_2 x_S] + (1+\Omega) = 1 + \Omega > 0. \end{aligned} \tag{5.20}$$

I conclude from $c<0$ and $a_2>0$ that – irrespective of the degree of input substitutability in corn production $(0<\sigma^C<\infty)$ – the economy is necessarily saddle-path stable and nonoscillating (that is, possesses roots $\eta_1 > 1$, $0 < \eta_2 < 1$).[15] The trajectories traced out by discrete-time system [(5.15), (5.16)] are, therefore, qualitatively the same as those of its saddle-path stable $(c<0)$ continuous-time approximation

$$\dot{\pi} = \phi(\pi, x),\ \phi_1 > 0,\ \phi_2 < 0;\ \dot{x} = \psi(\pi, x),\ \psi_1 < 0,\ \psi_2 > 0. \tag{5.21}$$

In what follows, I accordingly rely on the phase portrait of (5.21).

Consider the dynamic consequences of an unanticipated and permanent preference shift toward consumption services ($d\gamma > 0$; see figure 5.2). Across stationary states (A_0, A_1), the economy's wage fund and employment expand $(\bar{x}_1 > \bar{x}_0)$, and do so by enlarging the service sector at unchanged prices, rentals, and profit rates – thus, at an unchanged level of employment

[14] The dependence of $\bar{x}$ on Ω (not shown) is, as usual, ambiguous in sign; also, by the Ricardo–Bortkiewicz–Sraffa theorem, $\bar{x}$ is a function of corn technology only, not of a_{CS}.

[15] Note the contrast with MARX–SRAFFA [(4.15), (4.31)]. In the Leontief case $(\sigma^C = 0)$, even though $c<0$, $a_2 = 1+\Omega > 0$ as well, one has degeneracy, since from (5.9), (5.13) $p_1 \to \infty$, $p_2 \to -\infty$, thus, $\phi_i, \psi_i \to |\infty|$ $(i=1,2)$, $c \to -\infty$. Leontief dynamics nonetheless are well defined (see supplement C.2).

and output in the corn sector. The reason prices must change on impact – even at given expectations – is, of course, the presence of a market for nonbasics: Demand for perishable consumption services must equal supply of such services in each temporary equilibrium, not merely across steady states as in the case of aggregate demand for corn. Consequently, $d\gamma > 0$ gives rise to a flow excess demand for consumption services on impact that pushes up their relative price and the rental on the input, corn, used intensively in their production. This is accompanied by a shift of wage funds and employment from the corn to the service sector. Because, at prevailing asset prices, the net yield $r^C - 1$ on equity in wage funds tends to move above that expected on titles to land, the bourse responds by lowering $p^T = \pi$ for yield equality and stockmarket equilibrium. The extent of the drop in the price of land depends, in a way that should by now be familiar, on the model's assumption regarding expectations.

If the latter are static, (5.15) is replaced by $\Delta\pi^e \equiv 0 = \phi(\pi, x)$, which turns the corresponding $\hat{\pi} = \phi(\cdot) = 0$-curve in figure 5.2 into a temporary-equilibrium locus and yields point b as the initial impact position.[16] If, on the other hand, the stockmarket correctly anticipates that land prices will recuperate from their currently depressed levels, the $\hat{\pi}^e$-term in (5.11) turns positive and prevents π from falling as much as under static expectations: It drops to point a, located on the saddle path of the economy. The system's subsequent motion is clear from the figure and dictated by the fact that the profit rate has jumped above Ω on impact; therefore, K and $X^C = \bar{w}L$ must now both be growing. One period later, the increased stock of wage goods occasions a Rybczynski expansion of nonbasics output, an excess supply thereof, and a consequent downward correction in its price, the rental of corn, and the profit rate. With growth persisting, these corrections continue in later periods until the original price and profit rate situations have been reestablished at A_1. In the process, the initial withdrawal of wage funds from the corn sector is progressively reversed, with newly accumulating wage funds taking the place of funds pulled out of corn production on impact.

[16] The static-expectations system's subsequent motion along that locus is again assumed governed by an accumulation equation of the form $\Delta K = [(\rho - \Omega)/(1 + \Omega)]K + \bar{T}\Delta\pi$ [compare (1.28) and recall footnote 12 in chapter 4] or $\Delta x = \{p[\tilde{\pi}(x), x]a_{CS}^{-1} - 1 - \Omega\}(x + \pi)/(1 + \Omega) \equiv \tilde{\psi}(x)$, where $\pi = \tilde{\pi}(x)$ is the solution of $\phi(\pi, x) = 0$ for π and where $\tilde{\pi}' = -\phi_2/\phi_1 > 0$, $\tilde{\psi}' = (x + \pi)\Omega p_2/(1 + \Omega)a_{CS}\phi_1 < 0$. Dynamic stability $|\tilde{\psi}' + 1| < 1$ is not guaranteed. A monotonic approach to the stationary state $(0 < \tilde{\psi}' + 1 < 1)$ obtains if $\sigma^C \equiv \theta_{TC}/\epsilon > (1 - \gamma)\theta_{TC}/\theta^C_{X,K}$, that is, if the elasticity of input substitution σ^C – which now *does* matter for stability, unlike under perfect foresight – is high, or if consumption spending out of surplus income falls heavily on nonbasics ($\gamma \approx 1$; $\epsilon \equiv -q^{C''}x/q^{C'} > 0$ here is the elasticity of labor's marginal product in corn, $\theta^C_{X,K} \equiv X^C_C/(X^C_C + p^T\bar{T})$ the share of wage funds in corn-sector capital). See also supplement C.1 on the one-sector model.

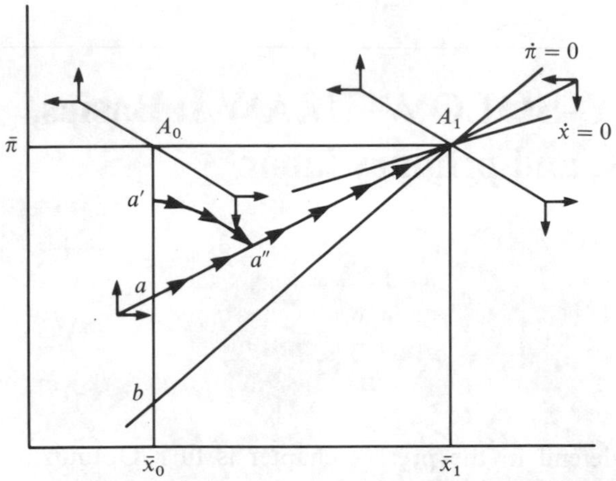

Figure 5.2 Dynamics of RICARDO under a neoclassical corn technology; adjustment following a preference shift toward consumption services

The effects of a correctly anticipated permanent future preference shift toward consumption services are portrayed by path $A_0 - a' - a'' - A_1$ in figure 5.2. They imply the following interesting result: Expectations of a future increase in consumption demand for a particular good must, in the Ricardian model, lead to a *drop* in its current equilibrium price. The mechanism is simple. When, today, a future demand shift away from corn becomes expected, the stockmarket correctly foresees one of its consequences – a post-impact period of depressed land prices. This anticipation must force down the price of land today (from A_0 to a'). By lowering wealth, the drop in $p^T = \pi$ in turn reduces today's demand for and price of consumption services. Therefore, expectations of a *rise* in demand for nonbasics have brought about a *decline* in their current equilibrium price.

6

RAMSEY–SOLOW–UZAWA: Basics, nonbasics, and primary labor

6.1 Introduction

The claim I wish to defend in the present chapter is this: Optimizing neoclassical models of exogenously driven one- and two-sector growth are structurally identical to the corresponding one- and two-sector versions of the Ricardian model.[1] Two ingredients account for this isomorphism: Nonreproducible neoclassical labor mimics Ricardian land as an input; and labor's shadow asset price mirrors the stockmarket price of human capital in an economy with voluntary slavery.

6.2 RAMSEY–SOLOW: A single basic and primary labor

I start by considering RICARDO'S one-sector variant,[2] in which land and corn (fixed-wage labor) produce the system's sole output, corn. Three simple, structure-preserving alterations are sufficient to transform it into a RAMSEY–SOLOW model:

1 Instead of nonreproducible land, let T denote primary labor, that is nonreproducible human capital. Like Ricardian land, human capital is thus strictly exogenous and either fixed or growing – in natural or efficiency units – at a fixed rate $n>0$. To interpret exogenous human-capital growth correctly, it is helpful to think of it by analogy to the role such growth would play in the Ricardian framework: In the latter, each unit of a fixed number of physical acres of land – owned by members of a capitalist class of fixed size – would be envisioned as undergoing land-augmenting technological progress at rate n. In other words, increasing total numbers of Harrodian land-efficiency units would, over time, be associated with the same

[1] See Ramsey (1928), Solow (1956), Cass (1965), Koopmans (1965) for the one-sector, Uzawa (1961,1963,1964) and Srinivasan (1964) for the two-sector neoclassical growth model.

[2] See supplement C.1.

unchanging number of physical units of land, ownership titles thereto, and capitalists.

In what follows, I treat growth in the economy's exogenous stock of human capital in just this manner. Since, unlike with land, natural population growth is a fact,[3] I put forward two metaphors about the system's worker-capitalists:

(a) The economy is composed of a fixed number of identical, infinitely lived dynastic households, each of which is headed by a benevolent patriarch; he is the sole repository of its legal persona and property rights, including rights over the single dynastic unit of human capital he embodies. Therefore, $\bar{T}$ will measure both the economy's invariant stock of primary human capital and the number of its dynasties. Natural growth occurs strictly within dynasties, representing "efficiency" growth (in the procreative sense) of the underlying unit of patriarchal human capital – no new dynasties are founded and no new primary human capital emerges.

(b) The economy again consists of a fixed number $\bar{T}$ of dynastic neoclassical worker-capitalists, all of whom own one unit of primary human capital. But now the size of a dynasty is fixed and the source of its human-capital growth is technological: Each worker-capitalist enjoys constant Harrodian labor-augmenting efficiency growth at rate $n>0$ in his unit of human capital.

Either of the two scenarios (a), (b) is captured by

$$\tilde{T}(\tau)=\tilde{T}(t)\exp[n(\tau-t)], \qquad \tilde{T}(t)=\bar{T}>0, \qquad n>0, \tag{6.1}$$

where $\bar{T}$ is the aggregate stock of primary human capital (number of dynasties); $\tilde{T}(\tau)$ its measure in natural or technological efficiency units at a moment in time τ ($\tau \geq t$, where t is some initial moment); and n the exogenous rate of growth, assumed strictly (but inessentially) positive by analogy to Solow (1956).[4]

The economy's capital, measured in its single output, corn, is given by

$$K(\tau)\equiv p^C(\tau)X^C(\tau)+p^T(\tau)\bar{T}\equiv p^C(\tau)X^C(\tau)+\tilde{p}^T(\tau)\tilde{T}(\tau), \tag{6.2}$$

where X^C is the stock of physical capital and p^C its price; p^T and $\tilde{p}^T$ the price

[3] Whether, in theory, that fact is better approached along Malthus–Marx–Lewis lines or via the present neoclassical exogeneity assumption is not at issue here.

[4] The two scenarios fail to be equivalent if the dynastic head under (a), but not its counterpart under (b), uses a Benthamite intertemporal utility function that weighs the felicity of each generation by the generation's numerical size. The discount factor in the Benthamite utility function is $\exp[-(\Omega-n)t]$ instead of $\exp(-\Omega t)$, and the steady-state interest rate $\bar{\rho}=\Omega$ instead of $\bar{\rho}=\Omega+n$. I neglect this complication since (provided $\Omega>n$) it does not affect the model's dynamic behavior.

of, respectively, a natural and an efficiency unit of human capital; and where $\tilde{p}^T$ has been defined such that $\tilde{p}^T\tilde{T} \equiv p^T T$ or, using (6.1),

$$\tilde{p}^T(\tau) = p^T(\tau)\exp[-n(\tau - t)]. \qquad (6.3)$$

I now discuss $\tilde{p}^T$ and p^T further.

2 The analogy drawn between a Ricardian model with land and a neoclassical model with primary labor would be strict, if ownership claims to human capital were, like titles to land, freely alienable in the bourse. Prohibitions against voluntary slavery preclude this.[5]

Intertemporal utility maximization by the representative neoclassical household, however, entails an economy that exactly replicates one in which no prohibitions against voluntary slavery exist. Provided the system contains a fully developed capital market, lenders will be willing to instantaneously extend credit – accept a bond mortgaged on human capital, in lieu of an equity in human capital – up to the full capitalized value of the borrower's future earnings from labor.

I now discuss this idea more fully. It makes use of two insights developed in chapter 2. The first is that, for a decentralized sequence economy to replicate the planner's optimal allocation of resources, a stockmarket is generally necessary – its absence leads to a missing-markets problem analogous to that of missing futures markets in the Arrow–Debreu system. There are two exceptions, however. Under them, a stockmarket is redundant, provided we have intertemporal consumption optimization by households and myopic profit maximization by firms. The two exceptions are the RICARDO–RAMSEY–SOLOW–UZAWA economies, which contain a single basic, and the WALRAS-IV pure-exchange system (chapter 8), which contains no produced inputs at all. The condition for the redundancy

[5] The issue of the alienability of labor is discussed by a segment of the philosophical literature on the contractarian basis of liberal democracy [see, for instance, Nozick (1974), Philmore (1982), Ellerman (1985)]. According to it, there exists a substantial, but neglected, "alienist" or nondemocratic strand in liberal thought, which goes back to Grotius and Hobbes (Nozick being its modern representative) and which condones contracts of political subjection and of voluntary self-enslavement. As pointed out by Ellerman, the issue that differentiates that strand from the "inalienist" or democratic tradition in liberal thought (originating in Locke) is not consent – which is required in both traditions – but whether or not consent can validly alienate the right to self-government (in the case of a group) or to self-determination (in the case of an individual). Ellerman persuasively argues that the employment (self-rental, as opposed to self-sale) contract between a firm and a worker involves the surrender of self-determination, albeit for a limited duration and within a limited scope. It is, thus, associated with the alienist, not the Lockean, tradition in liberal thought. He completes his argument by observing that in the decentralized Arrow–Debreu economy utility maximization leads to the conclusion of (Pareto-efficient) employment contracts over the entire future horizon, thus, to self-enslavement of unlimited duration (though still of limited scope, since it excepts leisure time).

of the stockmarket thus is that the economy contain no more than one reproducible input (it may contain any number of nonreproducible inputs). Should this be the case, all that is needed for a Pareto-optimal decentralized resource allocation are flow markets for outputs, for inputs, and for capital (loanable funds), plus myopic profit maximization by entrepreneurs and intertemporal utility maximization by consumers. In *all other* sequence economies, a Pareto-optimal allocation is not achievable in the absence of a stockmarket.[6]

The second insight is that, in the special case of a logarithmic felicity function, the shadow price of wealth λ and the equity price vector π do not move autonomously. Therefore, only one of them is needed to derive the economy's path; standard practice in the model at hand is to focus on λ.[7] Utility-maximizing household consumption decisions then yield convergent λ, x-dynamics and an associated path for the economy's interest rate ρ. Using this interest-rate path, agents will discount future labor income from human capital into a current shadow equity price of such capital that is *identical* to its stockmarket price under alienability. This has the following implication: Given logarithmic felicity, I may analyze the neoclassical RAMSEY–SOLOW–UZAWA economies of the present chapter *as if* they were operating under a system of voluntary slavery – that is, I may focus on π instead of on λ, obtaining the same path for the system as in the standard approach focusing on λ.[8]

To see how this works in some detail, consider the behavior of agents in the capital market, assuming absence of a stockmarket in human capital. Looking forward from, say, t, potential lenders will agree with a potential borrower that his unitary endowment of human capital is worth

$$p^T(t) = \int_t^\infty r^T(\tau)\exp[-\int_t^\tau \rho^C(s)ds]d\tau, \tag{6.4}$$

[6] The reason, as we recall from chapter 2 and supplement A.2, is that, whenever there are two (or more) basics, π is an autonomous forward-looking state variable whose value is treated as parametric by households and whose transversality condition is enforced by profit-maximizing speculators, not by households; that is, π moves independently from households' shadow price of wealth λ and the latter's motions, though autonomous except under logarithmic felicity, recursively depend on π.

[7] The reason for this focus is the practice of working with the general CRRA felicity function (rather than its special logarithmic form), together with a Non-Ponzi-Game (NPG) condition (or, equivalently, an intertemporal budget constraint); the latter guarantees that convergence of λ implies convergence of the shadow price $\pi = p^T$ of the model's nonproduced human capital. Recall footnote 9 in chapter 2.

[8] At the end of this section I show that, by imposing a static-expectations assumption on capital gains in an economy with voluntary slavery, I obtain a system indistinguishable from one with inalienable human capital and myopic (nonoptimizing) households. Its dynamics following unanticipated perturbations turn out to be qualitatively the same as those under perfect foresight, as usual.

where $\{r^T\}_{\tau=t}^{\infty}$, $\{\rho^C\}_{s=t}^{\infty}$ are the sequences of expected wage and interest rates, equal to actual rates along a utility-maximizing perfect-foresight path. (Observe that I have set $\rho=\rho^C$.) Using (6.1) and a definition of the efficiency wage $\tilde{r}^T$ such that [compare (6.3)]

$$\tilde{r}^T(\tau)=r^T(\tau)\exp[-n(\tau-t)], \qquad \tilde{r}^T\tilde{T}\equiv r^T T, \tag{6.5}$$

(6.4) may equivalently be expressed in terms of efficiency-unit prices and rentals as

$$\tilde{p}^T(t)=\int_t^{\infty}\tilde{r}^T(\tau)\exp\{-\int_t^{\tau}[\rho^C(s)-n]ds\}d\tau. \tag{6.6}$$

Though a shadow, not a market price, p^T or $\tilde{p}^T$ will affect the RAMSEY–SOLOW economy in a manner indistinguishable from a corresponding stockmarket price. To see this, differentiate (6.4) and (6.6) with respect to time, obtaining

$$\rho^C(t)=\frac{r^T(t)}{p^T(t)}+(\hat{p}^T)^{\mathrm{e}} \tag{6.4.1}$$

$$\rho^C(t)=\frac{\tilde{r}^T(t)}{\tilde{p}^T(t)}+n+(\hat{\tilde{p}}^T)^{\mathrm{e}} \tag{6.6.1}$$

respectively, where $r^T(t)/p^T(t)=\tilde{r}^T(t)/\tilde{p}^T(t)$ and $\hat{p}^T(t)=\hat{\tilde{p}}^T(t)+n$ from (6.3), (6.5). The reader will immediately recognize (6.4.1) as an implicit form of arbitrage equation (5.10) of the Ricardian system. It remains to render explicit the yield components of ρ^C.

3 Let the Ricardian model's stock of circulating corn wage goods X^C represent fixed capital, as in VON NEUMANN I. Let time be continuous and allow X^C to depreciate at the constant exponential rate δ, $0\leq\delta<\infty$. It then follows from (6.4.1) that the quasi-arbitrage condition of the RAMSEY–SOLOW model,

$$\rho^C\equiv\frac{r^C}{p^C}-\delta=\frac{r^T}{p^T}+(\hat{p}^T)^{\mathrm{e}}\equiv\rho^T, \tag{6.7}$$

is formally the same as stockmarket arbitrage condition (5.10) of the Ricardian model, but for replacement of $\delta^C=1$ by $0\leq\delta\equiv\delta^C<\infty$ and a continuous-time assumption. ρ^T is the shadow yield on human capital.

Given considerations 1–3, it is easy to show the isomorphism between RAMSEY–SOLOW and the one-sector version of RICARDO. To do this, I now write down the former's structure *in extenso*. Efficiency units of labor, $\tilde{T}$, and natural units of corn capital, X^C,[9] produce corn output according to

[9] Corn-augmenting technical progress is zero throughout.

a neoclassical production function identical to RICARDO's (5.4), (5.4.1),

$$\begin{aligned} &Q^C = Q^C(X^C, \tilde{T}) \equiv q^C(x)\tilde{T}, \qquad x \equiv X^C/\tilde{T} \\ &\quad q^{C\prime} > 0, \quad q^{C\prime\prime} < 0, \quad q^C(0) = 0, \quad q^C(\infty) \to \infty \\ &\quad q^{C\prime}(0) \to \infty, \quad q^{C\prime}(\infty) = 0. \end{aligned} \tag{6.8}$$

The model's zero-entrepreneurial-profit condition is

$$p^C = 1 = a_{CC}(x) r^C + a_{\tilde{T}C}(x)\tilde{r}^T, \tag{6.9}$$

where the efficiency-labor and corn-capital rentals must, by profit maximization, equal the corresponding physical marginal products,

$$\tilde{r}^T = q^C(x) - x q^{C\prime}(x) \equiv \tilde{r}^T(x), \qquad \tilde{r}^{T\prime} = -x q^{C\prime\prime}(x) > 0 \tag{6.10}$$

$$r^C = q^{C\prime}(x) \equiv r^C(x), \qquad r^{C\prime} = q^{C\prime}(x) < 0. \tag{6.11}$$

Equation (6.11) fully determines the system's momentary interest rate [I use (6.7), (6.9)],

$$\rho^C = r^C(x) - \delta \equiv \rho(x), \qquad \rho' = r^{C\prime} < 0. \tag{6.12}$$

Under nonalienability of human capital, the economy's marketable wealth consists of a single type of equity – claims to corn capital. Therefore, no portfolio composition problem and no stockmarket exists; thus, no temporary stock-equilibrium condition seemingly need be satisfied. Moreover, instantaneous flow-equilibrium conditions for nonbasics are absent. Nevertheless, the economy's temporary equilibrium is, as of (6.12), not yet closed: Its representative worker-capitalist still needs to determine his optimal rate of saving $\dot{K} = (\rho - \Omega)K$ at the momentary rate of interest $\rho(x)$,

$$\dot{K} = [\rho(x) - \Omega](x + \pi)\tilde{T}, \qquad \pi \equiv \tilde{p}^T/p^C, \tag{6.13}$$

which, for given x, requires him to place a relative value π on the stock of his efficiency human capital. As explained earlier, this valuation will be provided by capitalization (6.6) or, alternatively, by the law of motion (6.6.1) that valuation implies. Given (6.10), (6.12), and $\pi = \tilde{p}^T$, the latter may be written as

$$\chi(\pi; x, \hat{\pi}^e \ldots) \equiv r^C(x) - \delta - \frac{\tilde{r}^T(x)}{\pi} - n - \hat{\pi}^e = 0, \tag{6.14}$$

which, for given $\hat{\pi}^e$, determines the sought after shadow value π (or $p^T = \pi\tilde{T}/\bar{T}$). Equation (6.14) confirms that in temporary equilibrium RAMSEY–SOLOW operates as if under voluntary slavery and a corresponding stockmarket.

Turning to dynamics, the law of motion of the relative shadow equity price π is, from (6.14) and assuming myopic foresight $\hat\pi^e = \hat\pi \equiv \dot\pi/\pi$,

$$\dot\pi = \pi\{r^C(x) - [\tilde r^T(x)/\pi] - (\delta + n)\} \equiv \phi(\pi, x), \quad \phi_1 > 0, \phi_2 < 0. \quad (6.15)$$

From the definition of the aggregate capital stock in (6.2) and using (6.9), I have $\dot K \equiv \dot X^C + \tilde p^T \dot{\tilde T} + \tilde T \dot{\tilde p}^T$ so that, recalling $\hat{\tilde T} = n$, (6.13), and (6.15),

$$\begin{aligned} \dot x \equiv x(\hat X^C - \hat{\tilde T}) &= [r^C(x) - (\Omega + \delta + n)](x + \pi) - \phi(\pi, x) \\ &\equiv \psi(\pi, x), \quad \psi_1 = -\phi_1 < 0, \quad \psi_2 = 0 \end{aligned} \quad (6.16)$$

provides the law of motion of the economy's physical-to-human-capital (or "capital–labor") ratio $x \equiv X^C/\tilde T$. The simultaneous differential equation system [(6.15), (6.16)] is locally saddle-path stable,

$$-\phi_2\psi_1 < 0, \quad (6.17)$$

and illustrated in figure 6.1.[10] From my discussion in chapter 2 and supplement A.2, intertemporal utility maximization by the representative worker-capitalist guarantees that the economy will converge to the steady state along the stable saddle path – thus replicating the consequences of profit maximization by stockmarket speculators in an analogous economy with voluntary slavery.

The system's steady-state equilibrium $\dot\pi = \dot x = 0$ is easily seen to be characterized by

$$\begin{aligned} & r^C(x) - \delta = \bar\rho = \Omega + n, \text{ thus } \bar x = \bar x(\Omega + \delta + n), \ \bar x' < 0 \\ & \frac{\tilde r^T(x)}{\pi} + n = \bar\rho = \Omega + n, \text{ thus } \bar\pi = \frac{\tilde r^T(\bar x)}{\Omega} \equiv \bar\pi(\delta + n, \Omega), \quad \bar\pi_i < 0 \ (i = 1,2). \end{aligned} \quad (6.18)$$

Note that, since $\hat p^T = \hat{\tilde p}^T + n$, $\dot\pi = \dot{\tilde p}^T = 0$ implies a constant steady-state rate $n > 0$ of shadow capital gains on human capital.

It may be illuminating to discuss RAMSEY–SOLOW in the more conventional consumption/capital–labor-ratio state space. Writing normalized consumption as $e \equiv E/\tilde T$, I have, from the accumulation equation for corn $\dot X^C = Q^C(\cdot) - \delta X^C - E$,

$$\begin{aligned} & \dot x = q^C(x) - (\delta + n)x - e \equiv \psi^*(e, x) \\ & \qquad \psi_1^* < 0, \quad \psi_2^* = \rho - n \gtrless 0, = \Omega > 0 \text{ near a steady state,} \end{aligned} \quad (6.19)$$

as a representation of $\dot x$ alternative to (6.16).

[10] The discrete-time version of RAMSEY–SOLOW has the same phase space as the (one- or two-sector) RICARDO model, namely figure 5.2 (see supplement C.1). Derived on the basis of a discrete-time dynamical system, figure 5.2 differs slightly from the continuous-time phase space in figure 6.1 (on account of the difference between the discrete- and the continuous-time consumption function): Unlike in (6.16), in RICARDO one has $\psi_2 > 0$, which renders the $\dot x = 0$-locus positively sloped, as in figure 5.2, rather than horizontal, as in figure 6.1. The direction of the stable and unstable branches of the saddle point remains, however, unaffected.

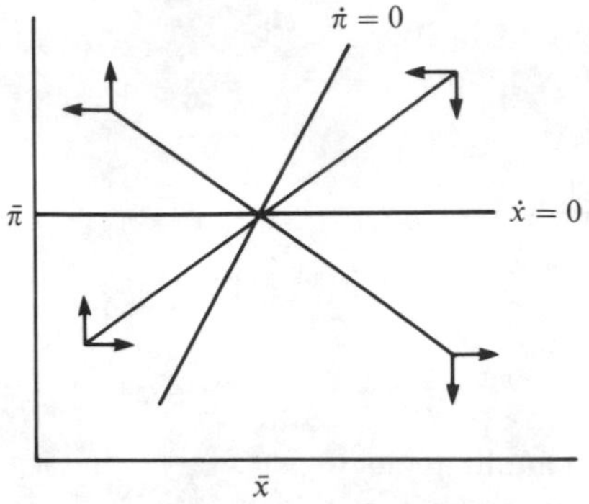

Figure 6.1 Dynamics of RAMSEY–SOLOW

The law of motion of consumption per efficiency worker follows from the optimizing consumption function $E = \Omega K$ or $e = \Omega(x + \pi)$: Solving for $\pi = (e/\Omega) - x$ and substituting in $\dot{\pi} = \phi(\pi, x)$ [(6.15)], I obtain $\dot{\pi} = \phi^*(e, x)$; differentiating the consumption function with respect to time and using $\psi^*(\cdot)$, $\phi^*(\cdot)$ gives

$$\dot{e} = \Omega[\psi^*(e,x) + \phi^*(e,x)] \equiv \xi(e,x), \qquad \xi_1 = 0, \qquad \xi_2 = \Omega\phi_2 < 0, \quad (6.20)$$

the desired law of motion of consumption. Since

$$-\psi_1^*\xi_2 < 0, \quad (6.21)$$

the e, x-system is, of course, also locally saddle-path stable.[11] The reader will recognize its representation in figure 6.2 as the conventional neoclassical optimal-growth diagram. From it, one may derive, in the usual fashion, the dynamic consequences of anticipated or unanticipated perturbations in technology, time preference, and labor-force growth.[12]

Before concluding my discussion of RAMSEY–SOLOW, I briefly want to return to the issue of optimization. The analysis so far has been predicated on the assumption of intertemporal utility maximization, which in turn required perfect foresight: Only by looking forward to the infinite horizon could the representative worker-capitalist pick the convergent path of the shadow price of wealth λ – or, equivalently, of the shadow price π of human capital – that would assure intertemporal consumption optimization. Is it possible to construct a meaningful nonoptimizing version of RAMSEY–SOLOW, requiring merely myopic consumption behavior? The answer is yes and may be approached in two steps.

[11] Observe from $e = \Omega(x + \pi)$ that continuity in π implies, and is implied by, continuity in e. The steady-state value of e is given by $\bar{e} = q^c(\bar{x}) - (\delta + n)\bar{x} \equiv \bar{e}(\delta + n, \Omega)$, $\bar{e}_i < 0$ $(i = 1,2)$.

[12] These consequences are well-known and will not be discussed; they are not affected by the restriction to a logarithmic (instead of to a general CRRA) felicity function.

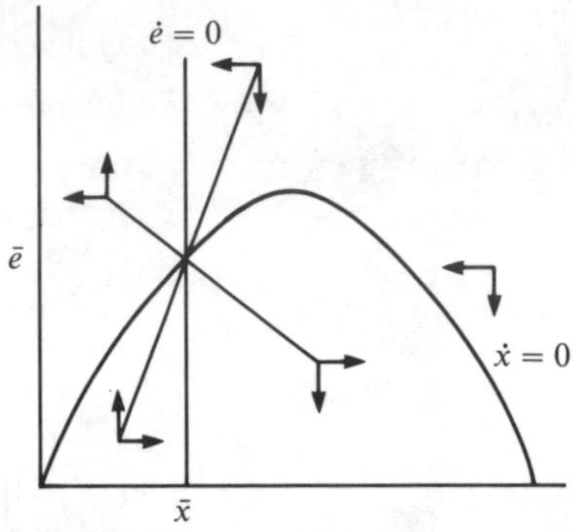

Figure 6.2 Dynamics of RAMSEY–SOLOW in e,x-space

First, it is clear that if ownership claims to human capital were freely tradable, an operative stockmarket would emerge in the model and be represented (given entrepreneurial profit maximization) by equation (6.14). In that instance, my usual treatment of the static-expectations case would go through: I would set $\hat{\pi}^e$ equal to zero ($\hat{\pi}^e \equiv 0 \gtreqless \hat{\pi}$) and solve (6.14) for the corresponding temporary-equilibrium value of π. When paired with an accumulation equation of the form [recall (1.28) and compare (6.13)]

$$\dot{K}=[\rho(x)-\Omega](x+\pi)\tilde{T}+\tilde{T}\dot{\pi}, \tag{6.23}$$

this would produce a stable dynamic model with adjustment characteristics (following unanticipated shocks) similar to those of its perfect-foresight cousin.[13]

Second, if voluntary slavery is excluded, I may construct a model that is mathematically isomorphic to the preceding system. Assume worker-capitalists do not look into the future in capitalizing their wage earnings, but instead myopically calculate $\tilde{p}^T$ to be

$$\tilde{p}^T=\tilde{r}^T(x)/[\rho(x)-n]\equiv\tilde{p}^T(x), \qquad \tilde{p}^{T\prime}>0, \tag{6.24}$$

that is, equal to the shadow price rendering the current yield on efficiency human capital $[\tilde{r}^T(x)/\tilde{p}^T]+n$ equal to the current yield on physical capital, $\rho^C=\rho(x)$. Furthermore, assume that in making their spending decisions agents continue to use

$$E=\Omega(p^C X^C+\tilde{p}^T\tilde{T}) \tag{6.25}$$

[13] In figure 6.1, $\dot{\pi}=0$ would denote the static-expectations system's temporary-equilibrium locus; the $\dot{x}=0$-schedule would be a vertical line through $\bar{x}$, with points to the right (left) implying $\dot{x}<0$ ($\dot{x}>0$).

as their (now nonoptimizing, but not implausible) consumption function. A little reflection shows that [(6.14), $\hat{\pi}^{e} \equiv 0 \gtreqless \hat{\pi}$] and (6.23) again will characterize the dynamic behavior of this economy, which thus is indistinguishable from a static-expectations system with alienable human capital.

6.3 UZAWA: Adding a nonbasic

I now briefly examine an extension of RAMSEY–SOLOW to two sectors, along the lines of Uzawa (1961,1963,1964) and Srinivasan (1964). My purpose is to demonstrate that UZAWA and the two-sector version of RICARDO examined in the last chapter are structurally identical, and to do so within a framework respectful of my axiom of sectoral immobility of existing resources. Since I do not as yet wish to model the investment processes associated with overcoming such immobility and since corn now represents, not a Ricardian wage fund, but asymptotically decaying fixed capital, I am thrust back to the single-specific-input technology. Despite its simplicity, that technology is capable of producing all the results of Uzawa's more complex framework – without the latter's inadmissible assumption of costless point-in-time factor mobility across sectors.

The resulting model has the following features. Exogenously growing efficiency labor produces the basic good corn. Corn produces a flow of nonbasic consumption services, whose market must clear at each moment. Given inalienability of human capital, no stockmarket exists. But as in RAMSEY–SOLOW, capitalization of wage earnings yields an analogue to the stockmarket–arbitrage equation, both under perfect foresight and under static expectations.

With my assumptions about human-capital ownership and growth unchanged from RAMSEY–SOLOW, equations (6.1)–(6.6) continue to apply. I repeat (6.2) for convenience (omitting the time index),

$$K \equiv p^{C} X^{C} + p^{T} \bar{T} \equiv p^{C} X^{C} + \tilde{p}^{T} \tilde{T}, \tag{6.26}$$

where X^{C} is the stock of physical capital and $\tilde{T}$, as before, refers to exogenously growing ($n > 0$) efficiency units of an unchanging amount of primary human capital, $\bar{T}$. As earlier [(6.3)], $\hat{\tilde{p}} = \hat{p}^{T} - n$ defines the relationship between the associated shadow prices, the latter again measured in terms of flow corn. The model's quasi-arbitrage equation remains (6.7) or

$$\rho^{C} \equiv \frac{r^{C}}{p^{C}} - \delta = \frac{\tilde{r}^{T}}{\tilde{p}^{T}} + n + (\hat{\tilde{p}}^{T})^{e} \equiv \rho^{T} \tag{6.27}$$

from (6.6.1).

UZAWA's production structure is given by[14]

[14] Recall the corresponding structure [(5.3), (5.4.4)] in RICARDO.

$$Q^S = a_{CS}^{-1} X^C \equiv a_{CS}^{-1} x \tilde{T}, \quad x \equiv X^C/\tilde{T} \tag{6.28}$$

$$Q^C = a_{\tilde{T}C}^{-1} \tilde{T}, \tag{6.29}$$

where Q^S, Q^C are outputs of consumption services and of corn, respectively; the a_{ij} fixed input–output coefficients; and x the system's capital composition or capital–labor ratio.

The economy's zero-entrepreneurial-profit conditions are given by

$$p = a_{CS} r^C \tag{6.30}$$

$$p^C = 1 = a_{\tilde{T}C} \tilde{r}^T, \tag{6.31}$$

where p is the price of nonbasics and p^C the equity price of corn capital, equal to the unitary price of corn output. Thus, at a given technology, $\tilde{r}^T$ is invariant, whereas r^C moves proportionately with p.

The essential difference with RAMSEY–SOLOW lies in the fact that, as in RICARDO, the flow market for consumption services must clear in temporary equilibrium. Using the supply function (6.28) and maintaining my usual assumptions about agent preferences – they spend a fraction $0 < \gamma \leq 1$ of their intertemporally optimal consumption expenditures $\Omega(X^C + p^T\tilde{T})$ on services, the remainder on corn – I have

$$z^S(p, \pi; x, \gamma, \Omega) \equiv a_{CS}^{-1} x - \gamma\Omega(x + \pi)/p = 0, \qquad \pi \equiv \tilde{p}^T/p^C = \tilde{p}^T \tag{6.32}$$

as the economy's normalized zero-excess-flow-supply equation for nonbasics ($z^S \equiv Z^S/\tilde{T}$; the definition of π is unchanged from RAMSEY–SOLOW). Equation (6.32) may be solved explicitly for p,

$$\begin{aligned} &p = \gamma\Omega(x + \pi)a_{CS}/x \equiv p(\pi; x, \gamma, \Omega) \\ &p_i > 0 \ (i = 1,3,4), \ < 0 \ (i = 2). \end{aligned} \tag{6.33}$$

Since, using (6.30) and (6.31), I may rewrite (6.27) as

$$\chi(p, \pi; \hat{\pi}^e, n + \delta) \equiv p a_{CS}^{-1} - (a_{\tilde{T}C}^{-1}/\pi) - (\delta + n) - \hat{\pi}^e = 0, \tag{6.34}$$

the model is seen to have a temporary-equilibrium structure, in which a flow-equilibrium condition $z^S(p, \pi; x \ldots) = 0$ and a quasi-stock-equilibrium condition $\chi(p, \pi; \hat{\pi}^e \ldots) = 0$ simultaneously determine the system's point-in-time p and π values, given x, $\hat{\pi}^e$, and parameters.[15] Importantly, as against RAMSEY–SOLOW [(6.12)], the system's temporary-equilibrium interest rate $\rho^C = a_{CS}^{-1} p[\pi(\cdot); x, \gamma, \Omega] - \delta \equiv \rho(\hat{\pi}^e, x, \gamma, \Omega \ldots)$ depends not just on the capital–labor ratio, but also on expectations $\hat{\pi}^e$ and preferences γ, Ω.

[15] Observe that this parallels the temporary-equilibrium structure of VON NEUMANN II and of the neoclassical version of RICARDO, but not that of RICARDO's specific-factors version (in which $z_1^S = 0$ as against $z_1^S > 0$ in (6.32); see equation (C2.8) in supplement C.2).

Inspection of (6.33) and (6.34) reveals – and the dynamic analysis to follow confirms – that the Ricardo–Bortkiewicz–Sraffa theorem again holds: Doubling service-sector productivity a_{CS}^{-1} leads to an instantaneous halving of p, but leaves ρ unchanged.

The sequence of UZAWA's temporary equilibria is readily derived along by now familiar lines. Substituting (6.33) in (6.34) and making the perfect-foresight assumption, I obtain the law of motion of the shadow price of efficiency human capital,

$$\begin{aligned}\dot{\pi} = \pi[a_{CS}^{-1}p(\pi, x) - (a_{\tilde{T}C}^{-1}/\pi) - (\delta + n)] \equiv \phi(\pi, x) \\ \phi_1 > 0, \qquad \phi_2 < 0.\end{aligned} \tag{6.35}$$

From my optimal savings equation, $\dot{K} = (\rho - \Omega)K$, and the definition of K in (6.26), I moreover have $\dot{X}^C + \pi\tilde{T}n + \tilde{T}\dot{\pi} = (\rho - \Omega)K$, or

$$\begin{aligned}\dot{x} = [a_{CS}^{-1}p(\pi, x) - (\Omega + \delta + n)](x + \pi) - \phi(\pi, x) \equiv \psi(\pi, x) \\ \psi_i < 0 \ (i = 1,2),\end{aligned} \tag{6.36}$$

the dynamic law governing the economy's capital composition. The resultant simultaneous differential equation system [(6.35), (6.36)] is locally saddle-path stable,

$$\phi_1\psi_2 - \phi_2\psi_1 < 0, \tag{6.37}$$

and characterized by the following steady-state prices:

$$\begin{aligned}a_{CS}^{-1}p - \delta = \bar{\rho} = \Omega + n, \text{ thus } \bar{p} = (\Omega + \delta + n)a_{CS} \\ (a_{\tilde{T}C}^{-1}/\pi) + n = \bar{\rho} = \Omega + n, \text{ thus } \bar{\pi} = a_{\tilde{T}C}^{-1}/\Omega.\end{aligned} \tag{6.38}$$

I may use (6.38) in (6.32) to explicitly solve for the steady-state capital–labor ratio $\bar{x}$,

$$\begin{aligned}\bar{x} = \gamma\{a_{\tilde{T}C}[(1-\gamma)\Omega + (\delta + n)]\}^{-1} \equiv \bar{x}(\gamma, \Omega, \delta + n) \\ \bar{x}_1 > 0, \qquad \bar{x}_i < 0 \ (i = 2,3).\end{aligned} \tag{6.39}$$

The phase portrait of UZAWA is given by figure 6.3, which has the same properties as the corresponding phase diagram of RICARDO (figure 5.2).[16] Thus, the two models have the same dynamical structure. Moreover, economic behavior will in each case impose on that structure the same end-point boundary conditions. For, as in RAMSEY–SOLOW, intertemporal utility maximization by the representative worker-capitalist guarantees that, despite the absence of a stockmarket for T, the economy jumps on to

[16] The difference in the sign of the partial derivative ψ_2, thus, in the slope of the $\dot{x} = 0$-locus (which is due to the difference between the discrete- and the continuous-time consumption function – recall footnote 10 above) does not affect the slopes of the stable and unstable branches of the saddle point.

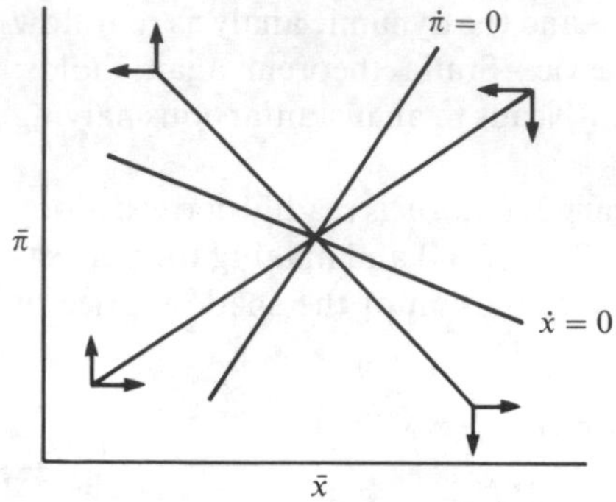

Figure 6.3 Dynamics of UZAWA

the convergent saddle path on impact of an unanticipated shock – thus behaving as if RICARDO'S profit-maximizing stockmarket speculation were present. Moreover, an UZAWA economy with myopic households that merely maximize the *current* shadow yield on inalienable human capital [as in (6.24)] again produces a dynamics which, for unanticipated shocks, closely resembles that obtaining under intertemporal optimization (it replicates the motions of RICARDO's static-expectations stockmarket economy).

I close my discussion of UZAWA with two observations, undoubtedly obvious from what has been said. First, apart from obeying the Ricardo–Bortkiewicz–Sraffa theorem, UZAWA exhibits long-run nonsubstitution behavior à la Samuelson ($d\bar{p}/d\gamma = 0$ from (6.38)). Surprisingly, this fact is rarely made use of in (say, trade-theoretic) applications of the neoclassical two-sector model, of which UZAWA and its smooth-substitution cousin are the natural dynamic representatives. Second, one may modify the model's technology in a Leontief direction by replacing (6.28), (6.29) with

$$Q^S = a_{CS}^{-1} X_S^C \tag{6.28.1}$$

$$Q^C = \min[a_{CC}^{-1} X_C^C, a_{\tilde{T}C}^{-1} \tilde{T}], \qquad \tilde{T} \leq \tilde{T}(\tau), \tag{6.29.1}$$

in which $\tilde{T}(\tau)$ denotes the predetermined supply of human capital at instant τ and $\tilde{T}$ the temporary-equilibrium entrepreneurial demand for it. This Uzawa–Leontief structure yields a dynamic theory of temporary unemployment of neoclassical labor, whose features are similar to my Ricardo-Leontief account of unemployed Ricardian land.[17]

[17] Recall [(5.3), (5.4.2)] and the corresponding discussion in supplement C.2.

7

WALRAS AND CAPITAL: Basics-only economies with multiple primary resources

7.1 Introduction

How does a basics-only economy – in which all of several outputs also represent inputs, as in VON NEUMANN I – adjust to a perturbation in the presence of one or several nonreproducible inputs? This is the question the present chapter seeks to address. By combining a VON NEUMANN I input–output structure with irremovable Walrasian input scarcities, it closes the doctrinal circle of production models.

Rather than costless reallocations of existing resources and instantaneous clearing of flow markets in response to a disturbance, the pure stock-equilibrium point of view here adopted emphasizes costless reallocations of existing portfolios and instantaneous clearing of the stockmarket – followed by the slow rearrangement in the economy's capital composition the perturbation and the consequent investment decisions give rise to. In such a perspective, flow supply does not equal flow demand except across steady states.[1]

I discuss two models. The first, WALRAS I (section 7.2), posits two basics like VON NEUMANN I, but adds a single nonproduced resource (exogenously growing efficiency labor). It is motivated by the Samuelson nonsubstitution theorem and the following question: What non-steady-state price and quantity dynamics underpin the theorem?[2]

The second model, WALRAS II (section 7.3), expands WALRAS I to multiple nonproduced inputs, namely two (labor and land). The nonsubstitution result no longer obtains – shifts in consumption preferences across

[1] Recall the introduction to chapter 3.

[2] Notwithstanding the title of Mirrlees's (1969) paper, no dynamic – that is, non-steady-state – analysis of the theorem (in a heterogeneous-capital context) exists in the literature. Recall that the Samuelson nonsubstitution theorem asserts that in a constant-returns-to-scale, no-joint-production economy with a single nonproduced input and an unchanging profit rate, shifts in demand will leave prices and production techniques unaltered.

outputs now must alter long-run relative prices and do so in the expected Walrasian direction. My point, however, will be that despite the Walrasian character of its steady-state equilibria, the model's behavior *outside the steady state* remains governed by a sequence of pure stock equilibria of the kind first encountered in VON NEUMANN I.

In supplement D, I use WALRAS II to criticize the theory of capital advanced in the *Elements of Pure Economics*.

7.2 WALRAS I: Multiple basics and primary labor

Consider an economy consisting of two social classes: Exogenously given identical workers, $\bar{T}$ in number, and a class of identical, infinitely lived, nonworking capitalists. Workers' only ownership claims are to their stock of human capital $\bar{T}$. Capitalists, who are the economy's sole savers, own its stocks of reproducible capital goods,

$$K \equiv p^C X^C + p^S X^S, \tag{7.1}$$

where K is capitalist wealth and the p^i, X^i respectively refer to equity prices and stocks of corn and steel ($i = C, S$). The system's numéraire is, as usual, corn output. Note that the two-class assumption could be dropped in favor of a worker-capitalist agent à la RAMSEY–SOLOW. The present set-up allows me to neglect the shadow price of human capital and, thus, to reduce the state variable space by one dimension. For the dynamic exercise considered below, no loss in generality is entailed.[3]

The economy's exogenous labor endowment is fixed in natural units, but growing in efficiency units $\tilde{T}$ at the rate

$$\tilde{T}(\tau) = \tilde{T}(t)\exp[n(\tau - t)], \qquad \tilde{T}(t) = \bar{T} > 0, \qquad n > 0, \tag{7.2}$$

which is the same as (6.1).[4]

Efficiency labor produces corn under constant returns,

$$Q^C = a_{\tilde{T}C}^{-1}\tilde{T} \equiv q^C\tilde{T}. \tag{7.3}$$

A fully automated production process[5] uses the services of steel and corn

[3] The reason is this: The shadow price of human capital has a law of motion that, though autonomous, recursively depends on the relative equity price $\pi \equiv p^S/p^C$ of the two produced inputs. (The same temporary-equilibrium recursivity obtains from $\rho = \rho^C = \rho^S$ to ρ^T as from $\rho = \rho^C$ to ρ^T in (6.7), (6.12) of RAMSEY–SOLOW.) Note another simplifying assumption: As earlier, I abstract from nonmarket uses of inputs. In the presence of neoclassical labor this is not trivial since, unlike changes in output preferences γ, alterations in labor–leisure tastes will, at given expectations, directly impinge on temporary-equilibrium prices and the profit rate, even in a basics-only (pure-stock-equilibrium) context.

[4] One may set $n = 0$ and obtain a model with a stationary state, as in WALRAS II below.

[5] Recall the automated production structure of VON NEUMANN I.

capital to produce steel by means of a standard neoclassical production function,

$$Q^S = Q^S(X^C, X^S) \equiv q^S(x)X^S, \qquad x \equiv X^C/X^S, \qquad q^{S\prime} > 0, \qquad q^{S\prime\prime} < 0, \tag{7.4}$$

plus the other Inada properties enumerated earlier.[6] Note the definition of the system's physical capital composition, x.

The zero-entrepreneurial-profit condition gives[7]

$$p^C = 1 = a_{\tilde{T}C}\tilde{r}^T \tag{7.5}$$

$$p^S = p = a_{CS}r^C + a_{SS}r^S, \tag{7.6}$$

where p is the flow price of steel; the r^i $(i = C, S)$, $\tilde{r}^T$ refer to rental rates on physical and efficiency human capital, respectively; and the a_{ij} $(i = C, S, \tilde{T}; j = C, S)$ as usual denote input–output coefficients. (7.5) fixes the economy's efficiency wage rate at the invariant level

$$\tilde{r}^T = a_{\tilde{T}C}^{-1} \equiv q^C. \tag{7.7}$$

It is an implication of entrepreneurial profit maximization that input services into steel are paid their value marginal products,

$$r^C = pq^{S\prime}(x) \tag{7.8}$$

$$r^S = p[q^S(x) - xq^{S\prime}(x)]. \tag{7.9}$$

As usual, stockmarket arbitrage reflects portfolio holders' insistence on a uniform expected yield across equity claims to stocks of corn and steel. Given $p^C = 1$ from (7.5), such arbitrage yields

$$\rho^C = r^C - \delta = \frac{r^S}{\pi} - \delta + \hat{\pi}^e = \rho^S, \qquad \pi \equiv p^S/p^C = p^S, \tag{7.10}$$

where the ρ^i denote expected equity yields; π is the price of steel equity in terms of corn equity; and the rate of fixed-capital depreciation δ has been assumed uniform for simplicity. Given (7.8), (7.9), I may as usual rewrite (7.10) as

$$\chi(\pi; x, \hat{\pi}^e) \equiv \pi q^{S\prime}(x) - [q^S(x) - xq^{S\prime}(x)] - \hat{\pi}^e = 0, \qquad \chi_1 > 0, \qquad \chi_i < 0 \ (i = 2, 3), \tag{7.11}$$

which closes the economy's temporary equilibrium by determining π on the basis of given stocks x, as yet parametric capital-gains expectations $\hat{\pi}^e$, and steel technology. According to (7.11), a shift in the composition of the

6 See for instance (6.8).

7 Inequalities are precluded for the same reasons as in (1.4), (1.5) of VON NEUMANN I (observe that (7.3) and (7.4) define a rectangular production-possibility frontier).

stocks of physical capital away from steel toward corn ($dx>0$) must, at given expectations, lead to a jump in the equity and flow price of steel $\pi=p$: It raises, at given prices, steel's rental and current yield by increasing its marginal physical product and it lowers that of corn correspondingly; the resultant incipient yield differential in favor of steel creates a stock excess demand for the latter, which drives up its equity price ($d\pi/dx=-\chi_2/\chi_1>0$, through corn-equity short-sales by arbitrageurs).

Recall that workers consume the entirety of their wage income $r^T\bar{T}\equiv\tilde{r}^T\tilde{T}$, of which they spend a constant fraction $0<\gamma<1$ on steel, the remainder on corn. Capitalists, on the other hand, use optimizing consumption function $E=\Omega K$. Though it would be possible to allow for capitalist consumption diversification, much simplicity is gained and, for my purposes, not much generality lost by restricting capitalist consumption to steel. The two classes' demand functions are thus given by

$$D_T^S=\gamma\tilde{r}^T\tilde{T}/p, \quad D_T^C=(1-\gamma)\tilde{r}^T\tilde{T}; \quad D_K^S=\Omega K/p, \tag{7.12}$$

where $D_T^j(j=C,S)$ and D_K^S are the demands of workers and of capitalists, respectively.

Before writing down the accumulation equations implied by (7.12), I establish the system's law of motion for π. Solving (7.11) for $\hat{\pi}^e$ and setting $\hat{\pi}=\hat{\pi}^e$ for myopic foresight, I obtain

$$\dot{\pi}=\pi[(x+\pi)q^{S\prime}(x)-q^S(x)]\equiv\phi(\pi,x), \quad \phi_1=\pi\chi_1>0, \quad \phi_2=\pi\chi_2<0. \tag{7.13}$$

From (7.3), (7.7), and (7.12), corn capital is accumulated at the rate $\dot{X}^C=Q^C-\delta X^C-(1-\gamma)\tilde{r}^T\tilde{T}\equiv X^C[(\gamma q^C/x^C)-\delta]$ or

$$\begin{aligned}\dot{x}^C\equiv x^C(\hat{X}^C-\hat{\tilde{T}})=x^C[(\gamma q^C/x^C)-(\delta+n)]\equiv\xi(x^C),\ x^C\equiv X^C/\tilde{T}\\ \xi'=-(\delta+n)<0,\end{aligned} \tag{7.14}$$

which is an autonomous differential equation in the single state variable x^C. Since the law of capital accumulation is as usual given by

$$\dot{K}=(\rho-\Omega)K, \quad \dot{K}\equiv\dot{X}^C+\pi\dot{X}^S+X^S\dot{\pi}, \tag{7.15}$$

the rate of growth of steel stocks will obey $\dot{X}^S=\pi^{-1}[(\rho-\Omega)K-\dot{X}^C-X^S\dot{\pi}]$ $=(X^S/\pi)\{[\pi q^{S\prime}(x)-(\Omega+\delta)](x+\pi)-x\hat{X}^C-\phi(\pi,x)\}$, where I have used (7.13) and temporary-equilibrium profit-rate uniformity $\rho=\rho^C$ in (7.10). Combining the expression for $\dot{X}^S$ with that for $\dot{X}^C$ discussed earlier, I finally obtain

$$\begin{aligned}\dot{x}\equiv x(\hat{X}^C-\hat{X}^S)=-x\{[\pi q^{S\prime}(x)-(\gamma q^C/x^C)-\Omega][(x/\pi)+1]\\ -\phi(\pi,x)/\pi\}\equiv\psi(\pi,x,x^C)\\ \psi_1=-(x/\pi)^2\phi_1<0, \quad \psi_2=0, \quad \psi_3=-(\delta+n)x(\pi^{-1}x+1)/x^C<0,\end{aligned} \tag{7.16}$$

as the law of motion of the system's capital composition (near a steady state).

[(7.13), (7.14), (7.16)] constitutes a three-dimensional differential equation system with Jacobian matrix

$$J \equiv \begin{bmatrix} \phi_1 & \phi_2 & 0 \\ \psi_1 & 0 & \psi_3 \\ 0 & 0 & \xi' \end{bmatrix} \tag{7.17}$$

and roots

$$\begin{aligned} \eta_1 &= \tfrac{1}{2}[\phi_1 + (\phi_1^2 + 4\psi_1\phi_2)^{\frac{1}{2}}] > 0 \\ \eta_2 &= \tfrac{1}{2}[\phi_1 - (\phi_1^2 + 4\psi_1\phi_2)^{\frac{1}{2}}] < 0 \\ \eta_3 &= -(\delta + n) < 0. \end{aligned} \tag{7.18}$$

The system's saddle-path motions are given by[8]

$$\begin{aligned} \pi(t) - \bar{\pi} &= A_2 y_{21} \exp(\eta_2 t) + A_3 y_{31} \exp(\eta_3 t) \\ x(t) - \bar{x} &= A_2 \exp(\eta_2 t) + A_3 \exp(\eta_3 t) \\ x^C(t) - \bar{x}^C &= A_3 y_{33} \exp(\eta_3 t), \end{aligned} \tag{7.19}$$

where the y_{hj} are elements of the eigenvector $y_h \equiv [y_{h1}\ 1\ y_{h3}]'$ associated with the root $\eta_h (h=2,3)$; overbars denote the system's steady-state values; and the A_h are constants determined by initial conditions.[9] Differentiating (7.19) with respect to time and writing the $A_h \exp(\eta_h t)$ in terms of y_{hj} and alternative pairs of the differences $\pi(t) - \bar{\pi}$, $x(t) - \bar{x}$, $x^C(t) - \bar{x}^C$, I obtain the system's stable motions in the three state-variable planes (π, x), (π, x^C), and (x, x^C). In the (π, x)-plane, these motions are given by

$$\begin{aligned} \dot{\pi} &= [(\eta_2 y_{21} - \eta_3 y_{31})(\pi - \bar{\pi}) + y_{21} y_{31}(\eta_3 - \eta_2)(x - \bar{x})]/(y_{21} - y_{31}) \\ &\equiv \phi^*(\pi, x), \qquad \phi_1^* = \phi_1 > 0, \qquad \phi_2^* = \phi_2 < 0 \\ \dot{x} &= [(\eta_2 - \eta_3)(\pi - \bar{\pi}) + (\eta_3 y_{21} - \eta_2 y_{31})(x - \bar{x})]/(y_{21} - y_{31}) \\ &\equiv \psi^*(\pi, x), \qquad \psi_1^* = -(\phi_1 - \eta_2)(\phi_1 - \eta_3)/\phi_2 > 0 \\ &\qquad\qquad\qquad\; \psi_2^* = (\eta_3 + \eta_2) - \phi_1 < 0, \end{aligned} \tag{7.20}$$

as illustrated by figure 7.1a.[10] The motions in the other two planes are similarly derived (see the appendix) and illustrated by figures 7.1b and 7.1c.

[8] Observe that either δ or n must be nonzero, otherwise $\eta_3 = 0$ and the system exhibits hysteresis (dependence on initial conditions). Recall footnote 4.

[9] The y_{hj} are derived in the appendix to this chapter.

[10] In addition to the usual dynamic loci $\dot{\pi} = 0, \dot{x} = 0$, figure 7.1a also depicts the (π, x)-plane projection of the two eigenvectors y_2, y_3 associated with the roots η_2, η_3. These projections have slope $y_{h1}/y_{h2} = y_{h1} = -\phi_2/(\phi_1 - \eta_h)$ $(h=2,3)$, that of the dominant eigenvector being larger (thus, figure 7.1a assumes $\eta_3 > \eta_2$). The appendix proves that the relative steepness of the dynamic loci and the y_h-curves is as indicated.

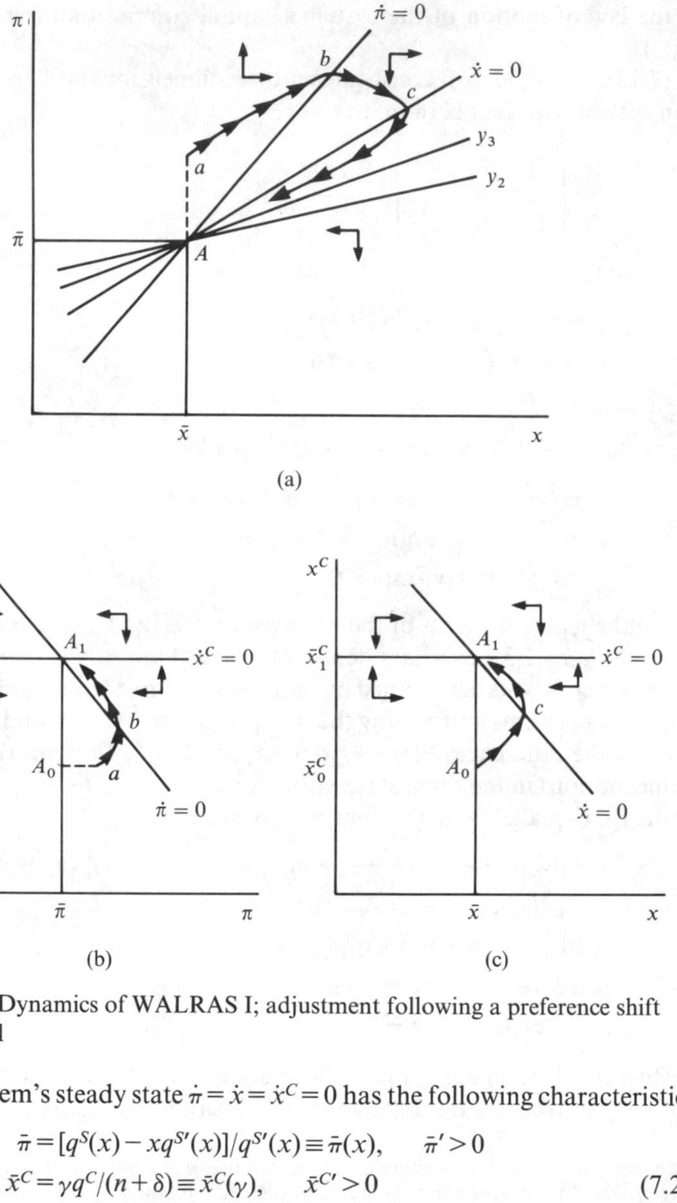

Figure 7.1 Dynamics of WALRAS I; adjustment following a preference shift toward steel

The system's steady state $\dot{\pi}=\dot{x}=\dot{x}^C=0$ has the following characteristics:

$$\begin{aligned}
&\bar{\pi}=[q^S(x)-xq^{S\prime}(x)]/q^{S\prime}(x)\equiv\bar{\pi}(x), \qquad \bar{\pi}'>0\\
&\bar{x}^C=\gamma q^C/(n+\delta)\equiv\bar{x}^C(\gamma), \qquad \bar{x}^{C\prime}>0 \qquad\qquad (7.21)\\
&q^S(x)-xq^{S\prime}(x)-\delta=\bar{\rho}=\Omega+n, \text{ or } \bar{x}=\bar{x}(\Omega+n), \qquad \bar{x}'>0.
\end{aligned}$$

According to (7.21), the model obeys a long-run Samuelson nonsubstitution theorem: $d\bar{p}/d\gamma=d\bar{\pi}/d\gamma=0$. To understand this, observe from the first equation that the function of the relative price $\bar{p}=\bar{\pi}$ is not to clear flow markets, but to equalize the own-rates-of-return $\bar{\rho}^i$ of the two physical capital stocks. Since from the third equation the own-rate-of-return on steel $\bar{\rho}^S \equiv q^S(x) - xq^{S\prime}(x) - \delta$ is fixed by the long-period profit rate $\bar{\rho} = \Omega + n$ – thus independent of the preference parameter γ – the nonsubstitution result ensues.

In the instance, a shift in consumption preferences does not affect the composition of the economy's physical capital stock either: $d\bar{x}/d\gamma = 0$. Instead, $d\gamma > 0$ leads to an equiproportionate increase in the ratio to exogenous efficiency labor of the two endogenous capital stocks ($\hat{\bar{x}}^C = \hat{\bar{x}}^S = \hat{\gamma} > 0$, where $x^S \equiv X^S/\tilde{T}$). From (7.3), (7.4), this supports an expansion of the steel relative to the corn industry sufficient to meet, at unaltered prices, the change in relative consumption demand.[11]

In the non-steady-state analysis to follow, I focus on the consequences of a preference shift toward steel that is unanticipated and permanent. Note first the diagrammatic representation of the steady-state effects of such a perturbation: The long-run equilibrium point remains unaltered at A in figure 7.1a and shifts up vertically from A_0 to A_1 in figures 7.1b and 7.1c. Since both x and x^C are non-jumping (thus, stationary at $\bar{x}$, $\bar{x}_0^C$ on impact), I can immediately infer the x, x^C trajectory in figure 7.1c. That trajectory implies $\dot{x} > 0$ on impact, which in turn means that in figure 7.1a the economy's position will be at some point vertically above A. Thus, the price of steel $\pi = p$ – and the uniform profit rate $\rho = \rho^C(\pi, x)$ – must jump on impact. To determine the magnitude of this jump in π – that is, to ascertain which among the candidate paths in the (π, x)-plane actually represents the system's stable manifold – I set $t = 0$ in (7.19) to obtain

$$\pi(0) - \bar{\pi} = \frac{y_{31} - y_{21}}{y_{33}}(\bar{x}_0^C - \bar{x}_1^C) > 0, \qquad \frac{y_{31} - y_{21}}{y_{33}} < 0, \tag{7.22}$$

which also determines the discrete impact movement from A_0 to a in figure 7.1b. The trajectories of the perfect-foresight system's three state variables π, x, x^C (and, by implication, the path of $x^S \equiv x^C/x$) are now straightforwardly determined and summarized in the time paths of figure 7.2.[12]

To understand the economics behind these time paths, it is helpful to turn to the case of static expectations by setting $\hat{\pi}^e \equiv 0$ in (7.11) and solving for $\pi = \pi(x)$, $\pi' > 0$. The adjustment story is now similar to that discussed in VON NEUMANN I and runs as follows. When, starting from a steady

11 By contrast, since they impinge on the steady-state profit rate – consequently, on the economy's long-run physical capital composition $\bar{x}$ – both a change in capitalist time preference and in the rate of efficiency-labor growth must alter steady-state relative prices: $d\bar{\pi}/d(\Omega + n) > 0$.

12 The appendix demonstrates that, as illustrated in the bottom diagram of figure 7.2, the perfect-foresight trajectory of x^S may either be monotonic or nonmonotonic ($\partial\dot{x}^S/\partial\gamma \gtrless 0$ on impact).

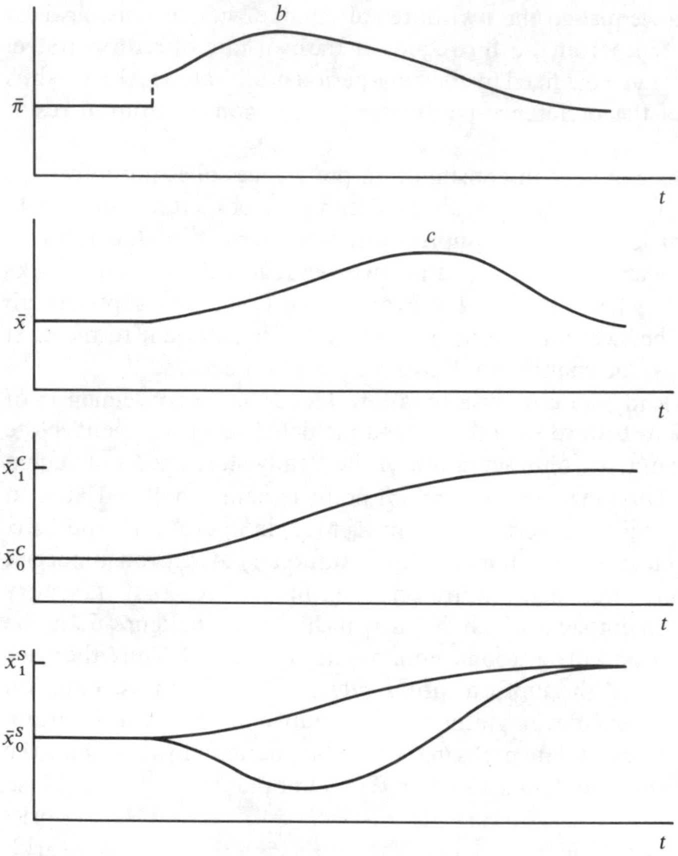

Figure 7.2 Time paths of WALRAS I following a preference shift toward steel

state, flow consumption demand for steel initially rises, the demand increase simply leads to a reduction in the rate of steel investment $\hat{X}^S$ below n.[13] The accompanying decline in corn consumption correspondingly allows $\hat{X}^C$ to rise above n. Though together this makes for $\dot{x} > 0$ on impact, stock levels – therefore, $x = \bar{x}$ and the physical productivities of corn and steel – are as yet unchanged. Since, consequently, neither stock supplies of nor stock demands for the X^i are altered, the price $\pi = p$ of steel must remain unchanged on impact.

From what has been said, x rises above $\bar{x}$ immediately following the

[13] Therefore, under static expectations $\dot{x}^S < 0$ necessarily on impact. As in VON NEUMANN I, I assume that stocks of corn and steel can be consumed. Thus, the account goes through when $n = 0$ or, more generally, when the demand shift is large relative to nX^i, necessitating consumption out of stock on impact.

impact period. By lowering the marginal productivity of corn and by raising that of steel [(7.8), (7.9)], this creates an incipient yield differential in favor of steel. The stockmarket responds by pushing up the latter's equity price π; the flow price p follows suit via entrepreneurial profit maximization. Diagrammatically, the static-expectations economy starts to move up its temporary-equilibrium locus $\dot{\pi}=0$ in figure 7.1a. By raising the uniform profit rate, subsequent increases in the steel price progressively decelerate the growth of corn relative to steel stocks, bringing it to a halt and to a reversal when the maximum non-steady-state profit rate is reached; thereafter, the economy moves back to point A along the $\dot{\pi}=0$-schedule.[14]

The preceding conveys the essence of the adjustment process that characterizes WALRAS I. Evidently, though prices do move in the expected direction following a flow disturbance, they do so only temporarily, with a lag, and for reasons quite foreign to the standard Walrasian market-clearing argument. The flow price of a good changes because its equity price does. And equity prices move because of emergent yield differentials in the representative capitalist's portfolio and consequent incipient stockmarket disequilibria. Such yield differentials – the immediate cause of the flow-price movement – cannot be said to be proximately related to the initiating flow disturbance, as flow excess demands in the Walrasian account certainly can be. Instead, their impetus comes from movements in the system's capital composition and the changes in production techniques such movements evoke. At given expectations, a demand disturbance first acts on relative rates of accumulation and thence on capital composition – not on relative prices. Any observed instantaneous flow-price response, such as that found under perfect foresight, will be a reflection of asset-price movements that are currently stockmarket clearing, not flow-market clearing. It is only across steady states that flow markets can be said to clear in response to a flow disturbance. Moreover, they will do so via adjustments in quantities alone: As implied by the Samuelson nonsubstitution theorem, in the long run relative prices must return to their initial value.

[14] Note $d\rho(x)/dx = d[\pi(x)q^{s\prime}(x) - \delta]/dx = -xq^{s\prime\prime} > 0$ under static expectations. The stability of the static-expectations process in x, x^c is easily shown from a phase space that has the same properties as figure 7.1c. It is evident why, in contrast to x^c, the static-expectations behavior of x^s must be nonmonotonic. On impact, $\dot{x}^s$ is exclusively affected by the demand shift toward steel: it drops discretely from zero to $\dot{x}^s < 0$. However, under the influence of a rising profit rate – which lifts $\dot{x}^s$, but not $\dot{x}^c$ [(7.14)] – in time it will switch sign: The economy must accelerate the accumulation of steel, relative to both labor and corn, so as to assure the proportional steady-state increase $\hat{\bar{x}}^s = \hat{\bar{x}}^c = \hat{y} > 0$ noted earlier. The replacement of static expectations by a perfect-foresight assumption adds little to the account just given. $\pi = p$ and the uniform profit rate now do jump on impact of the demand increase, since at that moment speculators correctly foresee a period of increasing steel prices, thus of continued capital gains on equity in steel (see path a–b). This may allow $\dot{x}^s > 0$ on impact already, though $\hat{x}^c > \hat{x}^s > 0$ necessarily.

7.3 WALRAS II: Multiple basics, primary labor, and land

How does an economy with multiple nonproduced inputs – say, neoclassical labor and land – differ from the single-primary-input system just discussed?

I first note that an economy with multiple long-run scarcities possesses a long-run equilibrium only if the exogenous (natural-plus-efficiency) growth rates of its primary inputs coincide – for instance, at zero. Second, the single-primary-input assumption of the nonsubstitution theorem is violated and an intratemporal preference shift now must alter long-run relative prices and the corresponding profit rate.

For instance, in a model in which a fixed amount of labor $\bar{T}_1$ plus variable quantities of corn X^C produce steel, while similarly fixed land $\bar{T}_2$ plus steel X^S produce corn,

$$Q^S = Q^S(X^C, \bar{T}_1) \equiv q^S(x^C)\bar{T}_1, \quad x^C \equiv X^C/\bar{T}_1 \tag{7.23}$$

$$\begin{gathered} Q^C = Q^C(X^S, \bar{T}_2) \equiv q^C(x^S)\bar{T}_2, \quad x^S \equiv X^S/\bar{T}_2, \\ q^{j\prime} > 0, \quad q^{j\prime\prime} < 0, \quad j = C, S, \end{gathered} \tag{7.24}$$

a preference shift toward steel must raise steel's stationary-state unit cost and flow price. Though Walrasian in appearance, this result is produced by a sequence of stockmarket equilibria alone, not by any temporary-equilibrium flow-market clearing.

To see how this works, assume static expectations for simplicity and note that, on impact, the demand shift will leave relative prices completely unperturbed, being satisfied at prevailing values out of inventory. In the next period, stocks of steel will be lower and stocks of corn higher, which must drive down the rental r^{T_2} of inflexibly supplied land and raise the wage r^{T_1} of scarce labor, since

$$r^{T_1} = p[q^S(x^C) - x^C q^{S\prime}(x^C)] \equiv r^{T_1}(p, x^C), \quad r_i^{T_1} > 0 \ (i = 1,2) \tag{7.25}$$

$$r^{T_2} = q^C(x^S) - x^S q^{C\prime}(x^S) \equiv r^{T_2}(x^S), \quad r^{T_2\prime} > 0, \tag{7.26}$$

by entrepreneurial profit maximization.

Next, assume that wages accrue to a class of nonsaving workers and land rents to a class of nonsaving landlords who, *à la* Ricardo, view their landed capital as a nonalienable source of rents exclusively.[15] A third class, made up of capitalists, saves and holds a portfolio of claims to the system's two produced capital goods X^C, X^S. It is clear that

$$\rho^C = \pi q^{S\prime}(x^C) - \delta = [q^{C\prime}(x^S)/\pi] - \delta + \hat{\pi}^e = \rho^S, \ \pi \equiv \frac{p^S}{p^C} = p^S = p, \ \hat{\pi}^e \equiv 0, \tag{7.27}$$

[15] These simplifying assumptions about the behavior of primary-resource owners are not essential to the argument.

will be the economy's arbitrage equation, where $\pi q^{S\prime}(x^C)=r^C$ is the rental on corn, $q^{C\prime}(x^S)=r^S$ the rental on steel, and other symbols have the usual interpretation. Evidently, the process of price determination remains exactly as in WALRAS I: At given primary and produced resource stocks (thus, x^i), expectations ($\hat{\pi}^e$, identically zero by assumption), and technologies, the relative equity price π of steel – therefore steel's flow price p – is uniquely determined via the requirement for stockmarket equilibrium. By lowering x^S (increasing $q^{C\prime}$) and by raising x^C (reducing $q^{S\prime}$), the demand shift under consideration creates, in the first post-impact period, an incipient yield differential in favor of steel. This gives rise to short-selling of corn equity that pushes up π, which in turn enables steel entrepreneurs to supply new steel output at a higher price $p=\pi$. The story so far runs exactly as in WALRAS I. Consider now some differences.

In a stationary state,[16] it must be true that $\bar{\rho}=\Omega$, so that (7.27) becomes

$$\Omega=\pi q^{S\prime}(x^C)-\delta=[q^{C\prime}(x^S)/\pi]-\delta, \tag{7.28}$$

a system of two equations in the three unknowns $\bar{\pi}$, $\bar{x}^C$, $\bar{x}^S$. It may be solved in terms of $\bar{x}^S$, Ω, and technology. Disregarding the latter two arguments, this yields

$$\bar{\pi}=\bar{\pi}(\bar{x}^S), \qquad \bar{\pi}'<0 \tag{7.29}$$

$$\bar{x}^C=\bar{x}^C(\bar{x}^S), \qquad \bar{x}^{C\prime}<0. \tag{7.30}$$

A *ceteris-paribus* increase in $\bar{x}^S$, by lowering the physical marginal product of steel $q^{C\prime}$, tends to reduce its stationary-state rental and yield. However, since the latter cannot fall below the economy's uniform profit rate Ω, the stock price of steel must decline proportionately, stabilizing $\bar{\rho}^S$ at Ω ($\bar{\pi}'<0$). The flow price of steel $\bar{p}$ falls *pari passu*, which tends to depress the value of the marginal product of corn. In order to avert a resultant drop in the long-run yield of corn below Ω, $\bar{x}^C$ will decline sufficiently to raise $q^{S\prime}$ by a percentage equal to the fall in $\bar{p}=\bar{\pi}$. I conclude that, at a constant rate of time preference, a rise in $\bar{x}^S$ is associated with an opposite movement in $\bar{x}^C$ and a fall in $\bar{\pi}=\bar{p}$. It remains to explain what determines $\bar{x}^S$.

To that effect, consider the long-run flow-equilibrium condition for corn $Q^C-\delta X^C-(1-\gamma)r^{T_1}\bar{T}_1\equiv Z^C(\cdot)=\dot{X}^C=0$, where as in WALRAS I, I for simplicity assume that only workers consume corn. From (7.24), (7.25), (7.27) I may write $Z^C(\cdot)=0$ explicitly as

$$\begin{aligned} &Z^C(\bar{\pi},\bar{x}^C,\bar{x}^S,\gamma)\equiv q^C(\bar{x}^S)\bar{T}_2-[\delta\bar{x}^C+(1-\gamma)r^{T_1}(\bar{\pi},\bar{x}^C)]\bar{T}_1=0 \\ &\quad Z_i^C<0\ (i=1,2),\ >0\ (i=3,4). \end{aligned} \tag{7.31}$$

16 The appendix demonstrates the local dynamic stability of the static-expectations system.

Substituting for $\bar{\pi}$ and $\bar{x}^C$ from (7.29), (7.30), I successively obtain

$$Z^C[\bar{\pi}(\bar{x}^S), \bar{x}^C(\bar{x}^S), \bar{x}^S, \gamma] \equiv \bar{Z}^C(\bar{x}^S, \gamma) = 0 \qquad \bar{Z}_i^C > 0 \ (i = 1,2) \tag{7.32}$$

$$\bar{x}^S = \bar{x}^S(\gamma), \qquad \bar{x}^{S\prime} < 0. \tag{7.33}$$

That is, a shift in demand away from corn ($d\gamma > 0$) will, across stationary states, be accommodated by a contraction in steel capital that lowers supply of corn and raises $\bar{\pi}$, $\bar{x}^C$ – thus, demand for corn at the lower $(1-\gamma)$ – sufficiently to ensure $Z^C(\cdot) = \dot{X}^C = 0$. Substituting (7.33) in (7.29) yields

$$\bar{\pi} = \bar{\pi}[\bar{x}^S(\gamma)] \equiv \bar{\bar{\pi}}(\gamma), \qquad \bar{\bar{\pi}}' > 0, \tag{7.34}$$

so that a shift in demand preferences toward steel, by moving the economy's capital composition $\bar{x} \equiv \bar{X}^C/\bar{X}^S$ away from steel ($\bar{x}^{S\prime} < 0$) toward corn ($d\bar{x}^C/d\gamma > 0$),[17] tends to create a stationary-state yield differential in favor of steel and a corresponding stock excess demand for and rise in the long-run equity price of steel. It is the rise in steel's equity price that allows entrepreneurs to permanently increase its flow supply price. This will just compensate them for the rise in long-run steel unit cost $\overline{UC}^S$,

$$d\overline{UC}^S/d\gamma = a_{T_1S}\, d\bar{r}^{T_1}/d\gamma > 0, \qquad \overline{UC}^S \equiv a_{T_1S}(\bar{x}^C)\bar{r}^{T_1} + a_{CS}(\bar{x}^C)\bar{r}^C, \tag{7.35}$$

they have suffered as a consequence of the higher stationary-state wage.[18]

At this point, the reader may be tempted to conclude that the preceding account fully agrees with the conventional Walrasian adjustment story. This is indeed the case – provided Walrasian equilibria are taken to refer to stationary states only.

To see this, consider the inverse of the function appearing in (7.29),

$$\bar{x}^S = \bar{x}^{S*}(\bar{\pi}), \qquad \bar{x}^{S*\prime} < 0, \tag{7.36}$$

and solve the first equation in (7.28) for $\bar{x}^C$ in terms of $\bar{\pi}$,

$$\bar{x}^C = \bar{x}^{C*}(\bar{\pi}), \qquad \bar{x}^{C*\prime} > 0. \tag{7.37}$$

Using $\bar{\pi} = \bar{p}$ and substituting (7.36), (7.37) in the flow-market-clearing condition (7.31), I obtain

$$Z^C[\bar{p}, \bar{x}^{C*}(\bar{p}), \bar{x}^{S*}(\bar{p}), \gamma] \equiv \bar{Z}^{C*}(\bar{p}, \gamma) = 0, \qquad \bar{Z}_1^{C*} < 0, \quad \bar{Z}_2^{C*} \equiv Z_4^C > 0, \tag{7.38}$$

[17] Recall that these are the directions in which the two capital stocks move on impact ($\dot{x}^S < 0$, $\dot{x}^C > 0$). Thus, unlike in WALRAS I, both of the system's state variables x^C, x^S will approach the new stationary state monotonically.

[18] $d\bar{r}^{T_1}/d\gamma = r_1^{T_1}\bar{\bar{\pi}}' + r_2^{T_1}(d\bar{x}^C/d\gamma) > 0$. Recall from (7.28) that $\bar{r}^C$ is invariant (tied down by $\Omega + \delta$) and that, at a point of cost minimization, $r^{T_1}da_{T_1S} + r^C da_{CS} = 0$, where a_{T_1S} and a_{CS} are the labor and corn input–output coefficients in steel.

a standard zero-flow-excess-supply condition that yields

$$\bar{p}=\bar{p}^*(\gamma), \qquad \bar{p}^{*\prime}>0. \tag{7.39}$$

To wit, at a given rate of time preference, the long-run supply curve of corn in the market for corn output is upward sloping because of increasing marginal costs imposed by scarce land. The corresponding demand schedule for corn is well behaved, too, and unambiguously downward sloping.[19] Should it shift leftward $[d(1-\gamma)<0]$, a flow excess supply of corn at the initial stationary-state corn flow price $1/\bar{p}_0$ must emerge. The Walrasian auctioneer now enters the picture and engages households and firms in a tatonnement process that, *across stationary states*, lowers that price to the market-clearing level $1/\bar{p}_1<1/\bar{p}_0$.

[19] My class-specific consumption assumptions preclude perverse distribution effects.

8

WALRAS AND EXCHANGE: Nonbasics-only economies with multiple primary resources

8.1 Introduction

I finally turn to an issue I have repeatedly alluded to but not addressed so far: The manner in which capital theory suggests one ought to think about the intersectoral transfer of existing resources. By condoning the postulate of "perfect factor mobility," current general-equilibrium literature simply assumes the problem away.[1]

From the laws of physics, intersectoral movements of existing resource stocks cannot help but be time-and-energy-consuming material processes. Thus, they are undoubtedly costly from an economic point of view – frequently more so than the creation of new resources. Both the movement of existing and the creation of new resources involve an investment decision, and both require a prior act of saving. Analytically, the error of assuming instantaneous resource mobility amounts to a conflation of steady-state analysis (in which time- and location-indexed stocks appear as variables) with the study of temporary equilibria (in which such stocks are predetermined).

That the assumption of perfect factor mobility is tolerated appears to be due to three beliefs, two of which are erroneous: (a) the process of intersectoral resource reallocation must play a central role in the theory of price (true); (b) the process operates via the intersectoral transfer of a fixed stock of resources (false); (c) a general-equilibrium representation of costly resource transfers is both intractable and unimportant (false). To a reader of the earlier chapters, the erroneousness of (b) need hardly be argued: Resource reallocation can be conceptualized as a rearrangement over time in the composition of the economy's growing stock of reproducible capital.

[1] This is not true of the Arrow–Debreu model, which indexes commodities by location; see, by contrast, the general-equilibrium literature in the theory of international trade [Jones (1965, 1971), Ruffin (1984), Smith (1984)]. Existing attempts at modeling resource movements as an investment decision, such as Mussa (1978), are marred by exogeneity assumptions on the interest rate and relative prices.

In other words, an economy intersectorally moves its produced inputs mainly through a rechanneling of its gross investment flows. The transfer across sectors of existing stocks of produced inputs is empirically insignificant, a fact easily explained by high moving relative to reproduction costs. Undeniably this contrasts with intersectoral movements of stocks of *nonproduced* inputs, such as neoclassical labor, which *are* important. Again, however, such movements will be costly and subject to an investment decision on the part of the agents involved.

In section 8.2, I accordingly develop a model (WALRAS III) containing primary inputs that are intersectorally movable over time via an investment process. As always, I use the quasi-Hamiltonian system [(0.1), (0.2)]. My goal is to convince the reader that, as against belief (c), a general-equilibrium analysis of such resource transfers is both feasible and important. The key insight afforded by such an analysis is that reallocations of primary labor involve adjustment costs and that these adjustment costs temporarily force the economy to consume inside its static production-possibility frontier. In other words, the future fruits of an improved labor allocation are always bought at the cost of a cut in current consumption, the question being – exactly as in the theory of growth – how to balance future benefits and current costs. (As will be seen, costs are higher the faster the pace of economic restructuring.) WALRAS III shows how a decentralized economy solves this problem.

WALRAS III also reveals the polar nature of two seemingly unrelated assumptions: That of perfect factor mobility and that of pure exchange. For it yields, first, a capital-theoretic interpretation of perfect factor mobility as a limiting instance of movability. Second, by considering the polar opposite, namely complete immovability of primary inputs, one is led directly to the Walrasian model of pure exchange.

The latter, entitled WALRAS IV, is laid out in the final section of this concluding chapter. As promised in chapter 1, it structurally stands in symmetry to VON NEUMANN I. The Walrasian model of pure exchange, therefore, provides a natural closing argument to my claim that a quasi-Hamiltonian dynamics in π and x represents the unifying core of classical and neoclassical value theory.

8.2 WALRAS III: Movable primary inputs

Consider a two-sector economy in which a fixed stock of a nonproduced resource $\bar{T}$ (labor) produces two nonbasics, consumption services (S) and nonstorable corn (C). Furthermore, whenever the long-run equilibrium of this economy is perturbed, some of the $\bar{T}$-resource will be removed from C- or S-production, combined with another fixed resource $\bar{T}^M$ (land), and engaged in the costly process of raising $\dot{T}_C \equiv -\dot{T}_S$ from zero to some optimal nonzero value, where T_C and T_S are the momentarily predetermined labor allocations to the two sectors.[2]

The preceding amounts to the following possible scenarios. (i) We have on hand an economy of voluntary slavery in which ownership claims to both land and human capital are freely tradable. Unlike human capital – which is temporarily sector-specific and costly to move – ownership claims thereon are instantaneously and costlessly tradable via the stockmarket. (ii) By reasoning similar to that outlined in RAMSEY–SOLOW, the stockmarket economy can be shown to be strictly analogous to one with inalienable human capital, but a fully developed capital market and intertemporally consumption-optimizing households.[3]

The fact that resources are used to transfer resources expresses the costliness of the intersectoral moving process. It implies the presence of a resource-moving activity (M) employing labor and M-specific land to supply, for instance, relocation and retraining services.

Consider, then, an economy whose wealth is given by

$$K \equiv p_C^T T_C + p_S^T T_S + p^{T^M} \bar{T}^M, \tag{8.1}$$

where T_j is the stock of human capital momentarily located in sector j $(= C, S)$, $\bar{T}^M$ the fixed stock of M-specific land, and p_j^T, p^{T^M} the associated equity prices.[4] The numéraire is, as usual, corn output. Human capital is embodied in a fixed number

$$\bar{T} \equiv T_C + T_S \tag{8.2}$$

of behaviorally identical wealth-owning agents.[5]

The system produces, without a time lag, two nonbasics, nonstorable corn and consumption services,

[2] $\bar{T}^M$ may be thought of as scarce entrepreneurship similar to that giving rise to an independent investment function in VON NEUMANN III. For brevity, $\bar{T}^M$ will be referred to below as land.

[3] The reader will recall that the analogy holds because the present model contains less than two (namely zero) produced capital goods.

[4] As in VON NEUMANN II, subscripts refer to sectors, superscripts to physical kinds.

[5] Regarding the interpretation of $\bar{T}$, note the following: (i) Human capital is intrinsically the same across the economy, but is valued differently depending on its momentary sectoral location. (ii) There is a one-to-one relation between a wealth-owning agent and the amount of human capital embodied in him (say, one unit of human capital per agent). Thus, $\bar{T}$, T_C, T_S also refer to the number of worker-owners in the economy as a whole, in sector C, and in sector S, respectively. If human capital is inalienable, no single representative wealth owner exists – there must at least be two, differentiated by momentary sectoral location. However, the assumption that all wealth owners possess identical behavioral parameters γ, Ω allows the inalienable-human-capital model to function as if it were a model of alienable human capital with a single representative capitalist agent. For economy, my exposition will be in terms of the latter.

$$Q^C = q^C T'_C, \qquad q^C > 0 \tag{8.3}$$

$$Q^S = q^S T'_S, \qquad q^S > 0, \tag{8.4}$$

where the Q^j are flow outputs $(j = C, S)$ and the q^j fixed productivities. $T'_j \leq T_j$ denotes the level of employment of T_j in the production of Q^j. When $T'_j < T_j$ obtains, $T_j - T'_j > 0$ resources momentarily specific to sector j are employed in the moving industry.

Given (8.3) and (8.4), profit-seeking entrepreneurs see to it that rental (wage) rates r_j in the two sectors are competitively driven to

$$r_C = q^C \tag{8.5}$$

$$r_S = pq^S, \tag{8.6}$$

where p is the price of consumption services. Given resource immobility, no tendency exists at a point in time for r_C and r_S to equalize.

Though *immobile*, human capital is intersectorally *movable*. It is so over time and at a cost – that is, subject to an investment decision. Instead of equality between sectoral rental rates as in the standard account, this entails an instantaneous competitive relationship between the equity price of labor currently in the service sector, the equity price of labor currently in the corn sector, and the price (or cost) of moving labor between the two sectors,

$$p^M = |p_S^T - p_C^T| \equiv p_C^T|\pi - 1| = \begin{cases} p_C^T(1-\pi) > 0 \text{ in ALPHA } (\pi < 1) \\ p_C^T(\pi - 1) > 0 \text{ in BETA } \quad (\pi > 1) \\ p_C^T(\pi - 1) = 0 \text{ in ZETA } \quad (\pi = 1) \end{cases}$$

$$p_j^T > 0, \qquad p^M \geq 0, \qquad \pi \equiv p_S^T / p_C^T > 0, \tag{8.7}$$

where p^M is the supply price and unit cost of the moving services required to transfer one unit of human capital between the two sectors.[6] (8.7) is analogous to my usual flow-equals-equity-price condition.[7] It precludes situations in which $|p_S^T - p_C^T| > p^M$, that is, in which – say, because $p_S^T - p_C^T > p^M$ – entrepreneurs could reap pure profits by buying an ownership claim to T_C at price p_C^T, incurring the cost p^M of moving the underlying real capital good to the S-sector, and selling what has now become a claim on T_S at the asset demand price $p_S^T > p^M + p_C^T$. The corresponding pure per-unit profit $p_S^T - (p^M + p_C^T) > 0$ would be competed away instantaneously by a jump in the supply of moving services (thus, in p^M).[8] Under regime ALPHA or BETA, the M-industry is operating and just covers costs; as we shall see, at any $\pi \gtrless 1$ its supply of moving services is uniquely determined and fixes

[6] The asserted equality between supply price and unit cost, which is required [in addition to (8.7)] for zero entrepreneurial profits, is further discussed below [(8.10)].

[7] See, for instance, the first equality in (1.4) and (1.5).

[8] The M-production assumptions discussed below will preclude $p_M > |p_S^T - p_C^T|$.

the temporary-equilibrium amount of resource transfers $|\dot{T}_S|>0$ undertaken by the economy. Only in ZETA, which is the stationary-state regime, and in which its unit costs fall to zero, does the M-industry cease operation.

The production technology of the moving industry is given by a standard neoclassical production function

$$\begin{aligned}
&Q^M = Q^M(\bar{T}^M, T_{jM}) \equiv q^M(x_M)\bar{T}^M, \qquad x_M \equiv T_{jM}/\bar{T}^M \geq 0,\, j=C,S \\
&\quad q^M(0)=0,\, q^M(\infty)\to\infty,\, q^{M\prime}(\cdot)>0,\, q^{M\prime\prime}(\cdot)<0, \\
&\qquad q^{M\prime}(\infty)=0, \quad q^{M\prime}(0)\to\infty \\
&\lim_{x_M\to 0}[q^M(x_M)-x_M q^{M\prime}(x_M)] \equiv \lim_{x_M^{-1}\to\infty} \tilde{q}^{M\prime}(x_M^{-1})=0,
\end{aligned} \tag{8.8}$$

whose Inada properties ensure full employment of the specific input $\bar{T}^M$ whenever $Q^M>0$, where Q^M is output of moving services and T_{jM} human capital employed in their production.[9] T_{jM} equals one of the following:

$$\begin{aligned}
&T_{SM} = T_S - T'_S > 0 \text{ in ONE } \quad (r_C > r_S) \\
&T_{CM} = T_C - T'_C > 0 \text{ in TWO } \quad (r_C < r_S) \\
&T_{CM} = T_{SM} = 0 \qquad \text{in ZETA } (r_C = r_S).
\end{aligned} \tag{8.9}$$

Competitive behavior among M-entrepreneurs guarantees that p^M just covers unit costs (the $a_{i,j}(\cdot)$ are input–output coefficients, r^{T^M} the land rental),

$$p^M = \min_{j=C,S}\{a_{T^M,M}(x_M)r^{T^M} + a_{T_{jM},M}(x_M)r_j\}. \tag{8.10}$$

According to (8.9) and (8.10), the moving industry chooses the sectoral source of its human-capital input so as to minimize cost; for example, if $r_C<r_S$ (which defines regime TWO), it will supply its retraining and relocation services by hiring staff from the corn industry. Given that choice, a cost-minimizing land–labor combination entails

$$x_M = x_M(\omega), \qquad x'_M > 0, \qquad \omega \equiv r^{T^M}/r_j. \tag{8.11}$$

Denoting prices measured in terms of M-output by a tilde, one finds

$$\begin{aligned}
&\tilde{p} = (1/q^j)\tilde{r}_j \\
&1 = a_{T^M,M}(\omega)\tilde{r}^{T^M} + a_{T_{jM},M}(\omega)\tilde{r}_j \\
&\qquad j = \begin{cases} S \text{ in ONE } (\tilde{p} \equiv p/p^M) \\ C \text{ in TWO } (\tilde{p} \equiv 1/p^M), \end{cases}
\end{aligned} \tag{8.12}$$

to be the pair of price equations dual to the pair of quantity equations [(8.4), (8.8)] and [(8.3), (8.8)], respectively. The Stolper–Samuelson property,

[9] $q^{M\prime}$ and $q^M - x_M q^{M\prime}$ represent the marginal products of labor and of land, respectively; note that $\tilde{q}^M(x_M^{-1}) = Q^M/T_{jM}$.

$$\omega = \omega(\tilde{p}), \qquad \omega' < 0, \tag{8.13}$$

then follows from division of the first by the second equality in (8.12) and the envelope property that, at a cost minimum, $\tilde{r}^{TM} da_{TM,M} + \tilde{r}_j da_{T_{jM},M} = 0$. (8.12) and (8.13) may now be used in the profit-maximizing condition that the rental $\tilde{r}^{TM}$ of land equal its physical marginal product $q^M - x_M q^{M\prime}$; this yields

$$\begin{aligned} \tilde{r}^{TM} &= q^M\{x_M[\omega(\tilde{p})]\} - x_M(\cdot)q^{M\prime}(\cdot) \equiv \tilde{r}^{TM}(\tilde{p}) \geq 0 \\ \tilde{r}^{TM\prime} &= -\frac{\tilde{r}^{TM}}{\tilde{p}}\frac{1-\theta_{TM}}{\theta_{TM}} \leq 0, \qquad \theta_{TM} \equiv \frac{\tilde{r}^{TM}\bar{T}^M}{Q^M} \leq 1 \\ r^{TM}(p^M, p) &\equiv p^M \tilde{r}^{TM}(\tilde{p}), \qquad r_1^{TM} \geq 0 \text{ in ONE, TWO} \\ & \qquad\qquad r_2^{TM} \leq 0 \text{ in ONE, } = 0 \text{ in TWO,} \end{aligned} \tag{8.14}$$

where the weak inequalities turn into equalities at the stationary state (since, from (8.8) and ZETA in (8.9), the marginal product of land and the wage share $1-\theta_{TM}$ in the moving industry must be zero at that point; note that the property $\tilde{r}^{TM} = 0 = \tilde{r}^{TM\prime}$ carries over to the rental r^{TM} measured in corn, and its partial derivatives). As we will see, this means that, for local perturbations around a long-run equilibrium, the role of land in the system's dynamics may be neglected.

I next consider the determinants of the instantaneous allocation of human capital between the C- or S-sector and the moving industry. For this purpose, it is useful to develop a relationship $\omega^*(\pi)$ between the rental–wage ratio ω and the relative equity price π of the two types of human capital. It comes from combining the inverse of (8.13), $\tilde{p} = \tilde{p}(\omega)$, with the expression for p^M in terms of π in (8.7). The latter gives the function $1/\tilde{p} = \frac{1}{\tilde{p}}(\pi)$ (near a stationary state with $\pi = 1$), so that

$$\frac{1}{\tilde{p}(\omega)} = \frac{1}{\tilde{p}}(\pi), \text{ thus } \omega = \omega^*(\pi), \ \omega^{*\prime} \begin{cases} <0 \text{ in ALPHA} \\ >0 \text{ in BETA, ZETA,} \end{cases} \tag{8.15}$$

where the sign of $\omega^{*\prime}$ follows from (8.7) and $\tilde{p}'(\omega) < 0$ [(8.13)]. I next define the allocation variable $\lambda_j \equiv T_j'/T_j$ – which denotes the fraction of j-sector human capital *not* working in the moving industry – and relate it to the function $\omega^*(\pi)$ just discussed. Observe that $x_M \equiv T_{jM}/\bar{T}^M \equiv (T_j/\bar{T}^M) - (T_j'/\bar{T}^M) \equiv (T_j/\bar{T}^M)(1-\lambda_j)$, so that

$$\begin{aligned} \text{ALPHA/ONE: } & \lambda_S(\pi, x) \equiv 1 - (1+x)x_M[\omega^*(\pi)] < 1, \ \lambda_C = 1 \\ & \lambda_{S1} = -(1+x)x_M'\omega^{*\prime} > 0, \ \lambda_{S2} = -x_M = 0 \\ \text{BETA/TWO: } & \lambda_C(\pi, x) \equiv 1 - (1+x^{-1})x_M[\omega^*(\pi)] < 1, \ \lambda_S = 1 \\ & \lambda_{C1} = -(1+x^{-1})x_M'\omega^{*\prime} < 0, \ \lambda_{C2} = \frac{x_M}{x^2} = 0 \end{aligned} \tag{8.16}$$

$$\text{ZETA: } \lambda_S = \lambda_C = 1$$
$$0 < \lambda_j \equiv T'_j/T_j \leq 1, \; x \equiv T_C/T_S, \; \bar{T}/\bar{T}^M = 1,$$

where partial derivatives have been evaluated at a stationary state and where I set $\bar{T} = \bar{T}^M$ without loss of generality. As shown in (8.16), I henceforth limit my non-stationary-state analysis to two combinations of equity price and wage regimes: ALPHA-*cum*-ONE and BETA-*cum*-TWO. My justification is (apart from limitations of space) that, near a stationary state, these are the only combinations possible, since there expected capital gains approach zero, so that expected-yield equality requires the relative equity price π to mirror the relative rental r_S/r_C. The intuition behind (8.16) is simple: For instance, in ALPHA ($\pi < 1$)/ONE ($r_C > r_S$), a diminution in the excess $p_C^T - p_S^T > 0$ of the equity price of human capital in the C-sector over that of labor in the S-sector reduces the moving industry's production incentive $p^M = p_C^T(1-\pi) > 0$, thus its employment $T_{SM} \equiv T_S(1-\lambda_S)$ of low-wage S-workers out of the predetermined pool T_S.[10]

I now turn to the economy's market-clearing conditions. As usual, holders of ownership claims to the capital stocks T_C, T_S, $\bar{T}^M$ will insist on equal expected yields,

$$\rho_C^T \equiv \frac{r_C}{p_C^T} + (\hat{p}_C^T)^e = \frac{r_S}{p_S^T} + (\hat{p}_S^T)^e \equiv \rho_S^T, \qquad \rho_C^T = \frac{r^{TM}}{p^{TM}} + (\hat{p}^{TM})^e \equiv \rho^{TM}, \qquad (8.17)$$

where the ρ_j^T, ρ^{TM} are instantaneous expected yields, the r_j/p_j^T, r^{TM}/p^{TM} current yields, and the $(\hat{p}_j^T)^e$, $(\hat{p}^{TM})^e$ expected capital gains. Substituting for r_j from (8.5), (8.6) and introducing the additional relative equity price π^M, I may rewrite (8.17) as

$$\chi(\pi, p_C^T, p; \hat{\pi}^e) \equiv (1/p_C^T)\left(q^C - \frac{pq^S}{\pi}\right) - \hat{\pi}^e = 0$$
$$\chi^M[\pi, \pi^M, p_C^T, p; (\dot{\pi}^M)^e] \equiv (1/p_C^T)\{q^C\pi^M - r^{TM}[p^M(\pi), p]\} - (\dot{\pi}^M)^e = 0$$
$$\chi_h > 0 (h=1), < 0 (h=3,4), = 0 (h=2)$$
$$\chi_h^M > 0 (h=2), < 0 (h=5), = 0 (h=1,3,4); \; \pi^M \equiv p^{TM}/p_C^T, \qquad (8.18)$$

where $\partial r^{TM}/\partial\pi = 0 = \partial r^{TM}/\partial p$ at a stationary-state point.[11] (8.18) guarantees stockmarket equilibrium at zero entrepreneurial profits.

In addition to a stockmarket, the economy contains a capital market and

[10] Observe that it is only changes in π that lead to alterations in the T_{jm}; at given π and near a stationary state, variations in the economy's sectoral labor allocation $x \equiv T_C/T_S$ have no Rybczynski-type effect on M-employment ($\lambda_{j2} = 0$). Also, note for future reference that a technology shock in the M-industry (say, $d\mu > 0$) shifts the function $x_M[\omega^*(\pi), \mu]$, thus alters $\lambda_j(\pi, x, \mu)$ at given π.

[11] Recall from (8.7), (8.14) that $p^M = p^M(\pi)$, $r_h^{TM} = 0$ ($h = 1,2$) at such a point.

three flow markets for nonbasics: A market for corn, a market for consumption services, and a market for moving services. Given capital-market equilibrium (equality between demand for and supply of loanable funds, discussed below), it will by Walras's Law be sufficient for these three nonbasics markets to clear if two are in balance. It is useful – for the determination of temporary-equilibrium prices in fact necessary – to focus on the two consumption markets and to keep the market for the investment services of moving initially in the background.[12] Given my usual consumption demand functions $D^S \equiv \gamma \Omega K/p$ and $D^C \equiv (1-\gamma)\Omega K$ for services and for corn, I obtain $Z^S \equiv Q^S - \gamma \Omega K/p = 0$ and $Z^C \equiv Q^C - (1-\gamma)\Omega K = 0$ as two independent temporary-flow-equilibrium conditions; using (8.1), (8.3), (8.4), (8.16) and normalizing by T_S (thus, $z^j \equiv Z^j/T_S$), this gives

$$
\begin{aligned}
&z^S(\pi, \pi^M, p_C^T, p; x, \gamma) \equiv q^S \lambda_S - \gamma \Omega[x + \pi + \pi^M(1+x)]p_C^T/p = 0 \\
&\left.\begin{aligned}&\text{ALPHA/ONE } (0 < \lambda_S(\pi) < 1): z_1^S \gtrless 0 \\ &\text{BETA/TWO, ZETA } (\lambda_S = 1): z_1^S < 0\end{aligned}\right\} z_h^S < 0 (h = 2,3,5,6),\ z_4^S > 0 \\
&z^C(\pi, \pi^M, p_C^T; x, \gamma) \equiv q^C x \lambda_C - (1-\gamma)\Omega[x + \pi + \pi^M(1+x)]p_C^T = 0 \\
&\text{ALPHA/ONE}(\lambda_C = 1), \text{ BETA/TWO}(0 < \lambda_C(\pi) < 1): \\
&\qquad z_h^C < 0 (h = 1-3),\ > 0 (h = 4,5),
\end{aligned} \tag{8.19}
$$

where, as earlier, all partial derivatives have been evaluated at a stationary state.[13]

Observe that the temporary-equilibrium price system is now closed: (8.18), (8.19) are four equations that, whatever the regime, are sufficient to determine the four temporary-equilibrium prices π, π^M, p_C^T, p (thus, p^M and rentals), given expectations $\hat{\pi}^e \equiv \dot{\pi}^e/\pi, (\dot{\pi}^M)^e$, the predetermined state variable x, and parameters. It is useful to solve $z^C(\cdot) = 0$ in (8.19) for $p_C^T(\pi, \pi^M \ldots)$ and, given the latter solution, $z^S(\cdot) = 0$ for $p(\pi, \pi^M \ldots)$; this yields

$$p_C^T = p_C^T(\pi, \pi^M; x, \gamma),\ p_{Ch}^T < 0 (h = 1,2),\ > 0 (h = 3,4) \tag{8.20}$$

$$p = p(\pi; x, \gamma),\ p_1 < 0,\ p_h > 0 (h = 2,3), \tag{8.21}$$

under either ALPHA/ONE or BETA/TWO.[14]

12 The reason is simple. Walras's Law implies $Z^C + pZ^S + p^M Z^M \equiv (\rho - \Omega)K - T_C \dot{p}_C^T - T_S \dot{p}_S^T - \bar{T}^M \dot{p}^{TM}$ [compare (1.13)], yet as seen below equilibrium in the M-market, $Z^M \equiv Q^M(\pi) = |\dot{T}_j| \geq 0$, will hold *identically* for any temporary-equilibrium π-value (no independent investment demand $|\dot{T}_j^d|$ for moving services is defined). Thus, although M is a perishable output (a nonbasic), its market behaves as if it were a basic: M-suppliers lock p^M into π [(8.7)] and determine the economy's equilibrium amount $|\dot{T}_S| \equiv |\dot{T}_C| \geq 0$ of resource transfers from the supply side alone. That M has the status of a quasi-basic will be confirmed in a moment.

13 They are given explicitly in the appendix to this chapter and use $\bar{\pi}^M = 0$; also, in deriving (8.19) recall $\bar{T}^M = T_C + T_S$ by normalization in (8.16).

14 Since π^M (unlike π) only has an effect on wealth (demands D^j), but not on the resource allocation variable λ_j (supplies Q^j), π^M does not affect the equilibrium relative price p of

Determination of the temporary-equilibrium quantity of resource transfers and of their sectoral direction is easily achieved if we now refer to the market for moving services and the market for capital. Considering the latter first, it requires balance between demand for loanable funds $(p_C^T\dot{T}_C+p_S^T\dot{T}_S)$ and supply of such funds $[(\rho-\Omega)K-(T_C\dot{p}_C^T+T_S\dot{p}_S^T+\bar{T}^M\dot{p}^{TM})]$, or

$$\dot{K}=(\rho-\Omega)K, \quad \dot{K}\equiv p_C^T\dot{T}_C+p_S^T\dot{T}_S+T_C\dot{p}_C^T+T_S\dot{p}_S^T+\bar{T}^M\dot{p}^{TM}. \tag{8.22}$$

Next, from the expression for equilibrium in the market for moving services (I use (8.8), (8.11), (8.15)),

$$Z^M\equiv\bar{T}^M q^M\{x_M[\omega^*(\pi)]\}=|\dot{T}_j|\geq 0, \tag{8.23}$$

we see that, given a temporary-equilibrium π-value, the *amount* $|\dot{T}_S|\equiv|\dot{T}_C|\geq 0$ of equilibrium resource movements is uniquely determined by the M-industry's supply decision $Q^M(\pi)\geq 0$. From (8.7), (8.23), $p^M Z^M$ is nonnegative and, from (8.19) and Walras's Law, identically equal to the supply of loanable funds;[15] that is, the economy must be saving (net of capital gains) whenever the M-industry is operating. For capital market equilibrium, the demand $p_C^T\dot{T}_C+p_S^T\dot{T}_S\equiv\dot{T}_S p_C^T(\pi-1)$ for loanable funds must, therefore, be nonnegative as well. Since whether $(\pi-1)>0$ or <0 has already been settled by the temporary-equilibrium price solution, the *direction* $\dot{T}_S\equiv-\dot{T}_C\gtreqless 0$ of the resource transfer $|\dot{T}_S|\equiv|\dot{T}_C|$ is now uniquely determined: $\dot{T}_S\gtreqless 0$ as $(\pi-1)\gtreqless 0$ (which does not come as a surprise).

It is, at this point, simple to derive the system's dynamics under the two non-stationary-state regimes being considered. For both, the stockmarket equilibrium conditions $\chi(\cdot)=\chi^M(\cdot)=0$ in (8.18), together with the myopic-foresight assumption $\dot{\pi}=\dot{\pi}^e$, $\dot{\pi}^M=(\dot{\pi}^M)^e$, give the equity-price dynamics

$$\dot{\pi}=(1/p_C^T)[\pi q^C-p(\pi,x)q^S]\equiv\phi(\pi,x), \quad \phi_1>0, \quad \phi_2<0 \tag{8.24}$$

$$\dot{\pi}^M=(1/p_C^T)\{\pi^M q^C-r^{TM}[p^M(\pi),p(\pi,x)]\}\equiv\phi^M(\pi^M), \quad \phi^{M\prime}>0, \tag{8.25}$$

where I have employed (8.21) and the fact, discussed earlier, that $\partial r^{TM}/\partial\pi=0=\partial r^{TM}/\partial x$ when evaluated at the system's restpoint. Given (8.24), (8.25), the motions of x follow from (I have used $\dot{T}_S\equiv-\dot{T}_C$ and (8.17) in (8.22))

consumption goods (note that the D^j exhibit unitary spending elasticities). Recalling $\lambda_j(\pi,x,\mu)$ from footnote 10 and considering, say, BETA/TWO, observe that $z^C(\cdot)$, thus $p_C^T(\cdot)$, must also be a function of M-technology μ, so that the temporary-equilibrium profit rate $\rho=\rho_C^T=[q^C/p_C^T(\cdot)]+(\hat{p}_C^T)^e$ [(8.5), (8.17)] will be altered by $d\mu>0$. This confirms the status of M-output as quasi-basic in the sense of the Ricardo–Bortkiewicz–Sraffa theorem ("quasi" because the property does not extend to the stationary-state profit rate). It is easily checked from (8.18), (8.19) that the two consumption commodities, by contrast, represent genuine nonbasics in terms of the theorem.

15 Recall footnote 12.

$$\hat{T}_S = (\pi - 1)^{-1} \left\{ \left(\frac{q^C}{p_C^T(\pi, \pi^M, x)} - \Omega \right)[x + \pi + \pi^M(1+x)] - (1+x)\dot{\pi}^M - \dot{\pi} \right\} \tag{8.26}$$

and are given by

$$\dot{x} \equiv -(1+x)\hat{T}_S = \frac{-(1+x)}{(\pi - 1)} \left\{ \left(\frac{q^C}{p_C^T(\pi, \pi^M, x)} - \Omega \right)[x + \pi + \pi^M(1+x)] - (1+x)\phi^M(\pi^M) - \phi(\pi, x) \right\} \equiv \psi(\pi), \quad \psi' < 0, \tag{8.27}$$

under both ALPHA/ONE and BETA/TWO (that is, irrespective of whether $\pi < 1$ or $\pi > 1$).[16]

The linearized form of dynamic system [(8.24), (8.25), (8.27)] has roots

$$\begin{aligned} \eta_1 &= \phi^{M\prime} = \Omega > 0 \\ \eta_2 &= \tfrac{1}{2}[\phi_1 + (\phi_1^2 + 4\psi'\phi_2)^{\frac{1}{2}}] > 0 \\ \eta_3 &= \tfrac{1}{2}[\phi_1 - (\phi_1^2 + 4\psi'\phi_2)^{\frac{1}{2}}] < 0 \end{aligned} \tag{8.28}$$

and is, thus, saddle-path stable. Observe that (8.25) and [(8.24), (8.27)] form two autonomous dynamical subsystems that may be analyzed in complete independence from each other,[17] provided we limit ourselves to local perturbations and motions in the vicinity of the restpoint. Subsystem [(8.24), (8.27)] is illustrated in figure 8.1.

Before pursuing the discussion of dynamics further, it is useful to consider the characteristics of the economy's long-run equilibrium. In it, all prices are unchanging, $\dot{p}_j^T = \dot{p}^{TM} = \dot{\pi} = \dot{\pi}^M = 0$, sectoral input stocks are stationary, $\dot{T}_j = \dot{x} = 0$, and the moving industry has ceased operation, $Q^M = x_M = 0$, $\lambda_C = \lambda_S = 1$. Stationarity of prices and of input stocks means that wealth is invariant, $\dot{K} = 0$, so that

$$\bar{\rho} = \Omega \tag{8.29}$$

from (8.22): The long-run rate of interest equals the rate of time preference. $\bar{\rho}$, in turn, anchors the yields, $\bar{\rho}_j^T$, $\bar{\rho}^{TM}$ and equity prices, $\bar{p}_j^T$, $\bar{p}^{TM}$ in arbitrage equation (8.17). These, moreover, must reflect the fundamental fact that

$$\bar{p}^M = 0, \text{ thus } \bar{\pi} = 1 \text{ or } \bar{p}_C^T = \bar{p}_S^T \equiv \bar{p}^T \tag{8.30}$$

[16] As the appendix shows, the dynamic partial derivatives appearing in (8.24) and (8.27) differ across regimes, but their *signs* near the restpoint do not. From the information provided in the appendix – or by inspection of (8.23) – it is easy to see that $\partial\dot{x}/\partial x = \partial\dot{x}/\partial\pi^M = 0$ at that point.

[17] That is, as if possessing two separate saddle points, a regular one in π, x-space and a degenerate one on the π^M-line.

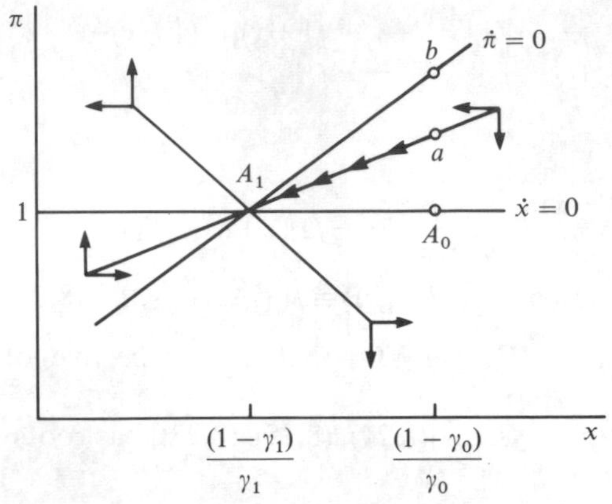

Figure 8.1 Dynamics of WALRAS III; adjustment following a preference shift toward consumption services

from (8.7). $\bar{p}^M$ is zero because the unit costs $a_{T^M,M}\bar{r}^{T^M} + a_{T_{jM},M}\bar{r}_j$ of the moving industry have fallen to zero. They have so on account of a cost-minimizing $a_{T_{jM},M}$-value that is zero (since $T_{jM} = 0$) and a rental $\bar{r}^{T^M}$ on M-specific land that is zero as well.[18]

But $\bar{\pi} = 1$ and absence of expected capital gains means that equity in the two types of human capital T_C, T_S will be willingly held, if and only if it earns the same dividends,

$$\bar{r}_S = \bar{r}_C = q^C, \tag{8.31}$$

where I have used (8.5) and the first arbitrage equation in (8.17). It is this equity-arbitrage argument – not an illusory costless mobility of physical labor – that explains why, in the long run, wages tend to equalize across sectors.[19]

Entrepreneurial profit maximization, finally, sees to it that the long-run relative price $\bar{p}$ reflects labor's relative productivity in C and S,

$$\bar{p} = q^C/q^S, \tag{8.32}$$

from (8.6) and (8.31).

I summarize this discussion of long-run price determination by writing down the stationary-state arbitrage equations:

$$\Omega = \frac{q^C}{\bar{p}^T} = \frac{\bar{p}q^S}{\bar{p}^T} = \frac{\bar{r}^{T^M}}{\bar{p}^{T^M}}, \quad \bar{p}^T = \frac{q^C}{\Omega} > 0, \quad \bar{p}^{T^M} = \frac{\bar{r}^{T^M}}{\Omega} = 0 = \bar{\pi}^M, \tag{8.33}$$

18 Both of these follow from (8.8) and (8.14), the former because an infinite marginal product $q^{M\prime}(0) \to \infty$ of labor implies an infinite average product $a^{-1}_{T_{jM},M}$.

19 As demonstrated in supplement A.3, a similar portfolio-theoretic argument shows why, given discrete time and storable outputs, short-run rental rates fail to equalize even if one assumes perfect physical factor mobility.

where the zero long-run land rental $\bar{r}^{TM}=0$ is now seen to be mirrored in a zero asset price $\bar{p}^{TM}=0=\bar{\pi}^{M}$ of land.[20]

From (8.32) and $\bar{Q}^{M}=0$ it is clear that the system possesses a standard straight-line Ricardian production-possibility schedule and that (provided the economy remains closed) intratemporal preferences can have no effect on $\bar{p}$. Instead, as in all nonsubstitution models, these preferences determine the long-run capital composition $\bar{x}\equiv\bar{T}_C/\bar{T}_S$,

$$\bar{x}=(1-\gamma)/\gamma\geq 0, \tag{8.34}$$

from (8.19) and the price results just discussed. This closes my discussion of the stationary state.

My next task is to consider the economy's behavior outside it. As usual, it proves useful to first approach the question from the static-expectations perspective. I accordingly set the capital-gains expectations $(\hat{p}_j^T)^e, (\hat{p}^{TM})^e$ that appear in arbitrage equations (8.17) equal to zero and, at the same time, assume that any consequent unexpected capital gains $[\hat{p}_j^T-(\hat{p}_j^T)^e]p_j^T T_j \neq 0$, $[\hat{p}^{TM}-(\hat{p}^{TM})^e]p^{TM}\bar{T}^M\neq 0$ are saved. This gives, from (8.18),

$$\pi=r_S/r_C=pq^S/q^C, \qquad \pi^M=r^{TM}[p^M(\pi),p]/q^C\equiv\pi^M(\pi,p), \pi_h^M=0\ (h=1,2), \tag{8.35}$$

and, from the analogue of capital-market-equilibrium equation (8.22),[21]

$$\dot{T}_S=\frac{1}{\pi-1}(\rho-\Omega)K/p_C^T. \tag{8.36}$$

which may be compared to (8.26). The goods-market-equilibrium price function $p=p(\pi,x,\gamma)$ in (8.21) continues to hold and may be substituted in (8.35) to yield a function

$$\pi=\pi(x,\gamma), \qquad \pi_h>0\ (h=1,2), \tag{8.37}$$

that determines the static-expectations behavior of the temporary-equilibrium relative equity price. (8.37) may then be substituted in the other goods-market-equilibrium price function $p_C^T=p_C^T[\pi(\cdot),x,\gamma]$,[22]

$$\begin{aligned} p_C^T=p_C^T(x,\gamma), \qquad & p_{Ci}^{T,\alpha 1}>0\ (i=1,2), \\ & p_{Ci}^{T,\beta 2}<0\ (i=1,2), \end{aligned} \tag{8.38}$$

[20] The ratio $\bar{r}^{TM}/\bar{p}^{TM}$ thus remains well-defined and equal to Ω.

[21] Namely, $\dot{K}\equiv\sum_{C,S}T_j\dot{p}_j^T+\sum_{C,S}p_j^T\dot{T}_j+\bar{T}^M\dot{p}^{TM}=\rho K+\sum_{C,S}[\dot{p}_j^T-(\dot{p}_j^T)^e]T_j+[\dot{p}^{TM}-(\dot{p}^{TM})^e]\bar{T}^M-\Omega K$, with $(\dot{p}_j^T)^e\equiv 0\equiv(\dot{p}^{TM})^e$ due to static expectations.

[22] See (8.20), in which I omit π^M given its constancy from (8.35). As shown in (8.38) (and demonstrated in the appendix), the response of p_C^T to variations x and γ depends – unlike that of $\pi(\cdot)$ in (8.37) – on whether the economy is in (or moving into) regime ALPHA/ONE ($\alpha 1$) or BETA/TWO ($\beta 2$).

which will determine the behavior of the static-expectations interest rate $\rho = q^C/p_C^T(\cdot)$.

The dynamic consequences of, say, a preference shift $d\gamma > 0$ away from corn toward consumption services are now easy to trace. The immediate impact is to create, at the prevailing long-run equilibrium prices and as yet unchanged supplies, an excess demand for consumption services and an excess supply of corn. Since stock equilibrium requires π to move positively with and in proportion to p [(8.35)], the only adjustment in the price of consumption services consistent with temporary stock-and-flow equilibrium is for p to rise. As it does, π increases in step, which tends to reduce the necessary upward adjustment in p (since $p_1 < 0$ in (8.21)) but, by an argument *a contrario*, can never obviate it. Observe the consequences of this rise in π and p: In its wake, p^M becomes positive [(8.7)] and the S-sector wage r_S rises above r_C [(8.35)], so that the M-industry finds it profitable to hire corn-sector labor and to commence operations [(8.9)]. That is, the economy has moved into non-stationary-state regime BETA/TWO on impact.

What is the sectoral direction of the resulting resource movement? Given $\pi > 1$ in the new short-run equilibrium (8.36) tells us that the answer to that question depends on the interest-rate response: Should ρ rise on impact, $\dot{T}_S \equiv -\dot{T}_C > 0$ and resources will begin to be moved out of corn into consumption services (and vice versa, if ρ falls on impact). Given the assumed demand shift, the former response is what we expect and require for convergence to a new stationary state. Since under static expectations such convergence (dynamic stability) always obtains, ρ must indeed jump on impact (that is, p_C^T will fall in (8.38)). It is worth examining this result a little further. For note that it implies that the *opposite* demand shift, $d\gamma < 0$, must lead to the same ρ- and p_C^T-response as under $d\gamma > 0$. Only in this way can we have $\dot{T}_S < 0$ in (8.36), given that now $\pi < 1$ on impact. The point, of course, is that any resource reallocation, of whatever sectoral direction, must be accompanied by a temporarily raised real rate of interest: Only this will bring about the *cut in current consumption* that is necessary to *finance the resource transfer*.[23]

The economy's subsequent dynamic adjustment is straightforward. With $\dot{T}_S \equiv -\dot{T}_C > 0$ (thus, $\dot{x} \equiv -(1+x)\hat{T}^S < 0$) on impact, employment and output must be higher (lower) in the S-sector (C-sector) in the next period. At the impact equilibrium prices, this will create an excess supply of consumption services (an excess demand for corn) that drives down the equilibrium value of p. This, in turn, reduces the rental r_S, thus, the expected yield ρ_S^T on S-sector human capital; yield uniformity then requires a proportionate decline in π. The moving industry thereby experiences a diminution in its

[23] The argument also follows from the fact (footnote 12) that, in temporary equilibrium and from Walras's Law, the value of M-sector output identically equals net saving.

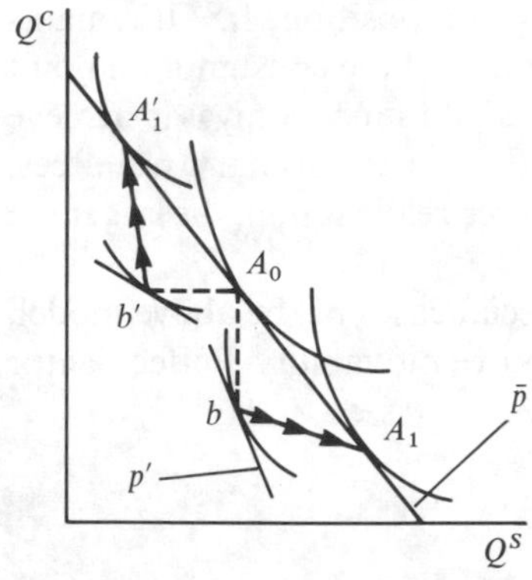

Figure 8.2 Production-possibility curve of WALRAS III; adjustment following preference shifts

demand price $p_S^T - p_C^T \equiv (1/p_C^T)(\pi - 1) > 0$, consequently, a reduction in its profit-maximizing output $Q^M = \dot{T}_S > 0$. However, as long $p_S^T - p_C^T = p^M$ remains positive, the moving process will continue – and, over time, drive all prices back to their initial value. It follows that across stationary states the demand disturbance will turn out to have been accommodated entirely by a change in resource allocation (capital composition) at unchanged, technology-determined prices. Moreover, in the new long-run equilibrium the moving industry will once again be out of operation, forcing land back into its original status as an unemployed resource.

The process may be summarized on a standard Ricardian PPC diagram (figure 8.2). On impact of $d\gamma > 0$, the economy's consumption point vertically drops from A_0 to b, as p rises from $\bar{p}$ to p', pulling C-resources into the moving industry through the creation of an equity-price differential $p_S^T - p_C^T = p^M > 0$. Observe that the value of aggregate consumption $E = Q^C + p'Q^S = r_C^T T_C' + r_S^T T_S$ at point b falls short of the value of national income $\rho K = Q^C + p'Q^S + p^M Q^M = r_C^T T_C' + r_S^T T_S + r_C^T T_{CM}$ at point A_0.[24] The reason is simple: Given that the rate of interest – the cost of present relative to future consumption – has jumped above the rate of time preference, the economy is currently saving, and investing in the resource transfer, an amount equalling $r_C^T T_{CM} (= A_0 b)$ when measured in corn output. Over time, this *consumption cost of resource reallocation* will be declining, for the pace $\dot{T}_S \equiv -\dot{T}_C > 0$ of resource transfers gradually approaches zero as the

[24] The former is measured by the Q^C-axis intercept of the price line p' (tangent to the indifference curve at point b); the latter by the Q^C-axis intercept of the same price line drawn through point A_0. Recall that $r^{TM}\bar{T}^M$ is second-order small and that expectations are here treated as static.

economy moves along b–A_1 to the new long-run position A_1.[25] It remains that a present sacrifice – a temporary movement of the consumption point inside the PPC – has been shown to be required, if the economy is to achieve the future benefits of an improved allocation of its primary resources. Moreover, the greater the speed of that resource reallocation, the larger the current consumption cost.[26]

I conclude by briefly juxtaposing two special cases of the above model, embodying limiting assumptions about resource movability: Perfect factor mobility and resource immovability.

Perfect factor mobility

Human capital is physically "perfectly mobile" across sectors in the present model, if in (8.8) I replace $q^{M''}(x_M)<0$, $x_M \geq 0$, by

$$q^{M''}(x_M)=0, \qquad x_M \geq 0, \tag{8.39}$$

but retain $q^{M'}(0)\rightarrow\infty$. It follows that the marginal cost $r_j/q^{M'}$ of moving resources is now zero not just at $x_M=0$, but fails to increase above zero at any $x_M>0$.[27] This formally expresses the idea that human capital may be moved across sectors costlessly. A moving industry can not, in these circumstances, come into existence: $r^{TM}=a_{T_{jM},M}=0=p^M$ competitively in (8.10) for any allocation $x_M \geq 0$ to the M-sector, so that the equilibrium allocation will always be $x_M=0=Q^M$, $\lambda_j=1$. Since moving services are infinitely elastically supplied at (any price slighty higher than) $p^M=0$, no equity-price differential $\pi \gtrless 1$ can ever emerge [(8.7)]. In consequence, ownership claims to T_C and T_S are willingly held if and only if they earn the same dividend at each moment. Put differently and more familiarly, sectoral wage rates must be instantaneously uniform,

$$r_C=r_S. \tag{8.40}$$

Entrepreneurial profit maximization (8.5), (8.6) then implies that the price

[25] The adjustment trajectory $A_0-b'-A_1'$ in figure 8.2 illustrates the response to the opposite disturbance $d\gamma<0$: On impact the rise in the real rate of interest and the consequent cut in consumption is now mirrored in a contraction of S-output from A_0 to b'.

[26] Figure 8.1 shows the system's adjustment path A_0-a-A_1 following an unanticipated permanent increase in γ under perfect foresight. As usual, the story is qualitatively the same as under static expectations, except that the relative asset price $1/\pi$ of C-sector human capital need not decline as much on impact, given the correct anticipation of relative capital gains $-\hat{\pi}>0$ on such capital along the saddle path. That is, instead of to point a, under static expectations π jumps to b, located on the temporary-equilibrium locus $\dot{\pi}=0$. (The $\dot{x}=0$-locus shown applies to the perfect-foresight system only; the corresponding dynamic locus under static expectations is vertical from (8.36), (8.38), and $\dot{x}\equiv-(1+x)\hat{T}_S$.)

[27] Recall that $q^{M'}(\cdot)$ is the marginal product of labor in the moving industry; the marginal cost to M-firms of producing an additional unit of moving services Q^M then is $r_j\partial T_{jM}/\partial Q^M \equiv r_j/(\partial Q^M/\partial T_{jM}) \equiv r_j/q^{M'}$, where r_j is the (minimum) wage rate they face.

of consumption services remains invariant at $p=q^C/q^S$. Therefore, all temporary-equilibrium prices are fixed and are so at what earlier was merely their long-run value [(8.29)–(8.33)]. Only one variable is left to ensure instantaneous output-market clearing: x, whose temporary-equilibrium value is easily shown to be $(1-\gamma)/\gamma$. As a state variable x therefore vanishes and the economy's price dynamics collapse into

$$\dot{\pi}=(q^C/p_C^T)(\pi-1)\equiv\phi(\pi), \qquad \phi'=\Omega>0, \tag{8.41}$$

and (8.25), which together form a (locally separable) dynamical system with repeated root $\lambda_1=\lambda_2=\Omega>0$ and a degenerate saddle point in π, π^M-space.

Resource immovability

Assume now that the marginal cost of moving resources $r_j/q^{M'}$ rises very steeply, namely

$$q^{M''}(0)\rightarrow-\infty, \tag{8.42}$$

so that $q^{M'}$ in (8.8) drops from $+\infty$ to zero when the first increment of T_{jM} is applied. In consequence, the unit cost of moving services in (8.10) is zero at $Q^M=x_M=0$, but becomes unbounded at any positive x_M, given that average labor productivity $1/a_{T_{jM},M}$ drops to zero.[28] It follows that (compare (8.7))

$$|p_S^T-p_C^T|<p^M\rightarrow\infty \qquad x_M\epsilon(0,T_j/\bar{T}^M]. \tag{8.43}$$

Thus, no configuration of finite equity prices p_j^T exists that can render intersectoral resource movements profitable. This makes for

$$\dot{T}_S\equiv-\dot{T}_C=0=\dot{x} \tag{8.44}$$

at all times.

In sum, what we have here is an economy in which sectorally immovable resource stocks $\bar{T}_C$, $\bar{T}_S$ of a primary resource $\bar{T}$ produce invariant quantities $\bar{Q}^C$, $\bar{Q}^S$ of two nonbasics. Evidently, this is a structure indistinguishable from one in which agents receive and trade two exogenous, nonstorable endowment flows – in other words, indistinguishable from the Walrasian model of pure exchange. To the latter I now turn.

8.3 WALRAS IV: The pure-exchange economy

Consider a competitive economy consisting of a large number of identical agents each of whom receives an exogenous endowment of milk, Q^M, and

[28] In (8.10), recall that $r^{TM}=r_h^{TM}=0$ $(h=1,2)$ at $x_M=0$, but $r_j>0$.

honey, Q^H.[29] Assume, to begin with, that the economy is static: It lasts for a single period, at the beginning of which agents are born and receive, trade, and consume their endowments; and at the end of which they – and the economic universe – expire. If the representative agent's preferences are Cobb–Douglas, his utility-maximizing demands for milk and honey will be

$$D^M = (1-\gamma)Y, \qquad D^H = \gamma Y/p, \qquad Y \equiv Q^M + pQ^H, \tag{8.45}$$

where $0<\gamma<1$ is a constant propensity to consume honey, Y endowment income, and p the price of honey (the system's numéraire is milk).

Define $Z^i \equiv Q^i - D^i$ to be an agent's excess supply of $i(=M,H)$. By Walras's Law,

$$Z^M + pZ^H \equiv 0. \tag{8.46}$$

For the economy to be in overall equilibrium it will, accordingly, be sufficient if one of the two goods markets clears, say,

$$Z^H \equiv Q^H - \gamma(Q^M + pQ^H)/p = 0, \tag{8.47}$$

where I have normalized the number of agents to one. (8.47) yields the system's equilibrium price,

$$p = \frac{\gamma}{1-\gamma}\frac{Q^M}{Q^H}. \tag{8.48}$$

The latter is seen to be a function of agents' preferences and (relative) endowments.

I next place the two-good exchange economy in real – that is to say, unbounded – time. Agents are infinitely lived, have perfect foresight, and receive endowments of instantaneously perishable milk and honey at the fixed exogenous flow-rates Q^M and Q^H per unit of time, *ad infinitum*.

Specifically, assume Q^M, Q^H flow forth from a fixed number of non-produced, infinitely lived milk and honey fountains $\bar{T}^M$, $\bar{T}^H$,

$$Q^i = q^i \bar{T}^i, \qquad q^i > 0 \; (i = M, H), \tag{8.49}$$

where q^i is the constant output flow of a type-i fountain. To each fountain is attached an ownership claim – an equity – entitling the holder (a) to bar others from access to the fountain, and (b) to freely alienate the latter by instantaneously and costlessly transferring the equity thereon to another

[29] I will, for once, allow myself a change of commodity labels, trading off invariance of nomenclature for convenience of imagery: nonstorable corn (C) turns into milk (M), consumer services (S) into honey (H), with M and H assumed to flow forth from stocks of non-produced fountains $\bar{T}^M$, $\bar{T}^H$. The switch from sub- to superscripts on the T's as between this and the last section reflects my convention that subscripts refer to differences in location, superscripts to differences in physical kind.

agent at an agreed upon price. If that price, p^i, is competitively determined,

$$K \equiv p^M \bar{T}^M + p^H \bar{T}^H \tag{8.50}$$

will be the representative owner's capital or wealth.[30]

Clearly, though to the economy as a whole the composition $\bar{T}^M, \bar{T}^H$ of its capital is rigidly given, to any individual portfolio manager j the desired make-up T^{Mj}, T^{Hj} of his equity portfolio will appear as a choice variable, subject to the wealth constraint $p^M T^{Mj} + p^H T^{Hj} \leq K$. That is, he considers the composition of his current wealth to be instantaneously variable through costless equity transactions in the bourse. Portfolio managers, being rational income maximizers, will therefore willingly hold the economy's existing stock of equities if and only if expected instantaneous yields ρ^M and ρ^H on the two types of claims are the same. That is to say, the arbitrage equation

$$\rho^M \equiv \frac{r^M}{p^M} + (\hat{p}^M)^e = \frac{r^H}{p^H} + (\hat{p}^H)^e \equiv \rho^H \tag{8.51}$$

must hold at all times, where $(\hat{p}^i)^e$ stands for the percent capital gain expected on equities of type i and where the zero-entrepreneurial-profit conditions

$$1 = (1/q^M) r^M \tag{8.52}$$

$$p = (1/q^H) r^H \tag{8.53}$$

determine the dividends $r^M = q^M$, $r^H = pq^H$ earned on fountains of milk and of honey, respectively.[31] The uniform expected equity yield $\rho \equiv \rho^M = \rho^H$ implied by (8.51) defines the system's point-in-time interest rate. Substituting in (8.51) from (8.52), (8.53) and rearranging, I obtain

$$\begin{gathered} \chi(\pi, p^M, p; \hat{\pi}^e \ldots) \equiv (1/p^M)\left(q^M - \frac{pq^H}{\pi}\right) - \hat{\pi}^e = 0, \qquad \pi \equiv p^H/p^M \\ \chi_1 > 0, \chi_j < 0 \ (j = 3,4), = 0 \ (j = 2), \end{gathered} \tag{8.54}$$

[30] The account to follow assumes that ownership claims are tradable through a stockmarket. Recall from my discussion in chapters 2 and 6 that the model of pure exchange is one of the cases in which such tradability is not in fact necessary for decentralized optimality, provided households are intertemporal optimizers who can freely borrow and lend through the capital market. My point, however, will be that *if* we view ownership claims as tradable – and, unlike in the case of human capital, there is no reason in the model of pure exchange why we should not (Fisherian lenders certainly will view the $\bar{T}^i$ backing their debtors as potentially tradable) – intertemporal price coordination requires a forward-looking stockmarket.

[31] The pure-exchange economy is thus indistinguishable from a production economy with sectoral unit-cost functions $(1/q^i)r^i$, competitive rentals r^i, and infinite relocation costs, as considered at the end of last section.

my usual expression for stockmarket equilibrium under zero entrepreneurial profits (evaluated at a stationary state).

Demands for milk and honey by capitalist households are given by

$$D^M = (1-\gamma)\Omega K, \qquad D^H = \gamma\Omega K/p, \tag{8.55}$$

where $\Omega K = E$ is consumption function (1.8) used throughout.[32]

The temporary-equilibrium closure of the model is now straightforward. Since milk and honey are instantaneously perishable, at each point in time we must have

$$Z^i(\cdot) \equiv Q^i - D^i = 0 \qquad (i = M, H). \tag{8.56}$$

Unlike in the static version of the exchange economy, these two flow-market-equilibrium conditions are *independent*. To see this, observe that in the infinite-horizon system Walras's Law implies, not (8.46), but[33]

$$Z^M + pZ^H \equiv (\rho - \Omega)K - (\bar{T}^M \dot{p}^M + \bar{T}^H \dot{p}^H). \tag{8.57}$$

Identity (8.57) confirms that two of the *three* flow restrictions $Z^M = 0$, $Z^H = 0$ and

$$\dot{K} = (\rho - \Omega)K, \qquad \dot{K} \equiv \bar{T}^M \dot{p}^M + \bar{T}^H \dot{p}^H, \tag{8.58}$$

must be independently satisfied. I choose to keep capital-market-equilibrium equation (8.58) in the background and to focus on the market-clearing conditions for nonbasics (8.56). After normalization by $\bar{T}^H$ ($z^i \equiv Z^i/\bar{T}^H$), I rewrite $Z^M = 0$ and $Z^H = 0$ as

$$\begin{aligned} &z^M(\pi, p^M; \bar{x}, \gamma\ldots) \equiv q^M\bar{x} - (1-\gamma)\Omega(\bar{x}+\pi)p^M = 0 \\ &\quad z_j^M < 0 \ (j=1,2), > 0 \ (j=3,4) \\ &\quad \bar{x} \equiv \bar{T}^M/\bar{T}^H \end{aligned} \tag{8.59}$$

$$\begin{aligned} &z^H(\pi, p^M, p; \bar{x}, \gamma\ldots) \equiv q^H - \gamma\Omega(\bar{x}+\pi)p^M/p = 0 \\ &\quad z_j^H < 0 \ (j=1,2,4,5), > 0 \ (j=3), \end{aligned} \tag{8.60}$$

which are two independent equations in the three unknowns π, p^M, and p.

The temporary-equilibrium system is thus fully determinate: Given expectations $\hat{\pi}^e$, capital composition $\bar{x}$, technology q^i, and preference parameters γ, Ω, equations (8.54), (8.59), and (8.60) solve for the momentary prices p^M, π (thus $p^H \equiv p^M\pi$), and p. In particular, (8.59) may be solved for the price of equity claims to milk fountains,

$$\begin{aligned} &p^M = \frac{q^M\bar{x}}{(1-\gamma)\Omega(\bar{x}+\pi)} \equiv p^M(\pi; \bar{x}, \gamma\ldots) \\ &\quad p_j^M < 0 \ (j=1), > 0 \ (j=2,3); \end{aligned} \tag{8.61}$$

[32] Compare (8.55) with (8.45). [33] Compare (1.13) in VON NEUMANN I.

(8.60) for the price of honey,

$$p = \frac{\gamma}{1-\gamma}\frac{q^M}{q^H}\bar{x} \equiv p(\bar{x}, \gamma \ldots), \qquad p_j > 0 \; (j=1,2), \tag{8.62}$$

after substitution from (8.61); and (8.54) implicitly for the price of honey-fountain equity in terms of milk-fountain equity,

$$\pi = \pi(\hat{\pi}^e, \bar{x}, \gamma \ldots), \qquad \pi_j > 0 \; (j = 1-3), \tag{8.63}$$

after substitution from (8.62).

The most interesting feature of the above temporary-equilibrium system is (8.62): The Walrasian terms of exchange p are independent of equity prices and the rate of time preference – they are a function only of intratemporal preferences γ and exogenous flow endowments $(q^M/q^H)\bar{x} \equiv Q^M/Q^H$, exactly as in the static version of the pure-exchange model [(8.48)]. In other words, the system seems to dichotomize: The flow price p feeds into the stockmarket, but the stock price π is without influence on flow markets. I will remark further on this apparent dichotomy in a moment.

Turning to the model's dynamics, I have from (8.54), (8.62), and the myopic-foresight postulate $\hat{\pi} = \hat{\pi}^e$,

$$\dot{\pi} = \frac{\pi q^M}{p^M}\left(1 - \frac{\gamma}{1-\gamma}\frac{\bar{x}}{\pi}\right) \equiv \phi(\pi), \qquad \phi' > 0, \tag{8.64}$$

the law of motion of the relative equity price. Since $x = \bar{x}$, accumulation equation (8.58) does not generate an x-dynamics. Instead, it may be rewritten as $K\hat{p}^M + p^H \bar{T}^H \hat{\pi} = [q^M/p^M + (\hat{p}^M)^e - \Omega]K$, which yields

$$\dot{\pi} = \left(\frac{q^M}{p^M} - \Omega\right)(\bar{x} + \pi), \tag{8.65}$$

given $\hat{p}^M = (\hat{p}^M)^e$. By substituting for p^M from (8.61), equation (8.65) is easily seen to be the same as (8.64) (near a stationary state with $q^M/p^M = \Omega$). The economy's motions are thus governed by a one-dimensional differential equation system in π, whose linearized form has root

$$\phi' = \Omega > 0 \tag{8.66}$$

and whose singularity is a degenerate saddle point.

In conclusion, I reconsider the question of how the framework just laid out compares to the static exchange model and how one is to interpret dichotomy (8.62) between flow and stock prices.

What static model (8.45)–(8.48) – which is Walras's model of pure exchange [Walras (1874, 1954)] – omits is this: By focusing exclusively on the terms at which agents are willing to *trade endowments*, it fails to enquire about the conditions under which agents are willing to *hold the ownership claims attached to the sources of these endowments*. Throughout this book, two alternatives to holding ownership claims have been put forth:(i) the decision to, say, instantaneously sell, in the aggregate, $\bar{T}^M$ claims to milk flows in exchange for $\bar{T}^H$ titles to honey flows – the motive being an attempt to arbitrage away a perceived yield differential between the two types of equities; (ii) the decision to reduce both $\bar{T}^M$ and $\bar{T}^H$ at a finite rate, in the attempt – necessarily unsuccessful in equilibrium but not, for that matter, impossible *ex ante* – to raise the level of current consumption ΩK above that of current income ρK. As stockmarket-equilibrium condition (8.51) and capital-market-equilibrium condition (8.58) show, both alternatives are open to agents in the pure-exchange economy, once I drop the assumption of single-period existence.

Next, what should we make of dichotomy (8.62) between flow and stock prices – is it satisfying or disturbing? The former response would base itself on the implied robustness of the Walrasian theory of price determination: Even when extended to an infinite horizon by means of a forward-looking market in ownership claims, the theory's goods price p and the derived factor prices r^i remain at all times solely determined by tastes and endowments, as in the static model. That is, even if convergence to $\bar{\pi}$ should for some reason fail and allow the system to move along an asset-price bubble, flow markets continue to clear at the invariant Walrasian price (8.48)$\equiv$(8.62). This works because along any such path the two capital-gain terms $\dot{p}^i$ will have opposite signs and move such that

$$\dot{K} \equiv \bar{T}^M \dot{p}^M + \bar{T}^H \dot{p}^H = (\rho - \Omega)K = 0 \tag{8.67}$$

at all times, ensuring

$$\rho = \bar{\rho} = \Omega. \tag{8.68}$$

The underlying economics is simple: Clearing of the market for milk, $\bar{Q}^M = (1-\gamma)\Omega K$, requires consumption spending ΩK – therefore, wealth and, from (8.67), the profit rate – to remain invariant along an explosive equity-price path. The invariance of p now follows from clearing of the market for honey, $\bar{Q}^H = \gamma \Omega K / p$.

It is not difficult to see where the argument just presented goes astray. Any asset-price bubble must burst in *finite* time (say, at $t = \tau < \infty$), since

$$\pi \rightarrow 0 \text{ or } \pi \rightarrow \infty \text{ as } t \rightarrow \tau < \infty, \tag{8.69}$$

but π is bounded at zero and infinity. Therefore, at $t = \tau$ at the latest, the stockmarket will fail to clear and capital-gains expectations $\hat{\pi}^e$ will be disappointed. With two conditions necessary for a perfect-foresight competitive-equilibrium path thus violated,[34] the Walrasian equilibrium price becomes inoperative,

[34] See my discussion in supplement A.2.

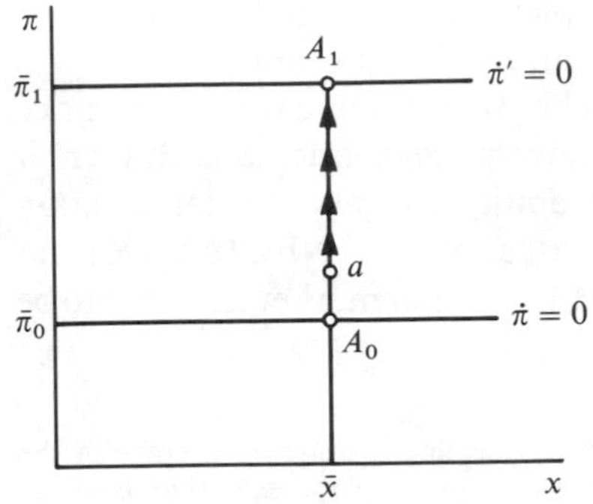

Figure 8.3 Adjustment following anticipations of a preference shift toward honey in WALRAS IV

$$p(t) \gtrless p(\bar{x}, \gamma \ldots), \qquad t \geq \tau, \tag{8.70}$$

since, at $t = \tau$ and beyond, $p(t)$ is no longer determined within the given model. It follows that a *necessary* condition for $p(\bar{x}, \gamma \ldots)$ to represent an equilibrium price is that the current stockmarket-equilibrium price $\pi(t)$ be such that the transversality condition [I use (8.54), (8.62)]

$$\pi(t) \to \bar{\pi} = \frac{\gamma}{1-\gamma}\bar{x} \qquad \text{as } t \to \infty \tag{8.71}$$

is satisfied.

To appreciate the significance of (8.71), observe that only in the absence of anticipated shocks does the condition entail $\pi(t) = \bar{\pi}$, all t. Consider, by contrast, a demand shift $d\gamma > 0$ toward honey correctly anticipated today (at $t = t_0$) to occur at some point $t = t_1 > t_0$ in the future (see figure 8.3). It will give rise to continued and accelerating increases in the relative price π of honey fountains, after an initial jump

$$\Delta\pi(t_0) \equiv \pi(t_0) - \bar{\pi}_0 = (\bar{\pi}_1 - \bar{\pi}_0)\exp[-\Omega(t_1 - t_0)] \tag{8.72}$$

from point A_0 to point a.[35] π reaches the new long-run price $\bar{\pi}_1$, without discontinuity, exactly on impact of the demand shift. Throughout, p and ρ have remained invariant at (8.62) and (8.68) (p jumps on impact). The condition $\pi(t_1) = \bar{\pi}_1$ simultaneously represents two profit-maximizing requirements for stockmarket speculators: A transversality condition and a continuity condition. Should transversality obtain, but continuity fail – that is to say, should π have to jump discontinuously at t_1 in order to reach its new long-run value $\bar{\pi}_1$ – the Walrasian price (8.62) will again fail to clear

[35] Equation (8.72) follows from the law of motion $\pi(t) = A\exp\Omega(t - t_0) + \bar{\pi}_0$ and the condition $\pi(t_1) = \bar{\pi}_1$ [recall (8.64), (8.66), (8.71)].

the economy's flow markets.[36] Consequently, both transversality and continuity are necessary for (8.62) to be an equilibrium price.

I draw the following conclusion. The Walrasian equilibrium price $p(\bar{x}, \gamma\ldots)$ is not independent of the equity price π after all. Rather, it critically hinges on the stockmarket's ability to gain the information necessary to speculatively anchor π in $\bar{\pi}$. Just as in VON NEUMANN I and all the other models my book has examined, the stockmarket turns out to be the linchpin of the decentralized pricing system.

[36] To see this intuitively, think of $\gamma = \gamma(\gamma_r, \gamma_s)$ as representing a weighted average of the consumption preferences $\gamma_r \neq \gamma_s$ of two groups of speculators r and s, one of which contains an agent who alone correctly anticipates the discrete jump in π ultimately required: By transferring, at t_0, the entirety of unexploited capital gains to himself, he will change the relative weights of γ_r and γ_s in γ – therefore, render the initial value of $p(\bar{x}, \gamma\ldots)$ non-market-clearing at t_0 despite as yet unchanged γ_r, γ_s-parameters. In other words, p has become a function of $[\bar{\pi}_1 - \pi(t_1)]\int_{t_0}^{t_1} \exp[-\int_{t_0}^{t} \rho(s)ds]dt$, the present value of the per-unit capital gain reaped by the agent.

Supplements

A Supplement to chapter 2

A.1 Introduction

The implications of the two theoretical supplements (A.2 and A.3) to follow were discussed in general terms in chapter 2. The purpose of the present introductory note is to acquaint the reader with their specific content and their organization by section and subsection.

Supplement A.2 contains four sections. The first (A.2.1) is entitled "Consumption optimization and the consumption function." It discusses the capitalist household's problem of maximizing intertemporal utility from consumption under a general constant-relative-risk-aversion (CRRA) felicity function, whose special logarithmic form is shown to entail myopic consumption function (1.8). (The appendix to chapter 4 discusses the corresponding consumption function in discrete time.) The section also shows the sense in which maximized utility can be said to behave like an asset stock that is subject to the economy's uniform-yield requirement. The second section (A.2.2), entitled "The market solution," has two subsections, of which the first (A.2.2.1) deals with the conditions *necessary* for the VON NEUMANN I economy to possess a perfect-foresight-competitive-equilibrium (PFCE) path – that is, an intertemporal trajectory which is forever profit maximizing, stockmarket clearing, and expectations fulfilling. (A PFCE path may not involve forward-looking consumption optimization by households; when viewed under an appropriate welfare function, such a path may nevertheless turn out to be optimal – recall Kurz's (1968) "inverse optimum".) The necessary conditions are distinguished from the *necessary-and-sufficient* conditions, discussed in the next subsection, in that they only require speculators to possess *myopic* foresight (knowledge of next period's stockmarket prices, that is, knowledge of the righthand derivative of $\pi(t)$), not *long-run* or "perfect" foresight (the capacity to extend myopic foresight to an infinite horizon and, thereby, ensure equity-price transversality). I discuss the dynamics implied by the necessary conditons first under a general CRRA felicity function – in which case the household's shadow price of wealth (λ) functions as an autonomous state variable – and then under logarithmic felicity (here λ is not autonomous, unlike the relative equity price π). In the logarithmic case, the economy's motions collapse into [(0.1), (0.2)], which I show to be the perturbed canonical equations of a descriptive national-income Hamiltonian in π and x. I examine the latter's mathematical and economic significance in some detail and later contrast it with the corresponding Pontryagin, or optimal-control, Hamiltonian. As mentioned, the second subsection (A.2.2.2) deals with conditions necessary-and-sufficient for a PFCE path. The question here is: What assures that a competitive equilibrium path with foresight obtains not only in the short and medium run, but over an *infinite* horizon? I show that it is profit maximization by forward-looking stockmarket speculators that does so. For instance, in the logarithmic VON NEUMANN I economy speculative-profit maximization under long-run foresight is sufficient to guarantee fulfillment of the system's single transversality condition (TVC). Loosely speaking, stockmarket speculation forces a readjustment in the economy's price structure whenever the system is setting off on a path that can be seen, with sufficient foresight, to be an unsustainable bubble. The supplement's third section (A.2.3) is entitled "The planning solution" and demonstrates (under a general CRRA felicity function) that the PFCE path of VON NEUMANN I coincides with the trajectory that would be adopted by a social planner. The decentralized VON NEUMANN I economy thus is Pareto optimal and implicitly obeys the two theorems of welfare economics. This section also compares the descriptive with the optimal-control Hamiltonian. Moreover, it contrasts the decentralized CRRA household's single TVC with the CRRA planner's *two* TVC's – the second of which corresponds to the decentralized TVC enforced by stockmarket speculators. The last section (A.2.4) of the first supplement briefly comments on models that, unlike those of the present book, possess an infinite-horizon PFCE path that fails to converge to a saddle point (exhibiting, say, a closed limit cycle instead). That section also mentions some recent work linking Hamiltonians in economics with Hamiltonians and conservation laws in physics.

I now turn to supplement A.3. It comprises two sections, the first of which (A.3.1) is entitled "Dorfman–Samuelson–Solow on dynamic efficiency." As discussed in chapter 2, that section critically reexamines – using an example similar to VON NEUMANN I – the well-known Dorfman *et al.* (1958) analysis of decentralized dynamic production efficiency. The analysis is found wanting, and wanting in a way suggestive of what accounts for the seeming absence of a stockmarket from the Arrow–Debreu economy. That this absence is apparent only, section A.3.2, entitled "A Hamiltonian interpretation of the Arrow-Debreu economy," demonstrates.

A.2 Market, plan, and intertemporal price coordination

A.2.1 Consumption optimization and the consumption function

1 Assume the representative capitalist household maximizes

$$\max_{D^S, D^C} \int_0^\infty U[D^S(t), D^C(t)]\exp(-\Omega t)\, dt, \qquad \text{(A2.1)}$$

where the felicity function U is specialized to

$$\left.\begin{aligned} U(\cdot) &\equiv \{[D^S(t)]^\gamma [D^C(t)]^{1-\gamma}\}^{1-R}/(1-R) \\ &\equiv \{[d^S(t)]^\gamma [d^C(t)]^{1-\gamma} \exp(gt)\}^{1-R}/(1-R) \end{aligned}\right\} \text{for } R>0,\ R\neq 1$$
$$\left.\begin{aligned} U(\cdot) &\equiv \ln\{[D^S(t)]^\gamma [D^C(t)]^{1-\gamma}\} \\ &\equiv \gamma \ln d^S(t) + (1-\gamma)\ln d^C(t) + gt \end{aligned}\right\} \text{for } R=1. \qquad \text{(A2.2)}$$

In (A2.2), $\{\cdot\}$ is a Cobb–Douglas index $(0 \leq \gamma \leq 1)$ of consumption of steel, $D^S(t) \equiv d^S(t)\exp(gt)$, and of corn, $D^C(t) \equiv d^C(t)\exp(gt)$; $\exp(gt)$ a detrending factor that normalizes quantities for steady-state growth at rate g; and $R>0$ a curvature index whose inverse can be shown to equal the elasticity of intertemporal consumption substitution (in a stochastic context of expected-utility maximization R is the coefficient of constant-relative-risk-aversion (CRRA); see Blanchard and Fisher (1989), for instance). $R=1$ provides the logarithmic specialization of $U(\cdot)$ used throughout the book.

The maximization problem is solved subject to the constraints

$$\begin{aligned} &\dot{K}(t) = \rho(t)K(t) - E(t) \text{ or } \dot{k}(t) = [\rho(t) - g]k(t) - e(t) \\ &K(t) \equiv k(t)\exp(gt) \geq 0,\ E(t) \equiv e(t)\exp(gt) \equiv D^C(t) + p(t)D^S(t) \geq 0 \\ &K(0) = k(0) \geq 0 \text{ given,} \end{aligned} \qquad \text{(A2.3)}$$

where $E(t)$ is consumption spending; $K(t) \equiv X^C(t) + \pi(t)X^S(t)$ wealth; $\{p(t)\}_{t=0}^\infty$, $\{\pi(t)\}_{t=0}^\infty$ the expected path of the relative output and the relative equity price of steel, respectively (by entrepreneurial profit maximization, the two will coincide as will the unitary flow and stock price of the numeraire good corn [(1.4), (1.5)]); and $\{\rho(t)\}_{t=0}^\infty$ the expected path of the uniform profit (interest) rate.

A meaningful interpretation of problem (A2.1)–(A2.3) requires three observations. First, as mentioned earlier, the problem presupposes – in the accumulation equation of (A2.3) – the existence of a *uniform* rate of profit or interest. In other words, the problem is meaningless in the absence of the prior fulfillment of uniform-yield or arbitrage condition (1.6). (I will have more to say on this later.) Second, given that $K(t)$ covers all sources of income, borrowing is synonymous with the sale of equity owned by the household; in other words, it is indistinguishable from decumulation. $K(t)$ is thus nonnegative by definition, so that the issue of overborrowing and of the fulfillment of the No-Ponzi-Game (NPG) condition by the household can not arise (nor will it arise in my other models, given a proper definition of wealth and of foresight; on the NPG condition, see Blanchard and Fisher (1989), chapter 2). Third, for problem (A2.1)–(A2.3) to be meaningful, the integral in (A2.1) must be bounded; that is, the term inside the integral must go to zero as t goes to infinity,

$$\lim_{t\to\infty} \exp\{[g(1-R)-\Omega]t\}\, u(\cdot)=0,$$

$$u[d^C(t),d^S(t)]\equiv\frac{\{[d^S(t)]^{\gamma}[d^C(t)]^{1-\gamma}\}^{1-R}}{1-R} \quad \text{for } R>0,\quad R\neq 1 \tag{A2.4}$$

$$\lim_{t\to\infty} \exp(-\Omega t)[v(\cdot)+gt]=0,$$

$$v[d^C(t),d^S(t)]\equiv\gamma \ln d^S(t)+(1-\gamma)\ln d^C(t) \quad \text{for } R=1.$$

Since the d^i ($i=C,S$) are constant in the steady state, (A2.4) requires

$$\Omega>g(1-R) \text{ for } R>0,\ R\neq 1;\ \Omega>0 \text{ for } R=1, \tag{A2.5}$$

which will be assumed.

2 Suppose now that a solution to (A2.1)–(A2.3) exists (it may not, even if (A2.5) holds; on this and what follows, see Arrow and Kurz (1970), pp. 45–51). The corresponding optimal paths will necessarily fulfill certain conditions. Given a current-value Hamiltonian written in terms of detrended quantities, namely $H[d^C(t),d^S(t),k(t),\lambda(t),t]\equiv U[d^C(t),d^S(t),t]+\lambda(t)\{[\rho(t)-g]k(t)-e(t)\}$, these necessary Pontryagin (1962) conditions for optimality are $H_1=H_2=0$, $\dot{\lambda}=\Omega\lambda-H_3$, $\dot{k}=H_4$, that is, respectively,

$$\begin{aligned}&\{[d^S(t)]^{\gamma}[d^C(t)]^{1-\gamma}\exp(gt)\}^{-R}(1-\gamma)[d^S(t)/d^C(t)]^{\gamma}\exp(gt)=\lambda(t)\\ &\qquad \text{for } R>0,\ R\neq 1;\\ &(1-\gamma)/d^C(t)=\lambda(t) \text{ for } R=1\end{aligned} \tag{A2.6}$$

$$\begin{aligned}&\{[d^S(t)]^{\gamma}[d^C(t)]^{1-\gamma}\exp(gt)\}^{-R}\gamma[d^C(t)/d^S(t)]^{1-\gamma}\exp(gt)=\lambda(t)p(t)\\ &\qquad \text{for } R>0,\ R\neq 1;\\ &\gamma/d^S(t)=\lambda(t)p(t) \text{ for } R=1\end{aligned} \tag{A2.7}$$

$$\dot{\lambda}(t)=\lambda(t)\{\Omega-[\rho(t)-g]\}, \tag{A2.8}$$

and the second equation in (A2.3). $\lambda(t)$ is the costate variable associated with $k(t)$; it represents the shadow value of wealth to the household, that is, the intertemporal utility increment obtainable from an additional unit of wealth. Solving (A2.6), (A2.7) for $d^C(t)$, $d^S(t)$ and thus for consumption spending $e(t) \equiv d^C(t) + p(t)d^S(t)$, I have

$$d^C(t) = \left\{[\frac{\gamma}{p(t)}]^{\gamma(1-R)}(1-\gamma)^{1-\gamma(1-R)}[\exp(-gt)]^{(R-1)}\lambda(t)^{-1}\right\}^{1/R} \quad \text{(A2.9)}$$

$$d^S(t) = \left\{[\frac{\gamma}{p(t)}]^{(1-\gamma)R+\gamma}(1-\gamma)^{(1-\gamma)(1-R)}[\exp(-gt)]^{(R-1)}\lambda(t)^{-1}\right\}^{1/R} \quad \text{(A2.10)}$$

$$e(t) = \left\{[\frac{\gamma}{p(t)}]^{\gamma(1-R)}(1-\gamma)^{(1-\gamma)(1-R)}[\exp(-gt)]^{(R-1)}\lambda(t)^{-1}\right\}^{1/R}. \quad \text{(A2.11)}$$

3 I next derive the household's optimizing consumption function. Integration of (A2.8) and of the second equation in (A2.3) gives, respectively,

$$\lambda(t) = \lambda(0)\exp\{-\textstyle\int_0^t[\rho(\tau)-(\Omega+g)]d\tau\} \quad \text{(A2.8.1)}$$

$$k(t)\exp\{-\textstyle\int_0^t[\rho(r)-g]dr\} = k(0) - \int_0^t e(r)\exp\{-\int_0^r[\rho(\tau)-g]d\tau\}dr. \quad \text{(A2.3.1)}$$

The lefthand side of (A2.3.1) goes to zero as $t \to \infty$, if $k(t)$ does not grow too quickly (for instance, if it converges to a constant steady-state value, as will be shown to be the case). This yields the agent's intertemporal budget constraint,

$$\textstyle\int_0^\infty e(t)\exp\{-\int_0^t[\rho(\tau)-g]d\tau\}dt = k(0), \quad \text{(A2.12)}$$

after a change in the variable of integration from r to t.

I next substitute for $\lambda(t)$ from (A2.8.1) in (A2.11), and then substitute the resulting expression for $e(t)$ in (A2.12). Solving the latter for $\lambda(0)$, one finds

$$\lambda(0) = [\alpha(0)k(0)]^{-R}, \qquad \alpha(0) \equiv (1-\gamma)^{(1-\gamma)(R-1)/R}/\delta(0)$$

$$\delta(0) \equiv \int_0^\infty \left[[\frac{\gamma}{p(t)}]^{-\gamma}\exp\{-\textstyle\int_0^t[\rho(\tau)-\Omega]d\tau\}\right]^{\frac{(R-1)}{R}}\exp[-\textstyle\int_0^t \Omega d\tau]dt. \quad \text{(A2.13)}$$

The choice of origin is arbitrary, so that I may let t stand for the origin and rewrite (A2.13) as

$$\lambda(t) = [\alpha(t)k(t)]^{-R}, \qquad \alpha(t) \equiv (1-\gamma)^{(1-\gamma)(R-1)/R}/\delta(t)$$

$$\delta(t) \equiv \int_t^\infty \left[[\frac{\gamma}{p(\tau)}]^{-\gamma}\exp\{-\textstyle\int_t^\tau[\rho(s)-\Omega]ds\}\right]^{\frac{(R-1)}{R}}\exp[-\textstyle\int_t^\tau \Omega ds]d\tau$$

$$\text{for } R>0,\ R\neq 1,$$

$$= \Omega^{-1} \text{ for } R=1. \quad \text{(A2.13.1)}$$

Substituting for $\lambda(t)$ from (A2.13.1) in (A2.11), one finds the representative capitalist's optimizing consumption function to be

$$e(t)=\beta(t)k(t)$$
$$\beta(t)\equiv\left\{\left[\frac{\gamma}{p(t)}\right]^{-\gamma}\exp(-gt)\right\}^{\frac{(R-1)}{R}}/\delta(t) \text{ for } R>0,\ R\neq 1, \quad \text{(A2.14)}$$
$$=\Omega \text{ for } R=1,$$

where $\beta(t)$ is the propensity to consume out of wealth, and where the logarithmic case ($R=1$) provides consumption function (1.8) used in all my models.

4 (A2.3) and (A2.6)–(A2.8) are necessary, but not sufficient, for optimality. Substitution from (A2.9)–(A2.10) and (A2.13.1) in $H(d^C, d^S, k, \lambda, t)$ gives the maximized Hamiltonian $H(k, \lambda, t)$. It may be shown that the latter is, for given λ and t, a concave function of k. It follows by a well-known sufficiency theorem in the theory of infinite-horizon optimal control [Arrow and Kurz (1970), p. 49] that any consumption path satisfying (A2.3), (A2.6)–(A2.8) and the transversality condition (TVC)

$$\lim_{t\to\infty}\lambda(t)\exp(-\Omega t)\geq 0,\ \lim_{t\to\infty}\lambda(t)k(t)\exp(-\Omega t)=0, \quad \text{(A2.15)}$$

must be optimal. (I will show later that (A2.15) is in fact necessary for optimality.) Observe that, though the second condition in (A2.15) may be written as containing both $\lambda(t)$ and $\pi(t)$,

$$\lim_{t\to\infty}\lambda(t)\{x^S(t)[\pi(t)+x(t)]\}=0,$$
$$x^S(t)\equiv X^S(t)\exp(-gt),\ x(t)\equiv X^C(t)/X^S(t), \quad \text{(A2.15.1)}$$

the shadow price $\lambda(t)$ and the market price $\pi(t)$ play completely different roles in the satisfaction of TVC (A2.15). The household treats the expected trajectory $\{\pi(t)\}_{t=0}^{\infty}$ (or, equivalently, $\{\rho(t)\}_{t=0}^{\infty}$) as given to it by the financial markets; by contrast, it *sets* $\lambda(0)$ – namely, such that the subsequent household accumulation decisions conform to the optimal motions (A2.3), (A2.8), (A2.15). I will come back to this when comparing the household's TVC (A2.15) with that of the planner.

5 Suppose the representative capitalist has, for a given path of expected equity prices and interest rates, maximized the infinite-horizon utility functional (A2.1). The latter may now be written as a value function $J(K_0, t_0)$ of beginning-time t_0 and of initial capital $K_0=K(0)\equiv k(0)$, where the partial derivative of J with respect to K_0 gives the shadow price of wealth, $\partial J/\partial K_0=\lambda(0)$ [see Arrow and Kurz (1970), p. 47; Intriligator (1971),

pp. 351–3]. One may instead focus on the partial derivative $\partial J/\partial t_0$ and inquire how J changes as we allow beginning time $t_0 = t\epsilon[0, \infty)$ to recede, holding constant initial wealth at $K_0 = K(0)$. After rewriting $J(\cdot)$ as a function of K_0 and t and normalizing it with K_0,

$$\phi(t) \equiv \frac{J(K_0, t)}{K_0} \equiv \text{Max}\int_t^{\infty} \frac{u[d^C(\tau), d^S(\tau)]}{K_0} \exp[g(1-R) - \Omega](\tau - t)d\tau, \tag{A2.16}$$

this gives, under the general CRRA felicity function,

$$\dot{\phi}(t) = [\Omega - g(1-R)]\phi(t) - [u(t)/K_0], \tag{A2.16.1}$$

and, in the logarithmic case,

$$\phi'(t) \equiv \phi(t) - \frac{g}{\Omega^2 K_0} \equiv \text{Max}\int_t^{\infty} \frac{v[d^C(\tau), d^S(\tau)]}{K_0} \exp[-\Omega(\tau - t)]d\tau \tag{A2.17}$$

$$\dot{\phi}'(t) = \dot{\phi}(t) = \Omega\phi'(t) - [v(t)/K_0], \tag{A2.17.1}$$

from (A2.2), (A2.4), where $\phi \equiv J/K_0$ is the maximized value of lifetime utility per unit of initial wealth. (In (A2.17), note the integral of the discounted logarithmic trend term $g(\tau - t)\exp[-\Omega(\tau - t)]/K_0$, which is a constant $g/\Omega^2 K_0$ independent of t.) In the steady state, $\dot{\phi} = 0$ and

$$\bar{\phi} = \frac{\bar{u}(\bar{d}^C, \bar{d}^S)/K_0}{\Omega - g(1-R)} \quad \text{for } R > 0,\ R \neq 1 \tag{A2.16.2}$$

$$\bar{\phi} = \frac{\bar{v}(\bar{d}^C, \bar{d}^S)/K_0}{\Omega} + \frac{g/K_0}{\Omega^2} \quad \text{for } R = 1. \tag{A2.17.2}$$

We may recall (A2.8) and, after solving the latter and (A2.16.1), (A2.17.1) for $\Omega - g(1-R)$, write down the uniform-yield conditions

$$\frac{u(t)/K_0}{\phi(t)} + \hat{\phi}(t) = \Omega - g(1-R) = \frac{r_K(t)}{\lambda'(t)} + \hat{\lambda}'(t) \quad \text{for } R > 0,\ R \neq 1$$
$$r_K \equiv \lambda'\rho,\ \lambda' \equiv \lambda[\exp(-gt)]^{(2-R)} \tag{A2.16.3}$$

$$\frac{[v(t) + g\Omega^{-1}]/K_0}{\phi(t)} + \hat{\phi}(t) = \Omega = \frac{r_K(t)}{\lambda'(t)} + \hat{\lambda}'(t) \quad \text{for } R = 1. \tag{A2.17.3}$$

Suppose for a moment that these arbitrage conditions refer to a world in which the assets involved (discussed further below) are tradable – namely, tradable through a stockmarket whose equilibrium conditions are (A2.16.3), (A2.17.3); in which "util" is the numéraire; and in which agents treat the util prices ϕ, λ' as parametric and the associated quantities as decision variables. The *lefthand side* in the above equations then represents the yield currently expected by the household on claims to the stock K_0 of wealth (the latter measured in corn) initially set aside for the generation of utility income. Its value in utils, $\phi(t)K_0$, represents the household's *stock of utility*, while $u(t)/K_0$ (or $[v(t)+g\Omega^{-1}]/K_0$) is the household's current *flow of utility* per unit of K_0 owned.

The following parable may be useful. Think of claims to K_0 as equity shares in a trust whose pattern of future investments and income disbursements were fixed inalterably at $t_0=0$. The beneficiaries of the trust may freely trade their shares of the trust's founding capital (at current stockmarket price $\phi(t)$). Observe that at no point will they actually have an incentive to sell their shares, or to accumulate capital independently from what is being accumulated for them by the trustees. Put differently, at no point will they come to regret their initial decision to commit *all* their wealth W_0 (say) to the trust fund K_0 – which, by definition of intertemporal utility maximization, they must have done ($W_0=K_0$).

This becomes clear once we look at the *righthand side* of the equations. It represents the yield on "new," or non-trust, capital $K(t)$ owned at t through the sale of trust equity in the stockmarket or through saving out of trust income disbursements. Since the trustees' optimal investment policy (A2.8) guarantees that $(r_K/\lambda')+\hat{\lambda}'\equiv\rho+\hat{\lambda}'$ never exceeds the yield $\Omega-g(1-R)$ on trust equity, no independent capital is ever acquired by the beneficiaries and all capital increments are held by the trust. For the logarithmic case, this is confirmed by

$$\begin{aligned} &d[\lambda'(t)K^N(t)]/dt=0, \text{ thus } \dot{W}(t)=\dot{\phi}(t)K_0 \\ &W(t)\equiv\phi(t)K_0+\lambda'K^N(t)=\phi(t)K_0 \text{ if } K^N(0)=0. \end{aligned} \tag{A2.18}$$

That is, if the nontrust component K^N of the beneficiaries' total wealth W was (by utility maximization) initially zero, it will remain so forever. (In deriving the "conservation law" $d(\lambda'K^N)/dt=0$ in (A2.18), I have used (A2.3), (A2.8), and (A2.14); an expression similar to (A2.18) – involving the discounted prices $\phi(t)\omega(t)$, $\lambda'(t)\omega(t)$, $\omega(t)\equiv\exp\{-\int_0^t[\Omega-g(1-R)-\beta(\tau)]d\tau\}$ – holds in the general CRRA case.) Finally, nothing in the above account depends on the use of utils as numéraire and of the corresponding constant utility interest rate $\Omega-g(1-R)$. I may recast the story in terms of a corn numéraire and a corresponding variable corn interest rate ρ by rewriting the arbitrage equation as

$$\frac{\tilde{u}(t)/K_0}{\tilde{\phi}(t)}+\hat{\tilde{\phi}}(t)=\rho(t) \qquad \text{for } R>0,\ R\neq1;\ \tilde{\phi}\equiv\phi/\lambda',\ \tilde{u}\equiv u/\lambda' \tag{A2.16.4}$$

$$\frac{[v(t)+g\Omega^{-1}]/K_0\lambda'(t)}{\tilde{\phi}(t)}+\hat{\tilde{\phi}}(t)=\rho(t) \qquad \text{for } R=1, \tag{A2.17.4}$$

where $\tilde{\phi}$ is the stockmarket price of an equity claim to trust (or "old") wealth K_0, $\tilde{\phi}$ being in terms of current corn output or "new" wealth $(\Delta)K(t)$.

($\tilde{\phi} \equiv \phi/\lambda'$ has units [utils/K_0]/[utils/(Δ)$K(t)$], where K_0 is in units of period-t_0 corn, $K(t)$ in units of current stock-corn, $\Delta K(t)$ in units of current flow corn, the stock and flow price of current corn coinciding by entrepreneurial profit maximization.) Observe that this links intertemporal utility maximization to my usual arbitrage or stock equilibrium condition (1.6). Using the latter, I may, for instance, rewrite (A2.16.4) as (recall $\pi = p^S$)

$$\frac{\tilde{u}(t)/K_0}{\tilde{\phi}(t)} + \hat{\tilde{\phi}}(t) = \frac{r^S(t)}{\pi(t)} - \delta + \hat{\pi}(t), \qquad \text{(A2.16.5)}$$

which shows maximized lifetime utility $\tilde{\phi}$ per unit of initial wealth to be the corn-price of a particular nonaugmentable asset K_0 that produces a certain rental income (namely, the utility income $\tilde{u}$ valued in corn) and that stands in continuous arbitrage competition with other forms of holding wealth (say, steel equity), productive of other forms of income (steel dividends $r^S X^S$).

The neoclassical theory of intertemporal utility maximization is thereby *subsumed* under the general theory of portfolio arbitrage and the classical principle of the uniform rate of profit that gave birth to it.

A.2.2 The market solution

This subsection has two parts which, respectively, discuss necessary (A2.2.1) and necessary-and-sufficient (A2.2.2) conditions for a perfect-foresight-competitive-equilibrium (PFCE) path.

A.2.2.1 PFCE paths: Necessary conditions

In what follows, I first discuss conditions necessary for the VON NEUMANN I economy to possess a PFCE path under a general CRRA felicity function. I then specialize to the logarithmic case. Finally, I demonstrate that the necessary conditions in the latter case – or, equivalently, in the case of an independently given consumption function (1.8) – coincide with the canonical equations of a perturbed Hamiltonian system in relative equity prices and relative resource stocks.

Necessary PFCE conditions under CRRA felicity

Assuming households optimize CRRA felicity function (A2.2), the following conditions (A)–(E) are necessary for a trajectory of VON NEUMANN I to represent a PFCE path:

(A) Entrepreneurs maximize profits. This yields $\{p(t)\}_{t=0}^{\infty} = \pi\{(t)\}_{t=0}^{\infty}$ [recall (1.4), (1.5)].

(B) At the capital-gains expectations $\dot{\pi}^e(t) \equiv \pi(t)\hat{\pi}^e(t)$ – which are taken as given from speculators, discussed below – stockmarket arbitrageurs maximize profits and thereby instantaneously clear the stockmarket (as discussed in chapter 1). This yields arbitrage equation (1.6).

(C) The representative capitalist household maximizes [(A2.1), (A2.2)] subject to (A2.3) and given sequences of expectations $\{p(t)\}_{t=0}^{\infty}=\{\pi(t)\}_{t=0}^{\infty}$ and $\{\rho(t)\}_{t=0}^{\infty}$. This yields (A2.8) as the motion of the shadow price of wealth. (In what follows the number of households is normalized to one, so that individual and aggregate consumption coincide.)

(D) Flow-equilibrium equation $\dot{X}^S=Q^S-\delta X^S-D^S$ [or (1.14)] holds. Given (B), such flow equilibrium obtains identically.

(E) Stockmarket speculators maximize profits and possess *myopic* foresight, in the sense that actual capital gains $\dot{\pi}$ coincide with expected capital gains $\dot{\pi}^e$ (speculators correctly predict the righthand derivative of $\pi(t)$). Also, expectations across agent groups are uniform, with arbitrageurs and households passively accepting speculators' $\pi(t)$-forecast. The conditions under which (i) myopic foresight entails *long-run* foresight (over an unbounded horizon), and (ii) $\pi(0)$ and $\lambda(0)$ can be treated as known, remain to be clarified. Both will be dealt with when I discuss necessary-and-sufficient PFCE conditions. It is there also that the behavioral assumption that speculators maximize profits takes on significance.

Dropping the time index and writing optimizing consumption as (recall (A2.11), (A2.14))

$$\begin{aligned} &e(\pi,\tilde{\lambda})=\eta(\pi)\tilde{\lambda}^{-1/R}, \qquad e_1 \gtreqless 0 \text{ as } R \gtreqless 1,\ e_2<0 \\ &\tilde{\lambda}\equiv\lambda[\exp(-gt)]^{(1-R)} \\ &\eta(\pi)\equiv(\beta/\alpha)[\exp(gt)]^{(R-1)/R}\equiv[(\gamma/\pi)^{\gamma}(1-\gamma)^{(1-\gamma)}]^{(1-R)/R}, \end{aligned} \tag{A2.14.1}$$

one finds that necessary PFCE conditions (A)–(E) yield the following dynamic system:

$$\dot{\pi}=\pi(\pi q^S-q^C\pi^{-1})\equiv\phi(\pi), \qquad \phi'>0 \tag{A2.19}$$

$$\dot{\tilde{\lambda}}=\tilde{\lambda}[\Omega+Rg-\rho(\pi)]\equiv\nu(\pi), \qquad \nu'<0 \tag{A2.20}$$

$$\begin{aligned} &\dot{k}=k[\rho(\pi)-g-e(\pi,\tilde{\lambda})k^{-1}]\equiv\eta(\pi,\tilde{\lambda},k), \\ &\qquad\qquad \eta_1\gtreqless 0,\ \eta_i>0\ (i=2,3) \end{aligned} \tag{A2.21}$$

$$\begin{aligned} \dot{x}\equiv x(\hat{X}^C-\hat{X}^S)&=(x+\pi)\{q^S(\pi-x)-[1-\gamma(1+x\pi^{-1})]e(\pi,\tilde{\lambda})k^{-1}\} \\ &-\phi(\pi)\equiv\tilde{\psi}(\pi,\tilde{\lambda},k,x), \qquad \tilde{\psi}_i\gtreqless 0\ (i=1\text{–}3),\ \tilde{\psi}_4<0, \end{aligned} \tag{A2.22}$$

where (A2.19) embodies (A), (B), (E) [recall (1.17)]; (A2.20) and (A2.21) incorporate (A)–(C) [recall (A2.3), (A2.8), and (A2.14)]; and (A2.22) uses (A2.19) and, in addition, embodies (C) and (D) [recall (1.18)]. [(A2.19)–(A2.22)] constitutes a recursive four-dimensional dynamic system in the state variables π, $\tilde{\lambda}$, x, and k [or $x^S \equiv X^S\exp(-gt)$, $k \equiv x^S(\pi + x)$] and roots $r_1 = \phi' > 0$, $r_2 = 0$, $r_3 = \eta_3 > 0$, $r_4 = \tilde{\psi}_4 < 0$. Setting $\dot{\pi} = \dot{\tilde{\lambda}} = \dot{k} = \dot{x} = 0$, one finds that its steady state is characterized by

$$\bar{\pi} = (q^C/q^S)^{\frac{1}{2}} > 0, \qquad \bar{\rho} = \bar{\pi}q^S - \delta > 0 \tag{A2.23}$$

$$g = \bar{\rho} - \bar{\beta} = R^{-1}(\bar{\rho} - \Omega) \equiv s\bar{\rho} \geq 0, \qquad s \equiv (\bar{\rho} - \Omega)/\bar{\rho}R \tag{A2.24}$$

$$\bar{\beta} = R^{-1}[\Omega - (1 - R)\bar{\rho}] > 0 \tag{A2.25}$$

$$\bar{x} = [q^C - (1 - \gamma)\bar{\beta}\bar{\pi}]\bar{\pi}/[q^C - \gamma\bar{\beta}\bar{\pi}] > 0, \tag{A2.26}$$

where g represents the economy's endogenous rate of steady-state growth (nonnegative by assumption); $g = s\bar{\rho}$ the Cambridge savings equation, s being the long-run propensity to save out of profits; and where the long-run propensity to consume out of wealth $\bar{\beta} = \bar{e}/\bar{k}$ is easily shown to be positive from (A2.5). The model's parameter restrictions may accordingly be summarized by

$$\bar{\rho} \geq \Omega > (1 - R)g \tag{A2.27}$$

where the first inequality guarantees nonnegative long-run growth and the second a bounded utility integral from (A2.5).

Necessary PFCE conditions under logarithmic felicity

Note that, though $\bar{\pi}$ and $\bar{x}$ are uniquely determined, neither the steady-state value of the independent state variable k (or x^S), nor that of $\tilde{\lambda}$ will so be: Both depend on the initial condition $x^S(0) \equiv X^S(0)$ (or, alternatively, $x^C(0) = X^C(0)$). Dynamical system [(A2.19)–(A2.22)] is thus not autonomous.

To render it so, I specialize (A2.2) to the logarithmic case. Setting $R = 1$ in [(A2.19)–(A2.22)], I find that $\tilde{\lambda}$ (or λ) and k (or x^S) vanish as independent state variables. This leaves

$$\dot{\pi} = \phi(\pi), \qquad \phi' > 0 \tag{A2.19) \equiv (1.17}$$

$$\dot{x} = \psi(\pi, x), \qquad \psi_i < 0 \; (i = 1,2), \tag{A2.28) \equiv (1.18}$$

which is the autonomous, saddle-path-stable system in π,x and roots $r_1 = \phi' > 0$, $r_2 = \psi_2 < 0$ discussed in chapter 1.

Necessary PFCE conditions from a descriptive Hamiltonian

I now show how, given consumption function (1.8)[$\equiv$(A2.14), $R = 1$], dynamic system [(A2.19), (A2.28)] can be derived directly from the quasi-canonical equations of a descriptive Hamiltonian function. (Recall that (1.8) is implied by intertemporal maximization of (A2.2), $R = 1$, but may also be viewed as primitive or as rationalized on grounds other than intemporal optimization.)

The analysis proceeds in two steps (1 and 2), a breakdown helpful for my later comparison of this section's descriptive Hamiltonian with the optimal-control Hamiltonian of the planning problem. I examine, as a candidate Hamiltonian function, first a four-argument national-income function in two equity prices and two detrended capital stocks; its canonical equations are modified by a set of perturbation terms (in the same variables) that reflect stock- and flow-market clearing. The resulting dynamical system turns out to be nonautonomous, in the sense that it is incapable of tying down, independently of initial conditions, the detrended steady-state stocks of the two capital goods. (The reason is the same as that accounting for the indeterminacy of the size of the firm under constant returns to scale.) What the dynamical system does uniquely tie down is the economy's capital *composition*, that is, the size of steady-state capital stocks relative to one another. This is suggested by an alternative two-argument Hamiltonian function (in the relative equity price and the ratio of capital stocks), which I introduce in step 2 of the analysis.

1 Recalling (1.2)–(1.5), consider the detrended national-income function

$$\begin{aligned} H(p^C, p^S, x^C, x^S) &\equiv [Y^G - (\delta + g)K]\exp(-gt) \\ &= [r^C X^C + r^S X^S - (\delta + g)K]\exp(-gt) \\ &= p^S q^S x^C + p^C q^C x^S - (\delta + g)(p^C x^C + p^S x^S) \qquad \text{(A2.29)} \\ H_{p^C} &= q^C x^S - (\delta + g)x^C, \; H_{p^S} = q^S x^C - (\delta + g)x^S, \\ H_{x^C} &= p^S q^S - (\delta + g)p^C, \; H_{x^S} = p^C q^C - (\delta + g)p^S, \end{aligned}$$

where the p^i are prices expressed in some accounting unit (not corn, that is; as usual, flow and stock prices coincide by entrepreneurial profit maximization); Y^G aggregate gross output, $Y^G - \delta K$ national income, $Y^G - (\delta + g)K$ national income net of the steady-growth capital requirement gK; and $x^i \equiv X^i\exp(-gt)$ the detrended capital stock X^i. The following quasi-canonical equations imply stock- and flow-market clearing:

$$\dot{p}^C = (\rho - g)p^C - H_{x^C} \qquad \text{(A2.30)}$$

$$\dot{p}^S = (\rho - g)p^S - H_{x^S} \qquad \text{(A2.31)}$$

$$\dot{x}^C = -d^C + H_{p^C} \qquad \text{(A2.32)}$$

$$\dot{x}^S = -d^S + H_{p^S}, \qquad \text{(A2.33)}$$

where the $(\rho - g)p^i$ and $d^i \equiv D^i\exp(-gt)$ are perturbation terms that modify the canonical form $\dot{p}^i = -H_{x^i}$, $\dot{x}^i = H_{p^i}$ of the equations of Hamilton. Some observations regarding system [(A2.30)–(A2.33)] are in order:

(i) Depending on whether ρ in the perturbation term $(\rho - g)p^i$ is written as ρ^S or ρ^C, it is either (A2.30) or (A2.31) that embodies stockmarket equilibrium condition $\rho^S = \rho^C$ and generates myopic-foresight price dynamics (A2.19) (the other equation yields the identity $\rho^i = \rho^i$, $i = C, S$). The dynamic quantity equations (A2.32), (A2.33), on the other hand, represent the output-market-balance conditions $\hat{X}^i(\pi, x) = (Q^i - \delta X^i - D^i)/X^i$ for corn and steel, respectively (thus, by Walras's Law, capital-market-equilibrium equation (1.12)). All of this is easily checked by substitution of the Hamiltonian partials from (A2.29).

(ii) The price equations (A2.30), (A2.31) take the canonical form $\dot{P}^i = -H^*_{x^i}$, if I replace current-value prices p^i and the current value Hamiltonian H by their present-value counterparts $P^i \equiv \tilde{\omega} p^i$, $H^* \equiv \tilde{\omega} H$, where $\tilde{\omega} = \tilde{\omega}(t) \equiv \exp\{-\int_0^t [\rho(\tau) - g] d\tau\}$ is a period-t discount factor with focal date zero ($\tilde{\omega}$ equals $\exp(-\Omega t)$, if ρ is unchanging). Thus, it is the presence of positive discounting of the future – an excess of current- over present-value prices – that accounts for the perturbation terms in (A2.30), (A2.31). (The canonical quantity equations remain unaltered from (A2.32), (A2.33), since $H^*_{p^i} = H_{p^i}$.)

(iii) In the static theory of the firm, functions like $H(\cdot)$ are known as revenue or restricted-profit functions. When extended across firms to the economy as a whole, they represent the entrepreneurially maximized value of national income at given output prices, input stocks, and technology (see Varian (1984), Dixit and Norman (1980)). To derive the dynamic paths of economies with heterogeneous capital goods, national-income functions have been used, implicitly or explicitly, by Samuelson and Solow (1956), Magill (1970, 1977), Cass and Shell (1976a), Brock and Malliaris (1989), and others. In such applications, the essential technical issues are as follows [for details, see the references just cited; also Levhari and Liviatan (1972), Samuelson (1972)]. Assume we have the Hamiltonian function $H(p, x)$ and the $2n$ associated (unperturbed) canonical equations $\dot{p} = -H_x(p, x)$, $\dot{x} = H_p(p, x)$ (where p and x are vectors of capital-goods prices p^i and of capital stocks x^i). By a theorem of Poincaré (1890, 1952), if the canonical equations are *linear* differential equations possessing a n-vector of characteristic roots r, then $-r$ must also be a n-vector of characteristic roots; that is, the system's restpoint is a saddle point. The question then arises as to whether such saddle-path stability carries over, locally or globally, to $H(p, x)$-functions that either do not generate linear canonical equations and/or whose canonical equations have been modified by perturbation terms (which are additive functions in p, x). For instance, assume that [(A2.30)–(A2.33)] forms an autonomous dynamical system and has been linearized at the rest-point $\bar{p}^i, \bar{x}^i$ ($i = C, S$): Will it exhibit local saddle-path stability near that point, despite the presence of the perturbation terms $[\rho(p^C, p^S) - g]p^i$, $d^i(p^C, p^S, x^C, x^S)$? If it does, the perturbed, or quasi-canonical, system [(A2.30)–(A2.33)] preserves, locally, the dynamical characteristics of the canonical system $\dot{p} = -H_x, \dot{x} = H_p$.

Most of the above-named Hamiltonian literature in capital theory strives for generality within some standard neoclassical framework (such as a single consumption good, a single non-produced input, and n capital goods). Within that structure, it seeks curvature restrictions on large-dimensional $H(p, x)$-functions (with perturbation terms due to discounting) that yield global stability, uniqueness and, in some cases, proofs of existence of bounded solution paths. (On global stability see, for instance, the contributions by Rockafellar (1976) in the Cass–Shell (1976b) volume; on existence, Gaines (1976) in the same collection.) Such generality is not the goal of the present work. It limits itself throughout to local stability analysis and proceeds by strong cases (generic examples), seeking the lowest possible dimension in which to make the desired point. That point invariably turns out to be the centrality of the stockmarket and of the Hamiltonian dynamics the market's arbitraging activity generates.

(iv) Finally, is [(A2.30)–(A2.33)] in fact an autonomous dynamical system? (It is so, if time enters only through the state variables.) As we have seen, (A2.30) or (A2.31) yields the law of motion (A2.19), $\dot{\pi} = \phi(\pi)$, while (A2.32), (A2.33) can be written as $\dot{x}^i = x^i[\hat{X}^i(\pi, x^C/x^S) - g]$, $i = C, S$. These laws must hold in a steady state, which gives the two implicit functions $\hat{X}^i(\pi, x) = g$, $i = C, S$, of which only one is independent and yields $\bar{x} = \bar{x}^C/\bar{x}^S$, given $\bar{\pi}$ from $\phi(\pi) = 0$ [recall (1.24)]. That is, the dynamical system solves for the path and steady-state value of the *ratio* of capital stocks independently of initial conditions, but not for the corresponding detrended *levels* of capital stocks $\bar{x}^i$. Thus [(A2.30)–(A2.33)] is not an autonomous dynamical system. (The reason, as mentioned, is the model's constant-returns-to-scale production structure.)

2 I will now propose a Hamiltonian function that, unlike (A2.29), *does* yield the autonomous VON NEUMANN I dynamics [(A2.19), (A2.28)]. Consider

$$
\begin{aligned}
H(\tilde{\pi}, x) &\equiv (\tilde{Y}^G - \delta\tilde{K})/X^S \equiv q^S x + \tilde{\pi} q^C - \delta(1 + \tilde{\pi} x) \\
H_{\tilde{\pi}} &= q^C - \delta x,\ H_x = q^S - \delta\tilde{\pi}; \quad \tilde{\pi} \equiv \pi^{-1},
\end{aligned}
\tag{A2.34}
$$

where $\tilde{Y}^G$ and $\tilde{Y}^G - \delta\tilde{K}$ are maximized aggregate gross and net output, respectively, and where a tilde refers to a variable measured in steel numéraire; the latter replaces the accounting numéraire of (A2.29) and the corn numéraire used in the rest of the text (note the symmetry in the ratios $\tilde{\pi} \equiv p^C/p^S$ and $x \equiv x^C/x^S$; a corn numéraire is convenient for the discussion of classical–neoclassical model symmetries). The quasi-canonical equations associated with (A2.34) are

$$\dot{\tilde{\pi}} = \tilde{\rho}^S \tilde{\pi} - H_x \equiv \tilde{\phi}(\tilde{\pi}), \qquad \text{or } \dot{\pi} \equiv -\pi^2 \dot{\tilde{\pi}} = \phi(\pi) \tag{A2.35}$$

$$\dot{x} = -x\left[\frac{D^C}{X^C}(\cdot) + \hat{X}^S(\cdot)\right] + H_{\tilde{\pi}} \equiv \zeta(\tilde{\pi}, x) \equiv \psi(\pi, x), \tag{A2.36}$$

where $\tilde{\rho}^S\tilde{\pi} = (\tilde{\pi}q^C - \delta)\tilde{\pi}$ and $-x[\cdot]$ are perturbation terms that ensure stock- and flow-market clearing. As before, consumption functions (1.8) allows these perturbation terms to be written as functions only of the Hamiltonian arguments $\tilde{\pi}, x$. Now, however, [(A2.35), (A2.36)] *is* an autonomous dynamical system – namely [(A2.19), (A2.28)].

This concludes my discussion of the Hamiltonian representation of the dynamics of VON NEUMANN I. Two final comments are in order. First, subsection A.2.3 wll show that the descriptive Hamiltonian system just discussed replicates the dynamics of a planned economy, as derived from an optimal-control Hamiltonian. Second, an important claim of this book is that the national-income Hamiltonian $H(\tilde{\pi}, x)$ and varying perturbation terms in $\tilde{\pi} \equiv \pi^{-1}$ and x are capable of characterizing the entire range of classical (Ricardo–Marx–Sraffa) and Walrasian competitive-equilibrium models. For all will be seen to be governed by the quasi-canonical equations [(0.1), (0.2)] such perturbed Hamiltonian systems generate. These dual equations, the book asserts, constitute the fundamental mathematical isomorphism linking the classical and the neoclassical theory of value.

A.2.2.2 PFCE paths: Necessary-and-sufficient conditions

We have seen above that conditions (A)–(E) are *necessary* for a PFCE path and that they imply, and are implied by, the laws of motion [(A2.19)–(A2.22)]. Provided they can be made to hold over an infinite horizon ($t \to \infty$), the conditions in question are also *sufficient* for such a path. As I will now show, in the logarithmic case this must obtain whenever the stockmarket can be made to clear over an unbounded horizon. (I briefly consider the general CRRA-case later.) Thus, the condition *necessary-and-sufficient* for a PFCE path under $R = 1$ is (A2.28) together with

$$r^C - \delta = \rho = \frac{r^S}{\pi} - \delta + \hat{\pi} \text{ or } \dot{\pi} = \pi(\pi q^S - q^C \pi^{-1}) \equiv \phi(\pi) \quad \text{for } t \in [0, \infty) \tag{A2.37}$$

or, equivalently, with

$$\pi(0) = F(0;t) \text{ for } t \in [0,\infty)$$
$$F(0;t) \equiv \int_0^t [r^S(\tau) - \delta\pi(\tau)]\exp[-\int_0^\tau \rho(s)ds]d\tau + \pi(t)\exp[-\int_0^t \rho(\tau)d\tau], \tag{A2.37.1}$$

where $F(0;t)$ – the forward integral of $\hat{\pi}$ in $\rho = (r^S/\pi) - \delta + \hat{\pi}$ – is the "fundamental" value of a steel equity held until time t, and then sold at price $\pi(t)$ ($r^S - \delta\pi$ is the steel-equity dividend, or net rental). What (A2.37.1) requires is that, however far into the future t recedes, the current price $\pi(0)$ of a steel equity must always equal the discounted sum of its expected dividends plus its resale value.

Before proceeding, I first demonstrate that for $R=1$ a VON NEUMANN I path fulfilling both the necessary conditions (A)–(E) and condition (A2.37) [that is, (A2.28) and (A2.37)] exists and that it is unique, in the sense that all other paths fulfilling (A)–(E) must violate (A2.37) in finite time.

That a VON NEUMANN I path fulfilling (A2.28), (A2.37) exists follows from the fact that system [(A2.19), (A2.28)] generates a saddle path. (I argue this further below.) As for uniqueness, it obtains because all other paths are explosive, that is, imply either $\pi = 0$ or $\pi \to \infty$ in *finite* time (see $\phi' > 0$ in (A2.19) and recall figure 1.2). But a zero relative price of steel (π) or of corn ($1/\pi$) is inconsistent with stockmarket equilibrium. Since capital goods are freely disposable, their price cannot become negative, so at $\pi = 0$ it must be true that $\dot{\pi} \geq 0$; it follows that $\rho^C = \pi q^S - \delta < (q^C/\pi) - \delta + \hat{\pi} = \rho^S$ at $\pi = 0$, creating an excess stock demand for steel. At $\tilde{\pi} \equiv 1/\pi = 0$ similarly $\tilde{\rho}^C = (q^S/\tilde{\pi}) - \delta + \hat{\tilde{\pi}} > \tilde{\pi} q^C - \delta = \tilde{\rho}^S$, entailing an excess stock demand for corn. Thus, any projected movement along a divergent trajectory offers – today, before its inception – unexploited profit opportunities.[1] For it will lead, in finite time, to a predictable stockmarket disequilibrium and a discrete adjustment in equity prices equaling $\Delta\pi(t) \equiv \pi(t^+) - \pi(t^-) \neq 0$, where $\pi(t^-)$ is the price immediately before the π-discontinuity, $\pi(t^+)$ the price on the saddle path after the market correction (both at $x = x(t)$). Any such expected price discontinuity has a present value of

$$\begin{aligned} B(0;t) &\equiv \pi(0) - F(0;t) \\ &= [\pi(t^+) - \pi(t^-)]\exp[-\int_0^t \rho(\tau)d\tau] \neq 0 \qquad (t < \infty), \end{aligned} \tag{A2.37.2}$$

[1] The argument just presented may also be applied to arbitrage between steel and lifetime utility discussed earlier (that is, to arbitrage equation (A2.16.5) and its logarithmic analogue). Since (A2.16.5) embodies conditions (A2.8) and (A2.16.1) *necessary* for lifetime utility maximization, its violation by a stockmarket disequilibrium at $\pi = 0$ or $1/\pi = 0$ is inconsistent with such maximization. It follows that a necessary condition for utility maximization is convergence of π.

and violates condition (A2.37.1), thus (A2.37). ($B(\cdot)$ stands for "bubble".)

(Observe that it also violates the assumption of myopic foresight $\dot{\pi}^e(t) = \dot{\pi}(t)$, which is one of the necessary PFCE conditions: An instant before $\pi = 0$ or $\tilde{\pi} = 0$ is reached, speculators predict $\dot{\pi} < 0$ or $\dot{\tilde{\pi}} < 0$, when in fact $\dot{\pi} \geq 0$, $\dot{\tilde{\pi}} \geq 0$ will obtain at that moment. Thus we could replace condition (A2.37) by $\dot{\pi}^e(t) = \dot{\pi}(t)$ for $t \epsilon [0, \infty)$ and then argue from unexploited profit opportunities due to erroneous market expectations, an erroneousness perceived and exploited by *some* speculators.)

By contrast to these divergent orbits, motions along the saddle path *do* fulfill (A2.37) and (A2.37.1), since along it $B(0; t) = 0$ for $t < \infty$ and

$$\begin{aligned} B(0; \infty) &\equiv \pi(0) - F(0; \infty) \\ &= \lim_{t \to \infty} [\pi(t^+) - \pi(t^-)] \exp[-\textstyle\int_0^t \rho(\tau) d\tau] = 0, \end{aligned} \tag{A2.37.3}$$

given that such motions converge on a constant π-value and thus satisfy the stockmarket transversality condition

$$\lim_{t \to \infty} \pi(t) \exp[-\textstyle\int_0^t \rho(\tau) d\tau] = 0 \tag{A2.38}$$

for both $\pi(t^+)$ and $\pi(t^-)$. This concludes my demonstration that a VON NEUMANN I trajectory obeying [(A2.28), (A2.37)] exists and is unique.

I now come back to the question of why fulfillment of [(A2.28), (A2.37)] *is* in fact necessary and sufficient for a PFCE path under $R = 1$. Recall that conditions (A)–(E) discussed earlier are not merely necessary but also sufficient for a PFCE path, if I can somehow ensure that each of them holds over an infinite horizon $t \epsilon [0, \infty)$. I claim that this is what (A2.37) – stockmarket equilibrium over an unbounded horizon – achieves in the case at hand.

To demonstrate this, I need only consider the two necessary PFCE conditions (C) and (E) involving forward-looking behavior, for only these are potentially imperiled by allowing the time horizon to become unbounded. First, consider necessary condition (C) that, along a PFCE path and provided they *are* in fact optimizers, households achieve what they perceive to be an intertemporal utility maximum. Recall that transversality condition (A2.15) is sufficient for such a maximum. But maximizing felicity function (A2.2), $R = 1$, necessarily satisfies TVC (A2.15), if (A2.37) obtains. This can be seen as follows. From (A2.20), (A2.24) and $\rho = \pi q^S - \delta$ it is clear that $\dot{\lambda}/\lambda$ ($= \dot{\tilde{\lambda}}/\tilde{\lambda}$, given $R = 1$) is a linear function of π that converges to zero as $\pi \to \bar{\pi}$. Convergence of π to $\bar{\pi}$ thus implies convergence of λ to some constant $\bar{\lambda}$ (a constant that will be a function of initial conditions $X^i(0)$). This guarantees that (A2.15) holds at the steady state. But we know that

(A2.37) *does* assure convergence of the economy to the steady state – thereby guaranteeing TVC (A2.15) and a utility maximum.[2]

What if optimization had been under the general CRRA felicity function (A2.2), $R \neq 1$? The necessary PFCE conditions now yield the motions [(A2.19)–(A2.22)], and the question is whether (A2.37) again implies that TVC (A2.15) is fulfilled. A glance at the structure of the dynamic system reveals the following. Though $\tilde{\lambda}$ now is an independent state variable, its motion remains recursively governed by that of π alone. By an argument analogous to that showing, under $R=1$, convergence of λ for a convergent π, $\tilde{\lambda}$ must converge to some constant value $\bar{\tilde{\lambda}}$, if π converges to $\bar{\pi}$. However, the system now has *two* unstable roots, so, even if the root $r_1 = \phi' > 0$ causing unstable behavior in the two prices $\pi, \tilde{\lambda}$ is cast out, the second unstable root $r_3 = \eta_3 > 0$ remains operative in the motions of the quantity variable k (or x^S). The resultant explosivity of k will violate TVC (A2.15), even if $\tilde{\lambda}$ is convergent. I conclude that, given a general CRRA felicity function, the necessary-and-sufficient conditions for a PFCE path must include *two* TVC's, namely (A2.37) and (A2.15), which now are independent boundary constraints. In the instance, infinite-horizon utility maximization by households and consequent enforcement by them of TVC (A2.15) therefore does contribute to convergence – namely convergence of *quantities* – separately from profit-maximizing stockmarket speculation.[3] Such speculation, however, remains sufficient for the infinite-horizon coordination of *market prices*.

I now consider the circumstances under which the *second* of the two forward-looking necessary PFCE conditions – profit maximization by stockmarket speculators with myopic foresight [(E)] – obtains over an unbounded horizon. That is, I want to examine the fundamental question of what is the relationship between (A2.37), or (A2.37.1), and the maximization of pure profits by stockmarket speculators. As is not difficult to see, the two imply each other,

$$\text{Profit maximization by speculators} \Leftrightarrow B(0;t) \equiv \pi(0) - F(0;t) = 0 \quad \text{for } t \in [0, \infty), \qquad \text{(A2.39)}$$

provided I extend PFCE condition (E) to include not just myopic, but *long-run* foresight. In other words, I now assume stockmarket speculators to be able to use (i) their myopic foresight $\dot{\pi}^e = \dot{\pi}$ and (ii) their knowledge of the

[2] From what has been said it is clear that whenever π evolves explosively, so will λ. But an explosively evolving λ must violate (A2.15). Since, as I have argued in the last footnote, convergence of π is necessary for utility maximization, it now follows that TVC (A2.15) is not merely sufficient, *but necessary*, for such maximization.

[3] That TVC (A2.15) is necessary for utility maximization in the general CRRA-case under consideration can be shown from Benveniste and Scheinkman (1982).

economy's static and dynamic structure so as to compute the infinite-horizon price path $\{\pi(t)\}_{t=0}^{\infty}$ implied by any initial $\pi(0), x(0)$ configuration.

The question of how the decentralized VON NEUMANN I economy discussed in chapter 1 solves the infinite-horizon price coordination problem has now finally found its answer. I summarize it as follows. The system contains a group of agents – stockmarket speculators – who know its structure and who possess myopic foresight. From that knowledge and that foresight they are able to compute, at $t=0$ and at the given endowments $x^i(0)$, the equity price paths $\{\pi(t) \mid \pi(0)\}_{t=0}^{\infty}$ implied by alternative $\pi(0)$-values. In so doing, they find that, for some $0<t<\infty$, all such price paths but one offer unexploited opportunities for pure speculative profits that equal, in present-value terms, $B(0;t) \equiv \pi(0) - F(0;t) \neq 0$ per steel equity. *All* speculators will perceive these opportunities, and all will seek to act on them through appropriate equity trades should the economy start to proceed along a nonconvergent path. By creating a stockmarket disequilibrium and corresponding instantaneous short-sales on the part of arbitrageurs, these trades force the $\pi(0)$-price on to the single PFCE trajectory free of anticipated future price jumps – the saddle path.[4]

A.2.3 The planning solution

1 In what follows I demonstrate that the PFCE path of VON NEUMANN I under a CRRA representative-agent felicity function coincides with the trajectory that would be adopted by a social planner under the same welfare function. In this sense, a market economy – including its logarithmic or non-maximizing variant with consumption rule (1.8) – can be said to be governed by a dynamic invisible hand that achieves a social optimum. (Recall that VON NEUMANN I households are pure capitalists all of whom are identical; distributional issues enter only in MARX–SRAFFA.) I also show how the optimal-control Hamiltonian of the social planning problem is related to the descriptive Hamiltonian $H(\tilde{\pi}, x)$ discussed earlier.

2 Assume a social planner who maximizes the social-welfare functional

$$\int_0^{\infty} U[D^S(t), D^C(t)] \exp(-\Omega t)\,dt, \qquad (A2.40)$$
$$D^S, D^C$$

of a centralized economy that consists of a fixed number $n(=1$ for simplicity) of identical, infinitely lived households with utility functional (A2.40). As earlier, the felicity function is assumed to take the CRRA form

[4] For a similar argument in a model of stockmarket trading under uncertainty, see Tirole (1982).

$$\left.\begin{aligned} U(\cdot) &\equiv \{[D^S(t)]^\gamma[D^C(t)]^{1-\gamma}\}^{1-R}/(1-R) \\ &\equiv \{[d^S(t)]^\gamma[d^C(t)]^{1-\gamma}\exp(gt)\}^{1-R}/(1-R) \end{aligned}\right\} \quad \text{for } R>0, R\neq 1$$

$$\left.\begin{aligned} U(\cdot) &\equiv \ln\{[D^S(t)]^\gamma[D^C(t)]^{1-\gamma}\} \\ &\equiv \gamma\ln d^S(t)+(1-\gamma)\ln d^C(t)+gt \end{aligned}\right\} \quad \text{for } R=1, \tag{A2.41}$$

where $D^i(t)\equiv d^i(t)\exp(gt)\geq 0$ and where all symbols have the meaning given to them in (A2.2). The maximization is subject to two flow constraints $(i=C,S)$

$$\dot{X}^i=Q^i-\delta X^i-D^i, \text{ or } \dot{x}^C=q^Cx^S-(\delta+g)x^C-d^C, \\ \dot{x}^S=q^Sx^C-(\delta+g)x^S-d^S, \tag{A2.42}$$

where $X^i(t)\equiv x^i(t)\exp(gt)\geq 0$, and to

$$X^i(0)=x^i(0)>0 \text{ given.} \tag{A2.43}$$

The optimal-control Hamiltonian corresponding to this problem is, when expressed in current-value terms and as a function of detrended variables,

$$\begin{aligned} H(d^C,d^S,x^C,x^S,\lambda^*,\mu,t) \equiv &\{[(d^S)^\gamma(d^C)^{1-\gamma}\exp(gt)]^{1-R}/(1-R)\} \\ &+\lambda^*[q^Cx^S-(\delta+g)x^C-d^C] \\ &+\mu[q^Sx^C-(\delta+g)x^S-d^S], \end{aligned} \tag{A2.44}$$

where λ^*, μ are the planner's *shadow prices* (costate variables) associated with corn and steel stocks, respectively. (An asterisk refers to the planning variant of a variable also used in a market context; to save on notation, I do *not* use an asterisk on the x^i and the d^i – their centralized or decentralized interpretation will be clear from the context.) The Pontryagin necessary conditions for optimality are $H_1=H_2=0$, $\dot{\lambda}^*=\lambda^*\Omega-H_3$, $\dot{\mu}=\mu\Omega-H_4$, $\dot{x}^C=H_5$, $\dot{x}^S=H_6$, or, respectively,

$$[(d^S)^\gamma(d^C)^{1-\gamma}\exp(gt)]^{-R}(1-\gamma)(d^S/d^C)^\gamma\exp(gt)=\lambda^* \tag{A2.45}$$

$$[(d^S)^\gamma(d^C)^{1-\gamma}\exp(gt)]^{-R}\gamma(d^C/d^S)^{1-\gamma}\exp(gt)=\mu \tag{A2.46}$$

$$\dot{\lambda}^*=\lambda^*[(\Omega+\delta+g)-(\mu/\lambda^*)q^S] \tag{A2.47}$$

$$\dot{\mu}=\mu[(\Omega+\delta+g)-(\lambda^*/\mu)q^C] \tag{A2.48}$$

$$\dot{x}^C=q^Cx^S-(\delta+g)x^C-d^C \tag{A2.49}$$

$$\dot{x}^S=q^Sx^C-(\delta+g)x^S-d^S. \tag{A2.50}$$

I next introduce the relative shadow price $\pi^*\equiv\mu/\lambda^*$: It indicates the value, to the planner, of (additions to) the stock of steel, the numéraire being units of corn stock X^C (instead of units of utility stock $\int_0^\infty U dt$, as in the case of μ). No distinction between the stock and the flow price of a good need be made, since, unlike in the decentralized economy, the planner simultaneously functions as holder of stocks and producer of additions to these stocks. Solving (A2.45), (A2.46) for d^C, d^S, I obtain

$$d^C(\tilde{\lambda}^*, \pi^*) = \left\{ \left(\frac{\gamma}{\pi^*}\right)^{\gamma(1-R)}(1-\gamma)^{1-\gamma(1-R)}/\tilde{\lambda}^* \right\}^{1/R},$$
$$\tilde{\lambda}^* \equiv \lambda^*[\exp(-gt)]^{(1-R)}, \ \pi^* \equiv \frac{\mu}{\lambda^*} \tag{A2.51}$$

$$d^S(\tilde{\lambda}^*, \pi^*) = \left\{ \left(\frac{\gamma}{\pi^*}\right)^{(1-\gamma)R+\gamma}(1-\gamma)^{(1-\gamma)(1-R)}/\tilde{\lambda}^* \right\}^{1/R}. \tag{A2.52}$$

Subtracting (A2.48) from (A2.47), one has

$$\dot{\pi}^* = \pi^*(\pi^* q^S - q^C/\pi^*) \equiv \phi(\pi^*). \tag{A2.53}$$

From (A2.53), (A2.19) and from (A2.47), (A2.51), (A2.20) one therefore finds, respectively,

$$\phi(\pi^*) = \phi(\pi) \tag{A2.54}$$

$$\dot{\tilde{\lambda}}^* = \tilde{\lambda}^*[\Omega + \delta + Rg - \pi^* q^S] \equiv \nu(\pi^*) = \nu(\pi). \tag{A2.55}$$

This coincidence between the price *motions* of the centralized and of the decentralized economy implies that the corresponding planning and market price *levels* will be the same as well, $\pi^*(t) = \pi(t)$, $\tilde{\lambda}^*(t) = \tilde{\lambda}(t)$, $t \epsilon [0, \infty)$, provided the planner and the stockmarket choose the same initial values $\pi^*(0) = \pi(0)$ and $\tilde{\lambda}^*(0) = \tilde{\lambda}(0)$. (Observe that, near a steady state, $\tilde{\lambda}^{(*)}(0)$ does not affect the rate of change $\dot{\tilde{\lambda}}^{(*)}(t)$; the level of the solution path $\tilde{\lambda}^{(*)}(t)$, however, will clearly depend on $\tilde{\lambda}^{(*)}(0)$, as will the levels of the solution paths of $x^{(*)}$, $k^{(*)}$ examined next.) To show that planning and market solutions for the quantity variables $x^i (i = C, S)$ coincide as well – as must, therefore, $x^{(*)} \equiv x^C/x^S$ and $k^{(*)} \equiv x^S(\pi^{(*)} + x^{(*)})$ – one substitutes $\hat{x}^C, \hat{x}^S, \hat{\pi}^*$ from (A2.49), (A2.50), (A2.53) in $\hat{k}^* \equiv \hat{x}^S + [\pi^*/(\pi^* + x^*)]\hat{\pi}^* + [x^*/(\pi^* + x^*)](\hat{x}^C - \hat{x}^S)$ and in $\hat{x}^* \equiv \hat{x}^C - \hat{x}^S$. From (A2.21), (A2.22) this yields

$$\dot{k}^* = \eta(\pi^*, \tilde{\lambda}^*, k^*) = \eta(\pi, \tilde{\lambda}, k) \tag{A2.56}$$

$$\dot{x}^* = \tilde{\psi}(\pi^*, \tilde{\lambda}^*, k^*, x^*) = \tilde{\psi}(\pi, \tilde{\lambda}, k, x), \tag{A2.57}$$

given (A2.54) [substituted in (A2.22)] and assuming $x^*(0) = x(0)$, $k^*(0) = k(0)$, $\tilde{\lambda}^*(0) = \tilde{\lambda}(0)$, $\pi^*(0) = \pi(0)$. It follows that $k^*(t) = k(t)$, $x^*(t) = x(t)$, $t \epsilon [0, \infty)$, provided $\tilde{\lambda}^*(0) = \tilde{\lambda}(0)$, $\pi^*(0) = \pi(0)$, and initial stocks $X^i(0)$ are identical across the two systems. (In deriving (A2.56), (A2.57), I have used $d^C/d^S = [(1-\gamma)/\gamma]\pi^*$ – which is obtained from division of (A2.46) by (A2.45) – and $e/k \equiv (\pi d^S + d^C)/x^S(\pi + x)$.)

In conclusion (A2.54)–(A2.57) demonstrates that, given identical initial endowments, the intertemporal path of a representative-household market economy with utility functional (A2.1) coincides with that of a corresponding planned economy – provided the planner and the market system choose the same initial values for $\tilde{\lambda}^{(*)}$ and $\pi^{(*)}$. But is the latter assumption warranted?

That it is, follows – at least for the logarithmic case, to which I now restrict myself for simplicity – from my earlier discussion of the decentralized choice of $\pi(0)$. Observe that, given $R=1$, the planned economy's dynamics [(A2.53), (A2.55)–(A2.57)] collapse into $\dot{\pi}^*=\phi(\pi^*)$, $\dot{x}^*=\psi(\pi^*,x^*)$, so that $\tilde{\lambda}^*=\lambda^*$ is no longer an independent state variable. This two-dimensional dynamic system, however, generates a unique convergent saddle path identical to that of the corresponding market economy. Along it, the planner's two transversality conditions

$$\lim_{t\to\infty}\lambda^*(t)\exp(-\Omega t)\geq 0, \qquad \lim_{t\to\infty}\lambda^*(t)x^C(t)\exp(-\Omega t)=0 \qquad \text{(A2.58)}$$

$$\lim_{t\to\infty}\mu(t)\exp(-\Omega t)\geq 0, \qquad \lim_{t\to\infty}\mu(t)x^S(t)\exp(-\Omega t)=0, \qquad \text{(A2.59)}$$

are necessarily fulfilled, since convergence of $\pi^*\equiv\mu/\lambda^*$ and $x^*\equiv x^C/x^S$ to saddle point $\bar{\pi}^*$, $\bar{x}^*$ implies stationarity of μ, λ^*, and the x^i at that point (see (A2.47)–(A2.50) under $R=1$ and recall $\bar{\pi}^*q^S-\delta=(q^C/\bar{\pi}^*)-\delta=\Omega+g$ by analogy to (A2.24)). Like the household TVC (A2.15) discussed earlier, (A2.58) and (A2.59) are *sufficient* for optimality. However, for the question at hand – will the planner choose a $\pi^*(0)$-value that coincides with the $\pi(0)$ of the decentralized system? – it is important that these conditions also be *necessary*: This will guarantee $\pi^*(0)=\pi(0)$, for no other path than the saddle path will then be optimal. (Recall that all divergent paths entail $\pi^*\equiv\mu/\lambda^*=0$ or $1/\pi^*=0$, thus $\lambda^*\to\infty$ or $\lambda^*<0$, $\mu\to\infty$ or $\mu<0$ in finite time, which is inconsistent with (A2.58), (A2.59).) That the saddle path indeed is the planner's unique optimal path can be seen from the fact that all divergent paths must at some point violate condition (A2.53) necessary for optimality. ((A2.53) *is* necessary for optimality, for it is the simple difference between the two necessary Pontryagin conditions (A2.47), (A2.48), therefore necessary itself.) I conclude that the planner's TVC's are not only sufficient, but necessary for optimality. Therefore, an optimizing planner *must* set the initial price $\pi^*(0)$ at a level equal to the stockmarket-clearing $\pi(0)$ of the corresponding decentralized economy.

3 Before leaving the planner's TVC's (A2.58), (A2.59), I wish to point out an important difference, referred to several times already, between these and the decentralized household's TVC (A2.15). First, recall that in both the centralized and decentralized case the transversality conditions are necessary for optimality (I have shown this for $R=1$ and refer the reader to

Benveniste and Scheinkman (1982) for the more general case). Next, assume the decentralized economy has attained an optimum; then we know that, for $t\epsilon[0, \infty)$, $\pi(t) = \pi^*(t)$, $\lambda(t) = \lambda^*(t)$, and that, as $t \to \infty$, $\pi^{(*)}$ converges to a stationary value, while $\lambda^{(*)}$ (thus $\mu = \pi^*\lambda^*$) grows at an asymptotic rate $(1-R)g < \Omega$ – that is, less rapidly than a term $\exp(\Omega t)$ [recall (A2.5), (A2.20), and $\hat{\hat{\lambda}} \equiv \hat{\lambda} - g(1-R)$]. It must therefore be true that in the decentralized optimum

$$\lim_{t\to\infty} \lambda^*(t)\exp(-\Omega t) = \lim_{t\to\infty} \lambda(t)\exp(-\Omega t) = 0 \tag{A2.58.1}$$

$$\begin{aligned}
\lim_{t\to\infty} \mu(t)\exp(-\Omega t) &= \lim_{t\to\infty} [\lambda(t)\pi(t)]\exp(-\Omega t) = [\lim_{t\to\infty} \lambda(t)][\lim_{t\to\infty} \pi(t)]\exp(-\Omega t) \\
&= [\lim_{t\to\infty} \lambda(t)][\lim_{t\to\infty} \pi(t)]\exp[-\textstyle\int_0^t[\rho(\tau) + \hat{\lambda}(\tau) - g]d\tau] \\
&= \{\lim_{t\to\infty} \pi(t)\exp[-\textstyle\int_0^t\rho(\tau)d\tau]\}\ [\lim_{t\to\infty} \lambda(t)\exp(-\textstyle\int_0^t[\hat{\lambda}(\tau) - g]d\tau)] \\
&= 0,
\end{aligned} \tag{A2.59.1}$$

where, in (A2.59.1), I have used (A2.55), $\hat{\hat{\lambda}} \equiv \hat{\lambda} - g(1-R)$, and $\rho^* \equiv \pi^* q^S - \delta = \pi q^S - \delta \equiv \rho^C = \rho$. Observe that the first part of (A2.58.1), (A2.59.1) is the first component of the planner's TVC's (A2.58), (A2.59), respectively, while the second equation in (A2.58.1) is the first component of the decentralized household's TVC (A2.15). (Since stocks are positive, satisfaction of the TVC's under consideration requires the weak inequality they contain to hold as equality.) Also note that the first term – in swung brackets – of the last equation in (A2.59.1) must equal zero, given that its companion term diverges ($\hat{\lambda}(\tau) \to 0$ as $\tau \to \infty$, so $-\int_0^t[\hat{\lambda}(\tau) - g]d\tau \to \int_0^t g d\tau > 0$ as $t \to \infty$); (A2.59.1), therefore, represents the decentralized economy's stock-market transversality condition (A2.38). Two points follow. First, in seeking an optimum and corresponding fulfillment of TVC's (A2.58), (A2.59), the planner will solve both the problem of the optimizing household – which includes satisfaction of TVC (A2.15) – *and* the problem of the profit-maximizing speculator, which requires satisfaction of (A2.38).

Second, and conversely, the VON NEUMANN I *market* system cannot replicate the planner's optimal allocation – the latter requires satisfaction of (A2.59), (A2.59.1) – if it contains utility-maximizing households (and profit-maximizing entrepreneurs), but no stockmarket speculators.[5]

4 As promised, I close my analysis of the planned economy by juxtaposing its laws of motion – expressed in terms of the partial derivatives of the

[5] Becker (1981) reaches the correct conclusion that an "efficient-market hypothesis" [an infinite-horizon arbitrage condition similar to (A2.37)] must obtain for the decentralized system to be able to replicate the planner's optimum. Which agents and what markets are supposed to make the hypothesis come true is left unclear, however: Only households and firms engaging in flow transactions appear in the model.

utility-based optimal-control Hamiltonian $H(x^C, x^S, \lambda^*, \mu, t) \equiv H^{\text{Max}}(d^C, d^S, x^C, x^S, \lambda^*, \mu, t)$ and the perturbation terms $\Omega\lambda^*$, $\Omega\mu$ – with the laws of motion of the logarithmic market economy, expressed in terms of the partial derivatives of the national-income Hamiltonian $H(\tilde{\pi}, x)$ and the associated perturbation terms $\tilde{\rho}^S\tilde{\pi}$, $-x[(D^C/X^C)+\hat{X}^S]$. For this purpose, it is useful to note that one may show from the planning analogue of intertemporal budget constraint (A2.12) and integration of (A2.47) that, just as for the decentralized economy [recall (A2.13.1)],

$$\lambda^* = (\Omega k^*)^{-1} \text{ for } R=1. \tag{A2.60}$$

It follows that the partial derivatives of the maximized Pontryagin Hamiltonian $H^{\text{Max}}(d^C, d^S, x^C, x^S, \lambda^*, \mu, t)$ may be written as (recall (A2.44) and $\mu \equiv \pi^*\lambda^*$)

$$\begin{aligned}
\frac{H_3^{\text{Max}}(\cdot)}{\lambda^*} &\equiv \frac{H_{x^C}(x^C, x^S, \lambda^*, \mu, t)}{\lambda^*} \equiv \frac{H_{x^C}}{\lambda^*}(\pi^*) = \pi^* q^S - (\delta+g)\\
\frac{H_4^{\text{Max}}(\cdot)}{\mu} &\equiv \frac{H_{x^S}(\cdot)}{\mu} \equiv \frac{H_{x^S}}{\mu}(\pi^*) = (q^C/\pi^*) - (\delta+g)\\
\frac{H_5^{\text{Max}}(\cdot)}{x^C} &\equiv \frac{H_{\lambda^*}(\cdot)}{x^C} \equiv \frac{H_{\lambda^*}}{x^C}(\pi^*, x^*) = (q^C/x^*) - (\delta+g) - (1-\gamma)\Omega(x^*+\pi^*)/x^*\\
\frac{H_6^{\text{Max}}(\cdot)}{x^S} &\equiv \frac{H_{\mu}(\cdot)}{x^S} \equiv \frac{H_{\mu}}{x^S}(\pi^*, x^*) = (q^S x^*) - (\delta+g) - \gamma\Omega(x^*+\pi^*)/\pi^*,
\end{aligned} \tag{A2.61}$$

where I have used (A2.51), (A2.52), (A2.60) and $k^* \equiv x^S(x^*+\pi^*)$, $x^* = x^C/x^S$ to write $d^C = (1-\gamma)\lambda^* = (1-\gamma)\Omega(x^*+\pi^*)/x^*$ and similarly for d^S. Recalling the Pontryagin necessary conditions $\hat{\lambda}^* = \Omega - H_3^{\text{Max}}/\lambda^*$, $\hat{\mu} = \Omega - H_4^{\text{Max}}/\mu$, $\hat{x}^C = H_5^{\text{Max}}/x^C$, $\hat{x}^S = H_6^{\text{Max}}/x^S$ discussed earlier, I thus have $\dot{\pi}^* \equiv \pi^*(\hat{\mu} - \hat{\lambda}^*) = \pi^*\left[\frac{H_{x^C}}{\lambda^*}(\pi^*) - \frac{H_{x^S}}{\mu}(\pi^*)\right] = \phi(\pi^*)$ as in (A2.53), and $\dot{x}^* \equiv x^*(\hat{x}^C - \hat{x}^S) = x^*\left[\frac{H_{\lambda^*}}{x^C}(\pi^*, x^*) - \frac{H_{\mu}}{x^S}(\pi^*, x^*)\right] = \psi(\pi^*, x^*)$, as in (A2.57) for $R=1$. I may now use (i) the equivalence between planning and market dynamics of π and x [see (A2.54), (A2.57)], and (ii) the representation [in (A2.35), (A2.36)] of market dynamics as the perturbed canonical equations of the descriptive Hamiltonian function $H(\tilde{\pi}, x)$, to write

$$\hat{\pi}^* = \frac{H_{x^C}}{\lambda^*}(\pi^*) - \frac{H_{x^S}}{\mu}(\pi^*) = -\tilde{\rho}^S(\pi^{-1}) + \pi H_x(\pi^{-1}, x) = \hat{\pi} \tag{A2.62}$$

$$\begin{aligned}
\hat{x}^* &= -\frac{H\mu}{x^S}(\pi^*, x^*) + \frac{H_{\lambda^*}}{x^C}(\pi^*, x^*)\\
&= -[\hat{X}^S(\pi^{-1}, x) + \frac{D^C}{X^C}(\pi^{-1}, x)] + x^{-1}H_{\pi^{-1}}(\pi^{-1}, x) = \hat{x},
\end{aligned} \tag{A2.63}$$

given $\pi^*(0)=\pi(0)$, $x^*(0)=x(0)$. Expressions (A2.62), (A2.63) summarize the two alternative representations of the dynamics of VON NEUMANN I: One in terms of the utility-based optimal-control Hamiltonian $H^{\text{Max}}(d^C, d^S, x^C, x^S, \lambda^*, \mu, t)$ and the other in terms of the national-income-based descriptive Hamiltonian $H(\tilde{\pi}, x)$.

A.2.4 Other theoretical issues

This subsection briefly addresses two topics importantly related to the issues of this book, but receiving scant attention in it: Nonlinear dynamics and multiple restpoints; and conservation laws in physics and economics.

Closed orbits and multiple restpoints

All the models examined in this book generate a unique point of long-run equilibrium; the decentralized economy will necessarily reach it, given fulfillment of the infinite-horizon PFCE conditions discussed earlier. It is important to note, however, that models exist in which infinite-horizon PFCE paths do not converge to a restpoint, or to a restpoint that is unique. The implication is that, in choosing $\pi(0)$, speculators are not primarily concerned with assuring convergence to a particular steady state. What they *are* concerned with is to be on an infinite-horizon PFCE path – a path that is forever stockmarket-clearing and expectations-fulfilling. Convergence to a unique restpoint and movement along an infinite-horizon PFCE path need not be the same, as is suggested by two types of models: (i) small-scale centralized-growth models (and their implicit decentralized analogues) that yield, not a saddle point, but an optimal closed orbit, attainable under a proper choice of $\pi(0)$ [see Benhabib and Nishimura (1979)]; and (ii) models with multiple restpoints (some of which are unstable; see Liviatan and Samuelson (1969), Magill (1977), Calvo (1978), the latter being an overlapping-generations model). Multiple restpoints are interesting for their as yet unexplored potential to generate, within a fully causal context, the kinds of capital-theoretic anomalies – reswitching, capital-reversing – that were central to the Cambridge controversies of the sixties.

Conservation laws in economics?

Hamiltonians are, of course, an import from physics, where they play a fundamental role in mechanics, optics, and hydro- and electrodynamics. They typically come with one or several conservation laws – in classical mechanics, for instance, with the law of conservation of (potential-plus-kinetic) energy. Some economists (Samuelson (1970), Sato (1981), (1985); see also the papers in Sato and Ramachandran (1990)) have grappled with analogous conservation principles in economics, instances of which are (A2.18) and similar examples of conservation of capital value [on the latter, see also Burmeister (1980), chapter 2]. Mirowski (1989) has approached the topic from a history-of-thought point of view, but his focus is on links between conservative Hamiltonian dynamics in physics and static constrained-optimization techniques in economics. In light of Noether's theorem – which shows that conservation laws are *algebraic* symmetries that reflect the parameter structure of the underlying Hamiltonian – the methodological significance of the "discovery" of such laws in economics is unclear.

A.3 The Arrow–Debreu model: A reinterpretation

A.3.1 Dorfman–Samuelson–Solow on dynamic efficiency

1 I start with an Arrow–Debreu private-ownership economy [Debreu (1959), section 5.5] that has six commodities: Two goods, corn and steel ($i=C, S$), distinguished by three dates of availability ($t=1-3$, where $t=1$ is the beginning of the first, $t=3$ the end of the second and last period). The system contains competitive consumers (households), corn firms, and steel firms (all identical and equal in number, namely one). Given a vector of discounted prices $P\equiv[P^C \;\; P^S]$, $P^i\equiv[P_1^i \;\; P_2^i \;\; P_3^i]$, with focal date $t=1$, consumers maximize some preference ordering subject to the wealth constraint $P{\cdot}D\leq W\equiv P{\cdot}\omega+\Pi$, where W represents wealth, Π aggregate discounted producer profits (discussed below), and $\omega'\equiv[\omega^C \;\; \omega^S]$, $\omega^{i\prime}\equiv[X_1^i \;\; 0 \;\; 0]$, a vector of exogenous resource endowments. This maximization, I assume, leads to consumption plan $D'\equiv[D^C \;\; D^S]$, $D^{i\prime}\equiv[0 \;\; D_2^i \;\; D_3^i+X_3^i]$. (Note that a prime refers to a transpose; $D_1^i=0$ assumes initial consumption is out of initial output emerging at the end of the first period, not out of X_1^i; X_3^i is the stock of capital goods remaining at the end of the last period; technology will presently be assumed constant-returns-to-scale, so $\Pi=0$ in equilibrium.)

Given the same price vector P, producers formulate a production plan $y'\equiv[y^C \;\; y^S]$, $y^{i\prime}\equiv[-X_1^i \;\; y_2^i \;\; y_3^i+X_3^i]$, that maximizes each firm's, thus aggregate, discounted profits $\Pi\equiv P{\cdot}y$ under the given technology T. (Note that y_t^i is *net* i-output made available by producers to consumers in period t; $y_1^i=-X_1^i<0$ by definition; in the last period producers make available their gross output, $y_3^i+X_3^i$.)

Should P be such that

$$D-y=\omega, \tag{A3.1}$$

the Arrow–Debreu economy will be said to be in intertemporal equilibrium.

In what follows, I take as given households' consumption decision D and focus entirely on the interpretation of discounted-profit maximization by producers,

$$\max_{y} \Pi \equiv P\cdot y \ \text{ s.t. } \ P\cdot y^{*} \geq P\cdot y, \tag{A3.2}$$

where y^* is the profit-maximizing net-output vector at the given discounted prices P. (In this section, an asterisk denotes a maximum value.)

I now introduce the stock/flow distinction and a recursive production-period representation of technology T that reflects it. (For a similar analysis, see Malinvaud (1972), chapter 10, part B.) That is, instead of working with net output y and a representation of technology as $y \in T$ (where T is a production set in six-dimensional space) or as $g(y_1^C, y_2^C, y_3^C, y_1^S, y_2^S, y_3^S) \leq 0$ (where $g(\cdot)$ is a real differentiable function defined on that space), I adopt a production function written in terms of end-of-period gross output flows and beginning-of-period inputs stocks,

$$Q_t^i = Q^i(X_t^C, X_t^S) \qquad (i = C, S; t = 1, 2). \tag{A3.3}$$

Here Q_t^i (units: substance i/time) is the rate of flow of i-output emerging at the end of period t as a result of the availability, at the beginning of period t, of input stocks X_t^i (units: i-machines) that deliver a one-to-one amount of input services (units: i-machines time) over the unitary production period. (For instance: one steel-machine delivers one steel-machine year of input services over a one-year production period.)

The following is worth noting: (i) The *rate of flow of output* Q_t^i is related to the *quantity of input stocks* or *"funds of services"* X_t^i [Georgescu-Roegen (1971), chapter 9]; by contrast, *output* tQ_t^i (which represents the timeless difference between two stocks and, for $t = 1$, equals Q_t^i only in magnitude) is related to the *quantity of services* tX_t^i these funds generate. (ii) What can be owned – via an *equity* – are stocks of inputs and of consumption goods (X_t^i covers both), or timeless increments thereto. Quantities of input services and rates of flow of outputs are – via *contracts* – supplied and demanded, but neither can be owned.[6] (iii) Both equities and contracts have prices; examples of the former are the numéraire equity price p^S or the relative equity price $\pi \equiv p^S/p^C$ of steel, examples of the latter the flow, or output, price p and the rental rate r^S of steel.

Given these stock/flow distinctions, the relationship between y_t^i and Q_t^i may now be written as (for simplicity, I throughout assume rates of depreciation of zero, $\delta^i = 0$)

[6] Recall at this point my definition of a (non)basic and the reasons given for why it differs from that of Sraffa (see footnote 16 in the Introduction; for the equity-contract distinction, see chapter 3, footnote 5).

$$y^i_{t+1} \equiv Q^i_t - \Delta X^i_t \quad (t=1,2),\ y^i_1 \equiv -X^i_1,\ \Delta X^i_t \equiv X^i_{t+1} - X^i_t, \qquad \text{(A3.4)}$$

where the definition $y^i_1 \equiv -X^i_1$ ($\equiv -\Delta X^i_0$ in flow terms) was introduced earlier already. It is easy to check that, given (A3.1), (A3.4), and the definitions of D, y, and ω provided earlier,

$$\Delta X^i_t = Q^i_t - D^i_{t+1} \Leftrightarrow 0 = y^i_{t+1} - D^i_{t+1} \qquad (i=C,S; t=1,2), \qquad \text{(A3.5)}$$

so that the discrete-time versions of the VON NEUMANN I output-market flow-equilibrium conditions (1.11) imply, and are implied by, Arrow–Debreu equilibrium condition (A3.1) (given the definition of y^i_1). It follows that (A3.1) indeed represents a *flow* equilibrium condition; and that, if I can show (1.11) to be identities under certain conditions, (A3.1) must, under the same conditions, be an identity as well.

I now choose a specific version of (A3.3), namely

$$Q^S_t = Q^S(X^C_t, X^S_{S,t}),\ Q^C_t = a^{-1}_{SC} X^S_{C,t} \qquad (t=1,2), \qquad \text{(A3.6)}$$

where a^{-1}_{SC} is a fixed input-output coefficient and where $Q^S(\cdot)$ is constant-returns-to-scale and possesses all the standard neoclassical Inada (1963) properties. In consequence, full-employment condition

$$X^S_{S,t} + X^S_{C,t} = X^S_t \qquad \text{(A3.7)}$$

will obtain, through profit maximization by firms, at all combinations of the current output price p_t of steel and the predetermined aggregate input stocks X^i_t. Like (1.2), (1.3) in VON NEUMAN I, (A3.6) incorporates an Uzawa intensity assumption, though steel is now used in both sectors. (To convert (A3.6) into (1.2), (1.3), let $Q^S_2 \to 0$ and $Q^S_1 = a^{-1}_{CS} = q^s$.) Unlike VON NEUMANN I and all the other models examined in this book (except RICARDO), (A3.6) does not adhere to my – and Debreu's (1959) – axiom of location specificity of resources. The reason why I here assume costless instantaneous ("perfect") intersectoral factor mobility of steel is to equip myself for the dissection of the Dorfman–Samuelson–Solow analysis of dynamic efficiency (which proceeds under the perfect-factor-mobility assumption). This will also show that, as against an unquestioned theoretical tenet, perfect intersectoral factor mobility does not entail equalization of rental rates ($r^S_S = r^S_C$) across sectors; rather, it enforces equality of expected yields ($\rho^S_S = \rho^S_C$) on the underlying ownership claims. Except in the steady state, the two need not be the same.

2 Let me then begin with the discussion of dynamic (production) efficiency. (See Dorfman, Samuelson, and Solow (1958) [hereafter DOSSO], chapter 12; Burmeister (1980), chapter 2.) Consider a planner who seeks to maximize the end-of-time stock of steel X^S_3, subject to a prescribed stock of corn $\bar{X}^C_3$, given demands $\bar{D}^i_t$, and initial stocks $\bar{X}^i_1$,

$$\text{Max } X_3^S \text{ s.t. } \bar{X}_3^C \geqslant 0, \bar{D}_t^i \geqslant 0, \bar{X}_1^i > 0 \quad (i=C,S; t=1,2), \tag{A3.8}$$

given technology (A3.6), steel resource constraint (A3.7), and flow-equilibrium condition (A3.5). (Overbars will help keep track of variables that are predetermined.) The Lagrangian for this problem is

$$\begin{aligned} L(X_2^C, X_2^S; \lambda) &\equiv F^2(\bar{X}_3^C, X_2^C, X_2^S) + \lambda[F^1(X_2^C, \bar{X}_1^C, X_1^S) - X_2^S] \\ F^t(X_{t+1}^C, X_t^C, X_t^S) &\equiv Q^{S,t}[X_t^C, X_t^S - (X_{t+1}^C - X_t^C)a_{SC}] + X_t^S - \bar{D}_{t+1}^S \\ F_1^t \equiv \frac{\partial F^t}{\partial X_{t+1}^C} &= -Q_2^{S,t}a_{SC}, \; F_2^t = Q_1^{S,t} + Q_2^{S,t}a_{SC}, \; F_3^t = Q_2^{S,t} + 1, \end{aligned} \tag{A3.9}$$

where the function $F^t(\cdot) \equiv X_{t+1}^S = Q^{S,t}(\cdot) + X_t^S - D_{t+1}^S$ is as in DOSSO and embodies flow-equilibrium condition (A3.5). (I use the superscript t on the functional expression $Q^{S,t}(\cdot)$ as a shorthand to indicate the period of the inputs that produce the Q^S under consideration; technology is stationary.) First-order conditions for a maximum of X_3^S are

$$\begin{aligned} L_1 &= 0 = F_2^2 + \lambda F_1^1 = Q_1^{S,2} + Q_2^{S,2}a_{SC} - \lambda Q_2^{S,1}a_{SC} \\ L_2 &= 0 = F_3^2 - \lambda = Q_2^{S,2} + 1 - \lambda, \end{aligned} \tag{A3.9.1}$$

which immediately yields the DOSSO condition for dynamic efficiency,

$$F_3^2 = -\frac{F_2^2}{F_1^1}, \quad \text{or } Q_2^{S,2} + 1 = \frac{1 - (Q_1^{S,2}/a_{SC})}{1 - Q_2^{S,1}}, \tag{A3.10}$$

and the well-known equality $F_1^1 \equiv (\partial X_2^S/\partial X_2^C)_{|d\bar{X}_1^i=0} = -(\partial X_2^S/\partial X_2^C)_{|dX_3^i=0} \equiv -(F_2^2/F_3^2)$ of the marginal rates of transformation between X_2^S and X_2^C as outputs and as inputs, respectively. (Under a VON NEUMANN I production structure, $F_1^1=0$ so that (A3.10) is inapplicable; dynamic efficiency obtains trivially since the constraints in (A3.8) pin down X_3^S uniquely.)

I now turn to the issue of principle interest: Under what conditions will a decentralized economy mimic the above planner and achieve dynamic efficiency through the price system? Both DOSSO and Debreu take *forward-looking* profit maximization by producers to be an essential prerequisite. Debreu [(1959), section 6.4] does so by using, in his proof of the second theorem of welfare economics, maximization (A3.2) of discounted profits. I will return to Debreu and (A3.2) in a moment.

DOSSO introduce two requirements for decentralized dynamic efficiency. The first is the maximization, independently at each t, of "current" producer profits; that is, treating corn as numéraire and writing undiscounted prices in lower-case letters as usual,

$$\begin{aligned} &\text{Max } \Pi^t(X_t^C, X_{S,t}^S, X_{C,t}^S; p_{t+1}, r_t^C, r_t^S) \equiv \Pi^{S,t} + \Pi^{C,t} \qquad (t=1,2) \\ &\Pi^{S,t} \equiv p_{t+1}Q^{S,t}(X_t^C, X_{S,t}^S) - (r_t^C X_t^C + r_t^S X_{S,t}^S) \\ &\Pi^{C,t} \equiv a_{SC}^{-1} X_{C,t}^S - r_t^S X_{C,t}^S, \end{aligned} \tag{A3.11}$$

where Π^t, $\Pi^{i,t}$ denote, respectively, aggregate profits and profits of firm i in period t. (The authors use, in lieu of (A3.11), the equivalent profit function $\Pi^t(X^C_{t+1}, X^C_t, X^S_t; \ldots) \equiv p_{t+1}[F^t(X^C_{t+1}, X^C_t, X^S_t) - X^S_t] + (X^C_{t+1} - X^C_t) - (r^C_t X^C_t + r^S_t X^S_t)$, which incorporates (A3.7); but, as mentioned, (A3.7) is always fulfilled under (A3.6), so will not constrain (A3.11).)

The key point to note about (A3.11) is that firms are supposed to competitively choose levels of inputs for period t in the light, not of the known period-t output price p_t, but of the *expected* next-period price p_{t+1}. (Recall that inputs are chosen at the beginning of the period, when period-t markets are open; the latter completely determine the temporary-equilibrium prices $p_t(=\pi_t)$, r^i_t, given expectations for p_{t+1}.) Put differently, instead of myopically maximizing current profits in the light of current prices p_t, r^i_t, firms *speculate*.

First-order conditions for (A3.11) are $\Pi^t_h = 0$ $(h = 1-3)$ or, respectively,

$$p_{t+1}Q_1^{S,t} = r^C_t, \; p_{t+1}Q_2^{S,t} = r^S_t, \; a_{SC}^{-1} = r^S_t \quad (t = 1, 2). \tag{A3.11.1}$$

This means that (i) entrepreneurs hire inputs in competitive rental markets to the point where the current cost r^i_t of the input service equals the value of its current marginal product reckoned at next period's expected output price (p_{t+1} and 1 for S and C, respectively); (ii) these expected value marginal products are equalized across sectors for any mobile factor.

It is now easy to show – by using $p_{t+1}Q_2^{S,t} = a_{SC}^{-1}$ for $t = 1, 2$; setting $t = 2$ in the first and second equation of (A3.11.1); and substituting in (A3.10) – that (A3.10) will obtain, given producer profit maximization as in (A3.11), if and only if the second of DOSSO's conditions for decentralized dynamic efficiency [the first is (A3.11.1)], namely

$$r^C_t = \frac{r^S_t}{p_t} + \hat{p}_t \equiv \rho_t \;\text{ or }\; \rho^C_t = \rho^S_t \equiv \rho_t, \; \hat{p}_t \equiv \frac{p_{t+1}}{p_t} - 1 \quad (t = 1, 2), \tag{A3.12}$$

is met. (A3.12), of course, is nothing but my VON NEUMANN I arbitrage or uniform-expected-yield condition (1.6) (in discrete time and given equality between flow and stock prices of goods, $p^C_t = 1$, $p^S_t = p_t$; recall $\delta = 0$). In the words of DOSSO:

If perfectly atomistic competitors cause resources to be channeled into consumption and investment programs so as (1) to maximize their current net profits or in any case to prevent net profits from becoming negative, and (2) to make it a matter of indifference how further increments of investment are scheduled, then an efficient program of capital accumulation will result. This presumes no uncertainty so that ex ante expected prices or rates of change of prices – which each competitor knows but cannot himself affect – will correspond exactly to ex post observed prices. (p.319)

Though a justly celebrated high point of their study, and though mathematically correct, DOSSO's reasoning is economically flawed. For why indeed should constant-returns-to-scale firms, operating in perfect input and output markets, be concerned at any point with the *future* price of their output? They face a perfectly elastic demand for their output (at $p_t = \pi_t$ and 1, respectively) and perfectly elastic supplies of input services (at r_t^C, r_t^S); they face no adjustment costs of any sort; and they own no stocks (they rent all inputs and distribute the entirety of their output as rental payments), so are unconcerned with capital gains or losses. As Arrow (1964) has shown, it is by maximizing profits myopically within each period in the light of output and input prices prevailing in that period that such firms maximize the firm's present value (the discounted sum of current and future profits).

This suggests that (A3.11) should be replaced by

$$\begin{aligned} &\text{Max } \tilde{\Pi}^t(X_t^C, X_{S,t}^S, X_{C,t}^S; p_t, r_t^C, r_{S,t}^S, r_{C,t}^S) \equiv \tilde{\Pi}^{S,t} + \tilde{\Pi}^{C,t} \qquad (t=1,2) \\ &\tilde{\Pi}^{S,t} \equiv p_t Q^{S,t}(X_t^C, X_{S,t}^S) - (r_t^C X_t^C + r_{S,t}^S X_{S,t}^S) \qquad \text{(A3.13)} \\ &\tilde{\Pi}^{C,t} \equiv a_{SC}^{-1} X_{C,t}^S - r_{C,t}^S X_{C,t}^S. \end{aligned}$$

The first-order conditions $\tilde{\Pi}_h^t = 0$ $(h = 1-3)$ give, respectively,

$$p_t Q_1^{S,t} = r_t^C,\ p_t Q_2^{S,t} = r_{S,t}^S,\ a_{SC}^{-1} = r_{C,t}^S \qquad (t=1,2), \qquad \text{(A3.13.1)}$$

which should be compared to (A3.11.1): p_t has replaced p_{t+1}; and I have *not* assumed intersectoral equality of steel rental rates $r_{S,t}^S = r_{C,t}^S$ (though I do not preclude it). It is easy to check – by solving (A3.13.1) for $Q_1^{S,2}$, $Q_2^{S,1}$, $Q_2^{S,2}$, and substituting in (A3.10) – that dynamic efficiency (A3.10) now fails to obtain under (A3.12). In other words, myopic profit maximization by firms (A3.13), together with fulfillment of arbitrage condition (A3.12), do not give us a dynamically efficient decentralized economy.

To probe this further, I start by addressing the question why the $r_{i,t}^S$ can differ. The reason is simple: Owners of steel stocks insist on earning the same expected equity yield $\rho_{i,t}^S$ – not the same current service rental $r_{i,t}^S$ – wherever such stock is being used in supplying steel-input services. Since, as I will now show, expected capital gains on equity claims to steel inputs used in corn firms usually differ from expected capital gains on equity claims to steel inputs employed in steel production, yield equality $\rho_{S,t}^S = \rho_{C,t}^S$ – consequently, willing supply of steel-input services to both sectors – requires $r_{S,t}^S \neq r_{C,t}^S$.

To see this, observe that steel firms will pay out – at the end of production period t, when steel output emerges – a portion (agreed upon at the beginning of t) $Q_2^{S,t} X_{S,t}^S = (r_{S,t}^S / p_t) X_{S,t}^S$ of total steel output Q_t^S to steel-stock owners they have hired input services from (the remainder, $Q_t^S - Q_2^{S,t} X_{S,t}^S$, goes to owners of the sector-specific input corn). Steel owners or their stockmarket representatives – a distinction not necessary in what follows – possess myopic foresight, therefore understand at the beginning of t that they will be able to sell this increment to their steel holdings at a price p_{t+1}, once the $t+1$-equity market has opened at the beginning of $t+1$. That is, should $p_{t+1} \neq p_t$, they will earn a numéraire capital gain or loss $(p_{t+1} - p_t)Q_2^{S,t}X_{S,t}^S = \hat{p}_t r_{S,t}^S X_{S,t}^S \gtrless 0$ on the steel-value $Q_2^{S,t}X_{S,t}^S$ of the rental received from their employers for period t. In consequence, their total expected yield on owning equity in one unit of steel stock employed in the steel sector will be $\rho_{S,t}^S \equiv (r_{S,t}^S/p_t)(1+\hat{p}_t) + \hat{p}_t \equiv (r_{S,t}^S/p_t) + \hat{p}_t[1 + (r_{S,t}^S/p_t)]$, where $r_{S,t}^S/p_t$ denotes the current yield, $(r_{S,t}^S/p_t)\hat{p}_t$ the percent capital gain specific to steel engaged in steel production, and $\hat{p}_t$ the capital gain on steel wherever employed. Similar reasoning shows that owners of the sector-specific corn input will make a capital gain of $(p_{t+1} - p_t)\, Q_1^{S,t} X_t^C = \hat{p}_t r_t^C X_t^C \gtrless 0$ on their steel rental income $Q_1^{S,t} X_t^C$, which affords them an expected equity yield of $\rho_t^C \equiv r_t^C(1+\hat{p}_t)$ (recall $p_t^C = 1$). Consider, finally, the yield on steel stock used to supply input services of steel to the corn industry. The latter will pay out the entirety of its end-of-period corn output $Q_t^C = a_{SC}^{-1} X_{C,t}^S$ for such services; thus, $r_{C,t}^S X_{C,t}^S = a_{SC}^{-1} X_{C,t}^S$ will be the rental payments received by its steel-input suppliers. Since the price of corn is invariant at unity, no capital gain can be generated on the corn equity increment that corresponds to this rental income. The expected yield on owning equity in one unit of steel stock rented out to the corn sector will thus be $\rho_{C,t}^S \equiv (r_{C,t}^S/p_t) + \hat{p}_t$, the sum of a current yield $r_{C,t}^S/p_t$ plus a capital gain $\hat{p}_t$ on equity in steel wherever employed.

As usual, the absence of unexploited arbitrage profits requires that expected yields on all forms of property be equal,

$$\rho_t^C = \rho_{S,t}^S = \rho_{C,t}^S \equiv \rho_t, \text{ or}$$
$$r_t^C(1+\hat{p}_t) = \frac{r_{S,t}^S}{p_t}(1+\hat{p}_t) + \hat{p}_t = \frac{r_{C,t}^S}{p_t} + \hat{p}_t \equiv \rho_t \quad (t=1,2), \tag{A3.14}$$

which should be compared to the DOSSO arbitrage condition (A3.12).

Four points are noteworthy about (A3.14). First, it substantiates the earlier claim that equality of yields $\rho_{S,t}^S = \rho_{C,t}^S$ does not imply, nor is implied by, intersectoral equality of rentals $r_{S,t}^S = r_{C,t}^S$ – unless $\hat{p}_t = 0$ as in the steady state (or unless the duration of the period of production approaches zero as in continuous time, or outputs are nonstorable). Second, observe that $\rho_{S,t}^S = \rho_{C,t}^S$ and (A3.13.1) yield (given the neoclassical properties of $Q^{S,t}(\cdot)$)

$$p_{t+1} Q_2^{S,t}\left(\frac{X_t^C}{X_{S,t}^S}\right) = a_{SC}^{-1}, \text{ thus } \frac{X_t^C}{X_{S,t}^S} = \frac{X_t^C}{X_{S,t}^S}(p_{t+1}),\ Q_h^{S,t} = Q_h^{S,t}(p_{t+1})\ (t, h = 1,2), \tag{A3.15}$$

so that the current period-t allocation (at predetermined X_t^i) of steel inputs $X_{i,t}^S$ between the two sectors and the consequent marginal productivities $Q_h^{S,t}$ depend, via stockmarket speculation by steel-equity holders, on the expected price of steel p_{t+1} for next period.

Third, we may solve the arbitrage equation $\rho_t^C = \rho_{S,t}^S$ – that is, $r_t^C = (r_{S,t}^S/p_t) + [\hat{p}_t/(1+\hat{p}_t)]$ – for $\hat{p}_t$. Given (A3.13.1), $\rho_{S,t}^S = \rho_{C,t}^S$ [thus, $Q_h^{S,t'} = Q_h^{S,t'}(p_{t+1})$ from (A3.15)], and myopic foresight, this yields an implicit law of motion of the price of steel,

$$p_{t+1} = \frac{p_t}{1-[p_t Q_1^{S,t'}(p_{t+1}) - Q_2^{S,t'}(p_{t+1})]} \qquad (t=1,2). \tag{A3.16}$$

Equation (A3.16) may be linearized, then solved explicitly for p_{t+1} or $\Delta p_t \equiv p_{t+1} - p_t$, which gives

$$\Delta p_t = \phi(p_t) \text{ or } \Delta\pi_t = \phi(\pi_t) \qquad (t=1,2), \tag{A3.17}$$

the present economy's instantiation of Hamiltonian equation (0.2). (Observe that, like the corresponding law of motion (1.17) of VON NEUMAN I, equation (A3.17) does not depend on the state variable $x_t \equiv X_t^C/X_t^S$, which means that (A3.17) is decoupled from the economy's demand side $D' \equiv [D^C \;\; D^S]'$.)

Fourth, it is not difficult to show that (A3.17) – which is due, as we recall, to *forward-looking* (myopic-foresight) stockmarket arbitrage, as in (A3.14), coupled with *myopic* maximization of current profits by firms, as in (A3.13) – now *must* give us dynamic efficiency. To see this, proceed as follows: (i) Substitute in the $\rho_t^C = \rho_{S,t}^S$-equation of (A3.14) for r_t^C, $r_{S,t}^S$ from the profit-maximizing conditions (A3.13.1) and let $t=2$; (ii) substitute in the $\rho_{S,t}^S = \rho_{C,t}^S$-equation for $r_{S,t}^S$ and $r_{C,t}^S$ and solve for p_{t+1} under $t=1$ and $t=2$; this yields $p_2 = 1/Q_2^{S,1'} a_{SC}$ and $p_2/p_3 = Q_2^{S,1'}/Q_2^{S,2}$ which, when substituted in the expression for $\rho_2^C = \rho_{S,2}^S$ obtained under (i), gives dynamic efficiency (A3.10).

To summarize: By failing to distinguish sharply between producers – who optimize across current outputs and services of inputs – and property owners — who optimize across speculative portfolios of equity claims to input stocks – DOSSO have misinterpreted the conditions necessary for the decentralized achievement of dynamic efficiency.

A.3.2 A Hamiltonian interpretation of the Arrow–Debreu economy

1 That the distinction between the economy's producers and its property owners is not mere pedantry can be seen in the consequences of its neglect by the Arrow-Debreu model, to which I now return. (I use the shorthand A–D for Arrow–Debreu in the remainder of this supplement.) Here the distinction is not merely insufficiently sharp as in DOSSO – where, as we recall, "pure investors" and an arbitrage equation [(A3.12)] remain features of the model – but entirely obliterated. It is so despite Debreu's assertion that in a "private ownership [economy] . . . consumers own the resources and control the producers. Given a price system, each producer

maximizes his profit, which is distributed to consumer-shareholders" (1959, p.74). The truth is that nowhere in the A–D model can a discussion of share-holding – that is, of resource *ownership* as opposed to resource *use* – be found. Financial issues only emerge as a byproduct of the introduction of uncertainty (Arrow (1952)). Yet such issues are centrally present in the full-certainty model already, if it is interpreted as a perfect-foresight economy moving through time, rather than as a beginning-of-history, complete-futures-market system. (On sequence-economy interpretations of the A–D model, see Radner (1972), Hahn (1970, 1973).)

To show this, what I have to do is to demonstrate that the law of motion (A3.17) – which, to recall, embodies forward-looking stockmarket arbitrage by portfolio holders and myopic profit maximization by entrepreneurs – implies, and is implied by, the maximization of discounted A–D profits (A3.2) discussed earlier. This, of course, will also provide the essential element in the proof that the A–D model and the quasi-Hamiltonian system [(0.1),(0.2)] are mathematically isomorphic.

I start from technology (A3.6) and an analogue to (A3.2) that (as I shall show) preserves all of the latter's implications, but is recursive. It is recursive in the sense that discounted profits are maximized sequentially period by period, not across the entire horizon:

$$\begin{aligned} &\text{Max } \Pi^t(X_t^C, X_{S,t}^S, X_{C,t}^S; P_{t+1}^C, P_t^C, P_{t+1}^S, P_t^S) \equiv \Pi^{S,t} + \Pi^{C,t} \qquad (t=1,2) \\ &\Pi^{S,t} \equiv P_{t+1}^S Q^{S,t}(X_t^C, X_{S,t}^S) + (P_{t+1}^S - P_t^S) X_{S,t}^S + (P_{t+1}^C - P_t^C) X_t^C \\ &\Pi^{C,t} \equiv P_{t+1}^C a_{SC}^{-1} X_{C,t}^S + (P_{t+1}^S - P_t^S) X_{C,t}^S, \end{aligned} \tag{A3.18}$$

where P_t^i is the discounted or present-value price of good i in period t (focal date $t=1$). According to (A3.18), to maximize profits steel producers (say) maximize the difference between the *expected* "*value of the firm*" $P_{t+1}^S(Q_t^S + X_{S,t}^S) + P_{t+1}^C X_t^C$ at the beginning of $t+1$ and its known value $P_t^S X_{S,t}^S + P_t^C X_t^C$ at the beginning of t, both discounted to $t=1$. By contrast, recall that earlier, in (A3.13), producers were assumed to maximize profits by maximizing the difference between the *known value of output* ($p_t Q_t^S$ for steel) and its known input cost ($r_t^C X_t^C + r_{S,t}^S X_{S,t}^S$), both measured in current – that is, undiscounted – prices obtaining at the beginning of period t. The first-order conditions for (A3.18), $\Pi_h^t = 0$ $(h = 1-3)$, give

$$\begin{aligned} &P_{t+1}^S Q_1^{S,t} + (P_{t+1}^C - P_t^C) = 0, \qquad P_{t+1}^S(Q_2^{S,t} + 1) - P_t^S = 0, \\ &\qquad P_{t+1}^C a_{SC}^{-1} + (P_{t+1}^S - P_t^S) = 0, \end{aligned} \tag{A3.18.1}$$

and are easily shown to imply dynamic efficiency. (To do so, solve the first equation for $Q_1^{S,2}$; the second for $Q_2^{S,1}$ and $Q_2^{S,2}$; the third for P_3^C and P_1^S, substituting the result in $Q_1^{S,2}$ and $Q_2^{S,1}$, respectively; substitution for the terms in (A3.10) now results in an identity.)

Maximization rule (A3.18) thus possesses the *same* efficiency properties as a decentralized mechanism involving myopic profit maximization by firms [(A3.13)] and stockmarket arbitrage by portfolio holders with myopic foresight [(A3.14)]. What alternative story about the behavior of agents and the structure of markets does (A3.18) tell?

First, note that (A3.18) requires there to be discounted *market* prices P_t^i, P_{t+1}^i for all $i(=C,S)$ and for each period $t(=1,2)$. Second, (A3.18) pictures a firm (producers, entrepreneurs) as "owning" input stocks X_t^i, and as being able to instantaneously buy and sell such stocks, in any desired amount, at the prevailing market price P_t^i. In other words, the firm is capable, not just of selling its current output, but of "liquidating itself" – selling off its assets – in any given period. Clearly, what is implied here is the possibility of instantaneous transfers of *ownership claims* across firms. That is, firms are thought of as performing a role that model [(A3.13), (A3.14)] – as well as DOSSO (recall (A3.12) and its "pure investors") – attributes to the economy's portfolio-holding capitalists or their stockmarket representatives. This, I will now argue, is the *only* possible interpretation of (A3.18) and, by extension, of A–D producer-profit maximization (A3.2). All alternative accounts can be shown to either collapse into the one just given, or to be inconsistent with (A3.18).

Consider, for instance, an interpretation of (A3.18) according to which firms come to "own" their input stocks because households "sell" to them their initial equity claims (in X_1^i) and at no subsequent point come to hold equity again, keeping their changing level of wealth instead in Fisherian bonds issued by firms. Or assume households' equity remains fixed in all periods at the initial level X_1^i, and pays a dividend income that, if unconsumed, is lent to firms, which use it to purchase – become "owners" of – stocks of inputs $X_t^i(t \neq 1)$. Whatever the story, the fact is that firms may *possess* but, by definition, at no point can come to *own* input stocks. All they do, behind whatever financial veil we may care to construct, is *rent* the services of input stocks from the economy's capitalists. For this they are either charged an explicit market rental or charge themselves a shadow rental (user cost) equal to the latter. The user cost will be such as to just defray depreciation charges and dividend payments to the firm's owners – who are capitalists that have substituted, in their portfolios, equity in the firm "owning" the input stocks for direct equity in the stocks themselves. (The Modigliani–Miller (1958) theorem reflects the irrelevance of the debt–equity distinction for the question of ownership.)

Consider next an account inconsistent with (A3.18). According to it, firms adjust their physical capital stock over several periods through finite-flow adjustments, by purchasing new capital goods in the output markets and by allowing existing capital to depreciate. But this is unacceptable: No

Penrose adjustment costs are present in the model and (A3.18) requires firms to be able to make within-period stock-shifts in their capital structure. An unhelpful, though typical, response to the requirement that instantaneous shifts in capital stocks be possible is to look for *markets in used capital goods* – and to conclude that, since in the real world there are few of them, the theory has a problem. Malinvaud is illustrative of this reaction:

Let us now examine the origin of the property . . . [that] for a firm in a "competitive market", the optimal policy is separate maximization of the [discounted] profits relating to each period [as in (A3.18)]. This property assumes the existence of perfect markets for all commodities including equipment in use and products in course of manufacture. In particular, it implies that no transportation cost hinders the sale or purchase of second-hand material . . . In short, the property under consideration assumes that capital is freely transferable at each date, at well-defined prices. In the real situation, a large part of capital is 'fixed'. The cost of transferring it from one use to another is often prohibitive. Thus the general theory . . . ignores an aspect of reality which is important in certain cases. (1972, pp.259–60 – terms in brackets are mine)

For similar arguments on the "problem" posed by the absence of markets in used capital goods, see Shell and Stiglitz (1967), Burmeister (1980).

Contrary to these authors, what is at issue are not markets through which input stocks can be physically transferred from one firm to another, instantaneously and at zero transportation costs. By the laws of physics, such transfers cannot help but be costly and time-consuming investment processes. (I analyze them as such in WALRAS III; note also the clash with the A–D characterization of a commodity by its location.) Rather, what is required are markets in the equity claims that the property system attaches to every input stock when it comes into physical existence. It is these financial or "paper" claims that must be allowed to change hands, instantaneously and quasi-costlessly, if (A3.18) is to be possible.

One final remark regarding the interpretation of (A3.18) may be helpful. Once we allow (as in the absence of costs of adjustment we must) that firms can perform instantaneous changes in the structure of the input stocks X_t^i they "own" – thus, in the streams of input services they have access to – all the options open to a firm that merely *rents* input services must be open to them as well. This again shows that firms that buy and sell input stocks must end up imputing to the services of the latter a shadow rental just equal to the rental in the corresponding competitive rental market – a market that always exists (if only incipiently) given yield maximization across all possible ways of holding property.

2 I have dwelled, perhaps excessively, on (A3.18) and its interpretation for a simple reason: It is the bridge that connects the A–D model with my quasi-

Hamiltonian system – specifically, links (A3.2) with (A3.17). I have, as it were, been standing at the center of this bridge, looking around and trying to orient myself and the reader. I will now cross it in one direction, reaching (A3.17), myopic profit maximization by firms, and forward-looking stock-market arbitrage by portfolio holders at the end. Retracing my steps and crossing the bridge in the other direction, I shall alight in A–D land.

To reach (A3.17) from (A3.18), I need some well-known definitions that link the system of discounted prices P_t^i – whose numéraire is period-one corn, so that $P_1^C \equiv 1$ – to the system of undiscounted or current prices p_t^i (which, as usual, has a corn numéraire for all t; let stock corn play that role, thus $p_t^C \equiv 1$ and $p_t^S \equiv p_t^S/p_t^C \equiv \pi_t = p_t$). A commodity's own rate of return $\tilde{\rho}_t^i$ and its own discount factor v_t^i are defined as (see, for instance, Debreu (1959), chapter 2, and Burmeister (1980), chapter 2)

$$\tilde{\rho}_t^i \equiv (P_t^i/P_{t+1}^i) - 1,\ v_t^i \equiv P_t^i/P_1^i \equiv (1+\tilde{\rho}_t^i)v_{t+1}^i \equiv \left[\prod_{\tau=1}^{t-1}(1+\tilde{\rho}_\tau^i)\right]^{-1}. \quad \text{(A3.19)}$$

In any consistent system of discounting, changes in the focal date must leave the contemporaneous relative price $p_t^S/p_t^C \equiv p_t^S$ unaffected; thus,

$$P_t^S/P_t^C \equiv p_t^S/p_t^C \equiv p_t^S. \quad \text{(A3.20)}$$

This implies, from (A3.19),

$$(p_t^S/p_{t+1}^S) \equiv P_t^S/P_{t+1}^S(1+\tilde{\rho}_t^C) \quad \text{or } P_{t+1}^S \equiv v_{t+1}^C p_{t+1}^S \equiv v_{t+1}^C(1+\hat{p}_t^S)p_t^S. \quad \text{(A3.21)}$$

Finally, I *assert* that the numéraire own rate of return $\tilde{\rho}_t^C$ in the discounted-price system and the uniform expected yield ρ_t in the current price system with a corn numéraire are identical,

$$\tilde{\rho}_t^C \equiv \rho_t. \quad \text{(A3.22)}$$

That is, rather than trying to argue for (A3.22) on theoretical grounds – which I do not know how to do without introducing new and otherwise unnecessary terms, such as Fisherian "commodity loans" – I treat it as true by definition and show that its use (i) is free of contradiction, and (ii) generates the desired nexus between (A3.2) and (A3.17). This has the advantage that *none* of the expressions I have introduced in (A3.19)–(A3.22) to characterize the discounted-price system contains a theoretical proposition: Each is merely a tautology.

I may, at this point, rewrite the representative steel-firm's discounted t-period profit $\Pi^{S,t}$ in (A3.18) as $\Pi^{S,t} \equiv P_{t+1}^S\{Q^{S,t}(\cdot) + [1-(P_t^S/P_{t+1}^S)]X_{S,t}^S + (P_{t+1}^C/P_{t+1}^S)[1-(P_t^C/P_{t+1}^C)]X_t^C\}$ or, after substituting for P_{t+1}^S and P_t^S/P_{t+1}^S from the second and first equation of (A3.21), for P_{t+1}^C/P_{t+1}^S, P_t^C/P_{t+1}^C from (A3.20) and (A3.19), and using (A3.22), as

$$\Pi^{S,t} \equiv v^C_{t+1}[p^S_t Q^{S,t}(\cdot)(1+\hat{p}^S_t) + p^S_t(\hat{p}^S_t - \rho_t)X^S_{S,t} - \rho_t X^C_t]. \tag{A3.23}$$

Similar manipulation shows that t-period profit of corn-firms in (A3.18), $\Pi^{C,t} \equiv P^S_{t+1}(P^C_{t+1}/P^S_{t+1})\{a^{-1}_{SC} + (P^S_{t+1}/P^C_{t+1})[1-(P^S_t/P^S_{t+1})]\}X^S_{C,t}$, equals

$$\Pi^{C,t} \equiv v^C_{t+1}[a^{-1}_{SC} + p^S_t(\hat{p}^S_t - \rho_t)]X^S_{C,t}. \tag{A3.24}$$

Aggregate discounted t-period profits are $\Pi^t \equiv \Pi^{S,t} + \Pi^{C,t}$, so that problem (A3.18) may be written as (I add and subtract $r^C_t X^C_t + r^S_{S,t}X^S_{S,t}$)

$$\begin{aligned} \text{Max } \Pi^t \equiv v^C_{t+1}\{ & Y_t + [p^S_t Q^{S,t}(\cdot) - (r^C_t X^C_t + r^S_{S,t}X^S_{S,t})]\hat{p}^S_t \\ & - [\rho_t - \hat{p}^S_t r^C_t]X^C_t - [p^S_t(\rho_t - \hat{p}^S_t) - \hat{p}^S_t r^S_{S,t}]X^S_{S,t} \\ & - p^S_t(\rho_t - \hat{p}^S_t)X^S_{C,t}\}, \quad Y_t \equiv p_t Q^{S,t} + a^{-1}_{SC}X^S_{C,t} \quad (t=1,2). \end{aligned} \tag{A3.25}$$

After these definitional manipulations, I have reached a crucial stage in my argument: I will now show that, problem (A3.25) – which is identical to (A3.18) – collapses into problem (A3.13) of myopically maximizing undiscounted period-t producer profits, provided myopic-foresight stockmarket equilibrium (A3.14) obtains. Alternatively, given (A3.13), stockmarket equilibrium under myopic foresight implies maximization problem (A3.25)≡(A3.18). It follows that (A3.14) and the first-order conditions (A3.13.1) imply, and are implied by, the first-order conditions of (A3.25): Whenever the stockmarket clears and firms have myopically maximized their current profits $\tilde{\Pi}^{i,t}$, problem (A3.25)≡(A3.18) has been solved. (As usual, I assume satisfaction of second-order conditions.) To see this, it is sufficient to note that the equalities $\rho^S_{S,t} = \rho_t$, $\rho^C_t = \rho_t$, $\rho^S_{C,t} = \rho_t$ in (A3.14) respectively imply coefficients of X^C_t, $X^S_{S,t}$, $X^S_{C,t}$ in (A3.25) that equal r^C_t, $r^S_{S,t}$, and $r^S_{C,t}$; consequently,

$$\Pi^t/v^C_{t+1} \equiv (1+\hat{p}^S_t)\tilde{\Pi}^{S,t} + \tilde{\Pi}^{C,t}, \text{ given (A3.14)} \quad (t=1,2). \tag{A3.26}$$

In maximizing discounted profits, firms treat $v^C_{t+1} \equiv P^C_{t+1} \equiv \left[\prod_{\tau=1}(1+\rho_\tau)\right]^{-1}$ and $\hat{p}^S_t$ as given. It follows that

$$\text{Max } \Pi^t \Leftrightarrow \text{Max } \tilde{\Pi}^t, \text{ given (A3.14)} \quad (t=1,2), \tag{A3.27}$$

as claimed before. Since I have shown that (A3.13.1) together with (A3.14) imply, and are implied by, (A3.17), I may finally conclude that

$$\Pi^t = (\Pi^t)^* \Leftrightarrow \Delta\pi_t = \phi(\pi_t) \quad (t=1,2), \tag{A3.28}$$

which is the Hamiltonian end of my journey across the theoretical bridge that (A3.18) represents. (Recall that an asterisk indicates a maximum value.)

I will now retrace my steps and, starting again from (A3.18), seek to establish the nexus

$$\{\text{Max } \Pi^t\}_{t=1}^2 \Leftrightarrow \underset{y}{\text{Max}}\ \Pi \equiv P \cdot y \tag{A3.29}$$

between period-by-period maximization of the expected value of the firm, as in (A3.18), and across-horizon maximization of discounted A–D profits, as in (A3.2). This is straightforward provided I can assume "the existence of perfect markets for all commodities including equipment in use. . ." (Malinvaud) – or rather, as I have argued in my comments on Malinvaud, the existence of a *stockmarket* and a corresponding equity price $p_t^S \equiv \pi_t$ or, equivalently, $P_t^S \equiv P_t^C p_t^S \equiv v_t^C p_t^S \equiv \left[\prod_{\tau=1}^{t-1}(1+\rho_\tau)\right]^{-1} \pi_t$ (which is the equity price $p_t^S \equiv \pi_t$ discounted to focal date $t=1$ at the uniform equity yield ρ_τ; recall (A3.19), (A3.22)). A stockmarket I indeed do assume.

(A3.29) then results from merely adding Π^t over the two periods ($t=1,2$), and using (A3.7) and the definition of net supply y_{t+1}^i in (A3.4) $(Q_t^i + X_t^i \equiv y_{t+1}^i + X_{t+1}^i)$; after cancellation of terms, this gives

$$\sum_{t=1}^{2} \Pi^t = [-P_1^C X_1^C + P_2^C y_2^C + P_3^C(y_3^C + X_3^C)] + [-P_1^S X_1^S + P_2^S y_2^S + P_3^S(y_3^S + X_3^S)] \equiv P \cdot y \equiv \Pi. \tag{A3.30}$$

(It would be useful for the reader to work through the cancellations; this gives an appreciation for how A–D netting across firms and time periods analytically compresses the economy's intertemporal capital structure.) I now conclude that, as claimed in (A3.29),

$$\{\Pi^t = (\Pi^t)^*\}_{t=1}^2 \Leftrightarrow \Pi = \Pi^*. \tag{A3.29.1}$$

Combining (A3.28) with (A3.29.1), I finally have

$$\Pi = \Pi^* \Leftrightarrow \{\Delta\pi_t = \phi(\pi_t)\}_{t=1}^2, \tag{A3.31}$$

so that an A–D discounted-profit maximum $\Pi = \Pi^* \equiv P \cdot y^*$ implies, and is implied by, the Hamiltonian equation $\Delta\pi_t = \phi(\pi_t)$ – that is, by myopic maximization of current producer profits [(A3.13)], combined with stockmarket arbitrage under myopic foresight [(A3.14)].

3 The example I have used to prove (A3.31) I claim to be generic. (Recall that the example is based on a basics-only economy identical to VON NEUMANN I, except for postulating a neoclassical steel technology.) In other words, given proper consideration of nonbasic outputs and of nonreproducible resources, a formal equivalence between the A–D economy and its quasi-Hamiltonian analogue could be shown to hold for all the

models examined in this book. This would, in general, require a model's demand side D and flow-equilibrium condition (A3.1) to be brought into the picture. It is not hard to see why that was unnecessary in the case at hand.

First, after endogenizing D (for instance, by means of a CRRA utility function, not necessarily logarithmic), one would obviously find that the present economy's path of general-equilibrium prices is, like that of VON NEUMANN I, independent of intra- and intertemporal consumer preferences. For instance, in response to an intratemporal preference shift, the system would move along a Rybczynski locus that cuts successive bowed-out production possibility curves at points with constant slope

$$p_t = a_{SC}^{-1}/Q_2^{S,t\prime}(p_t) \qquad (t=1,2). \tag{A3.32}$$

This follows from stockmarket equilibrium, (A3.15), and $p_{t+1} - p_t = \Delta\pi_t = 0$ (the latter is an implication of *long-run* foresight and the model's saddle-point structure).

Second, with p_t and $\rho_t = \rho_{C,t}^{S} \equiv 1/a_{SC}p_t$ uniquely determined by $\Delta\pi_t = \phi(\pi_t)$ in any period, so must be the discounted prices $P_t^C \equiv \left[\prod_{\tau=1}^{t-1}(1+\rho_\tau)\right]^{-1}$, $P_t^S \equiv P_t^C p_t^S$ be. Using (A3.5) I may therefore conclude that (recall $y_1^i \equiv -X_1^i$)

$$\Delta\pi_t = \phi(\pi_t) \Rightarrow \Delta X_t^i \equiv Q_t^i - D_{t+1}^i \Rightarrow D - y \equiv \omega \qquad (i=C,S;\, t=1,2). \tag{A3.33}$$

Thus, given stockmarket equilibrium and myopic entrepreneurial profit maximization, A–D zero-excess-flow-demand condition (A3.1) is an *identity*. It cannot, therefore, play any role in the determination of the A–D discounted-price vector P.

B Supplement to chapter 4

Note on the neoclassical theory of endogenous growth

I claim at the beginning of chapter 4 (footnote 1) that recent neoclassical literature on endogenous growth in form represents but a return to the pre-Solovian growth theory of Marx, von Neumann, Lewis and Harrod–Domar. This can be seen as follows. The point of departure of the literature is a RAMSEY–SOLOW one-sector model with a neoclassical CRS-production function $Q^C = Q^C(X^C, T)$, where X^C is physical capital and T exogenously given "raw" labor (nonproduced human capital, which may be set equal to unity). It then proceeds to a two-sector VON NEUMANN I analogue by writing $Q^C = \tilde{\tilde{Q}}^C(X_C^C, hT) \equiv \tilde{Q}^C(X_C^C, h) \equiv Q^C(X_C^C, X^S)$, $Q^S = Q^S(X_S^C)$, where $hT \equiv X^S$ is the endogenously growing amount of efficiency or "skilled" labor (h represents efficiency units of human capital, produced by some CRS-process $Q^S(\cdot)$ that uses one or both of the economy's reproducible resources). Clearly, nothing but a relabeling of my VON NEUMANN I corn and steel inputs X^C, X^S is involved, plus the assumption that S is a pure investment good. (See, for instance, Lucas (1988), Sala-i-Martin (1990).)

A key question about human capital, starkly put by MARX–SRAFFA, is "Who *owns* the initial stocks of resources, $X^i(0)$ and $T(0)$, that alone make human capital accumulation possible?" If I am a Marx–Lewis laborer in infinitely elastic supply who receives a period-by-period subsistence wage advance from a capitalist, any accumulation of human capital I undertake (financed by, say, an "educational loan" from the capitalist that allows me to go to school during part of the working day) must leave my lifetime earnings unchanged, for all returns to human capital will be captured by the capitalist. It is only by being an *owner of a scarce resource* to begin with (that is, an owner of scarce raw labor $T(0)$, physical capital $X^C(0)$, or skills $X^S(0)$ – the latter perhaps received through public education) that I can increase my future income through saving and further accumulation of skills and physical capital.

The substantive contributions of the neoclassical endogenous-growth literature are three. First, like the present study and unlike Cambridge-U.K. growth theory, the neoclassical literature anchors endogenous growth in intertemporal optimization and non-steady-state initial conditions. Second, it studies the implications of externalities associated with human capital. For there are situations where, though the stock of human capital is well defined and though the size of its service stream stands in one-to-one relation with the size of the momentary stock, lack of material specificity of the human-capital services rendered makes for the latters' incomplete remuneration. As a result, the income generated by the stock of human capital is only in part appropriated by its owner. Third, the literature examines situations where, though both the stock of human capital and the service stream from that stock (say, copies of an industrial design) are materially specific, the momentary service stream lacks (a) locational specificity (copies can be made simultaneously available at different locations) and (b) a one-to-one link with the momentary stock (copies can be arbitrarily multiplied at quasi zero marginal cost). This leads to the definition of "nonrival" inputs [Romer (1990), Parrinello (1992)]. Nonrival inputs provide services that are (i) either completely inappropriable (basic scientific research is an example) or only partly appropriable (in which case they are similar to the services of human capital exhibiting external effects); and (ii), due to characteristic (b), the source of increasing returns to scale (unless there is strict complementarity to rival inputs).

C Supplement to chapter 5

C.1 Ricardo: The one-sector model

Below, I present a one-sector (basics-only) version of RICARDO and compare its stability properties with those of the two-sector model, both under perfect foresight and under static expectations.

Wealth continues to be given by (5.1). Its two constituents $X^C, \bar{T}$ produce the economy's single output, corn, using Inada technology (5.4), (5.4.1) with $X_C^C \equiv X^C$ and $x_C = x$. (5.6) applies and the corresponding profit-maximizing rentals are (compare (5.8))

$$\begin{aligned} r^C &= q^{C\prime}(x) \equiv r^C(x), \qquad r^{C\prime} = q^{C\prime\prime} < 0 \\ r^T &= q^C - xq^{C\prime} \equiv r^T(x), \qquad r^{T\prime} = -xq^{C\prime\prime} > 0. \end{aligned} \tag{C1.1}$$

Arbitrage equation (5.10) holds, where $\rho^C = r^C(x) - 1 \equiv \rho(x)$ is now predetermined in temporary equilibrium, unlike in the two-sector model. Stock-market equilibrium under entrepreneurial profit-maximization requires (compare (5.11))

$$\chi(\pi; x, \hat{\pi}^e) \equiv r^C(x) - 1 - [r^T(x)/\pi] - \hat{\pi}^e = 0, \qquad \pi \equiv p^T/p^C = p^T, \tag{C1.2}$$

and yields the myopic-foresight motions of the price of land,

$$\begin{aligned} \Delta\pi = \pi\{r^C(x) - [r^T(x)/\pi] - 1\} \equiv \phi(\pi, x), \qquad &\phi_1 = \Omega > 0 \\ &\phi_2 = q^{C\prime\prime}(\pi + x) < 0, \end{aligned} \tag{C1.3}$$

near a stationary state with $r^T/\pi = \Omega$. (5.14) again provides the accumulation dynamics (or, equivalently, the capital-market-equilibrium condition, which holds identically). Substituting in it for $\Delta\pi$ from (C1.3), one has the one-sector economy's second autonomous law of motion,

$$\begin{aligned} \Delta x = [\rho(x) - \Omega]\left[\frac{x+\pi}{1+\Omega}\right] - \phi(\pi, x) \equiv \psi(\pi, x), \qquad &\psi_1 = -\phi_1 < 0 \\ &\psi_2 = \frac{\Omega\phi_2}{1+\Omega} > 0. \end{aligned} \tag{C1.4}$$

As in (5.20), the linearized version of dynamical system [(C1.3), (C1.4)] may be collapsed into a second-order difference equation. The latter's coefficients

$$\begin{aligned} -a_1 &= (\phi_1 + 1) + (\psi_2 + 1) = \eta_1 + \eta_2 > 0 \\ c &= \phi_1\psi_2 - \phi_2\psi_1 = \phi_1\phi_2/(1+\Omega) = (\eta_1 - 1)(\eta_2 - 1) < 0 \\ a_2 &= c - a_1 - 1 = 1 + \Omega = \eta_1\eta_2 > 0 \end{aligned} \tag{C1.5}$$

have the same signs as those of the two-sector model (observe that $a_2 = 1 + \Omega > 0$ in both cases, guaranteeing nonoscillation since $-a_1 > 0; c < 0$ then assures saddle-path stability). Moreover, since the partial derivatives ϕ_i, ψ_i also have the same signs, the phase space is again given by figure 5.2.

Consider next the static-expectations version of the one-sector model. Its single difference equation is

$$\Delta x = [\rho(x) - \Omega]\left[\frac{x+\pi}{1+\Omega}\right] \equiv \tilde{\psi}(x), \qquad \tilde{\psi}' = \frac{q^{C''}(x+\pi)}{1+\Omega} < 0. \tag{C1.6}$$

Using the definition of the elasticity of input substitution $\sigma^C \equiv \theta_{TC}/\epsilon > 0$ given in (5.9) – or, equivalently, that of the elasticity $\epsilon \equiv \hat{r}^C(x)/\hat{x} \equiv -xq^{C''}/q^{C'} > 0$ of the marginal-product-curve of labor – one finds the root $\eta \equiv \tilde{\psi}' + 1$ of the linearized form of (C1.6) to be stable ($|\eta| < 1$) iff

$$\sigma^C > \theta_{TC}(1+\Omega)^2/2x(\pi + x), \tag{C1.7}$$

which need not obtain. It follows that, unlike in the perfect-foresight model, local instability *is* a possibility in the static-expectations economy whenever the elasticity of factor substitution is sufficiently low. Such instability in turn opens up the prospect of chaotic dynamics, as in Bhaduri and Harris (1987).

It is clear from the above, however, that chaotic Ricardian dynamics are impossible in the presence of a forward-looking stockmarket. Moreover, as mentioned in chapter 5 (footnote 16), the introduction of a second sector producing nonbasics, when paired with classical demand assumptions, eliminates the possibility of instability even under static expectations.

For this, it is easiest to focus on the condition for a nonoscillating static-expectations approach to the stationary state, $0 < \eta = \tilde{\psi}' + 1 < 1$: The second inequality is guaranteed by $\tilde{\psi}' < 0$, while the first is fulfilled whenever

$$\sigma^C > \frac{\theta_{TC}}{\theta_{X^C,K}} \text{ or } \epsilon < \theta_{X^C,K}, \qquad 0 < \theta_{X^C,K} \equiv \frac{X^C}{K} < 1 \tag{C1.8}$$

$$\sigma^C > \frac{(1-\gamma)\theta_{TC}}{\theta_{X^C_C,K_C}} \text{ or } \epsilon < \frac{\theta_{X^C_C,K_C}}{(1-\gamma)}, \qquad 0 < \theta_{X^C_C,K_C} \equiv \frac{X^C_C}{X^C_C + p^T\bar{T}} < 1 \tag{C1.9}$$

in the one- and in the two-sector model, respectively (θ_{TC} is the share of rent income in corn output [(5.8)], $\theta_{X^C,K}$ and $\theta_{X^C_C,K_C}$ the share of the wage fund in corn-sector capital). Since $\sigma^C \equiv \theta_{TC}/\epsilon$ is positive by definition, it follows that a stable and monotonic approach to the stationary state is guaranteed whenever consumption spending by surplus recipients is largely on non-basics – for instance, when $\gamma = 1$ as in the Ricardo–Pasinetti (1960) model. (Under the latter's assumption of a class-specific consumption pattern – with capitalists saving all profits ρX^C and landlords spending all rents $r^T\bar{T} = \rho p_T\bar{T}$ on nonbasics – (C1.9) simplifies to $\sigma^C > (1-\gamma)\theta_{TC} = 0$.)

C.2 Ricardo: Discrete technologies and the dynamics of unemployment

Below, I examine RICARDO under discrete alternatives to (5.4.1), starting with the single-technique Leontief case [(5.3), (5.4.2)] illustrated in figure 5.1b.

With isoquants in T, X_C^C-space rectangular instead of neoclassically smooth, $x_C = a_{CC}/a_{TC}$ is fixed, so that p disappears as an argument not just from nonbasics demand, but now also from nonbasics supply $q^S(\cdot)$, thus, from the flow-equilibrium condition $z^S(\cdot)=0$ for nonbasics.[1] The latter therefore solves for π as a function $\pi=\pi(x,\gamma\ldots)$ of the predetermined variable x and parameters; $\chi[p,\pi(x,\gamma\ldots),\hat{\pi}^e]=0$ [(5.11)] then yields $p=p[\pi(x,\gamma\ldots),\hat{\pi}^e]$.[2]

It is clear that the function $\pi=\pi(x,\gamma\ldots)$ precludes standard dynamics along a saddle path, since π is not free to jump on to such a path on impact of an unanticipated disturbance (for instance, given a current preference shift $d\gamma>0$, $d\pi$ is constrained to equal $\pi_2 d\gamma$ on impact, irrespective of the economy's transversality condition). Nevertheless, $\pi(x,\gamma,\ldots)$ *is* consistent with PFCE adjustments of two types: Movements from the original to the new stationary state within a single period, following an unanticipated perturbation; and multiperiod full-employment dynamics following the emergence of anticipations of a future perturbation.[3] Finally – and this will be the main insight gleaned from the Leontief model – the system may find it profit-maximizing to render the full-employment $\pi(x,\gamma\ldots)$-function inoperative by allowing some resource to become transitorily unemployed.

First, consider one-period jumps across full-employment stationary states in response to an unanticipated permanent preference shift that leaves long-run prices unaltered, but alters capital composition $\bar{x}$.[4] Though in the Leontief economy such single-period long-run adjustments are *feasible* for either $d\gamma>0$ (requiring accumulation of wage funds) or $d\gamma<0$ (allowing decumulation),[5] they will be *profit-maximizing* always (optimal

[1] Recall (5.12) and the reason, discussed in footnote 11 of chapter 5, why $\partial D^s/\partial p=0$.

[2] As mentioned earlier, the fact that the nonbasics flow-equilibrium condition here solves for the stock price π, whereas the stockmarket equilibrium condition $\chi(\cdot)=0$ determines the nonbasics price p naturally suggests the Marshallian temporary-equilibrium adjustment process M2 discussed in chapter 3. The same will be true for the specific-inputs technology [(5.3), (5.4.4)] analyzed below. I therefore postpone discussion of this issue.

[3] The point being that, though $\pi(x,\gamma)$ cannot, in the current period, jump in response to change in expectations $d\hat{\pi}^e \gtrless 0$, the nonbasics price $p[\pi(x,\gamma),\hat{\pi}^e]$ and the profit rate $\rho(p)$ *can* jump – thereby allowing $\pi(x,\gamma)$ to respond *in the subsequent period*, as x changes in reaction to the change in the rate of profit. The details of these anticipatory dynamics under a temporary-equilibrium function $\pi=\pi(x,\gamma)$ remain to be worked out.

[4] From the "non-substitution" theorem, as originally intended by Samuelson (1951) and others, the stationary-state results (5.17)–(5.19) indifferently apply to the neoclassical and the Leontief system.

[5] Feasibility follows from the fact that one-period adjustments are always feasible under the more restrictive specific-factors technology [(5.3), (5.4.4)] discussed later.

from the planning point of view) only for $d\gamma < 0$. This can be inferred from the fact that $d\gamma < 0$ is incompatible with unemployment (of wage funds – the rental on wage funds $r^C = pa_{SC}^{-1}$ declines as the price of consumption services p falls, but is not allowed to drop to zero since this would make the price of corn $1/p$ infinite), whereas $d\gamma > 0$ *is* compatible with unemployment (of land – the rental $r^T(p)$ on land falls as the price of corn $1/p$ declines and will reach zero before p reaches infinity, given that the cost of corn includes the remuneration of wage funds). To discuss a one-period jump across full-employment stationary states I shall, therefore, focus on a preference shift $d\gamma < 0$ toward corn. Conversely, to exposit the dynamics of land unemployment, I will concentrate on its opposite, $d\gamma > 0$.[6]

It is easy to see how a single-period perfect-foresight response to a preference shift toward corn works. Following the impact of $d\gamma < 0$ at the beginning of t, we have a fall in the price p of consumption services in reaction to their excess supply; this reduces the rental $r^C = pa_{CS}^{-1}$ on wage funds. The corresponding drop in the uniform interest rate $\rho = pa_{CS}^{-1} - 1$ is mirrored in a jump of the price π of land, which allows wealth $(\pi + x)\bar{T}$ to increase. It is this wealth increase (not the fall in p) that ends up stabilizing equilibrium demand for, thus output of, nonbasics at a level unchanged from before $d\gamma < 0$ – thereby allowing wage funds to remain fully employed across both sectors. (Note that service-sector wage funds cannot move into corn, given that corn output $Q^C = a_{TC}^{-1}\bar{T} = a_{CC}^{-1}X_C^C$ cannot increase.) By contrast, equilibrium consumption demand for corn *does* increase – by an amount just sufficient to bring down the quantity of wage funds reaccumulated at the end of the period to the new stationary state value $\bar{X}_1^C \equiv \bar{x}_1(\gamma_1)\bar{T} < \bar{x}_0(\gamma_0)\bar{T}$. (Recall $\Delta X^C = \bar{Q}^C - X^C - D^C$ or $\bar{Q}^C = X^C(t+1) + D^C(t)$.) Viewed differently, the expected capital loss on land $[\Delta\pi(t)]^e \equiv [\pi(t+1)]^e - \pi(t) = \bar{\pi} - \pi(t) < 0$[7] and the decline in $\rho(t)$ below Ω at the beginning of t together are such as to allow the accumulation equation to just produce, across the single period t, the requisite stationary-state capital-composition adjustment $\Delta\bar{x} \equiv \bar{x}_1 - \bar{x}_0 = \{[\rho(t) - \Omega]/[1 + \Omega]\}[\pi(t) + \bar{x}_0] - [\Delta\pi(t)]^e < 0$.[8]

I next turn to the opposite preference shift $d\gamma > 0$ and the multiperiod land-unemployment dynamics it may give rise to. Following the increase in

6 Even though a full-employment jump across long-run equilibria is feasible in the latter case as well and, for certain parameter configurations, optimal. (These configurations remain to be explored.)

7 Contrast this with the currently experienced unexpected capital gain $\pi(t) - \bar{\pi} > 0$.

8 Recall (5.14), (5.16). In sum, we have $(\partial\pi/\partial\gamma) = -(\partial\pi/\partial x)(d\bar{x}/d\gamma)$, consistently with the function $\pi = \pi(x, \gamma \ldots)$, $d\bar{\pi}/d\gamma = 0$, and perfect foresight. Namely, $\partial\pi/\partial\gamma$ is the unanticipated change in π at the beginning of t following $d\gamma < 0$, $\partial\pi/\partial x = (\partial\pi)^e/\partial x$ the perfectly anticipated change in π between the beginning of t and the beginning of $t+1$, and $d\bar{x}/d\gamma = -\bar{x}' < 0$ [(5.19)] the single-period contraction in long-run capital composition required by $d\gamma < 0$. See the appendix to chapter 5 for a rigorous proof.

the demand for nonbasics and the consequent tendency for their price p and the profitability $p - a_{CS}^{-1} r^C$ of producing them to increase, S-sector entrepreneurs will seek to hire wage funds (thus, workers) away from their C-sector competitors. Given the Leontief corn technology, the departure of a single wage-fund unit from the C-sector is sufficient, however, to leave some land unemployed – which in turn must instantaneously drive the remuneration of land, employed or unemployed, to zero ($r^T(p) = 0$).

For the first time in this book, *unemployment of a resource in fixed supply* has emerged.[9] Such unemployment will profoundly alter the system's dynamic behavior from what it was under the neoclassical and Leontief full-employment regimes studied so far. I start by considering the temporary equilibrium of a Ricardo–Leontief economy in which entrepreneurial demand for land, T, falls short of land supply, $\bar{T}$. I then discuss the dynamics that render such land unemployment dynamically self-correcting, thus ensuring the full-employment-stationary-state nonsubstitution results (5.17)–(5.19).

The neoclassical cost equations (5.5), (5.6) now must be replaced by[10]

$$p = a_{CS} r^C,\ p^C = 1 = a_{CC} r^C,\ \text{thus } \bar{\bar{p}} = \frac{a_{CS}}{a_{CC}},\ T < \bar{T} \text{ and } r^T = 0, \qquad \text{(C2.1)}$$

the arbitrage and $\chi(\cdot) = 0$ equations (5.10), (5.11) by

$$\begin{aligned} &\bar{\bar{\rho}} \equiv \rho^C = r^C - 1 = (\hat{p}^T)^e = \rho^T > 0 \\ &\chi(\hat{\pi}^e; \ldots) = a_{CC}^{-1} - 1 - \hat{\pi}^e = 0,\ \pi \equiv p^T/p^C = p^T, \end{aligned} \qquad \text{(C2.2)}$$

given $r^C = a_{CC}^{-1}$ from (C2.1). Thus, the return $\rho^T = (\hat{p}^T)^e$ on land equity will come from expected capital gains exclusively. These must at each instant equal the invariant yield $\rho^C = a_{CC}^{-1} - 1 > 0$ on wage funds, if land is to be willingly held in capitalist portfolios at a positive price.[11] The case of static expectations is instructive: Given $(\hat{p}^T)^e = \hat{\pi}^e \equiv 0$, unemployment of land implies not only $r^T = 0$, but also $p^T = 0$ (thus, $K = X^C$). In other words, whenever $T < \bar{T}$ under static expectations, not just the services of land, but land as an asset is free. The reason is simple: Since $\rho^T = 0 < \rho^C$, equity claims to land are willingly "held" in portfolios only at a zero price. By contrast, a fundamental insight of this supplement will be that, while the rental on land may fall to zero under perfect foresight, the price of land cannot: $r^T \geq 0$, but $p^T = \pi > 0$ at all times.

Since $x_S = x - x_C$ in the S-sector supply function $q^S(\cdot)$ of (5.9) must be

[9] Since no Keynesian problem of effective demand is present, simultaneous unemployment of *all* momentarily scarce inputs (land *and* wage funds) is impossible.

[10] A double overbar on a price variable refers to an invariant temporary-equilibrium value under unemployment of land.

[11] ρ^C or $\rho^C X_C^C \equiv (a_{CC}^{-1} - 1) X_C^C \equiv Q^C - X_C^C$ is assumed positive for Simon–Hawkins viability.

replaced by $x_S = (\bar{T}/T)x - \bar{\bar{x}}_C$,[12] nonbasics market-clearing condition (5.12) now appears as

$$z^S(T, \pi; x, \gamma, \Omega) \equiv a_{CS}^{-1}\left[\left(\frac{\bar{T}}{T}x - \bar{\bar{x}}_C\right) - \gamma\frac{\Omega}{1+\Omega}(x+\pi)\right] = 0,$$
$$\bar{\bar{x}}_C \equiv \frac{a_{CC}}{a_{TC}}, \qquad z_1^S < 0, \tag{C2.3}$$

all partial derivatives other than z_1^S remaining as in (5.12). Thus, instead of solving for p, as in (5.13), $z^S(\cdot) = 0$ will now determine the level of (un)employment of land $T(\pi, x\ldots) < \bar{T}$ as a function of land's stockmarket price π, capital composition $x \equiv X^C/\bar{T}$, and parameters.

The economy's dynamics are governed by the myopic-foresight ($\hat{\pi} = \hat{\pi}^e$) motions of the price of land, as implied by (C2.2),

$$\Delta\pi = \pi(a_{CC}^{-1} - 1) \equiv \phi(\pi) > 0, \qquad \phi' = a_{CC}^{-1} - 1 = \bar{\bar{\rho}} > 0, \tag{C2.4}$$

and by the law of accumulation (5.14) or, equivalently, by the motions $\Delta x = \Delta X^C/\bar{T}$ of capital composition,

$$\Delta x = \left(\frac{\bar{\bar{\rho}} - \Omega}{1+\Omega}\right)(\pi + x) - \phi(\pi) \equiv \psi(\pi, x), \qquad \psi_1 = -\frac{\Omega}{1+\Omega}a_{CC}^{-1} < 0$$
$$\psi_2 = \frac{\bar{\bar{\rho}} - \Omega}{1+\Omega} \gtrless 0. \tag{C2.5}$$

The roots of dynamic system [(C2.4), (C2.5)], inferable from $\phi_1\psi_2 \equiv (\eta_1 - 1)(\eta_2 - 1)$ as in (5.20), are given by

$$\eta_1 = 1 + \bar{\bar{\rho}} > 1, \; \eta_2 = 1 + \frac{\bar{\bar{\rho}} - \Omega}{1+\Omega} > 1 \text{ for } \psi_2 > 0$$
$$0 < \eta_2 = \frac{1+\bar{\bar{\rho}}}{1+\Omega} < 1 \text{ for } \psi_2 < 0. \tag{C2.6}$$

As shown by figure C1, it is only the unstable unemployment economy $(\eta_1 > 1, \eta_2 > 1; \psi_2 > 0)$ that possesses a dynamics capable of generating an increase in x as required by $d\gamma > 0$.[13]

[12] Recall from (5.2) that x_j is normalized by T, x by $\bar{T}$.

[13] In the saddle-path-stable case $(\eta_1 > 0, 0 < \eta_2 < 1; \psi_2 < 0)$, a one-period jump across full-employment stationary states remains possible as an adjustment response to $d\gamma > 0$. Three other points about these dynamics with unemployment are worth noting. First, neither of the two cases $\psi_2 > 0$, $\psi_2 < 0$ contains a viable stationary state. Second, they involve *linear* difference equations, with coefficients ϕ', ψ_i that are functions of the own-productivity of corn a_{CC}^{-1} and the rate of time preference Ω alone. System [(C2.4), (C2.5)] can thus be plotted globally, as in figure C1. (The independence from the parameters a_{CS}^{-1} and γ respectively reflects the Ricardo–Bortkiewicz–Sraffa and the nonsubstitution theorem.) Third, motions are always nonoscillating $(\eta_i > 0)$ and, thus, qualitatively indistinguishable from those of a continuous-time analogue $\dot{\pi} = \phi(\pi)$, $\dot{x} = \psi(\pi, x)$ to system [(C2.4), (C2.5)].

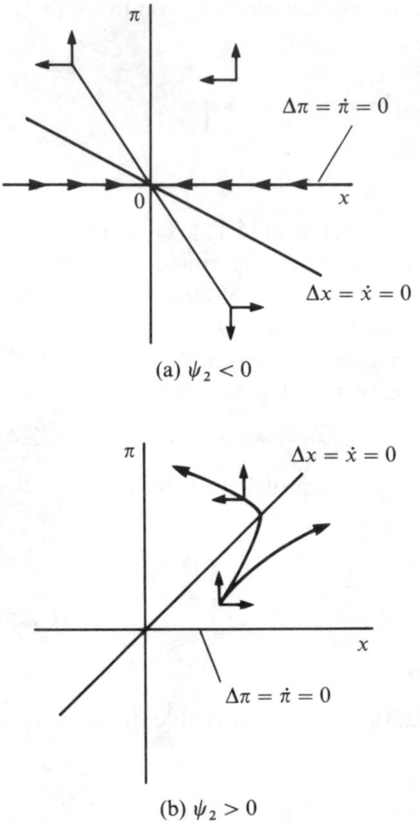

Figure C1 Dynamics of RICARDO under a Leontief technology and unemployment of land

The intertemporal consequences of a preference shift $d\gamma > 0$ toward consumption services at the beginning of period t are now easy to discern. Assume, to begin with, that perfect foresight obtains, that the perturbation is unanticipated and permanent, and that the economy starts out in a full-employment stationary state. On impact of $d\gamma > 0$, there will be an excess demand for (end-of-period) nonbasics, consequently, upward pressure on their (beginning-of-period) price $p(t)$. As indicated earlier, the rise in p will increase S-sector profitability and allow that sector's entrepreneurs to hire wage funds and workers away from corn producers, $dT = -\bar{\bar{x}}_C^{-1} dX_S^C < 0$ of whose land inputs consequently become unemployed (where $dX_S^C = -dX_C^C > 0$ is the beginning-of-t equilibrium increase in S-sector employment). The equilibrium rise in p on impact, $\bar{\bar{p}} - \bar{p} = a_{CS}(\bar{\bar{\rho}} - \Omega) > 0$, is rigidly prescribed by technology and time preference and independent of the size of the demand shift. The same is true of the jump $\bar{\bar{\rho}} - \bar{\rho} = (\bar{\bar{p}} - \bar{p}) a_{CS}^{-1}$ in the rate of

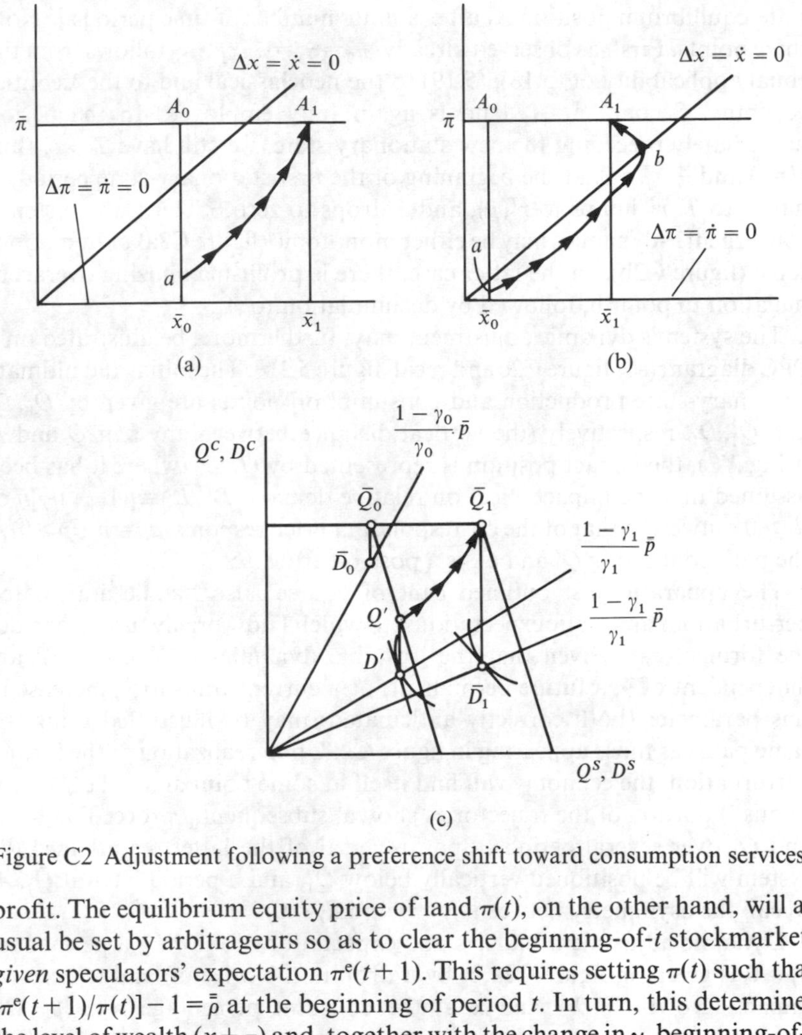

Figure C2 Adjustment following a preference shift toward consumption services

profit. The equilibrium equity price of land $\pi(t)$, on the other hand, will as usual be set by arbitrageurs so as to clear the beginning-of-t stockmarket, *given* speculators' expectation $\pi^e(t+1)$. This requires setting $\pi(t)$ such that $[\pi^e(t+1)/\pi(t)]-1=\bar{\bar{\rho}}$ at the beginning of period t. In turn, this determines the level of wealth $(x+\pi)$ and, together with the change in γ, beginning-of-t demand for nonbasics $D^S(t)/\bar{T}=\gamma_1[\Omega/(1+\Omega)]a_{CS}^{-1}[\bar{x}_0+\pi(t)]$, thus, supply of nonbasics $Q^S(t)=a_{CS}^{-1}\{[\bar{T}/T(t)]\bar{x}_0-\bar{\bar{x}}_C\}=D^S(t)$ and, consequently, the rate of equilibrium land unemployment $[\bar{T}/T(t)]-1$ the latter implies. Finally, (C2.5) gives the accumulation of wage funds $\Delta x(t)=x(t+1)-\bar{x}_0>0$ at the end of the production period.

The economy's perfect-foresight dynamics are illustrated in figure C2a, b and will pin down, by the usual transversality and continuity arguments, the variable $\pi^e(t+1)=\pi(t+1)$ left dangling in the above account. As can be seen, convergence occurs nonasymptotically along an unstable path a–A_1 (point a is the impact position), landing the economy at its new stationary-state-equilibrium position A_1 after a finite number of time periods.[14] Note three points. First, as observed already, $\bar{\pi}_0=\bar{\pi}_1=\bar{\pi}$, $\bar{x}_1>\bar{x}_0$ follows from the equal applicability of (5.18), (5.19) to the neoclassical and to the Leontief economy. Second, at A_1 land is again fully employed: In the period immediately preceding the new stationary state, we still have $T<\bar{T}$, thus $r^T=0$ and $\hat{\pi}=\bar{\bar{\rho}}>0$; at the beginning of the first stationary-state period, T jumps to $\bar{T}$, r^T jumps to $r^T(\bar{p})$, and $\hat{\pi}$ drops to zero.[15] Third, the system's convergent x-dynamics may be either monotonic (figure C2a) or nonmonotonic (figure C2b). In the latter case, there is profit-maximizing overaccumulation to point b, followed by decumulation to A_1.

The system's dynamic adjustment may, furthermore, be illustrated on a PPC diagram (see figure C2c and recall figure 5.1b): The initial and ultimate stationary-state production and consumption points are given by $\bar{Q}_0, \bar{D}_0$ and $\bar{Q}_1, \bar{D}_1$, respectively (the vertical distance between any pair Q and D being X^C); the impact position is represented by Q', D' (where it has been assumed that the impact effect on relative demand $D^C/D^S\equiv[(1-\gamma)/\gamma]p$ of $d\gamma>0$ outweighs that of the corresponding price response $dp=\bar{\bar{p}}-\bar{p}>0$);[16] the path connecting Q' and $\bar{Q}_1$ is a possible traverse.

The apparatus just outlined can, of course, also handle anticipated perturbations and static expectations, to which I now briefly turn. Consider the former first. Given that the unstable dynamics [C2.4), (C2.5)] are independent of γ, a future permanent, or a current transitory, increase in this parameter (both correctly anticipated) may be illustrated using the same paths as those appearing in figure C2: Upon realization of the former perturbation, the economy will find itself at some point along the ("continuous") portion of the trajectories shown, subsequently proceeding to A_1 and $\bar{Q}_1$ over several periods; upon reversal of the latter disturbance the system will be positioned vertically below $\bar{Q}_1$, and a period later at $\bar{Q}_1, A_1$ (recall the asymmetry between $d\gamma>0$ and $d\gamma<0$).[17]

Dynamic adjustment under static expectations following a permanent $d\gamma>0$ is given, in figure C2a,b, by a drop in the price of land to zero on impact, growth in X^C and x at the constant percentage rate $(\bar{\bar{\rho}}-\Omega)/$

[14] There is a switch from unemployment to full-employment dynamic regime at A_1.

[15] $d|\hat{\pi}|>dr^T$, given that ρ simultaneously falls from $\bar{\bar{\rho}}$ to $\bar{\rho}$ as p drops from $\bar{\bar{p}}$ to $\bar{p}$.

[16] Say the assumption fails to hold: The demand ray must then rotate *upwards* on impact, which – given the present supposition that $dQ^S>0$, thus $dQ^C<0$ on impact – necessarily implies a vertical distance $0\gtrless Q'-D'<\bar{Q}^0-\bar{D}^0$, thus $X^C(t+1)-\bar{X}^C_0<0$ or $\Delta x(t)<0$. But this is inconsistent with convergence (recall figure C1a, b). Also note, in figure C2c, the tangency of the intratemporal indifference curves to the relevant price slopes.

[17] If these anticipated perturbations had instead been changes in a_{CC} or Ω, the $\Delta x=\dot{x}=0$ locus would rotate on impact or reversal. By appropriate choice of initial π-value, speculators would see to it that at that instant the system is located at the intersection of the two relevant unstable trajectories, allowing π to remain stationary as required by the continuity condition.

$(1+\Omega)>0$ along the horizontal x-axis, and a vertical jump from that axis to A_1 upon attainment of the new stationary state. In figure C2c, adjustment is qualitatively the same as under perfect foresight.

This closes my discussion of Leontief technology [(5.3), (5.4.2)]. It remains to comment on the blueprints technology [(5.3), (5.4.3)] and the specific-inputs technologies [(5.3), (5.4.4)] and (5.4.5). The essential feature of a blueprints technology is that the PPC in figure 5.1c possesses a *region* RS of full-employment output combinations, rather than the single point Q characteristic of the single-technique Leontief system. This means that a process of dynamic multiperiod adjustment to, say, an unanticipated permanent $d\gamma>0$ need not necessarily involve unemployment of land on impact and/or during the traverse. Continuous full employment will obtain, if the economy's output point does not leave the segment RS on impact – the original stationary state necessarily lies on the latter or at its single-technique endpoints – nor the corresponding segment on the subsequent PPC's. (It is costless period-by-period shifts in the proportion in which profit-maximizing corn entrepreneurs mix the two available production technologies that keep $T(t)=\bar{T}$.) Should profit maximization, on the contrary, require land to become unemployed at some point during the adjustment process, unstable dynamics similar to those discussed for the Leontief case will guide the system back to full employment (which may obtain before the new stationary state is reached, unlike in the Leontief scenario).

Turning to the single-specific-input technology [(5.3), (5.4.4.)] used in most of my book and its anti-Uzawa alternative (5.4.5), it is easy to see that, as claimed earlier, the latter is not viable in the long run. It is not because, in finite or infinite time, the wage fund goes to zero or the finite-price assumption is violated (myopic foresight fails to obtain). To see this, recall first that the full-employment profit rate is now exogenously fixed at $\rho^C=a_{CC}^{-1}-1=\bar{\rho}$ but that, as accumulation equation $\Delta x=[(\rho-\Omega)/(1+\Omega)](\pi+x)-\Delta\pi$ [(5.14)] shows, a stationary state $\Delta x=\Delta\pi=0$ requires $\bar{\rho}=\Omega$. Except by fluke, a stationary state thus does not exist. Examination of the system's dynamics moreover shows that all motions not leading to the origin must, in finite time, violate one of the existence conditions $x(t)>0, \pi(t)<\infty, \pi(t)>0$ (see figure C3a,b). Such finite-time nonviability is produced by one out of three configurations of dynamic roots $(\eta_i>0, i=1,2)$.[18] The other two are only inconsistent with existence over an

[18] See the appendix to chapter 5 for details. As is easily checked there from the $z^S(p,\pi,x,\gamma)=0$-equation, $\pi\rightarrow\infty$ for instance implies $p\rightarrow\infty$, thus violates the finite-output-price assumption; at $\pi=0$, on the other hand, the stockmarket fails to clear and/or myopic foresight fails to obtain. In figure C3b, note that perpetual growth of both x and π is impossible, for the motions shown are explosive ($\pi\rightarrow\infty$ in finite time).

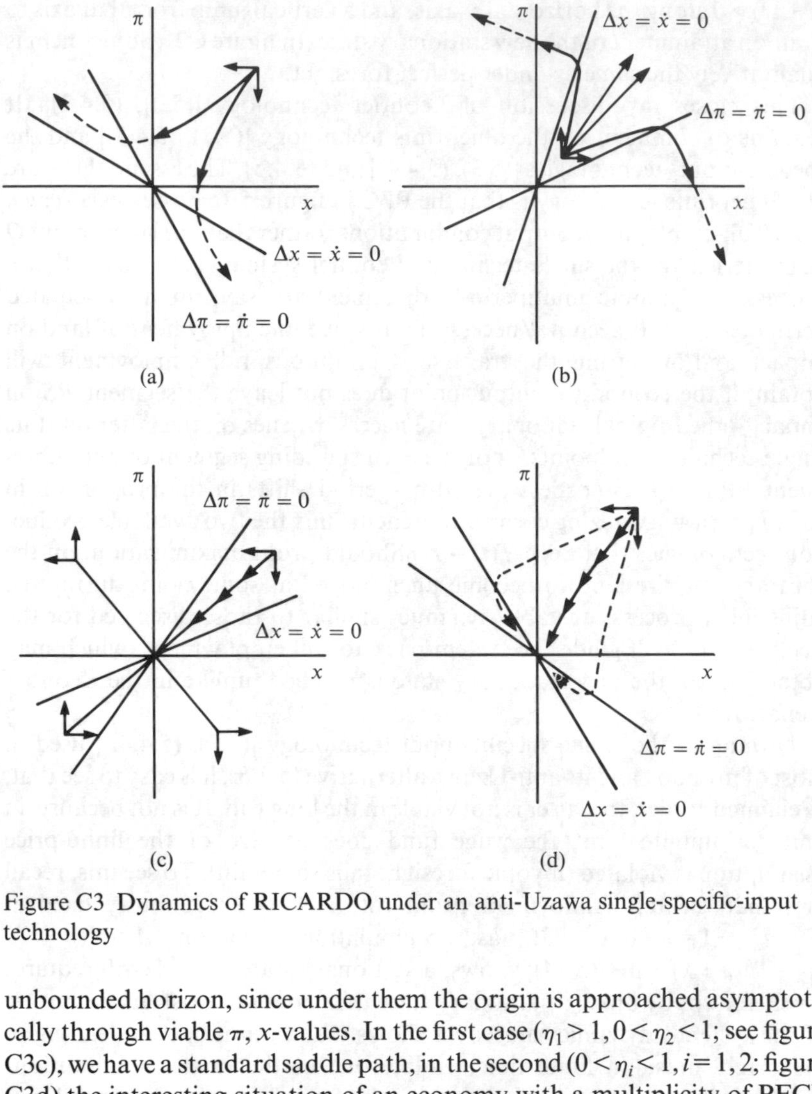

Figure C3 Dynamics of RICARDO under an anti-Uzawa single-specific-input technology

unbounded horizon, since under them the origin is approached asymptotically through viable π, x-values. In the first case ($\eta_1 > 1, 0 < \eta_2 < 1$; see figure C3c), we have a standard saddle path, in the second ($0 < \eta_i < 1, i = 1, 2$; figure C3d) the interesting situation of an economy with a multiplicity of PFCE trajectories, all of which asymptotically lead to the origin. Nevertheless, no indeterminacy exists, for stockmarket speculators would seek out the single path consistent with finite-time viability, $\pi(t) > 0, x(t) > 0, t\epsilon[0, \infty)$.

This leaves my standard specific-factors-cum-Uzawa-intensity technology [(5.3), (5.4.4)]. Since its zero-entrepreneurial-profit conditions are given by

$$p = a_{CS} r^C, \qquad p^C = 1 = a_{TC} r^T, \tag{C2.7}$$

r^T is now constant, instead of a negative function of p as in the Inada and Leontief cases. As easily seen, this leaves the properties of the stockmarket equilibrium equation $\chi(p, \pi, \hat{\pi}^e) = 0$ unaffected. What is affected by land being the sole input into corn is the model's other temporary-equilibrium condition,

$$z^S(\pi, x, \gamma, \Omega) \equiv a_{CS}^{-1} x - \gamma \frac{\Omega}{1+\Omega} a_{CS}^{-1}(\pi + x) = 0, \qquad \text{(C2.8)}$$

the flow-market-clearing equation for nonbasics. Unlike under a neoclassical corn technology, here momentary S-output $a_{CS}^{-1} x \bar{T}$ is rigidly fixed under full employment and, furthermore, cannot be altered by a profit-maximizing shift to unemployment, as in the Leontief model.[19] As in the latter's stationary state (but in the present model also in all non-stationary-state situations) there is, from (C2.8), *one* stockmarket price of land only that can clear the market for consumption services at a given instant: No other price apart from π enters $z^S(\cdot)$. It follows that, of the two Marshallian adjustment mechanisms (M1 and M2) discussed in chapter 3, it is the one (M2) in which stockmarket arbitrageurs clear the economy's instantaneous flow market that suggests itself.[20]

They do so by first setting π for a flow-market-clearing level of wealth – through short-selling, as explained in chapter 1 – and by then requiring (gross) shareholder dividends r^i from entrepreneurs such that, at the expected capital gains implied by π^e, stockmarket equilibrium condition[21]

$$\rho^C = r^C - 1 = \frac{\bar{r}^T}{\pi(x, \gamma, \Omega)} + \hat{\pi}^e = \rho^T, \qquad \hat{\pi}^e \equiv \frac{\pi^e}{\pi(\cdot)} - 1, \qquad \text{(C2.9)}$$

obtains for the flow-market-clearing asset price $\pi(x, \gamma \ldots)$. To now bring p into the picture, observe that such behavior on the part of portfolio managers forces S-sector entrepreneurs to set a price for consumption services

$$p \geq a_{CS} r^C[\pi(\cdot), \pi^e], \qquad \text{(C2.10)}$$

[19] It cannot be so altered because of the finite-price assumption on p and $1/p$: Unlike in the Leontief model, unemployment of land can only obtain at an infinite p that makes the rental on land in terms of nonbasics zero ($\bar{r}^T = (1/p) a_{TC}^{-1} = 0$); as in the Leontief model, unemployment of wage funds is also precluded since it requires $r^C = p a_{CS}^{-1} = 0$, thus an infinite price $1/p$ of corn. (See the rectangular PPC in figure 5.1d.) It is this property of the single-specific-input technology – absence of unemployment without the need for a neoclassical technology and a related factor-mobility assumption – that has recommended its adoption throughout this book.

[20] This is not mathematically necessary: The pseudo-dynamics underlying M1 remain stable even if the $z^S = 0$-locus in figure 3.2 (M1) is vertical.

[21] π^e is speculators' expectation $[\pi(t+1)]^e$ for next period's land price; recall the convention $\hat{\pi} \equiv \hat{\pi}(t) \equiv [\pi(t+1)/\pi(t)] - 1$.

enabling them to pay the required dividend $r^C[\pi(\cdot), \pi^e]$ without incurring losses. Competition with aspirants to entrepreneurship as usual guarantees an equality in (C2.10). So it is stockmarket arbitrage that has effectively enforced, via entrepreneurial profit maximization, the temporary-equilibrium Walrasian price

$$p = p[\pi(x, \gamma), \pi^e] \qquad \text{(C2.11)}$$

of nonbasics.[22]

I note, finally, that in response to *any* unanticipated disturbance the economy under consideration jumps to the new stationary state in a single-period.[23] The demonstration and economic intuition is similar to that provided earlier for the one-period adjustment to $d\gamma < 0$ by the fully employed Leontief economy. Unlike in the Leontief case – in which, as I have shown, a multiperiod dynamics with unemployed land is available as a possible response to the opposite shock $d\gamma > 0$ and the associated necessity $d\bar{x}/d\gamma > 0$ to accumulate wage funds – a one-period jump now always obtains under $d\gamma > 0$ as well. That is, on impact of $d\gamma > 0$ the rise in the real rate of interest *vis-à-vis* the rate of time preference will always be sufficiently steep for the economy to manage to increase its wage fund stock by the full amount $d\bar{x}/d\gamma > 0$ within a single period. In this light, the reason why the Leontief system would, by contrast, sometimes choose to approach the stationary state by leaving land unemployed is clear: Though a draconian one-period savings effort is feasible for it as well, that response may be suboptimal from a planner's perspective – that is, fail to be utility- and profit-maximizing from the decentralized system's point of view.

D Supplement to chapter 7

Walras's capital theory: A critique

The model of section 7.3 is well-suited to illustrate a serious flaw in Walras's theory of interest-rate determination, as presented in Parts V and VI of the *Elements of Pure Economics*. The point at issue is purely logical and

22 As discussed in chapter 3, the critical assumption in this flow-market-clearing story is that arbitrageurs know not only $\tilde{\chi}(\pi, r^i, \hat{\pi}^e)$, as in the stockmarket-clearing argument of chapter 1, but also $z^S(\pi, x, \gamma, \Omega)$ – in particular the consumption preferences γ, Ω. From my account of short-selling in chapter 1, arbitrageurs have an incentive to acquire this information.

23 As regards anticipated perturbations, observe that all momentary equilibria must obey the temporary-equilibrium function $\pi = \pi(x, \gamma, \Omega)$ since, in contrast to the Leontief economy, no unemployment regime is available. The question then arises how specific-inputs system [(5.3), (5.4.4)] can satisfy the continuity condition on π under an expected future perturbation, given that $\pi(x, \gamma, \Omega)$ renders π predetermined at the moment the expectation arises. Footnote 3 above gives a partial answer.

exegetically unambiguous. It concerns Walras's failure to grasp the role of the arbitrage equation in the closure of temporary equilibrium.[1]

I will first quote or summarize the most relevant passages from the *Elements* without comment and then proceed with my critique.

The author lays out his overall conception of capital and interest as follows:

All the foregoing relations we have established so far are not sufficient for [the] determination of [the interest rate] *i* and the prices of capital goods. Up to this point we have assumed that the quantities of land, personal faculties and capital proper are given, and that land-owners, workers and capitalists exchange all the services of their capital goods for consumers' goods and services... Under such circumstances, there could be no purchase or sale of capital goods, for these goods could only be exchanged for one another in ratios proportional to their net incomes; and such transactions, being theoretically without rational motive, could not give rise to any prices of capital goods in terms of numéraire. If there is to be a demand for, a supply of, and prices of capital goods, we must suppose that there are land-owners, workers and capitalists who purchase consumers' goods and services in amounts that either fall short of or exceed their incomes, thus leaving them either a surplus with which to buy capital goods or a deficit which compels them to sell their capital goods... [We now] have all the elements necessary for the solution of our problem. New capital goods are exchanged against the excess of income over consumption; and the condition of equality between the value of the new capital goods and the value of the excess gives us the equation required for the determination of the rate of net income [*i*] and consequently for the determination of the prices of [new] capital goods...

The particular groping which we have just described actually takes place in the stock exchange, which is the market for new capital goods, where the prices of these goods rise (or fall) through a fall (or rise) in the rate of net income, according as the demand for new capital in terms of the numéraire is greater (or less) than the supply.

The rate of net income and the prices of new capital goods having once been determined, the prices of all existing capital goods ... are determined ipso facto ... [for the] prices of existing capital goods ... are equal to the prices of new capital goods.[2]

In Walras's scheme of things, three steps – I to III below – are required to find a temporary equilibrium for an economy with capital.[3]

[1] The reader is referred to the critical fourth edition of the *Elements* by Jaffé [Walras (1954)]. For other commentary on Walras's capital theory, see Wicksell (1934), I. Fisher (1907, 1930), Jaffé (1942, 1953), Patinkin (1965), Diewert (1977), Morishima (1977), Eatwell (1987). It is Jaffé (1942) who comes closest to the argument advanced below. Unfortunately, in Jaffé (1953) the author retracts his earlier misgivings about the coherence of Walras's account of momentary interest-rate determination, on the basis of an inapplicable steady-state argument suggested by Samuelson.

[2] Lesson 23, par. 234; Lesson 25, par. 254; Lesson 28, par. 268. Terms in brackets are mine.

[3] I follow Walras and abstract throughout from expectations and realizations of capital gains (their neglect by Walras is not critical to my argument).

I Aggregate net saving must be brought into equality with the value of new capital goods,[4]

$$D'_k \frac{p'_k}{i' + \mu_k} + D'_{k'} \frac{p'_{k'}}{i' + \mu_{k'}} + \ldots \gtrless F_e(i'), \qquad \text{(D1.1)}$$

where $F_e(\cdot)$ is aggregate net saving; i' the arbitrary initial value of the interest rate; $D'_h(h = k, k' \ldots)$ the initial quantities of new capital goods and

$$\frac{p'_h}{i' + \mu_h} = P'_h, \qquad h = k, k' \ldots, \qquad \text{(D1.2)}$$

their initial price, with p'_h representing the initial gross rental and μ_h the rate of depreciation. (D1.2) of course implies arbitrage equation

$$i' = \frac{p'_k}{P'_k} - \mu_k = \frac{p'_{k'}}{P'_{k'}} - \mu_{k'} = \ldots \qquad \text{(D1.2.1)}$$

and, thus, yield uniformity. Walras says:[5]

Let us first examine the inequality [(D1.1)] and let us try to convert it into an equality [by means of a process of tatonnement toward temporary equilibrium]. The left-hand side is a decreasing function of i. We know from the facts underlying the function F_e that the right-hand side is a function of i which first increases from zero [as i increases] and then decreases to zero again (at $i = \infty$) . . . This being the case, we see at once that, in order to make an equality of this inequality, i' will have to fall or rise according as the left-hand side is less than or greater than the right-hand side for the initial value i'.

Diagrammatically, Walras's argument[6] may be illustrated as in figure D1, which is adapted from Jaffé (1942).

II Entrepreneurial profits must be eliminated, that is, the cost of production of new capital goods must be brought into equality with their price. This will determine the quantities $D_k, D_{k'}, \ldots$ of new capital goods produced along positively sloped supply schedules of the capital-goods producing industries.[7]

[4] Lesson 25, par. 253. Net saving is expressed by the author as a demand for perpetual numéraire income streams, which are represented by an imaginary commodity labeled E (e when in subscript) that enters consumers' utility function alongside ordinary goods. I use Walras's notation, in which (i) primes denote both alternative capital goods $k, k' \ldots$ and arbitrary initial conditions on prices or interest rates; (ii) upper-case (lower-case) P's signify prices (rentals) of capital goods. In (D1.1), (D1.2), I have slightly simplified the author's expression, without change in meaning.

[5] Ibid.; expressions in brackets are mine except for [as i increases], which is Jaffé's.

[6] The author seems to take the assertion "The left-hand side is a decreasing function of i" as requiring no further justification.

[7] See Lesson 23, par. 242; Lesson 25, par. 252, 256–8. Instantaneous input mobility across sectors allows Walras's temporary-equilibrium supply curves to be positively sloped rather than vertical.

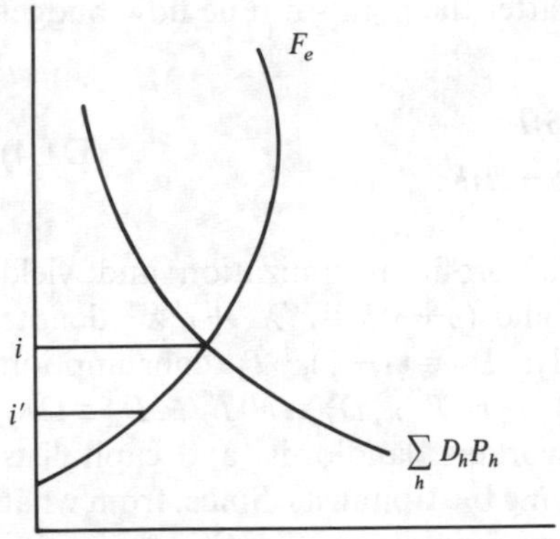

Figure D1 Interest-rate determination in Walras's theory of capital

III The rentals p_h having been determined via input and output markets; the rate of interest and the prices of new capital goods having been ground out by (D1.1) and (D1.2); the prices of existing capital goods now must adjust so as to equal the prices of new capital goods.

I turn to my comments.

1 Recall that, given an arbitrage equation such as (D1.2.1), in the eyes of equity holders capital goods $k, k' \ldots$ represent perfect substitutes. Holders therefore are indifferent as to the relative rates of accumulation of these capital goods, which leaves *ex-ante* investment flow demands for them undefined (no VON NEUMANN III-type installation costs are present). The output-market-clearing equation associated with each reproducible capital good therefore represents an identically holding inventory-accumulation equation that cannot possibly contribute to the determination of temporary-equilibrium prices. The function of determining these prices instead falls to an equal number of arbitrage equations.

2 Since the D_h $(h=k, k' \ldots)$ in (D1.1) thus cannot denote *ex-ante flow demands* for $k, k' \ldots$, they must be referring to *ex-ante flow supplies* of capital goods. However, as I now show, only under special assumptions will a model that, correctly, defines the D_h as profit-maximizing outputs of new capital goods throw up a capital-market-equilibrium condition

$$\dot{K}(i) = F(i), \tag{D1.3}$$

akin to (D1.1), that can be viewed as solving for the economy's temporary-equilibrium interest rate i ($\dot{K}(i)$ is aggregate investment, $F(i)$ aggregate saving). To explain this, I return to the basics-only economy WALRAS II.

A little reflection shows that in the latter the point-in-time flow budget constraint may be written as[8]

$$\begin{aligned} Q^C + \pi Q^S &\equiv r^{T_1}\bar{T}_1 + r^{T_2}\bar{T}_2 + (\rho+\delta)K \\ &\equiv D^C_{T_1} + \pi \sum_i D^S_i + (\rho+\delta-\Omega)K, \end{aligned} \tag{D1.4}$$

where I have assumed entrepreneurial profit maximization and yield equality [(7.25)–(7.27)]: $K \equiv X^C + \pi X^S$ and $(\rho+\delta)K \equiv r^C X^C + r^S X^S$ denote capital and gross profits, respectively; $D^C_{T_1} \equiv (1-\gamma) r^{T_1}\bar{T}_1$ consumption demand for corn by workers [(7.31)]; $D^S_{T_1} \equiv \gamma r^{T_1}\bar{T}_1/\pi$, $D^S_{T_2} \equiv r^{T_2}\bar{T}_2/\pi$, $D^S_K \equiv \Omega K/\pi$ consumption demand for steel by workers, landlords, and capitalists $(i = T_1, T_2, K)$; and $(\rho+\delta-\Omega)K$ gross saving by capitalists. Since, from what has been said, the individual rates of accumulation $\dot{X}^C = Q^C - \delta X^C - D^C_{T_1}$ and $\dot{X}^S = Q^S - \delta X^S - \sum D^S_i$ hold identically, (D1.4) may be rewritten as

$$\dot{X}^C + \pi \dot{X}^S \equiv (\rho - \Omega)K, \tag{D1.5}$$

which establishes an identity – not an equilibrium equality – between aggregate investment (demand for loanable funds) $\dot{K} \equiv \dot{X}^C + \pi \dot{X}^S$ and aggregate saving (supply of loanable funds) $F \equiv (\rho - \Omega)K$. I conclude that, whenever all outputs are basics, capital-market-equilibrium equation (D1.3) cannot possibly fulfill the role of an interest-rate-determining temporary-equilibrium condition Walras wishes to assign to it. The reason is simple: All prices and the interest rate have already been determined by profit maximization and the system's stock-equilibrium condition.[9]

This ought to give pause for thought. For it so happens that in his theory of capital Walras *does* assume all of his outputs to be storable and subject to arbitrage condition (D1.2.1).[10]

3 Consider next a slightly different model, seemingly more favorable to the author's attempt to interpret (D1.3) as an interest-rate-determining loanable-funds equation. Storable corn X^C and primary labor T_1 produce a nonbasic (instantaneously perishable consumption services, S); corn is produced by land T_2 alone, which like corn stocks is marketable in the bourse (landlords have been absorbed into the capitalist class). Workers and capitalists both diversify their consumption, spending an identical proportion $0 < \gamma < 1$ of their consumption on services. Assuming profit-

8 Recall again that, following Walras, I am neglecting expected and actual capital gains.

9 Recall arbitrage equation (7.27) – the WALRAS-II analogue to (D1.2.1) – which uniquely solves for $\pi(x^C, x^S)$ and $i \equiv \rho(x^C, x^S)$. The fact that, unlike Walras's own model, WALRAS II does not allow for point-in-time variations in factor-service supplies (the stocks x^C, x^S and the services they render are predetermined) is without consequence for the present argument.

10 See Part VI, Lesson 29, which contains the most explicit statement of the author's assumptions.

maximization, yield-arbitrage, and once again following Walras and abstracting from both expected and actual capital gains, the system's budget constraint now appears as

$$\begin{aligned} Q^C + pQ^S &\equiv r^{T_1}\bar{T}_1 + (\rho+\delta)K \\ &\equiv \sum_i D_i^C + p\sum_i D_i^S + (\rho+\delta-\Omega)K, \end{aligned} \tag{D1.6}$$

where p is the flow price of services in terms of corn; $K \equiv X^C + \pi\bar{T}_2$ and $(\rho+\delta)K \equiv r^C X^C + r^{T_2}\bar{T}_2$ represent the value of physical capital and gross profits, respectively ($\pi \equiv p^T/p^C = p^T$ is the equity price of land); $D_{T_1}^C \equiv (1-\gamma)r^{T_1}\bar{T}_1$, $D_K^C \equiv (1-\gamma)\Omega K$ consumption demand for corn by workers and capitalists; $\sum D_i^S \equiv \gamma(r^{T_1}\bar{T}_1 + \Omega K)/p$ $(i = T_1, K)$ the corresponding market demand for steel; and $(\rho+\delta-\Omega)K$ gross saving by capitalists. A little reflection shows that (D1.6) may again be written as identity (D1.5) if, for argument's sake, I label the excess supply of consumption services as $\dot{X}^S (\equiv Z^S \equiv Q^S - \sum D_i^S)$. However, unlike in WALRAS II, the fact that services are instantaneously perishable will enforce

$$\dot{X}^S = 0 \tag{D1.7}$$

at each moment: The flow market for consumption services must clear in temporary equilibrium. Substitution of equilibrium condition (D1.7) in identity (D1.5) allows me to express such flow-market clearing in the alternative form

$$\dot{X}^C = (\rho - \Omega)K. \tag{D1.8}$$

I now will show that (D1.8) in fact is Walras's loanable-funds equilibrium condition (D1.3). Note that in the present model stockmarket equilibrium requires [compare (7.27)]

$$\rho = \rho^C(p, x^C) \equiv r^C - \delta^C = (r^{T_2}/\pi) \equiv \rho^{T_2}(\pi) = \rho, \tag{D1.9}$$

where $r^C = pq^{S\prime}(x^C)$ and $r^{T_2} = q^C$ are the gross rentals on corn and land, respectively, and $\rho \equiv i$ the uniform profit and interest rate [recall $x^C \equiv X^C/\bar{T}_1$ from (7.23), $Q^C = q^C\bar{T}_2$, $\delta^{T_2} = 0$, and the static-expectations assumption $\hat{\pi}^e \equiv 0$]. The first and the last equation in (D1.9) may respectively be solved for p and π in terms of ρ,

$$p = p(\rho, x^C), \qquad \pi = \pi(\rho), \tag{D1.10}$$

which immediately yields (dots stand for parameters and predetermined variables)

$$\begin{aligned} \dot{K}(\rho;\ldots) \equiv \dot{X}^C &= q^C\bar{T}_2 - \delta X^C \\ &- (1-\gamma)\{p(\rho, x^C)[q^S(x^C) - x^C q^{S\prime}(x^C)]\bar{T}_1 + \Omega[X^C + \pi(\rho)\bar{T}_2]\} \end{aligned} \tag{D1.11}$$

and

$$F(\rho;\ldots)\equiv(\rho-\Omega)K(\rho;\ldots)\equiv(\rho-\Omega)[X^C+\pi(\rho)\bar{T}_2]. \qquad \text{(D1.12)}$$

(D1.11) – which holds identically, given (D1.9) – and (D1.12) – which is a definition – yield (D1.3) when substituted in flow-equilibrium condition (D1.8). The interest rate $i\equiv\rho$ can then indeed be solved for from a capital-market-equilibrium condition, as intended by Walras.

It thus appears that I have rescued Walras from himself by explicitly allowing for nonbasics in his theory of capital. This interpretation should, however, be resisted. For recall from the passages quoted that Walras repeatedly and unequivocally asserts that what (D1.3) determines, via (D1.2), is the price vector of *new* capital goods. Only once the latter has been solved for, will prices of *existing* capital goods recursively adjust to equal it. Evidently, what Walras has in mind is to put forth (D1.3) as a pure flow theory of interest-rate determination. This clearly is impossible: Even if we introduce instantaneously perishable outputs – which allows us to view (D1.3) as a reduced-form equilibrium condition – the latter will always reflect a situation of simultaneous flow *and* stock equilibrium. After all, $\dot{K}(i)=F(i)$ incorporates (D1.9) or (D1.2.1) – an arbitrage equation.

4 I summarize my case:

(i) In order for Walras's system to throw up a capital-market equilibrium condition that will determine the temporary-equilibrium interest rate irrespective of any assumption about the storability of outputs, the author needs well-defined *ex-ante* investment-flow-demand functions. Given absence of stock-adjustment (installation) costs, such functions are not available. So an assumption about output storability is necessary to make headway.

(ii) It turns out that Walras does in fact explicitly assume all outputs to be storable and subject to yield arbitrage. But this is precisely the case when a reduced-form savings-investment equilibrium condition in ρ that, correctly, posits investment to be supply-determined is unavailable.

(iii) Even if we generalize Walras's model to include nonbasics and instantaneous output market clearing – thus making possible a reduced-form capital-market-equilibrium condition in ρ – the latter will never represent the pure flow theory of interest-rate determination the author is after, for it always incorporates a stock-equilibrium condition.

In conclusion, it is evident that Walras's fundamental problem is his failure to grasp the significance of an arbitrage equation. Unlike in his discussion of zero-excess-flow-demand equations – whose economic function he invariably establishes by careful enunciation of the markets and adjustment processes that guarantee them – the author never seriously asks what, in (D1.2.1), is supposed to produce $i'_k = i'_{k'} = i'$ rather than[11]

$$i'_k \equiv \frac{p'_k}{P'_k} - \mu_k \gtrless \frac{p'_{k'}}{P'_{k'}} - \mu_{k'} \equiv i'_{k'}. \tag{D1.13}$$

Had he tried to address that question, he might have happened upon the concept of portfolio equilibrium and the distinction between the stock-market and the capital market it entails – with profound consequences not just for his theory of capital but, as shown in chapter 8, for his model of pure exchange as well.[12]

It is hard to escape the impression that it was the author's unexamined prior commitment to pure exchange – thus, flow equilibrium – as paradigmatic that was responsible for the fiasco of his capital theory. Had Walras approached his task with a capital-theoretic perspective from the outset, the question, What are the conditions under which agents are willing to *hold* (the claims to) their endowments? would have imposed itself and received the same attention as, What are the terms at which agents willingly *exchange* their endowments?

[11] I have found only two instances in which he briefly entertains the possibility of nonzero yield differentials (see Lesson 23, par. 233 and Lesson 28, par. 267). In both cases, instead of confronting the question of which markets and what market forces will eliminate these differentials, he contents himself with assertions such as "in an economy in normal operation which has only to maintain itself in equilibrium, we may suppose [yield equality] to be satisfied" (par. 267).

[12] Recall also that Fisherian capital theory is in all essentials a direct descendant of Parts V and VI of the *Elements* and that the concept of portfolio or stock equilibrium was not fully absorbed by the profession until Keynes's *General Theory*.

Appendices

The chapter appendices to follow contain (i) explicit forms of partial derivatives whose signs are not obvious from inspection of the corresponding function (all are evaluated at a restpoint and listed by text equation number); (ii) mathematical demonstrations referred to in the body of the text or in the supplements. Appendix equation numbers carry a prefix consisting of "a" and the corresponding chapter number.

Appendix to chapter 1

(i) Partial derivatives

$$\psi_1 = x(\hat{X}_1^C - \hat{X}_1^S) < 0, \hat{X}_1^C(\pi, x) = -(1-\gamma)\Omega x^{-1} < 0, \hat{X}_1^S = \gamma\Omega x\pi^{-2} > 0$$
$$\psi_2 = -(\pi + x)\hat{X}_2^S = -[(\pi + x)/\pi][g + \delta + (1-\gamma)\Omega] < 0 \qquad (1.18)$$

(ii) Anticipated productivity shocks

First, note that $\pi(t)$ is a function of the entire future path of technology $\{q^C(\tau), q^S(\tau)\}_{\tau=t}^{\infty}$ expected by stockmarket speculators,

$$\pi(t) = \bar{\pi}^2 \int_t^\infty \exp[-\phi'(\tau - t)] q^S(\tau) d\tau + \int_t^\infty \exp[-\phi'(\tau - t)] q^C(\tau) d\tau, \qquad (a1.1)$$

where (a1.1) is the forward solution of the linearized version of (1.17) in terms of its forcing functions.

I now specialize (a1.1) to a temporary corn-sector technology shock, as discussed in the text: $dq^C > 0$ unexpectedly at $t = t_0$, but the rise in q^C is correctly expected to be reversed at $t = t_1 > t_0$.

Before t_0, the economy is in steady-state equilibrium,

$$\pi(t) = \bar{\pi} = (q^C/q^S)^{\frac{1}{2}}. \qquad (a1.2)$$

For the system to evolve along an infinite-horizon PFCE path requires that it be on the saddle path after t_1, thus again move according to (a1.2) (recall that the saddle path coincides with the horizontal line $\pi = \bar{\pi}$). Moreover, an infinite-horizon PFCE path cannot at any point leave open unexploited opportunities for speculative profit in the form of anticipated discrete jumps in π (see my discussion in supplement A.2). Therefore, the economy's path during $(t_0, t_1]$ must be continuous and obey the transversality condition

$$\pi(t_1) = A\exp[\phi'(t_1 - t_0)] + \bar{\pi}' = \bar{\pi}, \qquad \text{(a1.3)}$$

where $\bar{\pi}' = (q^{C'}/q^S)^{\frac{1}{2}} > \bar{\pi} = (q^C/q^S)^{\frac{1}{2}}$, $q^{C'} \equiv dq^C + q^C$. (a1.3) yields

$$A = \exp[-\phi'(t_1 - t_0)]d\bar{\pi}, \qquad d\bar{\pi} \equiv -(\bar{\pi}' - \bar{\pi}) < 0, \qquad \text{(a1.4)}$$

as the unique value of the constant A consistent with a PFCE path. It immediately follows that, at t_0, the stockmarket-equilibrium price must jump by

$$\Delta\pi(t_0) = \pi(t_0) - \bar{\pi} = \{\exp[-\phi'(t_1 - t_0)] - 1\}d\bar{\pi} > 0 \qquad \text{(a1.5)}$$

to a point such as a' in figure 1.3, and subsequently move along path $a' - a'' - A$.

Appendix to chapter 3

Below I discuss (i) the dynamic loci of figure 3.3; (ii) the partial derivatives that appear in equations (3.30)–(3.47); and (iii) the impact result $dp/d\gamma > 0$ of VON NEUMANN III.

(i) Dynamic loci of figure 3.3

ALPHA: The partials appearing in (3.18), (3.19) are given by

$$\phi_1^\alpha = (q^C/\pi) + \gamma\Omega x > 0, \qquad \phi_2^\alpha = \gamma\Omega\pi^2 > 0$$
$$\psi_1^\alpha = (1-\gamma)\Omega x^2 > 0, \qquad \psi_2^\alpha = -[q^C - (1-\gamma)\Omega\pi]x < 0.$$

The corresponding loci $\dot{\pi} = 0$, $\dot{x} = 0$ are, respectively, defined by the equations $x = (q^C - \gamma\Omega\pi)/\gamma\Omega\pi^2$ and $x = (1-\gamma)\Omega/[q^C - (1-\gamma)\Omega\pi]$. The former implies $x = \bar{x}$ at $\pi = 1, x \to \infty$ at $\pi = 0$, and a negative slope $-\phi_2^\alpha/\phi_1^\alpha$ that is increasing; the latter $x < \bar{x}$ at $\pi = 1$ (from $g \geq 0$), $x = (1-\gamma)\Omega/q^C < x_{|\pi=1}$ at $\pi = 0$, and a positive slope $-\psi_2^\alpha/\psi_1^\alpha$ that is decreasing.

BETA: The partials appearing in (3.21), (3.22) are given by

$$\phi_1^\beta = \gamma\Omega x\pi > 0, \qquad \phi_2^\beta = \gamma\Omega\pi^2 > 0$$
$$\psi_1^\beta = x[q^C - (1-\gamma)\Omega]/\pi > 0, \qquad \psi_2^\beta = [q^C - (1-\gamma)\Omega] > 0.$$

The corresponding loci $\dot{\pi}=0, \dot{x}=0$ are segments of rectangular hyperbolae defined by, respectively, $\pi x=\bar{x}$ and $\pi x=(1-\gamma)\Omega/[q^C-(1-\gamma)\Omega]$.

(ii) Partial derivatives of VON NEUMANN III

$$\begin{aligned}&\Pi_1^C=\pi(a_{CS}^{-1}/q)-q\hat{X}'\gtrless 0, \quad \Pi_2^C=-(a_{CS}^{-1}/q)\pi<0, \quad \Pi_3^C=a_{CS}^{-1}>0\\&\Pi_1^S=-\hat{X}(1+T)\pi/q<0, \quad \Pi_2^S=\{[\hat{X}(1+T)/q]-q\hat{X}'\}\pi\gtrless 0,\\&\Pi_3^S=-\hat{X}(1+T)<0\end{aligned} \tag{3.30}$$

$$\begin{aligned}&\chi_1=-\chi_2=[\pi a_{CS}^{-1}+\hat{X}(1+T)]q^{-2}>0,\\&\chi_3=(a_{CS}^{-1}+\pi^{-2}a_{SC}^{-1})q^{-1}>0, \quad \chi_4=-1<0\end{aligned} \tag{3.33}$$

$$\begin{aligned}&z_1^C=-[(1-\gamma)\Omega(1+\pi x^{-1})+q\hat{X}']<0, \quad z_2^C=-q(1-\gamma)\Omega x^{-1}<0,\\&z_3^C=-[\hat{X}(1+T)+q(1-\gamma)\Omega]x^{-1}<0, \quad z_4^C=q\Omega(1+\pi x^{-1})>0,\\&z_5^C=-q(1-\gamma)(1+\pi x^{-1})<0, \quad z_6^C=-a_{SC}^{-2}x^{-1}<0\end{aligned} \tag{3.34}$$

$$\begin{aligned}&z_1^S=-[\gamma\Omega(1+\pi^{-1}x)+q\hat{X}']<0, \quad z_2^S=q\gamma\Omega x\pi^{-2}>0,\\&z_3^S=[q\gamma\Omega+\hat{X}(1+T)]x^{-1}>0, \quad z_4^S=-q\Omega(1+\pi^{-1}x)<0,\\&z_5^S=-q\gamma(1+\pi^{-1}x)<0, \quad z_6^S=-a_{CS}^{-2}x<0\end{aligned} \tag{3.35}$$

$$\begin{aligned}&\rho_1=(a_{CS}^{-1}-q\Omega)/q^2=\hat{X}(1+T)/q^2>0,\\&\rho_2=-\pi a_{CS}^{-1}/q^2<0, \quad \rho_3=-q\rho_2>0, \quad \rho_4=1>0\end{aligned} \tag{3.36}$$

$$q_h^i=-z_{h+1}^i/z_1^i \qquad (i=C,S; h=1-5) \qquad \text{(3.37), (3.38)}$$

$$\begin{aligned}&\phi_1=\pi[\Omega\pi^{-2}+\chi_1(q\pi^{-1}+q_1^C-q_1^S)]=\Omega\pi^{-1}+\chi_1 q^2\hat{X}'(\Omega+q\hat{X}')(z_1^Cz_1^S)^{-1}>0,\\&\phi_2=\pi\chi_1(q_2^C-q_2^S)<0\end{aligned} \tag{3.39}$$

$$\psi_i=x\hat{X}'(q_i^C-q_i^S)<0 \qquad (i=1,2) \tag{3.40}$$

$$\bar{\rho}'(\Omega\ldots)=\Omega/(\Omega+q\hat{X}')>0 \tag{3.46}$$

$$\begin{aligned}&\bar{x}_1=-z_4^C/z_3^C>0,\\&\bar{x}_2=a_{SC}^{-1}q\hat{X}'\bar{q}'D^{-2}(1-2\gamma)\gtrless 0 \text{ as } \gamma\gtrless\tfrac{1}{2},\end{aligned} \tag{3.47}$$

where D is the denominator of (3.47).

(iii) Proof of $dp/d\gamma>0$ on impact in VON NEUMANN III

Solving (3.39), (3.40) for the stable motion along the saddle path I find

$$\begin{aligned}&\pi(t)-\bar{\pi}=\frac{(\bar{x}_1-\bar{x}_0)\phi_2}{\phi_1-\lambda_2}\exp(\lambda_2 t)\\&x(t)-\bar{x}_1=-(\bar{x}_1-\bar{x}_0)\exp(\lambda_2 t),\end{aligned} \tag{a3.1}$$

where $\lambda_2 < 0$ is the system's stable root and $\bar{x}_1 - \bar{x}_0 \equiv \bar{x}_1(\gamma, \Omega \ldots)d\gamma$ the change in the steady-state value of x [(3.47)]. (a3.1) immediately yields

$$\pi(0) - \bar{\pi} \equiv d\pi = \frac{\phi_2 \bar{x}_1(\gamma, \Omega \ldots)}{\phi_1 - \lambda_2} d\gamma, \tag{a3.2}$$

or $d\pi/d\gamma = \phi_2 \bar{x}_1(\gamma, \Omega \ldots)/(\phi_1 - \lambda_2) < 0$, the drop of π on impact (at $t=0$).

From (3.31), (3.37), (3.38), and (a3.2) the corresponding change in p is

$$\begin{aligned} \frac{dp}{d\gamma} &= \frac{d\pi}{d\gamma} + \frac{d[q^C(\pi, \bar{x}_0, \gamma \ldots)/q^S(\pi, \bar{x}_0, \gamma \ldots)]}{d\gamma} \\ &= [q(\phi_1 - \lambda_2)]^{-1}[\chi_1(q + q_1^C - q_1^S)q_2^S\left(-\frac{q_3^C}{q_2^C} + \frac{q_3^S}{q_2^S}\right) + (q_3^C - q_3^S)(\Omega - \lambda_2)], \end{aligned} \tag{a.3.3}$$

which, since $q_3^C/q_2^C = q_3^S/q_2^S$, is seen to yield $dp/d\gamma > 0$.

Appendix to chapter 4

This appendix (i) gives explicit forms of the partial derivatives appearing in equations (4.11)–(4.35); (ii) derives the discrete-time optimizing consumption function (4.10).

(i) Partial derivatives of MARX–SRAFFA

$$\tilde{\hat{X}}_2^S = q^{S*}\left(1 - \gamma\frac{\Omega}{1+\Omega}\right) > 0 \tag{4.11}$$

$$\psi_1 = x(\hat{X}_1^C - \hat{X}_1^S) \gtrless 0$$

$$\hat{X}_1^C(\pi, x) = -(1-\gamma)\frac{\Omega}{1+\Omega}[(1+\pi x^{-1})q^{S*}(1+\phi') + (1+\rho)x^{-1}] < 0$$

[from:

$$\hat{X}^C(\pi, x) = q^C x^{-1} - 1 - (1-\gamma)\frac{\Omega}{1+\Omega}\left[\left(1 + \frac{\phi(\pi)}{\pi}\right)\pi q^{S*}\right](1+\pi x^{-1})]$$

$$\hat{X}_1^S(\pi, x) = -\frac{\gamma\Omega q^{S*}}{1+\Omega}[1 + (1 + x\pi^{-1})\phi'] < 0$$

[Note: due to the interest-rate factor $(1+\rho)$ in end-of-period consumption spending, $\hat{X}_1^S$ changes sign *vis-à-vis* $\hat{X}_1^S$ in VON NEUMANN I.]

$$\psi_2 = -(\pi + x)\hat{X}_2^S = -(\pi + x)\tilde{\hat{X}}_2^S < 0 \tag{4.14}$$

$$y_1 = \bar{w}(q^{S*} - \delta^S x^{-1}) > 0,\ y_2 = -\bar{w}(q^C - \delta^S)/x^2 = -\bar{w}\pi\rho/x^2 < 0 \tag{4.22}$$

$$\begin{aligned} r_1^C &= q^{S*} - \epsilon y_1/\bar{w} = (1-\epsilon)q^{S*} + \epsilon\delta^S x^{-1} > 0 \\ r_2^C &= \epsilon\pi\rho/x^2 \geq 0 \text{ as } \epsilon \geq 0;\ r_3^C = -y/\bar{w} < 0 \end{aligned} \tag{4.24}$$

$$\pi_i = -r^C_{i+1}/[r^C_1 + q^C\pi^{-2}] < 0(i=1), > 0(i=2)$$
$$\pi_3 = (1+r^C)/[r^C_1 + q^C\pi^{-2}] > 0 \tag{4.26}$$
$$\rho_i = r^C_{i+1}\{1 - [r^C_1/(r^C_1 + q^C\pi^{-2})]\} > 0(i=1), < 0(i=2)$$

[Note: also follows by inspection from π_i $(i=1,2)$ and $\rho = \rho^S = (q^C/\pi) - \delta^S + \hat{\pi}^e$.]

$$\rho_3 = r^C + r^C_1\pi_3 > 0$$

$$\tilde{\tilde{X}}^S_1 = -(\gamma_L \epsilon x/\bar{w})\frac{\partial y(\pi,x)/\pi}{\partial\pi} + \gamma_K\frac{\Omega}{1+\Omega}[(1+x\pi^{-1})q^C + (1+\rho)x]\pi^{-2}$$

$$> 0, \text{ since } \frac{\partial y(\pi,x)/\pi}{\partial\pi} = -\bar{w}(q^C x^{-1} - 1)\pi^{-2} = -\bar{w}(g + d^C)\pi^{-2} < 0$$

$$\tilde{\tilde{X}}^S_2 = q^{S*}\left(1 - \gamma_K\frac{\Omega}{1+\Omega}\right) - (\epsilon/\pi)\left\{\gamma_L[\rho + (\epsilon y/\bar{w})] - \gamma_K\frac{\Omega}{1+\Omega}y/\bar{w}\right\}$$

$$\gtrless 0, \approx q^{S*}\left(1 - \gamma_K\frac{\Omega}{1+\Omega}\right) > 0 \text{ for small } \epsilon \tag{4.27}$$

$$\phi_1 = [\pi/(1+r^C)][r^C_1 + (q^C/\pi^2)] > 0$$
$$\phi_2 = [\pi/(1+r^C)]\epsilon\pi\rho/x^2 \geq 0 \text{ as } \epsilon \geq 0 \tag{4.28}$$

$$\psi_1 \gtrless 0 \text{ [recall } \psi_1 \gtrless 0 \text{ for } \epsilon = 0 \text{ in (4.14)]}$$
$$\psi_2 \gtrless 0, \approx -(\pi + x)\hat{X}^S_2 = -(\pi + x)\tilde{\tilde{X}}^S_2 < 0 \text{ for small } \epsilon \tag{4.29}$$

[recall (4.27), (4.14)]

$$\bar{x}_i = -\bar{z}^S_{i+1}/\bar{z}^S_1 \gtrless 0\ (i=1),\ > 0\ (i=2,3) \quad \text{for small } \epsilon$$

$$\text{since } \bar{z}^S_1 = \tilde{\tilde{X}}^S_2 + \epsilon\frac{y_2}{\bar{w}}\left\{\frac{\tilde{\tilde{X}}^S_1}{r^C_1 + q^C\pi^{-2}} + \left[1 - \frac{r^C_1}{r^C_1 + q^C\pi^{-2}}\right](1+\Omega)^{-1}\right\}$$

$$\gtrless 0, \approx \tilde{\tilde{X}}^S_2 > 0 \text{ for small } \epsilon$$

$$\bar{z}^S_2 = \tilde{\tilde{X}}^S_1\bar{\pi}_2 + (\partial\tilde{\tilde{X}}^S/\partial\epsilon) - [\bar{\rho}_2/(1+\Omega)] \gtrless 0$$

[where $\partial\tilde{\tilde{X}}^S/\partial\epsilon = -\gamma_L yx/\bar{w}\pi < 0$]

$$\bar{z}^S_3 = \partial\tilde{\tilde{X}}^S/\partial\gamma_L < 0,\ \bar{z}^S_4 = \partial\tilde{\tilde{X}}^S/\partial\gamma_K < 0 \tag{4.34}$$

$$\bar{\bar{\pi}}_1 = \bar{\pi}_1\bar{x}_1 + \bar{\pi}_2 = \{-r^C_2(\partial\tilde{\tilde{X}}^S/\partial\epsilon) + r^C_3\tilde{\tilde{X}}^S_2\}/\bar{z}^S_1(r^C_1 + q^C\pi^{-2})$$

> 0 starting at small or zero ϵ. (4.35)

$$\bar{\bar{\pi}}_2 = \bar{\pi}_1\bar{x}_2 < 0,\ \bar{\bar{\pi}}_3 = \bar{\pi}_1\bar{x}_3 < 0 \text{ starting at small or zero } \epsilon$$

(ii) Derivation of optimizing consumption function (4.10)

Assume the representative capitalist household maximizes

$$\sum_{\substack{t=0\\ D^S,\, D^C}}^{\infty}(1+\Omega)^{-t}\ln\{[D^S(t)]^{\gamma}[D^C(t)]^{1-\gamma}\}, \tag{a4.1}$$

where $(1+\Omega)^{-t}$ is a discount factor based on the fixed rate of time preference $\Omega > 0$; $U(D^C, D^S) \equiv \ln\{\cdot\}$ a logarithmic felicity function [(1.10)]; and $\{(D^S)^{\gamma}(D^C)^{1-\gamma}\}$ a Cobb–Douglas index $(0 \leq \gamma \leq 1)$ of quantities of corn (D^C) and steel (D^S) consumed. [Recall the corresponding continuous-time VON NEUMANN I utility function (A2.1), (A2.2) in supplement A.2.] The maximization is subject to

$$\begin{aligned} &\Delta K(t) \leq \rho(t)K(t) - E(t) \text{ or } K(t+1) + E(t) \leq [1+\rho(t)]K(t) \\ &E(t) \equiv D^C(t) + p(t)D^S(t),\ K(0) > 0 \text{ given,} \end{aligned} \tag{a4.2}$$

where $E(t)$ is end-of-period consumption spending; $K(t)$ beginning-of-period wealth; and $\{p(t)\}_{t=0}^{\infty} = \{\pi(t)\}_{t=0}^{\infty}$, $\{\rho(t)\}_{t=0}^{\infty}$ the expected path of the price of steel and of the uniform profit (interest) rate, respectively. Given $\ln\{\cdot\}$ in (a4.1), the dynamic budget constraint in (a4.2) will necessarily hold with equality along an optimal path.

[(a4.1), (a4.2)] may be set up as a Lagrangian maximization problem in the three choice variables $D^C(t), D^S(t), K(t+1)$, and the dynamic multiplier $\lambda(t)$,[1]

$$\begin{aligned} &L[\{D^C(t),\ D^S(t),\ K(t+1);\ \lambda(t)\}_{t=0}^{\infty}] \equiv \\ &\sum_{t=0}^{\infty}(1+\Omega)^{-t}[\gamma \ln D^S(t) + (1-\gamma)\ln D^C(t)] - \\ &\sum_{t=0}^{\infty}\lambda(t)\{K(t+1) + E(t) - [1+\rho(t)]K(t)\} \equiv \\ &\sum_{t=0}^{\infty}(1+\Omega)^{-t}[\gamma \ln D^S(t) + (1-\gamma)\ln D^C(t)] - \\ &\sum_{t=0}^{\infty}\lambda(t)[D^C(t) + p(t)D^S(t)] - \\ &\sum_{t=0}^{\infty}\{\lambda(t) - \lambda(t+1)[1+\rho(t+1)]\}K(t+1) + \lambda(0)[1+\rho(0)]K(0). \end{aligned} \tag{a4.3}$$

The first-order necessary conditions are, for $t = 0, 1, \ldots, \infty$,

$$\begin{aligned} &\frac{\partial L}{\partial D^C(t)} = [(1+\Omega)^{-t}(1-\gamma)/D^C(t)] - \lambda(t) = 0 \\ &\frac{\partial L}{\partial D^S(t)} = [(1+\Omega)^{-t}\gamma/D^S(t)] - \lambda(t)p(t) = 0 \\ &\frac{\partial L}{\partial K(t+1)} = -\{\lambda(t) - \lambda(t+1)[1+\rho(t+1)]\} = 0 \end{aligned} \tag{a4.4}$$

[1] What follows is adapted from the elegant treatment of discrete-time optimization given, for the one-commodity case, in Foley (1991).

$$\frac{\partial L}{\partial \lambda(t)} = -\{K(t+1)+E(t)-[1+\rho(t)]K(t)\}=0.$$

Rearranging and summing the first two conditions gives $\lambda(t)[D^C(t)+p(t)D^S(t)]=(1+\Omega)^{-t}$ or, over an infinite horizon, $\sum_{t=0}^{\infty}\lambda(t)[D^C(t)+p(t)D^S(t)] = \sum_{t=0}^{\infty}(1+\Omega)^{-t} = \frac{1}{1-(1+\Omega)^{-1}} = \frac{1+\Omega}{\Omega}$, which – since the constraint function in $L[\cdot]$ must equal zero at an optimum – implies $(1+\Omega)/\Omega = \left[\sum_{t=0}^{\infty} -\{\lambda(t)-\lambda(t+1)[1+\rho(t+1)]\}K(t+1)\right] + \lambda(0)[1+\rho(0)]K(0)$. But note that the terms under the summation sign on the righthand side are zero (from the third condition in (a4.4)), so that we have $\lambda(0)=(1+\Omega)/\Omega[1+\rho(0)]K(0)$. The first and second condition in (a4.4), on the other hand, imply $\lambda(0)=(1-\gamma)/D^C(0)=\gamma/p(0)D^S(0)$. Since the choice of origin is arbitrary, one similarly must have, for any t, $(1+\Omega)/\Omega[1+\rho(t)]K(t)=\lambda(t)=(1-\gamma)/D^C(t)=\gamma/p(t)D^S(t)$ at a maximum. The optimal demand functions are thus given by $D^C(t)=(1-\gamma)[\Omega/(1+\Omega)][1+\rho(t)]K(t)$, $D^S(t)=\gamma[\Omega/(1+\Omega)][1+\rho(t)]K(t)/p(t)$, and the corresponding optimal consumption law by

$$E(t)=\frac{\Omega}{1+\Omega}[1+\rho(t)]K(t)=\Omega K(t+1), \qquad (a4.5)\equiv(4.10)$$

after substitution for $[1+\rho(t)]K(t)$ from (a4.2) to obtain the second equality. Consumption is thus proportional to end-of-period wealth gross ($[1+\rho(t)]K(t)$) or net ($K(t+1)\equiv K(t)+\Delta K(t)$) of end-of-period consumption $E(t)$, $\Omega/(1+\Omega)$ and Ω being the respective factors of proportionality ($K(t)=X^C(t)+\pi(t)X^S(t)$ is wealth at the beginning of the period, measured at the then obtaining temporary-equilibrium equity price $\pi(t)=p(t)=\pi[\hat{\pi}^e(t); q^C(t), q^{S*}(t)]$; recall (4.9)).

Appendix to chapter 5

This appendix provides technical detail on (i) single-period adjustment under a Leontief technology, and (ii) dynamics under anti-Uzawa technology (5.4.5). Both are discussed in supplement C.2 to chapter 5.

(i) Single-period adjustment to $d\gamma<0$ under a Leontief technology

Given technology [(5.3), (5.4.2)], the zero-entrepreneurial profit conditions are [compare (5.5), (5.6)]

$$p=a_{CS}r^C, \qquad p^C=1=a_{CC}r^C+a_{TC}r^T. \qquad (a5.1)$$

On impact of $d\gamma < 0$, full employment of both inputs must obtain (since r^C cannot fall to zero and r^T tends to rise). The nonbasics market-clearing equation therefore is given by [recall (5.9), (5.12)]

$$z^S(\pi; x, \gamma) \equiv a_{CS}^{-1}[(x - \bar{\bar{x}}_C) - \gamma\frac{\Omega}{1+\Omega}(\pi + x)] = 0, \quad \bar{\bar{x}}_C = a_{CC}/a_{TC}$$

$$z_1^S = -\gamma\frac{\Omega}{1+\Omega}a_{CS}^{-1} < 0, \; z_2^S = a_{CS}^{-1}\left(1 - \gamma\frac{\Omega}{1+\Omega}\right) > 0 \qquad \text{(a5.2)}$$

$$z_3^S = \frac{-\Omega}{1+\Omega}(\pi + x)a_{CS}^{-1} < 0,$$

and yields the function

$$\pi = \pi(x, \gamma), \qquad \pi_i = \frac{-z_{i+1}^S}{z_1^S} > 0 (i=1), \; < 0 (i=2), \qquad \text{(a5.2.1)}$$

discussed in C.2. Assume now that – following the impact of $d\gamma < 0$ on the stationary-state economy $[\pi(t-1) = \bar{\pi}, \; x(t-1) = x(t) = \bar{x}(\gamma_0) \equiv x_0]$ at the beginning of t and a resultant beginning-of-t temporary equilibrium $\pi(t) = \pi(x_0, \gamma_1)$, $x(t) = x_0$ – the system indeed attains the new stationary state at the beginning of $t+1$; given perfect foresight, speculators then form the expectation $\pi^e \equiv [\pi(t+1)]^e = \bar{\pi}$ at the beginning of t. Arbitrage condition (5.10) must hold at that moment and, given (a5.1), can be written as [compare (5.11)]

$$\chi(p, \pi; \bar{\pi}) \equiv pa_{CS}^{-1} - 1 - [r^T(p)/\pi] - \hat{\pi}^e = 0, \; \hat{\pi}^e = \frac{\bar{\pi}}{\pi} - 1, \; r^{T'} = -\bar{\bar{x}}_C a_{CS}^{-1} < 0$$

$$\chi_1 = a_{CS}^{-1}\left(1 + \frac{\bar{\bar{x}}_C}{\pi}\right) > 0, \; \chi_2 = \frac{1+\Omega}{\pi} > 0, \qquad \text{(a5.3)}$$

which yields the function (I omit $\bar{\pi}$ as an argument)

$$p = p(\pi), \qquad p' = -\chi_2/\chi_1 < 0, \qquad \text{(a5.3.1)}$$

and a corresponding rate of profit $\rho = \rho^C = p[\pi(x, \gamma)]a_{CS}^{-1} - 1$ after substitution from (a5.2.1). If the expectation $\pi^e = \bar{\pi}$ is to be validated, that rate of profit must generate x-dynamics [recall (5.16]

$$x(t+1) = \{p[\pi(x_0, \gamma)]a_{CS}^{-1} - 1 - \Omega\}\frac{[x + \pi(\cdot)]}{1+\Omega} - [\bar{\pi} - \pi(\cdot)] + x_0 \equiv \tilde{\psi}(x_0, \gamma) \qquad \text{(a5.4)}$$

such that $dx(t+1)/d\gamma = d\bar{x}/d\gamma \equiv \bar{x}'(\gamma)$, or

$$\bar{x}' = \tilde{\psi}_2 = p'\pi_2 a_{CS}^{-1}\left[\frac{x+\pi}{1+\Omega}\right] + \pi_2, \qquad \text{(a5.4.1)}$$

which is easily verified by substituting for $\bar{x}' = -z_3^S/z_2^S, p', \pi_2$, and using (a5.2).

(ii) Dynamics under anti-Uzawa technology (5.4.5)

Given technology (5.4.5), the zero-entrepreneurial-profit conditions are

$$p = a_{TS}r^T, \qquad p^C = 1 = a_{CC}r^C. \tag{a5.5}$$

The uniform profit rate is fixed at $\bar{\rho}^C = a_{CC}^{-1} - 1$ from (5.10) and (a5.5), which together yield the temporary stock-equilibrium condition

$$\chi(p, \pi, \hat{\pi}^e) \equiv \bar{\rho} - (p a_{TS}^{-1}/\pi) - \hat{\pi}^e = 0. \tag{a5.6}$$

Temporary flow-equilibrium for nonbasics requires

$$\begin{gathered} z^S(p, \pi, x, \gamma) \equiv a_{TS}^{-1} - \gamma \frac{\Omega}{1+\Omega} a_{CC}^{-1}(\pi + x)/p = 0 \\ z_1^S = a_{TS}^{-1}/p > 0,\ z_2^S = z_3^S = -\gamma \frac{\Omega}{1+\Omega} a_{CC}^{-1}/p < 0,\ z_4^S = \frac{-\Omega}{1+\Omega} a_{CC}^{-1}(\pi + x)/p < 0, \end{gathered} \tag{a5.7}$$

which gives a function

$$p = p(\pi, x, \gamma), \qquad p_1 = p_2 = -z_2^S/z_1^S > 0,\ p_3 = -z_4^S/z_1^S > 0, \tag{a5.7.1}$$

similar to (5.13) (but with the sign of z_3^S, thus of p_2, reversed in accordance with the Rybczynski theorem).

Under myopic foresight, $\hat{\pi}^e = \hat{\pi} \equiv \Delta\pi/\pi$, (a5.6) and (a5.7.1) yield the land-price motions

$$\begin{aligned} \Delta\pi &= \pi\bar{\rho} - p(\pi, x, \gamma) a_{TS}^{-1} \equiv \phi(\pi, x), \\ \phi_1 &= \bar{\rho} - p_1 a_{TS}^{-1} = [(\bar{\rho} - \Omega) + (1-\gamma) a_{CC}^{-1}\Omega]/(1+\Omega) \gtrless 0, \\ &\qquad > 0 \text{ if } \bar{\rho} > \Omega \\ \phi_2 &= -p_1 a_{TS}^{-1} < 0, \end{aligned} \tag{a5.8}$$

and the capital-composition dynamics [recall (5.16)]

$$\begin{aligned} \Delta x &= (\bar{\rho} - \Omega)\frac{x+\pi}{1+\Omega} - \phi(\pi, x) \equiv \psi(\pi, x) \\ \psi_1 &= \frac{\bar{\rho} - \Omega}{1+\Omega} - \phi_1 = -(1-\gamma)\Omega a_{CC}^{-1}/(1+\Omega) < 0 \\ \psi_2 &= \frac{\bar{\rho} - \Omega}{1+\Omega} - \phi_2 = [(\bar{\rho} - \gamma) + \gamma a_{CC}^{-1}\Omega]/(1+\Omega) \gtrless 0,\ > 0 \text{ if } \bar{\rho} > \Omega. \end{aligned} \tag{a5.9}$$

The partial derivatives in [(a5.8), (a5.9)] imply the following coefficients of the corresponding second-order difference equation [recall (5.20)]:

$$-a_1 = (\phi_1 + 1) + (\psi_2 + 1) = [2 + \bar{\rho}(2+\Omega) + \Omega]/(1+\Omega) = \eta_1 + \eta_2 > 0$$

$$c = \phi_1\psi_2 - \phi_2\psi_1 = \frac{\bar{\rho}(\bar{\rho}-\Omega)}{1+\Omega} = (\eta_1 - 1)(\eta_2 - 1) \gtrless 0, \ >0 \text{ if } \bar{\rho} > \Omega \quad \text{(a5.10)}$$

$$a_2 = c - a_1 - 1 = [\bar{\rho}(2+\bar{\rho}) + 1]/(1+\Omega) = \eta_1\eta_2 > 0.$$

Consequently, the three possible configurations of the two (necessarily positive) roots η_1, η_2 are

$$\begin{aligned} &\text{(a) } \eta_i > 1 \ (i=1,2) \\ &\text{(b) } \eta_1 > 1, 0 < \eta_2 < 1 \\ &\text{(c) } 0 < \eta_i < 1 \ (i=1,2) \end{aligned} \quad \text{(a5.11)}$$

and represent, respectively, a locally unstable (figure C3 a, b), saddle-path-stable (figure C3c, which shows one of three admissible configurations of dynamic loci), and stable (figure C3d) dynamical system.

Appendix to chapter 7

Below the reader will find the derivation of (i) the eigenvectors y_h associated with the stable roots η_h $(h=2,3)$ of WALRAS I; (ii) the relative slopes of the schedules appearing in figure 7.1a; (iii) the dynamic equations underlying figures 7.1b and c; (iv) the condition governing the sign of $\dot{x}^S$ on impact of $dy > 0$ in WALRAS I under perfect foresight; (v) the dynamic stability of WALRAS II under static expectations.

(i) Eigenvectors y_h

They are obtained by solving the homogeneous equation system

$$[J - \eta_h I]y_h = O, \qquad h = 2,3, \quad \text{(a7.1)}$$

for the elements of the vector $y_h \equiv [y_{h1} \ \ 1 \ \ y_{h3}]'$, where $y_{h2} = 1$ by normalization, J is given by (7.17), I is the identity matrix, O a null vector, and η_h denotes one of the two stable roots. Using (7.18), I immediately have the eigenvector elements

$$\begin{aligned} h=2:\ & y_{21} = -\phi_2/(\phi_1 - \eta_2) > 0 \\ & y_{22} = 1 \\ & y_{23} = 0 \\ h=3:\ & y_{31} = -\phi_2/(\phi_1 - \eta_3) > 0 \\ & y_{32} = 1 \\ & y_{33} = (\eta_2 - \eta_3)(\eta_2 + \eta_3 - \phi_1)/(\phi_1 - \xi')\psi_3 \gtrless 0 \text{ as } \eta_2 \gtrless \eta_3. \end{aligned} \quad \text{(a7.2)}$$

In deriving y_{33} and the partial derivatives in (7.20), (a7.5), (a7.6) below; impact effect (7.22); and the relative slopes in (a7.4) below, the following facts are useful:

$$\begin{aligned} \eta_2^2-\psi_1\phi_2 &= \phi_1\eta_2<0 \\ y_{31}-y_{21} &= (\eta_2-\eta_3)\phi_2/[(\phi_1-\eta_2)(\phi_1-\eta_3)] \gtreqless 0 \text{ as } \eta_3 \gtreqless \eta_2 \\ \eta_2 y_{21}-\eta_3 y_{31} &= (\eta_2-\eta_3)\phi_1\eta_2/(\phi_1-\eta_3)\psi_1 \gtreqless 0 \text{ as } \eta_2 \gtreqless \eta_3. \end{aligned} \tag{a7.3}$$

(ii) Relative slopes in figure 7.1a

$$\begin{aligned} &(d\pi/dx)_{\dot\pi=0}-(d\pi/dx)_{\dot x=0} = \eta_3(y_{21}-y_{31})^2\psi_1(\phi_1-\eta_3)/\phi_1(\eta_2-\eta_3)^2>0 \\ &(d\pi/dx)_{y_3}-(d\pi/dx)_{y_2} = (y_{31}/y_{32})-(y_{21}/y_{22}) = y_{31}-y_{21} \gtreqless 0 \text{ as } \eta_3 \gtreqless \eta_2 \\ &(d\pi/dx)_{\dot x=0}-(d\pi/dx)_{y_2} = \eta_2\phi_2/(\phi_1-\eta_2)(\phi_1-\eta_3)>0 \\ &(d\pi/dx)_{\dot x=0}-(d\pi/dx)_{y_3} = \eta_3\phi_2/(\phi_1-\eta_2)(\phi_1-\eta_3)>0. \end{aligned} \tag{a7.4}$$

(iii) Dynamic equations underlying figures 7.1b and 7.1c

(π, x^C)-plane:
$$\begin{aligned} \dot\pi &= [\eta_2 y_{33}(\pi-\bar\pi)+y_{31}(\eta_3-\eta_2)(x^C-\bar x^C)]/y_{33} \\ &\equiv \phi^{**}(\pi, x^C), \quad \phi_1^{**}=\eta_2<0,\ \phi_2^{**}=\frac{\phi_2\psi_3(\phi_1-\xi')}{(\phi_1-\eta_3)(\eta_2+\eta_3-\phi_1)}<0 \\ \dot x^C &= \eta_3(x^C-\bar x^C)\equiv \xi^*(x^C), \quad \xi^{*\prime}=\eta_3<0 \end{aligned} \tag{a7.5}$$

(x, x^C)-plane:
$$\begin{aligned} \dot x &= [\eta_2 y_{33}(x-\bar x)+(\eta_3-\eta_2)(x^C-\bar x^C)]/y_{33} \\ &\equiv \psi^{**}(x, x^C), \quad \psi_1^{**}=\eta_2<0,\ \psi_2^{**}=-\frac{\psi_3(\phi_1-\xi')}{(\eta_2+\eta_3-\phi_1)}<0 \\ \dot x^C &= \eta_3(x^C-\bar x^C)\equiv \xi^{**}(x^C), \quad \xi^{**\prime}=\eta_3<0. \end{aligned} \tag{a7.6}$$

(iv) Behavior of $\dot x^S$ on impact of $d\gamma>0$ in WALRAS I

Using the expression for $\dot X^S$ developed immediately after (7.15) and the definition $x^S \equiv X^S/\tilde T$, I obtain

$$\begin{aligned} \dot x^S &\equiv x^S(\hat X^S-n) = x^S\{[\pi q^{S\prime}(x)-(\Omega+\delta+n)](x\pi^{-1}+1) \\ &\quad -(\pi x^S)^{-1}\xi(x^C;\gamma)-\pi^{-1}\phi(\pi,x)\}\equiv \Gamma(\pi,\gamma\ldots) \\ \Gamma_1 &= x^C q^{S\prime}\pi^{-1}>0 \\ \Gamma_2 &= -q^C\pi^{-1}<0. \end{aligned} \tag{a7.7}$$

Therefore, the impact effect under consideration is

$$\partial \dot x^S/\partial\gamma = \Gamma_1\partial\pi/\partial\gamma+\Gamma_2 \gtreqless 0, \tag{a7.8}$$

where $\partial\pi/\partial\gamma \equiv -[(y_{31}-y_{21})/y_{33}]d\bar x^C/d\gamma>0$ from (7.22).

(v) Dynamic stability of WALRAS II

Under $\hat{\pi}^e \equiv 0 \gtrless \hat{\pi}$, (7.27) solves for the temporary-equilibrium relative equity price π,

$$\begin{gathered}\pi = [q^{C\prime}(X^S)/q^{S\prime}(X^C)]^{\frac{1}{2}} \equiv \pi(X^S, X^C) \\ \pi_1 = \tfrac{1}{2}q^{C\prime\prime}/q^{S\prime} < 0, \qquad \pi_2 = -\tfrac{1}{2}q^{S\prime\prime}/q^{S\prime} > 0,\end{gathered} \tag{a7.9}$$

where I normalize $\bar{\pi} = \bar{T}_1 = \bar{T}_2 = 1$ and evaluate partials near a stationary state with $\rho = \Omega$. Since only workers consume corn, the law of accumulation of corn is given by

$$\begin{aligned}\dot{X}^C = q^C(X^S) - \delta X^C - (1-\gamma)r^{T_1}[\pi(X^S, X^C), X^C] \equiv \psi(X^S, X^C) \\ \psi_1 = q^{C\prime} - (1-\gamma)r_1^{T_1}\pi_1 > 0 \\ \psi_2 = -\delta - (1-\gamma)(r_1^{T_1}\pi_2 + r_2^{T_1}) > 0,\end{aligned} \tag{a7.10}$$

where I have used (7.25) and (a7.9). Assuming static-expectations accumulation behavior identical to that in VON NEUMANN I [(1.27), (1.28)],

$$\dot{K} = (\rho - \Omega)K + (\dot{\pi} - \dot{\pi}^e)X^S, \qquad \dot{K} \equiv \dot{X}^C + \pi\dot{X}^S + X^S\dot{\pi}, \tag{a7.11}$$

which, given $\dot{\pi}^e \equiv 0$, (7.27), and (a7.10) yields

$$\begin{aligned}\dot{X}^S = \pi^{-1}\{[\pi(X^S, X^C)q^{S\prime}(X^C) - (\Omega + \delta)]K - \psi(X^S, X^C)\} \equiv \zeta(X^S, X^C) \\ \zeta_1 = q^{S\prime}K\pi_1 - \psi_1 < 0, \qquad \zeta_2 = (q^{S\prime\prime} + q^{S\prime}\pi_2)K - \psi_2 \gtrless 0.\end{aligned} \tag{a7.12}$$

Since $\zeta_1 + \psi_2 < 0$ and

$$\zeta_1\psi_2 - \zeta_2\psi_1 = (\Omega + \delta)K(\pi_1\psi_2 + \pi_2\psi_1) > 0, \tag{a7.13}$$

dynamic system [(a7.10), (a7.12)] exhibits local dynamic stability.

Appendix to chapter 8

Partial derivatives of WALRAS III

$z_1^S = q^S(\lambda_{S1} - \gamma) \gtrless 0$ in ALPHA/ONE, $z_1^S = -\gamma q^S < 0$ in BETA/TWO

$z_2^S = -q^S < 0$, $z_3^S = -\Omega q^S/q^C < 0$, $z_4^S = (q^S)^2/q^C > 0$

$z_5^S = -\gamma q^S < 0$, $z_6^S = -q^S/\gamma < 0$

$z_1^C = -(1-\gamma)q^C < 0$ in ALPHA/ONE, $z_1^C = q^C[x\lambda_{C1} - (1-\gamma)] < 0$ in BETA/TWO

$z_2^C = -(1-\gamma)q^C/\gamma < 0$, $z_3^C = -(1-\gamma)\Omega/\gamma < 0$, $z_4^C = \gamma q^C > 0$

$z_5^C = q^C/\gamma > 0$ (8.19)

$$p_1 = -\frac{z_1^S + z_3^S p_{C1}^T}{z_4^S} = \begin{cases} -(q^C/q^S)\lambda_{S1} < 0 \text{ in ALPHA/ONE} \\ (q^C/q^S)\lambda_{C1} < 0 \text{ in BETA/TWO} \end{cases}$$

$$p_2 = -\frac{z_5^S + z_3^S p_{C3}^T}{z_4^S} = \gamma q^C/(1-\gamma)q^S > 0 \tag{8.21}$$

$$p_3 = -\frac{z_6^S + z_3^S p_{C4}^T}{z_4^S} = q^C/q^S\gamma(1-\gamma) > 0$$

$$\phi_1 = \Omega[1 - (q^S/q^C)p_1] > 0,\ \phi_2 = -(q^S/q^C)\Omega p_2 < 0 \tag{8.24}$$

$$\phi^{M\prime} = \Omega > 0 \tag{8.25}$$

$$\psi' = \begin{cases} \dfrac{\Omega}{\gamma(\pi-1)}\lambda_{S1} < 0 \text{ in ALPHA/ONE} \\[2ex] \dfrac{(1-\gamma)\Omega}{\gamma^2(\pi-1)}\lambda_{C1} < 0 \text{ in BETA/TWO} \end{cases} \tag{8.27}$$

$$\begin{aligned} \pi_h &= \frac{(q^S/q^C)p_{h+1}}{1+\lambda_{S1}} > 0 \text{ in ALPHA/ONE } (h=1,2) \\ \pi_h &= \frac{(q^S/q^C)p_{h+1}}{1-\lambda_{C1}} > 0 \text{ in BETA/TWO } (h=1,2) \end{aligned} \tag{8.37}$$

$$\begin{aligned} p_{C1}^{T,\alpha 1} &= \frac{\gamma^2 q^C \lambda_{S1}}{(1-\gamma)\Omega(1+\lambda_{S1})} > 0 \text{ in ALPHA/ONE } (\alpha 1) \\ p_{C1}^{T,\beta 2} &= \frac{\gamma q^C \lambda_{C1}}{\Omega(1-\lambda_{C1})} < 0 \text{ in BETA/TWO } (\beta 2) \\ p_{C2}^{T,\alpha 1} &= p_{C1}^{T,\alpha 1}/\gamma^2 > 0 \text{ in ALPHA/ONE} \\ p_{C2}^{T,\beta 2} &= p_{C1}^{T,\beta 2}/\gamma < 0 \text{ in BETA/TWO} \end{aligned} \tag{8.38}$$

References

Abraham-Frois, G. and E. Berrebi (1979), *Theory of Value, Prices and Accumulation: A Mathematical Integration of Marx, von Neumann and Sraffa*, Cambridge: Cambridge University Press.

Afriat, S.N. (1987), *Logic of Choice and Economic Theory*, Oxford: Claredon Press.

Ahmad, S. (1991), *Capital in Economic Theory: Neo-classical, Cambridge and Chaos*, Aldershot: Edward Elgar.

Alexander, S.S. (1952), Effects of a devaluation on the trade balance, *IMF Staff Papers* 2: 263–78.

Allais, M. (1943), *A la recherche d'une discipline économique. Première partie: l'économie pure*, Paris: Ateliers Industria.

Arrow, K.J. (1952, 1964), Le rôle des valeurs boursières pour la répartition la meilleure des risques, in *International Colloquium on Economics*, Paris: CNRS; English translation 1964: The role of securities in the optimal allocation of risk-bearing, *Review of Economic Studies* 31: 91–6.

(1959), Toward a theory of price adjustment, in M. Abramowitz *et al.*, eds., *The Allocation of Economic Resources*, Stanford: Stanford University Press.

(1964), Optimal capital policy, the cost of capital, and myopic decision rules, *Annals of the Institute of Statistical Mathematics* 16: 21–30.

(1978), The future and present in economic life, *Economic Inquiry* 16: 157–69.

Arrow, K.J., H.D. Block, and L. Hurwicz (1959), On the stability of the competitive equilibrium, II, *Econometrica* 27: 82–109.

Arrow, K.J. and G. Debreu (1954), Existence of an equilibrium for a competitive economy, *Econometrica* 22: 265–90.

Arrow, K.J. and F. Hahn (1971), *General Competitive Analysis*, San Francisco: Holden-Day.

Arrow, K.J. and L. Hurwicz (1958), On the stability of the competitive equilibrium, I, *Econometrica* 26: 522–52.

Arrow, K.J. and M. Kurz (1970), *Public Investment, the Rate of Return, and Optimal Fiscal Policy*, Baltimore: Johns Hopkins Press.

Arrow, K.J. and D. Starrett (1973), Cost-theoretical and demand-theoretical approaches to the theory of price determination, in J.R. Hicks and W. Weber, eds., *Carl Menger and the Austrian School of Economics*, Oxford: Clarendon Press.

Barro, R.J. and H.I. Grossman (1971), A general disequilibrium model of income and employment, *American Economic Review* 61: 82–93.

Becker, R.A. (1981), The duality of a dynamic model of equilibrium and an optimal growth model: The heterogenous capital goods case, *Quarterly Journal of Economics* 96: 271–300.

Benassy, J.P. (1975), Neo-Keynesian disequilibrium theory in a monetary economy, *Review of Economic Studies* 42: 502–23.

Benhabib, J. and K. Nishimura (1979), The Hopf bifurcation and the existence and stability of closed orbits in multisector models of optimal economic growth, *Journal of Economic Theory* 21: 421–44.

Benveniste, L.M. and J.A. Scheinkman (1982), Duality theory for dynamic optimization models of economics: the continuous time case, *Journal of Economic Theory* 27: 1–19.

Bhaduri, A. and D.J. Harris (1987), The complex dynamics of the simple Ricardian system, *Quarterly Journal of Economics* 102: 893–901.

Bharadwaj, K. (1978), *Classical Political Economy and the Rise to Dominance of Supply and Demand Theories*, New Delhi: Orient Longman.

Bickerdike, C.F. (1920), The instability of foreign exchange, *Economic Journal* 30: 118–22.

Black, F. and M. Scholes (1973), The pricing of options and corporate liabilities, *Journal of Political Economy* 81: 637–54.

Blanchard, O.J. and S. Fisher (1989), *Lectures on Macroeconomics*, Cambridge, Mass.: MIT Press.

Bliss, C.J. (1975), *Capital Theory and the Distribution of Income*, Amsterdam: North-Holland.

Bortkiewicz, L. von (1907), Zur Berichtigung der grundlegenden theoretischen Konstruktion von Marx im dritten Band des 'Kapitals', *Jahrbücher für Nationalökonomie und Statistik* (July); English translation: appendix of P.M. Sweezy, ed. and trans. (1949), *Karl Marx and the Close of His System* by E. Böhm-Bawerk, New York.

Brems, H. (1986), *Pioneering Economic Theory 1630–1980*, Baltimore: Johns Hopkins University Press.

Brock, W.A. (1982), Asset prices in a production economy, in J.J. McCall, ed., *Economics of Information and Uncertainty*, Chicago: University of Chicago Press.

Brock, W.A. and A.G. Malliaris (1989), *Differential Equations, Stability and Chaos in Dynamic Economics*, Amsterdam: North-Holland.

Broome, J. (1983), *The Microeconomics of Capitalism*, London: Academic Press.

Bruno, M. (1969), Fundamental duality relations in the pure theory of capital and growth, *Review of Economic Studies* 36: 39–53.

Burgstaller, A. (1989), A classical model of growth, expectations and general equilibrium, *Economica* 56: 373–93.

Burmeister, E. (1980), *Capital Theory and Dynamics*, Cambridge: Cambridge University Press.

Calvo, G. (1978), On the indeterminacy of interest rates and wages with perfect foresight, *Journal of Economic Theory* 19: 321–37.

Cass, D. (1965), Optimum growth in an aggregative model of capital accumulation, *Review of Economic Studies* 32: 233–40.

(1972a), Distinguishing inefficient competitive growth paths: A note on capital overaccumulation, *Journal of Economic Theory* 4: 224–40.

(1972b), On capital overaccumulation in the aggregative neoclassical model of economic growth: A complete characterization, *Journal of Economic Theory* 4: 200–23.

Cass, D. and K. Shell (1976a), Introduction to Hamiltonian dynamics in economics, *Journal of Economic Theory* 12: 1–10.

(1976b), *The Hamiltonian Approach to Dynamic Economics*, New York: Academic Press.

Chakravarty, S. *et al.*, eds. (1989), *Von Neumann and Modern Economics*, Oxford: Clarendon Press.

Chick, V. (1987), Speculation, the rate of interest, and the rate of profit, *Journal of Post-Keynesian Economics* 10: 124–31.

Currie, M. and I. Steedman (1990), *Wrestling with Time*, Ann Arbor: University of Michigan Press.

Dasgupta, A.K. (1985), *Epochs of Economic Theory*, Oxford: Basil Blackwell.

Debreu, G. (1959), *Theory of Value*, New Haven: Yale University Press.

Diamond, P.A. (1965), National debt in a neoclassical growth model, *American Economic Review* 55: 1126–50.

Diewert, W.E. (1977), Walras' theory of capital formation and the existence of a temporary equilibrium, in G. Schwödiauer, ed., *Equilibrium and Disequilibrium in Economics*, Dordrecht: D. Reidel.

Dixit, A. (1981), The export of capital theory, *Journal of International Economics* 11: 279–94.

(1990), *Optimization in Economic Theory*, 2nd edn, Oxford: Oxford University Press.

Dixit, A.K. and V. Norman (1980), *Theory of International Trade*, Cambridge: Cambridge University Press.

Dobb, M. (1973), *Theories of Value and Distribution since Adam Smith*, Cambridge: Cambridge University Press.

Dorfman, R., P.A. Samuelson, and R.M. Solow (1958), *Linear Programming and Economic Analysis*, New York: McGraw Hill.

Dornbusch, R. (1976), Expectations and exchange rate dynamics, *Journal of Political Economy* 84: 1161–76.

Drèze, J.H. (1975), Existence of an exchange equilibrium under price rigidities, *International Economic Review* 16: 301–20.

Duffie, D. (1992), *Dynamic Asset Pricing Theory*, Princeton: Princeton University Press.

Duménil, G. and D. Lévy (1985), The classicals and the neoclassicals: a rejoinder to Frank Hahn, *Cambridge Journal of Economics* 9: 327–45.

Eatwell, J. (1987), Walras's theory of capital, in J. Eatwell, M. Milgate, and P. Newman, eds., *The New Palgrave*, vol. IV, New York: Stockton Press.

Ellerman, D.P. (1985), On the labor theory of property, *The Philosophical Forum* 16: 293–326.

Ethier, W.J. (1984), Higher dimensional issues in trade theory, in R.W. Jones and P. B. Kenen, eds., *Handbook of International Economics*, vol. I, Amsterdam: North-Holland.

Fisher, F.M. (1983), *Disequilibrium Foundations of Equilibrium Economics*, Cambridge: Cambridge University Press.

Fisher, I. (1907), *The Rate of Interest*, New York: Macmillan.

(1930), *The Theory of Interest*, New York: Macmillan.

Fleming, J.M. (1962), Domestic financial policies under fixed and floating exchange rates, *IMF Staff Papers* 9: 369–79.

Foley, D.K. (1991), Growth, Distribution and Money, manuscript, Barnard College, Columbia University.

Furuya, H. and K. Inada (1962), Balanced growth and intertemporal efficiency in capital accumulation, *International Economic Review* 3: 94–107.

Gaines, R.E. (1976), Existence of solutions to Hamiltonian dynamical systems of optimal growth, in D. Cass and K. Shell, eds. (1976b), *The Hamiltonian Approach to Dynamic Economics*, New York: Academic Press.

Georgescu-Roegen, N. (1971), *The Entropy Law and the Economic Process*, Cambridge, Mass.: Harvard University Press.

Goldstein, H. (1950), *Classical Mechanics*, Reading, Mass.: Addison-Wesley.

Goodwin, R. (1967), A growth cycle, in C.H. Feinstein, ed., *Socialism, Capitalism and Economic Growth*, Cambridge: Cambridge University Press; revised version in E.K. Hunt and J.G. Schwartz, eds. (1969), *A Critique of Economic Theory*, Harmondsworth: Penguin.

Gordon, D.F. and A. Hynes (1970), On the theory of price dynamics, in E.S. Phelps, ed., *Microeconomic Foundations of Employment and Inflation Theory*, New York: Norton.

Grossman, S.J. and J.E. Stiglitz (1980), On the impossibility of informationally efficient markets, *American Economic Review* 70: 393–408.

Hahn, F. (1966), Equilibrium dynamics with heterogeneous capital goods, *Quarterly Journal of Economics* 80: 633–46.

(1970), Some adjustment problems, *Econometrica* 38: 1–17.

(1973), *On the Notion of Equilibrium in Economics*, Cambridge: Cambridge University Press.

(1982a), The neo-Ricardians, *Cambridge Journal of Economics* 6: 353–74.

(1982b), Stability, in K.J. Arrow, and M.D. Intriligator, eds., *Handbook of Mathematical Economics*, vol. II. Amsterdam: North-Holland.

(1983), On general equilibrium and stability, in E.C. Brown and R.M. Solow, eds., *Paul Samuelson and Modern Economic Theory*, New York: McGraw Hill.

Harcourt, G.C. (1972), *Some Cambridge Controversies in the Theory of Capital*, Cambridge: Cambridge University Press.

Hayashi, F. (1982), Tobin's marginal and average *q*: A neoclassical interpretation, *Econometrica* 50: 213–24.

Heller, W.P. (1975), Tâtonnement stability of infinite horizon models with saddle-point instability, *Econometrica* 43: 65–80.

Hicks, J. (1939, 1946), *Value and Capital*, 2nd edn 1946, Oxford: Oxford University Press.

(1973), *Capital and Time: A Neo-Austrian Approach*, Oxford: Clarendon Press.
(1989), *A Market Theory of Money*, Oxford: Clarendon Press.
Hollander, S. (1979), *The Economics of David Ricardo*, Toronto: University of Toronto Press.
Hotelling, H. (1931), The economics of exhaustible resources, *Journal of Political Economy* 39: 137–75.
Huang, C. and R.H. Litzenberger (1988), *Foundations for Financial Economics*, New York: North-Holland.
Inada, K. (1963), On a two-sector model of economic growth: Comments and a generalization, *Review of Economic Studies* 30: 119–27.
Ingrao, B. and G. Israel (1990), *The Invisible Hand*, Cambridge, Mass.: MIT Press.
Intriligator, M. (1971), *Mathematical Optimization and Economic Theory*, Englewood Cliffs: Prentice Hall.
Jaffé, W. (1942), Leon Walras' theory of capital accumulation, in D. Walker, ed. (1983), *William Jaffé's Essays on Walras*, Cambridge: Cambridge University Press.
(1953), Walras's theory of capital formation in the framework of his theory of general equilibrium, *ibid.*
Johnson, H.G. (1971), *The Two-Sector Model of General Equilibrium*, London: George Allen and Unwin.
Jones, R.W. (1965), The structure of simple general equilibrium models, *Journal of Political Economy* 73: 557–72.
(1971), A three-factor model in theory, trade and history, in J. Bhagwati *et al.*, eds., *Trade, Balance of Payments, and Growth*, Amsterdam: North-Holland.
Jones, R.W. and J.A. Scheinkman (1977), The relevance of the two-sector production model in trade theory, *Journal of Political Economy* 85: 909–35.
Kaldor, N. (1937), The recent controversy on the theory of capital, *Econometrica* 5: 201–33.
(1939), Speculation and economic stability, *Review of Economic Studies* 7: 1–27.
Kemeny, J.G., O. Morgenstern, and J.L. Thompson (1956), A generalization of the von Neumann model of an expanding economy, *Econometrica* 24: 115–35.
Keynes, J.M. (1936), *The General Theory of Employment, Interest, and Money*, London: Harcourt Brace.
Koopmans, T.C., ed. (1951), *Activity Analysis in Production and Allocation*, New York: John Wiley.
Koopmans, T.C. (1965), On the concept of optimal growth, *The Econometric Approach to Development Planning*, Chicago: Rand McNally.
Kouri, P. (1976), The exchange rate and the balance of payments in the short run and in the long run, *Scandinavian Journal of Economics* 78: 255–75.
Kurz, M. (1968), The general instability of a class of competitive growth processes, *Review of Economic Studies* 35: 155–74.
Lancaster, K. (1973), The dynamic inefficiency of capitalism, *Journal of Political Economy* 81: 1092–109.
Lanczos, C. (1970), *The Variational Principles of Mechanics*, Toronto: the University of Toronto Press; reprint 1986, New York: Dover.

Leontief, W.W. (1951), *The Structure of the American Economy, 1919–1939*, 2nd edn, New York: Oxford University Press.

Lerner, A. (1944), *The Economics of Control*, London: Macmillan.

Levhari, D. and N. Liviatan (1972), On stability in the saddle-point sense, *Journal of Economic Theory* 4: 88–93.

Lindahl, E. (1939), *Studies in the Theory of Money and Capital*, London: George Allen and Unwin.

Liviatan, N. and P.A. Samuelson (1969), Notes on turnpikes: Stable and unstable, *Journal of Economic Theory* 1: 454–75.

Lucas, R.E., Jr. (1967), Adjustment costs and the theory of supply, *Journal of Political Economy* 75: 321–34.

(1978), Asset prices in an exchange economy, *Econometrica* 46: 1429–45.

(1988), On the mechanics of economic development, *Journal of Monetary Economics* 22: 3–42.

Magill, M.J.P. (1970), On a general economic theory of motion, in Beckmann, M. and H.P. Künzi, eds., *Lecture Notes in Operations Research and Mathematical Systems* (36), New York: Springer-Verlag.

(1977), Some new results on the local stability of the process of capital accumulation, *Journal of Economic Theory* 15: 174–210.

Majumdar, M. (1988), Decentralization in infinite horizon economies: An introduction, *Journal of Economic Theory* 45: 217–27.

Majumdar, M., T. Mitra, and D. McFadden (1976), On efficiency and Pareto optimality of competitive programs in closed multisector models, *Journal of Economic Theory* 13: 26–46.

Malinvaud, E. (1953), Capital accumulation and efficient allocation of resources, *Econometrica* 21: 233–68.

(1961), The analogy between atemporal and intertemporal theories of resource allocation, *Review of Economic Studies* 28: 143–60.

(1962), A corrigendum, *Econometrica* 30: 570–3.

(1972), *Lectures on Microeconomic Theory*, Amsterdam: North-Holland.

(1977), *The Theory of Unemployment Reconsidered*, Oxford: Basil Blackwell.

Marglin, S.A. (1984), *Growth, Distribution, and Prices*, Cambridge, Mass.: Harvard University Press.

Marshall, A. (1890), *Principles of Economics*, London: Macmillan.

McKenzie, L. (1963), Turnpike theorems for a generalized Leontief-model, *Econometrica* 31: 165–80.

(1982), Optimal economic growth and turnpike theorems, in K.J. Arrow and M.D. Intrilligator, *Handbook of Mathematical Economics*, vol. III, Amsterdam: North-Holland.

Mirowski, P. (1989), *More Heat than Light*, Cambridge: Cambridge University Press.

Mirrlees, J. (1969), The dynamic nonsubstitution theorem, *Review of Economic Studies* 36: 67–76.

Modigliani, F. and M. Miller (1958), The cost of capital, corporation finance and the theory of investment, *American Economic Review* 48: 261–97.

Morgenstern, O. and G.L. Thompson (1976), *Mathematical Theory of Expanding and Contracting Economies*, Lexington, Mass.: D.C. Heath.
Morishima, M. (1964), *Equilibrium, Stability and Growth*, London: Oxford University Press.
(1973), *Marx's Economics*, Cambridge: Cambridge University Press.
(1977), *Walras' Economics*, Cambridge: Cambridge University Press.
(1989), *Ricardo's Economics*, Cambridge: Cambridge University Press.
Mundell, R.A. (1963), Capital mobility and stabilization policy under fixed and flexible exchange rates, *Canadian Journal of Economics and Political Science* 29: 475–85.
Mussa, M. (1978), Dynamic adjustment in the Heckscher–Ohlin–Samuelson model, *Journal of Political Economy* 86: 775–91.
Nagatani, K. (1981), *Macroeconomic Dynamics*, Cambridge: Cambridge University Press.
Negishi, T. (1962), The stability of a competitive economy: A survey article, *Econometrica* 30: 635–69.
Neumann, J. von (1946), A model of general economic equilibrium, *Review of Economic Studies* 13: 1–9.
Nozick, R. (1974), *Anarchy, State, and Utopia*, New York: Basic Books.
Parrinello, S. (1992), Non pure commodities in the economics of production processes, mimeo, Universita di Roma "La Sapienza."
Pasinetti, L. (1960), A mathematical formulation of the Ricardian system, *Review of Economic Studies* 27: 78–98.
Patinkin, D. (1965), *Money, Interest, and Prices*, New York: Harper and Row.
Penrose, E.T. (1959), *The Theory of Growth of the Firm*, Oxford: Basil Blackwell.
Phelps, E.S. (1961), The golden rule of accumulation: a fable for growthmen, *American Economic Review* 51: 638–43.
(1965), Second essay on the golden rule of accumulation, *American Economic Review* 55: 793–814.
Philmore, J. (1982), The libertarian case for slavery, *The Philosophical Forum* 14: 43–58.
Poincaré, H. (1890), Sur le problème des trois corps et les équations de la dynamique, *Acta Math.* 13: 1–270; 1952 reprint in *Oeuvres de Henri Poincaré*, tome VII, 262–479, Paris: Gauthier-Villars.
Pontryagin, L.S. (1962), *Mathematical Theory of Optimal Processes*, New York: John Wiley.
Radner, R. (1961), Paths of economic growth that are optimal with regard only to final states: A turnpike theorem, *Review of Economic Studies* 28: 98–104.
(1972), Existence of equilibrium of plans, prices, and price expectations in a sequence of markets, *Econometrica* 40: 289–303.
Ramsey, F.P. (1928), A mathematical theory of saving, *Economic Journal* 38: 543–59.
Ricardo, D. (1951), *The Works and Correspondence of David Ricardo*, vols. I–X; *Essay on Profits* (1815) vol. IV; P. Sraffa, ed., Cambridge: Cambridge University Press.

Robinson, J. (1947), The foreign exchanges, in *Essays in the Theory of Employment*, 2nd edn, Oxford: Basil Blackwell.

Rockafellar, R.T. (1976), Saddle points of Hamiltonian systems in convex Lagrange problems having a nonzero discount rate, in D. Cass and K. Shell, eds. (1976b), *The Hamiltonian Approach to Dynamic Economics*, New York: Academic Press.

Roemer, J.E. (1982), *A General Theory of Exploitation and Class*, Cambridge, Mass.: Harvard University Press.

Romer, P.M. (1986), Increasing returns and long-run growth, *Journal of Political Economy* 94: 1002–37.

(1990), Are nonconvexities important for understanding growth?, *American Economic Review* 80: 97–103.

Ruffin, R. (1984), International factor movements, in R.W. Jones and P.B. Kenen, eds., *Handbook of International Economics*, vol. 1, Amsterdam: North-Holland.

Rybczynski, T.M. (1955), Factor endowment and relative commodity prices, *Economica* 22: 336–41.

Sala-i-Martin, X. (1990), Lecture notes on economic growth (II): Five prototype models of endogenous growth, NBER Working Paper No. 3564, Cambridge, Mass.: NBER.

Samuelson, P.A. (1937), Some aspects of the pure theory of capital, *Quarterly Journal of Economics* 4: 469–96.

(1951), Abstract of a theorem concerning substitutability in open Leontief models, in Koopmans, T.C., ed., *Activity Analysis in Production and Allocation*, New York: John Wiley.

(1953), Price of factors and goods in general equilibrium, *Review of Economic Studies* 21: 1–20.

(1957), Wages and interest: A modern dissection of Marxian economic models, *American Economic Review* 47: 884–912.

(1958), An exact consumption-loan model of interest with or without the social contrivance of money, *Journal of Political Economy* 66: 467–82.

(1959), A modern treatment of the Ricardian economy: I, II, *Quarterly Journal of Economics* 73: 1–35, 217–31.

(1960), Efficient paths of capital accumulation in terms of the calculus of variations, in K.J. Arrow *et al.*, eds., *Mathematical Methods in the Social Sciences*, Stanford University Press.

(1961), A new theorem on nonsubstitution, in H. Hegeland, ed., *Money, Growth and Methodology and Other Essays in Economics in Honor of J. Akerman*, Lund: CWK Gleerup.

(1970), Law of conservation of the capital-output ratio in closed von Neumann systems, Proceedings of the National Academy of Sciences, *Applied Mathematical Science* 67: 1477–9; reprinted in R. Sato and R.V. Ramachandran, eds. (1990), *Conservation Laws and Symmetry*, Boston: Kluwer.

(1971), Ohlin was right, *Swedish Journal of Economics* 73: 365–84.

(1972), The general saddlepoint property of optimal-control motions, *Journal of Economic Theory* 5: 102–20.

Samuelson, P.A. and R.M. Solow (1956), A complete capital model involving heterogeneous capital goods, *Quarterly Journal of Economics* 70: 537–62.

Sato, R. (1981), *Theory of Technical Change and Economic Invariance*, New York: Academic Press.

(1985), The invariance principle and income-wealth conservation laws, *Journal of Econometrics* 30: 365–89.

Sato, R. and R.V. Ramachandran, eds., (1990), *Conservation Laws and Symmetry*, Boston: Kluwer.

Schumpeter, J. (1934), *The Theory of Economic Development*, New York: Oxford University Press.

Shell, K., ed. (1967), *Essays on the Theory of Optimal Economic Growth*, Cambridge: MIT Press.

Shell, K. and J.E. Stiglitz (1967), The allocation of investment in a dynamic economy, *Quarterly Journal of Economics* 81: 592–609.

Smith, M.A.M. (1984), Capital theory and trade theory, in R.W. Jones and P.B. Kenen, *Handbook of International Economics*, vol. I, Amsterdam: North-Holland.

Solow, R.M. (1956), A contribution to the theory of economic growth, *Econometrica* 33: 671–84.

(1983), Modern capital theory, in E.C. Brown and R.M. Solow, eds., *Paul Samuelson and Modern Economic Theory*, New York: McGraw Hill.

Sonnenschein, H. (1972), Market excess demand functions, *Econometrica* 40: 549–63.

Sraffa, P. (1960), *Production of Commodities by Means of Commodities*, Cambridge: Cambridge University Press.

Srinivasan, T.N. (1964), Optimal savings in a two-sector model of growth, Econometrica 32: 358–73.

Steedman, I. (1981), Time preference, the rate of interest and abstinence from accumulation, *Australian Economic Papers* 20: 219–34.

Steedman, I., ed., (1979), *Fundamental Issues in Trade Theory*, New York: St. Martin's Press.

Stiglitz, J. (1970), Non-substitution theorem with durable capital goods, *Review of Economic Studies* 37: 543–53.

(1974), The Cambridge-Cambridge controversy in the theory of capital; a view from New Haven: A review article, *Journal of Political Economy* 82: 802–903.

Takayama, A. (1972), *International Trade*, New York: Holt, Rinehart and Winston.

Tirole, J. (1982), On the possibility of speculation under rational expectations, *Econometrica* 50: 1163–81.

Tobin, J. (1969), A general equilibrium approach to monetary theory, *Journal of Money, Credit and Banking* 1: 15–29.

Townshend, H. (1936), Liquidity-premium and the theory of value, *Ecomomic Journal* 47: 157–69.

Uzawa, H. (1961/3), On a two-sector model of economic growth, *Review of Economic Studies* 29/30: 40–7/105–18.

(1964), Optimal growth in a two-sector model of capital accumulation, *Review of Economic Studies* 31: 1–24.

(1969), Time preference and the Penrose effect in a two-class model of economic growth, *Journal of Political Economy* 76: 628–52.

Vanek, J. (1968), *Maximum Economic Growth*, Ithaca: Cornell University Press.

Varian, H.R. (1984), *Microeconomic Analysis*, 2nd edn, New York: Norton.

Walsh, V. and H. Gram (1980), *Classical and Neoclassical Theories of General Equilibrium*, New York: Oxford University Press.

Walras, L. (1874, 1954), *Elements of Pure Economics*, W. Jaffé, transl., Homewood, Ill.: Irwin.

Wan, H.Y. (1971), *Economic Growth*, New York: Harcourt Brace Jovanovich.

Weintraub, E.R. (1991), *Stabilizing Dynamics*, Cambridge: Cambridge University Press.

Weizsäcker, C.C. von (1971), Steady state capital theory, in Beckmann, M. and H.P. Künzi, eds., *Lecture Notes in Operations Research and Mathematical Systems* (54), New York: Springer-Verlag.

Wicksell, K. (1934), *Lectures on Political Economy*, vol. I, London: Routledge & Kegan Paul.

Index